The publisher gratefully acknowledges the generous contribution to this book provided by the Ahmanson Foundation Humanities Endowment Fund of the University of California Press Foundation.

Wagner Beyond Good and Evil

Photograph of Wagner taken on 1 May 1882 in the studio of Joseph Albert, Munich. Courtesy of the Theatermuseum, Munich.

Wagner Beyond Good and Evil

JOHN DEATHRIDGE

University of California Press

BERKELEY   LOS ANGELES   LONDON

University of California Press, one of the most distinguished university presses in the United States, enriches lives around the world by advancing scholarship in the humanities, social sciences, and natural sciences. Its activities are supported by the UC Press Foundation and by philanthropic contributions from individuals and institutions. For more information, visit www.ucpress.edu.

University of California Press
Berkeley and Los Angeles, California

University of California Press, Ltd.
London, England

Library of Congress Cataloging-in-Publication Data

Deathridge, John.
    Wagner beyond good and evil / John Deathridge.
        p.   cm.
    Includes bibliographical references and index.
    ISBN: 978–0–520-25453-4 (cloth : alk. paper)
        1. Wagner, Richard 1813–1883—Criticism and interpretation.
    2. Opera—19th century.   I. Title.

ML 410.W13D35   2008
782.1092—dc22   2008004589

Manufactured in the United States of America

17   16   15   14   13   12   11   10   09
10   9   8   7   6   5   4   3   2

This book is printed on New Leaf EcoBook 50, a 100% recycled fiber of which 50% is de-inked post-consumer waste, processed chlorine-free. EcoBook 50 is acid-free and meets the minimum requirements of ANSI/ASTM D 5634–01 (*Permanence of Paper*).

To my mother and in memory of my father

Contents

Preface

Much of this book was written after the end of the twentieth century when, as everyone knows, the world began to change with violent and very public events. It presents, I hope, a different and critical view of Richard Wagner based on new research and the conviction, which is not shared by everyone, that his works still have something to say to us. Against my own skepticism, I have been spurred on by George Bernard Shaw's remark in the preface to the fourth edition of his book *The Perfect Wagnerite*, in which, after describing with devastating brevity the outcome of the First World War's appalling series of catastrophes, he more or less confessed that he had changed his mind about Wagner's *Der Ring des Nibelungen*. In the first edition, published at the end of the nineteenth century, he accused Wagner of a disconcerting lurch toward a plump German brand of conservatism in the course of an epic that had begun with the best revolutionary credentials. In the light of what had happened since, he now wrote, "it says much for [Wagner's] grasp of things that his allegory should still be valid and important."

Shaw's point was that the social implications of the *Ring* in the 1920s were still intact, despite the rapid aging of some of its technical aspects. Wagner's music dramas are still enjoying full-scale productions, indeed more than ever before, and possibly for similar reasons. Good performances of *Der Ring des Nibelungen* and *Tristan und Isolde*—the two pinnacles of Wagner's achievement at the center of this book—still genuinely touch a great many people. Despite my skepticism, I do not know myself exactly why I get carried away. All I can say is that the will to present us with labyrinthine riddles about ourselves and the world we live in through the medium of opera, or rather the peculiar amalgam of allegory and myth that Wagner made from it, obviously has something to do with the abiding allure of these works.

I have deliberately excluded discussions of *Tannhäuser* and *Die Meistersinger von Nürnberg*, which are not among Wagner's works I cherish most. They are both about singing competitions (in the first deadly serious, in the second intended to be comic, but in fact even more deadly serious than in the first), and they are in my view equally problematic, though for opposite reasons: *Tannhäuser* because it verges on musical and dramatic incoherence, as Wagner himself confessed; and *Die Meistersinger* because it is overly stylized and all too cohesive, features that lend it a smug *bürgerlich* complacency without a trace of vulnerability on its golden surface, unlike nearly all of Wagner's other works. Why they have not stood the test of time as well as the other works—or, shall we say, why the problem of producing them convincingly seems to be well-nigh unsolvable in the twenty-first century—is a question I want to pursue in a separate study.

In some chapters I touch on Wagner's memories of different histories, from the history of his own life, recorded in his autobiographical writings, to that of the symphony and opera. In between are other histories of greater import, among them that of the "modern" world (as he liked damningly to apostrophize it) and the supposed decline of the human race. Wagner was not a fully paid-up follower of Hegel, perhaps the most influential philosopher of the nineteenth century, who to a degree invented the idea of "the end of history," which has gained some notoriety in Francis Fukuyama's book *The End of History and the Last Man* (1992). The "end" here means the achievement of a steady state in which the deepest needs of society have been satisfied and history no longer needs to "progress." Fukuyama projected this idea problematically onto liberal capitalist thinking of more recent times, as if to say that Hegel's ideal is at last in sight, despite the fact that huge parts of the world are still beset by poverty and violence.

But for Hegel's and Wagner's generation, history had a narrower, more Eurocentric focus that lent the notion of its end, in the above sense, a certain ethical weight. Envisaging a bright future for humanity, Wagner was on the side of the angels, advocating the "end" of the symphony and opera, and many things besides, including the conventional theater and even the layout of its auditorium, which he considered to reflect an outdated social norm. The famous result was the Bayreuth Festival Theatre with its amphitheater and clear lines of sight to the stage for all. And its creator was hardly averse to the idea of the "last" either, choosing *Rienzi, the Last of the Roman Tribunes* as the subject of his first major opera, writing of Beethoven's Ninth Symphony as the "last" symphony, and, as I note in this book, even referring to himself as the "last German" and to his final opera, *Parsifal,* as his "last card."

As Nietzsche was the first to remark, however, this seemingly humanistic investment in the future of the world existed in Wagner's imagination alongside its opposite: the idea of history driven by the irrational, the blindness of sexual instinct, racial conflict, the mindless ruination of nature, sacred ritual, sacrifice, and superstition. It was not an alternative notion, but one mixed in with the first, regardless of the contradictions. Even before reading the works of Schopenhauer, Hegel's great antipode, Wagner was enamored of the idea of the fundamental chaos of human existence and its endless circle of violence. More ominously, he also came to believe that there is very little we can do about it, that is, except to believe in our redemption through drama and a communal experience of theater, and by extension an imagined purity of life cleansed of all baseness grounded in unalterable racial difference and enmity toward the heroic. Dubious ethics and powerful art: with Wagner it is easy to lose one's head.

Voices like Nietzsche's were already objecting to the glittering attractions of the Wagnerian idea of redemption in the late nineteenth century. Especially after the Hitler era, we can see that their skepticism was justified. But it is far from being the whole story. I am basically suggesting that in order to resituate the idea, even if it means rejecting it in the end, we need to take into account some of the improbable goals Wagner placed in its path—encumbrances in and around his works that perhaps were always more eloquent about the modern world than the moments of its supposed redemption. I nearly called these essays "stumbling blocks on the way to Wagner." Apart from huge demands on performers, not to mention some famously fantastical scenic directions that could never be realized from the start, I am referring to Wagner's highly idiosyncratic staging of the modern in general. His often abstruse allegorizing, his broad and widely misunderstood inclusion of the sacred, and his penchant for baffling dialectics that also many times found their way into the structure of his music need to be confronted. And so do more notorious aspects, like the thickets of frequently indigestible supporting text in the prose works and the focus on female sacrifice and racial conflict that were already controversial in the nineteenth century. Generally admired features of the project are not so simple either, including the revival of tragedy on a par with the Greeks and the creation of symphonic drama comparable with the most powerful orchestral works of Beethoven. I would even go as far as to say that these most famous of all Wagner's ambitions can just as easily deflect attention from his real and very considerable achievements as usefully define them. In this book, I am interested in the obstacles.

The dedication is to my mother and late father in warm gratitude, and not only for sentimental reasons. They were amateur singers in the Birmingham Midland Music Makers in the United Kingdom. The society's quasi-Elgarian name disguised the fact that under the aegis of its director, Arthur Street, a distinguished metallurgist, it helped to introduce some significant works of international stature to opera enthusiasts in Britain at a time when they were little known. These included Berlioz's *Les Troyens* in 1948, and a few years later Rossini's *Guillaume Tell* and Musorgsky's *Boris Godunov* in its original orchestration, in which Leslie Deathridge sang the roles of Aeneas, Arnold, and Shuysky, respectively. My mother, Iris, took part in this yearly local operatic bonanza in Birmingham too, among other things assuming the role of Marguerite de Valois in Meyerbeer's *Les Huguenots* (with Leslie as Raoul). At the time, it was a brave attempt to recover a lost world in opera, which did not go unnoticed nationally by major critics. I have never forgotten it. Later in my life, the memory of it gave me a real insight into just how much Wagner owed to that world, despite his vehement opposition to it.

I owe a particular debt of gratitude to a number of German musicologists. As well as offering genuine friendship to a British scholar who found himself a bit lost in Munich in the 1970s, they introduced me to a far more rigorous approach to philology in the context of the Wagner Collected Edition, then in its initial stages, than I had ever encountered in Britain. Martin Geck was the first to alert me to the importance of this vast undertaking. Later I worked with Isolde Vetter, and especially with Egon Voss—whose knowledge of Wagner sources is without parallel—on the onerous detail of the sources themselves and, above all, on their implications for a less myth-laden approach to Wagner. It is also impossible to forget the late Carl Dahlhaus in this context, who gave me a job in the offices of the Wagner Collected Edition in Munich when I most needed it. I had some lively conversations with him, and I remain an admirer of his liberal spirit of debate—perhaps another way of saying that we were not always in agreement, especially about Wagner.

Alexander Goehr and the late Bernard Williams tempted me back to Britain in the early 1980s as a teacher at the University of Cambridge. I am indebted to them for many memorable conversations about Wagner's music and genuine encouragement in difficult times for academic life in Britain generally. I then went on to teach at King's College London, where I still find, in the middle of a great metropolis where all kinds of music are promoted to an extent that finds few parallels elsewhere, truly great friendliness and institutional support.

I would also like to record my special thanks to Patrick Carnegy and Jill Gomez, whose long-standing friendship and generous understanding of things Wagnerian and Epicurean (in about equal measure) I have always warmly appreciated. A special note of gratitude is due as well to a number of colleagues who took the trouble to engage with some of these texts at a detailed level and helped me improve them. In alphabetical order they are: Julie Brown, Majel Connery, Mervyn Cooke, Marion Kant, Thomas Grey, Arthur Groos, David J. Levin, Jean-Jacques Nattiez, Karen Painter, Roger Parker, and Peter Vergo.

Numerous colleagues and many of my former and present students have taken time to discuss Wagner with me. We were not always in agreement, but over the years they still invited me to explain my ideas about him in public broadcasts, lectures, colloquia, and articles, or took the trouble to engage with me personally about this decidedly thorny subject and help me understand it more clearly. I cannot possibly name them all, though I would like to record my special thanks to the following: Carolyn Abbate, Mike Ashman, Nikolaus Bacht, Robert Bailey, Warren Bebbington, George Benjamin, Mark Berry, Harrison Birtwistle, Tim Blanning, Caryl L. Clark, Eoin Coleman, Klaus Döge, Laurence Dreyfus, Lydia Goehr, Simon Goldhill, Robert Gutman, Robin Holloway, Julian Horton, Linda Hutcheon, Brian Hyer, Rena Charnin Mueller, Anna Papaeti, Clive Portbury, Philip Reed, Alex Rehding, Annegret Ritzel, Kriss Rusmanis, Edward Said, Áine Sheil, Stewart Spencer, Reinhard Strohm, Michael Tanner, Marc Weiner, Arnold Whittall, and Slavoj Žižek.

To Mary Francis, my lively and genial editor, the rest of her team at the University of California Press, in particular Mary Severance and my indefatigable copy editor Sharron Wood, and the publisher's reviewers, I owe many thanks for taking this project forward with great energy and for their keen-eyed criticisms and creative suggestions for improvement. Lastly, I would like to acknowledge the truly stoic patience of my wife Victoria Cooper and our daughter Julia, who generously tolerate my enthusiasm for Wagner without stinting on their invaluable help and warm support.

John Deathridge, King's College London,
February 2007

PART I

A Few Beginnings

1. Wagner Lives

Issues in Autobiography

Wagner's biography has been researched to within an inch of its life. It has been dissected, drenched with no end of detail, eroticized, vilified, heroicized, and several times filmed.[1] Its foundations are the collected writings, which in the first instance Wagner edited himself in the spirit of an autobiographical enterprise;[2] a separate and lengthy autobiography, *Mein Leben* (My life), dictated to his mistress and later second wife, Cosima, daughter of Franz Liszt;[3] notebooks and diaries;[4] photographs and portraits;[5] an unusually large number of letters;[6] mounds of anecdotal gossip; and no end of documentation on the way he lived and how his contemporaries saw him.[7] In this sense, he is almost the exact antithesis of Shakespeare, whose life, or at least what is safely known about it in terms of verifiable "facts," can be told in a relatively short space. I have summarized the history of Wagner biography elsewhere.[8] Here I want to look at Wagner's own portrayals of his life, some issues they raise, the philosophical spirit in which I believe they were attempted, and their effect on the generation that came immediately after him.

Biographers of Shakespeare have had to resort to imaginative reconstructions and not infrequently to knowingly forged documents that have accorded their subject more lives than a cat.[9] In stark contrast, there appears to be only one life for Wagner, which he did his best to determine in large part himself. It was also a singular life in another sense: he was a maverick, turbulent, exceptionally creative on many levels, never afraid to attempt the impossible, uncannily prescient of modern thinking about media and human psychology, genuinely revolutionary in aspiration, and yet prone to an institutionalism with protofascist traits that were largely, but not only, the result of posthumous aggrandizement on the part of his apostles and admirers.[10] In all its colorful detail, the story has been repeated so many

times—with its hero's adventures, amours, tribulations, and eventual acceptance among Western music's cultural elite all in their proper place—that
at first sight it seems like a never-changing biographical myth.

To speak of Wagner's life in the singular, however, is seriously to underestimate his own sophisticated view of biography and autobiography and the
appreciable distance of that view from the standard mapping of famous lives
in the nineteenth century. Lytton Strachey rightly spoke in his *Eminent Victorians* of the "air of slow, funereal barbarism"[11] of the (normally) two
leather-bound volumes produced by the biographical undertaker of Victorian
times, whose bounden duty it was to incarcerate the distinguished personage
in an everlasting literary mausoleum. There is no reason to suppose that Wagner would have disagreed with him. Strachey admitted the value of these
gloomy reservoirs of information for his speculative approach to biography.
And Wagner, too, was not slow to appoint an official biographer, Carl Friedrich
Glasenapp, who began with the obligatory two volumes, later expanding them
to six after Wagner's death.[12] A schoolteacher from Riga, Glasenapp not only
had frequent personal contact with the subject of the biography and hence
ample opportunity to get acquainted at first hand with his memories and
intentions, but he also obtained privileged access to many sources zealously
protected by his immediate family. These included the diaries of Cosima,
which she continued from day to day with a stubborn and almost bureaucratic
thoroughness for fourteen years until just before Wagner's death, supremely
conscious of the biographical burden that had been placed upon her.

THE "LIFE" AS A TOTALITY

Wagner began dictating *Mein Leben* to Cosima on 17 July 1865 in Munich
at the request of King Ludwig II of Bavaria. He finally finished its fourth and
last part (covering the years 1861–64) fifteen years later in Naples on 25
July 1880. The first page of the manuscript (entirely in Cosima's hand except for corrections and additions by Wagner) bears their entwined initials
"W[agner] R[ichard] C[osima]."[13] This signaling of a pact between them
was subsequently reinforced by the beginning of Cosima's diaries four
years later on 1 January 1869, effectively turning her for good into the historian of her husband-to-be (they were married on 25 August 1870), despite
her ostensible intention, expressed in the very first entry, to convey to her
children "every hour" of her life, and not his. There were occasional doubts:

> I want to convey the essence of R. to my children with all possible
> clarity, and in consequence try to set down every word he speaks, even

about myself, forgetting all modesty, so that the picture be kept intact for them—yet I feel the attempt is failing: how can I convey the sound of his voice, the intonations, his movements, and the expression in his eyes? But perhaps it is better than nothing, and so I shall continue with my bungling efforts.[14]

Still, Cosima's awareness that the aging composer would never have the inclination or the energy to complete *Mein Leben,* which ends with the young king calling Wagner to Munich in 1864 and pulling him out of a spiral of impecuniousness and anxiety, made her increasingly certain that she would be regarded as the authentic biographical conduit of his life's final stage. Not unjustly described by one prominent critic as "the foreign secretary of the Holy Grail,"[15] she soon became, after his death, the long-standing prime minister of everything concerning the perpetual refurbishment of his legacy. Only three days before he died, he told her that he still intended "to finish the biography."[16] Even this was only the last remnant of an earlier promise he had made to the king that he would continue *Mein Leben* up to the moment his wife had herself begun "to keep a most exact record of my life and work, so that after my death my whole life up to the last hour will one day be available in every detail *[lückenlos]* to my son."[17]

Wagner's ambition to present his life to his son in its totality with the aid of Cosima's diaries raises three complicated issues. First, in terms of its narrative strategy and underlying ideology, the concept depends to no small extent on the inclusion of his own death. Jean-Jacques Rousseau in his *Confessions,* the first part of which was published in 1782, placed the vanity of his life and its immediacy in the foreground—unremitting self-knowledge as a bastion against the untruth of the mere biographer's "ingenious fictions"[18]—and did not envisage the prospect of death because the present emotion of the subject and the reliving of the subject's history in the act of writing were for him all important. A certain confessional style and the reenactment of history subjectively in the moment were crucial for Wagner too, as we shall see. The creation of the self through writing, however, was conditioned in Wagner's case to a great extent by a score settling with the outer world. In turn this outer world was envisaged as a history in need of "correction" that must culminate, according to the metaphysics of pessimism that pervade his works and writings, in the welcome escape of the subject in death.

A second issue arises from the fact that anyone wanting to present his life in literary form—especially a life like Wagner's, which has been lived in the supposed spirit of a Greek tragic hero transposed into the mayhem of the modern world (a common male autobiographical model in the nineteenth century)—knows that it will be impossible to narrate the all-important death of the hero in his own words. To put it another way, the search for wholeness in autobiography is plagued by the difficulty that in the real world one cannot tell the tale from a position beyond the grave, unlike countless fictions (e.g., the film *Sunset Boulevard*) that take advantage of a narrator miraculously able to recount his own death and the logical steps of the life that led up to it. There is no doubt that the older Wagner became the more remorselessly he pursued this idea of the single life "up to the last hour" that could be presented to posterity as a unified vision. He did not enter into intimate relations with Cosima solely to ensure the survival of that vision. But she was nearly twenty-five years younger (and outlived him by forty-seven years), making it clear from the start that she would in all likelihood be in a position to finish the story on his behalf.

The much-discussed issue of gender relations in nineteenth-century biography and autobiography is a third issue,[19] if only because the striking narrative reticence of Cosima's diaries does not always conceal the real sentiments of a strong-willed woman under the severe constraints of obligatory self-erasure. On 21 November 1874, the momentous day that saw the completion of *Der Ring des Nibelungen* twenty-six years after it had been started, Cosima experienced some shabby treatment from her husband. Instead of uttering the usual passive words of the admiring wife, she involved her own feelings in the situation with some unusually revealing thoughts. Launching into a bitter description of how she and her children had burst into tears, she asked, not without self-pitying rhetoric, why she was being denied the right to celebrate the completion of the grand project to which she had dedicated her life "in suffering": "How could I express my gratitude other than through the destruction of all urges toward a personal existence? . . . If a genius completes his flight at so lofty a level, what is left for a poor woman to do [except] to suffer in love and rapture?" What follows in the diaries is still more eloquent. There are no entries at all until 3 December 1874: almost two weeks of complete silence.

The redoubtable Mrs. Oliphant, discussing Lucy Hutchinson's *Memoirs of the Life of Colonel Hutchinson* in *Blackwood's Edinburgh Magazine* in 1882, pointed out that this "noble memorial" to Lucy's deceased Roundhead husband was erected without a single "I" in the narrative, followed by Lucy effacing herself, "as if she died with him."[20] Cosima did use the "I," as we have just seen, though for much of the time it was part of a tense conformity to the ideology of female sacrifice in the name of male authority that included recording the life of that authority "up to the last hour." But on 13 February 1883, the day of Wagner's death, Cosima wrote nothing. She took no food for hours, insisted on being alone with his body for the rest of the day and night, cut off her hair and laid it in his coffin, accompanied the body from Venice back to Bayreuth in black robes, and remained hidden from sight for more than a year, receiving nobody and speaking only to her children. Only through Lucy Hutchinson's reticence about her role in her husband's life, Mrs. Oliphant suggested, did she achieve immortality for herself. Stung by rumors of an imminent decline in the fortunes of the Bayreuth Festival Theatre, Cosima returned from her condition of extreme self-denial to become its renowned guardian for more than twenty years— a right she knew she had earned in the eyes of society after years of discreet labor and self-effacement, most of them recorded faithfully by the diaries that were to secure her lasting fame.

THE REWRITTEN DIARY AND METAPHORS OF EXPERIENCE

In terms of genuine autobiography, Wagner's life remains a fragment to this day. Moreover, the fate of the diary he started when barely in his twenties in correct anticipation of his illustrious career is indicative of an unexpected complexity with respect to not only sources, but also the nuanced, and indeed modern, view he took of the whole enterprise. The early diary is known as "The Red Pocket-Book" *(Die rote Brieftasche)* because in *Mein Leben* Wagner reports that in August 1835 he began using "a large red pocket-book" to make notes for his "future [auto-]biography."[21] To King Ludwig he described this document as a means of sketching "vivid tokens of experience, as if for the eye" *(plastische Merkmale des Erlebten, gleichsam für das Auge)* in order to hold on to a quasi-visible memory of his impressions and their "inner feeling" *(des innerlich Empfundenen)*.[22] This striking statement transforms the diary at once from an omnium-gatherum of facts into tiny snapshots of a life serving to remind their creator of his subjective reactions to the events in it.

A few years later, Wagner's recording of his life became still more interesting. At the point in the dictation of *Mein Leben* when, within its narrative, his health and finances really began to take a turn for the worse (Easter 1846), he sat down—in February 1868—to create a second diary out of the first. These revised "vivid tokens of experience" are known as the "Annals," which in their complete form run to thirty-six pages of print.[23] Except for its first four pages, which only go as far as Wagner's arrival in Paris on 17 September 1839, the rest of "The Red Pocket-Book" is lost, most commentators assuming, though no proof exists, that Wagner simply destroyed it.

According to one, "the further forward he got in the portrayal of his life, the more he felt constrained by the fact that the Pocket-Book naturally contained a great deal that was impossible to dictate [in *Mein Leben*] to his friend and later wife." Given Cosima's forbearance in her diaries toward his past affairs, the observation is not entirely compelling. But the same scholar then came up with a less banal reason: "he also wanted to see some things *differently* to when he first made a note of them under the immediate impression of what he was experiencing at the time."[24]

All of a sudden we are in Proustian territory. To support the idea of autobiography as process—never finished, never complacent—Wagner clearly felt the need to confront experiences noted in the past with an immediate response in the present to his recorded memory of them. Or, as Georges Gusdorf put it in a seminal essay on autobiography, "a second reading of experience . . . is truer than the first because it adds to experience itself a consciousness of it."[25] The factual discrepancies between Wagner's earlier and later accounts of himself and their many striking changes of emphasis can therefore be accounted for by his instinct for a double-edged narrative informed by a philosophical awareness of its own process. He regarded his life as a totality—an epitaph configured by the element of death as an endpoint that paradoxically attempted to convey his life as he lived it. But he also wished to present his life as a series of lived "moments" that resist the idea of a finite end, a contradiction reflecting both an underlying discomfiture with the image of himself as eternal monument, and a hankering for the status that image enjoyed in the nineteenth century.

Skeptical observers with forensic instincts may wince at this argument, unable to quell suspicions of an elaborate ruse to justify some barefaced lying on Wagner's part. Indeed, the problematic aspect of Gusdorf's argument is the claim that the "literary, artistic function" of autobiography is of greater importance than its "historic and objective function in spite of the claims made by positivist criticism."[26] Gusdorf admits that the historian has a duty to countermand self-biography with cold facts and alternative narratives. But he is not prepared to concede the exposure of the "literary, artistic function" as ideology, or, to put it more benignly, to admit that the literary approach itself can serve to distort fact in the name of a larger vision with its own subjective "truth" that transforms harsh realities into positive and powerful images. Wagner's claim in *Mein Leben* that he heard Wilhelmine Schröder-Devrient sing Leonore in Beethoven's *Fidelio* in Leipzig in 1829 has no evidence to support it. And the scholarly fuss that ensued after the present author wrote that in *The New Grove Wagner* (1984) still failed to produce any.[27] The observation was not meant to discredit Wagner.

On the contrary, it was intended to draw attention to a deliberately constructed metaphor of huge psychological importance to him in his later years: the great singer of his youth as a redemptive "woman of the future," carrying the spirit of Beethoven and the destiny of true German art in her hands.

And this is not the only alternative story. Take the claim about the "impoverished" revolutionary in exile in Switzerland in the 1850s.[28] Contrary to the impression given in *Mein Leben*, Wagner was accorded privileged treatment from the outset and received substantial financial support, including huge sums from Otto Wesendonck, whose total patronage was second only to that of King Ludwig II.[29] But his royalist sympathies, anti-Semitism, ultraconservative friends (like Bernhard Spyri), dalliance with the archaic, love of ostentatious luxury (Liszt wrote to the Princess of Sayn-Wittgenstein of his "dandified" appearance and penchant for wearing "a hat of slightly pinkish white"), and elitist disdain for democracy gradually alienated most of his fellow émigrés with liberal views, including Georg Herwegh, who came to know a rather different Wagner from the one they were expecting. In *Mein Leben* Wagner needed the myth of the genius among the scrooges and inhibited intellectuals in "this little philistine state"[30] to downplay the support he had received from Otto and Mathilde Wesendonck, and for good measure to gloat that Zurich had thus forfeited its chances of becoming his Bayreuth.

The creator of the momentous artwork of the future may have invented a tendentious yarn about how he narrowly escaped the land of the cuckoo clock. Equally, in terms of his literary view of autobiography that has no qualms about the use of fictional strategies, the reasons for its tendentiousness are not entirely trivial. Wagner tells of exciting and dangerous expeditions up sheer-faced glaciers and precipitous descents from vertiginous peaks at this memorable moment in *Mein Leben*, all of these stories tinged with entertaining theatrical exaggeration. But a comment to the effect that a letter from Herwegh dragged him down from his "lofty Alpine impressions into the unpleasant everyday world"[31] immediately suggests that the exaggeration is actually a way of bringing home to the reader the contrasting "lives" of the artist: the one emphatically identified with subjective freedom and nature, the other marooned in the narrow confines of day-to-day living. Wagner's devout Swiss biographer, Max Fehr, who naïvely claimed that for all Wagnerians Switzerland is "hallowed soil,"[32] reports that in 1855 Wagner seriously considered as the festival site for the first production of *Der Ring des Nibelungen* the village of Brunnen on Lake Lucerne, a location in full view of the spectacular mountains of Uri and the famous Mythenstein near

Rütli, the birthplace of the Swiss confederation. Lake barges fastened together by carpenters in the bay of Brunnen would function as the stage, while the audience would be seated along the shore. Apparently the whole fantastic plan was only abandoned when the realization dawned that the waters in the bay could become disruptive in stormy weather. But whether the story is accurate or not (Fehr gives no source),[33] the very idea of striving for a myth-laden natural setting for the performance of the *Ring* is manna to the vivid Wagnerian imagination, immediately setting into relief as incidental the mere "facts" of the real life of the artist, which can be distorted at will to accommodate the larger picture.

This is still more obvious in a fascinating autobiographical essay, *A Communication to My Friends* (1851), written near the beginning of Wagner's stay in Switzerland, in which (in a move familiar to students of early romanticism) he not only depicts his life as opposed to the mundane world, in which he exists in reality, but he also equates it with the work of art itself. "I make *life*," he wrote, "the first and foremost condition of the phenomenon of the work of art," later defining this phenomenon as a "development *in time*."[34] As his emphases suggest, arid notions of timelessness and a "life" not lived to the fullest do not define the present; only the life of the true artist and the work of art together are its "moving, willing, and fashioning organ."[35] His view is not identical with the antichronological aesthetic of some of the new biographers in the 1920s (e.g., the self-styled "psychographer" Gamaliel Bradford),[36] though the striking psychological and philosophical ambition of *A Communication to My Friends* does place it well beyond those nineteenth-century biographies that he regularly read and criticized.[37]

Yet it is not generally realized how obsessed Wagner was with chronology; he often dated his manuscripts not just to the day, but to the exact time of day.[38] This Goethe-like ambition to determine history as his own philologist, so to speak, looks at first sight like an attempt to create a "timeless" archival monument in keeping with conventional nineteenth-century biographical ethics, contrary to his professed views on the subject. The logic of his narrative, however, suggests that the punctilious dating of manuscripts is merely the converse activity of the genuine artist who, as the dynamic "organ" of presence, is therefore all the more capable of escaping the chronological force of history. The ideal life is never equivalent to the mere dating of musical works, only to its exact opposite: the experience of time in the works' actual realization. Or, as he put it in the forward to his collected writings, "[The reader] will thus inwardly grasp that these are not the collected works of a writer, but a record of the life's work of an artist, who in his art, over and above the general pattern of things, sought life. This life, however, is precisely the *true music*, which I recognize as the only genuine art of the present and the future."[39]

THE COLLECTED WRITINGS AS AUTOBIOGRAPHY:
THE USES AND ABUSES OF CHRONOLOGY

Wagner edited ten volumes of his collected writings, the first nine appearing in the early 1870s and a tenth in 1883, the year of his death. In the foreword— in many respects a key text for understanding his entire output—he says that he is publishing his writings in chronological sequence in order to show "how the most diverse of occasions always awoke in me *one* motif that is at the core of my entire project as a writer, even though my writings are so dispersed." Almost in the same breath, however, he claims that ordering the writings according to when they were written "has the advantage of preventing the impression of a truly scientific system among so much that is disparate."[40] Nowhere is the contradiction explained. Wagner almost certainly knew that there could never be a truly unified method of bringing together such diverse subjects as autobiography, history, philosophy, politics, music theory, the texts of the works themselves, and performance practice as an ordered system. He also realized that in order to make his life seem like a consequential unfolding of events he had to modify the writings and their ordering at significant junctures. Indeed, the occasional manipulation of chronology, discreet addition, self-censorship, minor rewriting, telling omission, and many other modifications amounting to a "second" experience of the original texts are why, among other reasons, the ten-volume edition must count as one of the most illuminating parts of his autobiographical legacy.

The early "Autobiographical Sketch" (1843), placed right at the start of the collected writings (out of chronological order), is an early example of how Wagner presented his various "lives." The artist who has to fight for his existence in the real world of politics and poverty is set against the occasional episode when the artist experiences time creatively outside that world in a nearly mythic realm, as in the famous narrative about the ship's stormy journey from Riga to London via Norway that inspired him to write *Der fliegende Holländer*. The essay ends with a suddenly redemptive sentence that hankers after a mythical dimension of time beyond all pedantry and dryly objective chronology. Nothing could have better suited the intransigent Francophobe that Wagner had become in the meantime when he set about preparing the publication of his collected writings in 1871: "I left

[Paris] in the spring of 1842. For the first time I saw the Rhine: with glistening tears in my eyes I, poor artist, swore eternal fidelity to my German fatherland."[41]

But the Wagner of the early 1840s was not quite the fanatic nationalist of the early 1870s, and the essay had to have its wings clipped. A self-critical sentence in favor of Italian opera to the effect that "Germans who write operas" are incapable of writing an "independent free melody" had to go.[42] And other essays in the first volume—most of them originally written in Paris (1839–42)—had to succumb similarly to prudent makeovers. In the essay *On German Music*, which first appeared in a Parisian journal in 1840, an event like the successful international premiere of an opera by Rossini is set against a mythical primal scene of German music. Within the confines of this unsullied *Heimat*, according to the young Wagner, there exists an opportunity for the German genius to arise "out of his limited world . . . to create something universal."[43] And remarkably, Meyerbeer is cited as the prime example of the German composer who can set out, *must* set out, "in alien terrain" *(auf fremdem Terrain)* on the path of a truly universal art with its roots in his native land. For the fifty-eight-year-old composer who had long since made Meyerbeer his archenemy and celebrated the defeat of France in the Franco-Prussian War in 1871, this was simply unacceptable. In the version edited for the collected writings, the pro-French sentiments of his younger self are provided with ironic footnotes, and the passage praising Meyerbeer remorselessly cut.[44]

There is much more. The essay *The Wibelungen* in the second volume describes, among other things, a supposed relationship between a historical figure, Friedrich Barbarossa, and a mythical one, Siegfried. In his edition, Wagner placed the essay just before the libretto of *Siegfrieds Tod* (the first version of *Götterdämmerung*) as an example of a neat transition of the artist from history to myth, opera to music drama, and, above all, the final escape of the artist from the narrowing constraints of institutionalized culture into exile and subjective freedom. What he did not say—and not only because it would have seemed utterly pedantic—was that he continued to work on the essay for some time after the summer of 1848, when this famous peripeteia in his life is supposed to have taken place.[45] Had the essay been placed a year later, where it really belongs, and no longer antecedent to the Dresden Uprising, it would have muddied the core of the narrative: the beginning of the flight of the artist *before* the Dresden Uprising in May 1849 from the alienating world of Parisian historical opera, toward his creation *after* the revolution of a "true" music that presents a mythic "life" beyond history.

But *Der Ring des Nibelungen* did not escape the dramaturgical methods of the Parisians entirely; its concluding images of volatile nature and collapse alone are unthinkable without Auber's *La muette de Portici* or Meyerbeer's *Le prophète*. And famous readings of it as historical and political allegory like Shaw's *The Perfect Wagnerite* (1898) will always present a convincing, if partial, truth that contradicts its place in the collected writings as the desired removal of the artist from history and politics into myth. Indeed, the possibilities Wagner found in myth, which he claimed made possible a new kind of music of great authenticity and power (as opposed to music still rooted in the real world of facts and appearances), reflect only one side of his life and work at the time, suggesting that his chronology is more part of a vivid theatrical construct than an objective way of reflecting the messier reality of how he actually evolved as an artist. More generally, his method served to underpin the literary enactment of a life as a work of art, a "development *in time*," in which various contradictory strands, embracing both the mundane and the ideal, accordingly converged (and this is the narrative's monumentalizing moment) toward a final and crowning achievement. The tenth and last volume, edited posthumously "in chronological sequence" according "to the express intention of the Master,"[46] ends not with a last-written theoretical essay, open letter, or autobiographical communication, but with an artistic creation, the complete text of *Parsifal* (actually published some years before), and its last line: "Redemption to the Redeemer."

THE "LIFE" AFTER WAGNER

Wagner's original intention to bequeath to posterity a single "life" that included a description of his final hour by his wife was thwarted at the last minute by the very same (and very common) subjugation of the female subject that had made a continuous authentic narrative of that life seem possible in the first place. It was a small sign that the concept of his life as a totality was doomed to failure from the beginning. The four-year gap between the end of *Mein Leben* and the start of Cosima's diaries, to cite just one instance, is covered only by the "Annals," the rewritten diary Wagner created in 1868. Consequently, the part of the diary covering the years 1864–68 was published at the end of a modern German edition of *Mein Leben* in 1976 in the belief that, together with the first publication of Cosima's diaries in 1976–77, they would, in the words of the editor, at last enable everyone to survey Wagner's life in its entirety on the basis of an unbroken line of "autobiographical testimony" *(Selbstzeugnisse)*.[47] As the

English translators of the edition tactfully point out, however, while the "Annals" may be valuable material for the biographer, "they do not constitute autobiography."[48] And neither, for that matter, do Cosima's diaries, which, despite the impression of self-biography by proxy they may give to some, fuse the trivial with the important in almost surreal fashion, as diaries tend to do. What they cannot offer is a coherent narrative of a life. For critical Wagner biographers, often confronted in any case with a tortuous legacy of sex, lies, and invidious hype in the sources they have to deal with,[49] the task of piecing together his life on the basis of "authentic" documents is therefore less straightforward than it seems to be at first sight.

In the case of the autobiographer, Nietzsche's admonition comes to mind that a self-reflective account can be dangerous if it is seen to be "useful and important for one's activity to interpret it *falsely*."[50] It may not be wrong to suppose that this salutary warning has its origin in Nietzsche's experience with the first three volumes of the private edition of *Mein Leben*, the proofs of which he corrected when he was still on good terms with Wagner in the early 1870s. His involvement with *Mein Leben* even included the invention and supervision of the crest on the title pages of the volumes. The crest merges an image of the seven-star constellation called the Plough *(der Wagen)* with a vulture *(Geier)* that was duly provided by Nietzsche, on Wagner's recommendation, with a distinctive ruff to distinguish it from an eagle.[51] The image was meant to symbolize a "double" paternity, the natural father Friedrich Wagner and the stepfather Ludwig Geyer. Given the strikingly contrasted characters of the "fathers"— one an intellectual bureaucrat, the other an actor and painter—the crest poses an interpretative challenge for any truly alert biographer, as its inventor was the first to realize. Geyer was not Jewish, but his name had sufficient Jewish resonance for an older and more skeptical Nietzsche and his friend Heinrich Köselitz (a.k.a. Peter Gast) to play with the idea that Geyer was the real father, and Wagner hence possibly of Jewish extraction. Köselitz joked that on learning (incorrectly) that the mother, or one of her lovers, was called "Beer," he spent an entire evening referring to Wagner as "Geyerbeer."[52] More importantly—and fatefully—Nietzsche let hints of these malicious speculations spill over into a notorious footnote in the first postscript of his polemical *The Case of Wagner*. He writes, "Was Wagner a German at all? . . . His father was an actor by the name of Geyer. A Geyer [vulture] is practically an Adler [eagle].—What has hitherto circulated as "Wagner's Life" is *fable convenue* [a myth that has gained acceptance], if not worse. I confess my mistrust of every point attested to by Wagner himself."[53]

Concerning Wagner's life, this was not Nietzsche's only spectacular volte-face. In 1872 he complained to his friend Erwin Rohde that a newly published pamphlet, Theodor Puschmann's *Richard Wagner: A Psychiatric Study*, used tactics that spurned crude rejection for the more subtle approach of "insidious, deeply malicious innuendo" that would "undermine the confidence of the coming generation."[54] Five years after Wagner's death in 1888, he did not hesitate to use such tactics himself, claiming that "Wagner is a neurosis . . . Our physicians and physiologists confront their most interesting case [of degeneration] in Wagner, at least a very complete case."[55] Indeed, Nietzsche proved to be the leader in a more general desire to dent Wagner's posthumous (and massive) cultural authority by using aspects of his life to question his sanity, the stability of his body, his virility and sexual orientation, and even his racial character. In Wagner's case, already symptomatic of an age rapidly becoming disenchanted with masculine "genius," Nietzsche had finally opened up what Norma Clarke has trenchantly called the "dreadful prospect . . . of male failure."[56]

Soon after the appearance of Puschmann's pamphlet came the publication of sixteen letters from Wagner to a Viennese seamstress in the highly respected Viennese daily newspaper *Neue freie Presse*. The editor, Daniel Spitzer, prefaced the letters, which contained orders for satin bedspreads, silk ribbons, rose garlands, and countless satin dressing gowns, with Hunding's line from *Die Walküre*, "How like the woman he looks," which in its original context has quite a different meaning. The way was open for the adoption of Wagner by the leaders of the movement for homosexual emancipation in the third volume of Magnus Hirschfeld's *Yearbook for Sexual Intermediary Stages with Special Consideration of Homosexuality* (1901) and Hanns Fuchs's book *Richard Wagner and Homosexuality* (1903). And it was open for many other Wagners retrieved from notorious publications in the past in a classic essay by a modern scholar, Isolde Vetter. In these publications he was described, among other things, as a sadist, an effeminate male running around in bisexually suggestive lace drawers, a criminally insane egotist, an epileptic, a dermatitic fetishist (!), a transvestite and hemorrhoid sufferer, a megalomaniac hysteric, a non-Nordic sensualist, a paranoiac, a graphomaniac, and just a plain old degenerate.[57]

Even in Wagner's most intimate circle there were tremors of discontent, especially about *Mein Leben*. When Cosima wrote to King Ludwig II of Wagner's worry about the impression the "hopelessly repugnant experiences" in his life would make on the "cherished exalted one," she was herself already sounding apprehensive. "Had I not fervently implored him to say everything, everything, however embarrassing," she told the king, "he would not have taken note of many things."[58] The subjective tone of *Mein Leben* did indeed go beyond the boundaries of what was then acceptable in biography and autobiography. After obtaining a copy in 1892 that had been surreptitiously struck off by the printer of the private edition, Wagner's early biographer, Mrs. Burrell, clearly expecting something different, refused to believe that Wagner could be its author and became obsessed with the idea that he was "not responsible" for the book.[59] Its uninhibited subjectivity was probably also the reason why, after his death, Cosima asked the recipients of the edition (limited to fifteen and later eighteen copies) to return the volumes to Bayreuth, where most of them were destroyed. Even the king obliged. One of Wagner's Swiss friends, Jakob Sulzer, who had known the composer well in the years after the Dresden Revolution, wrote in a letter to Mathilde Wesendonck in August 1887 that he hoped *Mein Leben* would never come to light "in its authentic shape" because the moment of psychological self-examination at work in it could never do justice to the literal external truth it claims to finesse. "Wagner was an extremely subjective nature, his entire knowledge of the world, the entire knowledge that he wanted of the world, was what he got from the arbitrary reflection of it that he carried in his own consciousness."[60]

But that was precisely the point. Sulzer unwittingly put his finger on the reason for the existence of an autobiography that had consciously eschewed attempts to recall the past as accurately as was humanly possible in favour of a radical theodicy of selfhood. Quite apart from Wagner's deliberate attempts in his works and autobiographical writings to go far beyond the dialectical tension between the private and the public that had defined the romantic sense of self, even the involuntary gap, which Gusdorf sees between the avowed plan of autobiography to retrace the history of a life and "its deepest intentions,"[61] is blithely overridden by Wagner, who practically from the start set out to construct himself as an evolving subjective presence at odds with the "fact" of real chronological time, fully cognizant of the philosophical implications of such a move.

That this strategy came into conflict with Wagner's ambition to bequeath to his son and to posterity the authentic narrative of a life completely formed to the point of including his own death explains the insecurities not far beneath the surface of his autobiographical writings, not to mention those of his biographers. Far too many of them strive to treat the texts as if they are "straight" narratives, only quickly to come up against a blank wall of puzzled incomprehension when the realization dawns that the narrator is not telling the truth in any simple sense of the word. There is an air of repression about it all—the ego seeking involuntarily to evade certain

memories and feelings that could endanger its sense of wholeness and existence in the present—and the wounds Nietzsche and others sought to inflict on Wagner's cultural authority were no doubt the result of a shrewd
perception of the remarkable psychological radicalism of the texts, including some of his letters, which made him vulnerable to gleeful, hand-rubbing
posturing about the propriety of his behavior.

Nor is the problematic status of Wagner's writings about his life confined
to their interpretation by his critics. Worries among his closest allies, as we
have seen, also contributed to the bifurcation of his image into the ogre of
doubtful probity and "the *artist* and creator of so many immortal masterpieces, who should not and cannot be impugned,"[62] as (of all people) the
editor of the 1906 edition of his "letters to a seamstress" put it, at the same
time alluding to supposed sexual abnormalities that made no difference to
the genius of the music. It is no accident that *Mein Leben* had to wait for the
age of Freud and the "new biography" for its first public printing in 1911. But
even those who read it intelligently could not dislodge the already long-
standing cliché of a Wagner at once perverse and great, a grotesque parody
of his own division of himself into the artist rooted in a supposedly degenerate world and his heroic other who sought life in the *"true music."* The
candor of his writings about himself and misunderstandings of their raison
d'être, in other words, helped to create the myth of two apparently irrecon-
cilable Wagners that is still the line of least resistance in any untroubled admiration of his art. The irony is that it was Wagner himself who first set out
to challenge the apparent discrepancy. The naïve separation of the "so-called
genius"[63] from reality, and also from a direct warts-and-all subjectivism
well beyond romanticism, was one he rejected. It is exactly this insight,
however, together with his skeptical view of the role of autobiography in the
nineteenth century that places Wagner's narratives about himself among
the most remarkable and underappreciated of modern autobiographical tes-
timonies.

2. "Pale" Senta

*Female Sacrifice and the
Desire for* Heimat

We shall never know when Wagner first heard of the Flying Dutchman legend and exactly when he decided to turn it into an opera. There
is no doubt, however, that his source was Heinrich Heine's *Memoirs
of Herr von Schnabelewopski.*[1] In chapter 7—note the number—
Schnabelewopski enters a theater in Amsterdam where he sees a play
about a Dutch captain who "had sworn by all the devils in hell that, despite the storm that was raging, he would round a certain cape . . . despite
the heavy storm that was raging at the time, even if he had to keep on
sailing until the Day of Judgement." The Devil took the captain at his
word: "he would have to sail the seas until the Last Judgement, unless he
was redeemed by the fidelity of a woman's love." The Devil is stupid
enough not to believe in female constancy and allows the Dutchman to
go ashore every seven years to get married and to take the opportunity
to pursue his redemption. "Poor Dutchman! He's often only too happy
to be saved from marriage and the woman who wants to save him; so back
he goes to his ship again." This Wandering Jew of the Ocean, as the
Dutchman jokingly refers to himself, eventually meets Katharina, a
merchant's daughter, and receives her promise to be "true unto death."
Schnabelewopski catches sight of a pretty woman in the audience, an
"exquisitely beautiful Eve," who tempts him not with an apple *(Apfel)*
but with an orange *(Apfelsine)*. He leaves with his temptress, and by the
time they return to the theater "Mrs. Flying Dutchman" is wringing her
hands and about to plunge herself into the sea. She leaps, and the bedev-
iled Flying Dutchman is redeemed. The moral according to Heine is that
"women must be careful of marrying a Flying Dutchman; and we men
can see from the piece how, in the best of circumstances, women are the
ruin of us all."

RECRUITING HEINE TO THE WAGNERIAN CAUSE

The earliest surviving document connected with Wagner's opera is a scenario in French, which he wrote in 1840.[2] The essentials of Heine's story are all there: the reckless Dutchman, his somber ship with its ghostly crew, the merchant's daughter, and the fidelity unto death. But there are differences. For a start, there is another character, a young man passionately in love with the merchant's daughter and plagued by a strange inclination to dream about her. The daughter is without a name: she is simply a "young woman." As in Heine, she sits in front of the Dutchman's portrait, which shows him in somber Spanish-style dress; but whereas Heine does not bother to say much else about how the Dutchman looks, Wagner goes out of his way to emphasize that he is "pale and handsome," with features expressing a "profound and endless suffering" that touch the young woman to "the bottom of her heart." This is important. And so is the complete absence of Heine's irony.

On 6 May 1840, Wagner sent his scenario to Meyerbeer's librettist Eugène Scribe. He spoke in his cover letter of "a little opera in one act,"[3] clearly hoping that Scribe would write the libretto and effect a commission for him from the Paris Opéra to set it to music. Anticipating an audition with Scribe and Meyerbeer, Wagner composed three songs: the two songs of the ships' crews in the third act of the opera as we now know it, and a ballad for the young woman. Wagner later claimed, quite rightly, that the ballad was the beginning of the whole project and lay at the heart of it. The blood-red sails of the phantom ship are there, and so is the "pale man" (cet homme pâle),[4] who is the ship's commander. Wagner also invented a parody text, probably strictly for private use, that easily fits the music:

> the poor devil dances well
> his pig's foot doesn't spoil it
> Houih! he dances well
>
> *Le pauvre diable danse bien,*
> *son pied de porc n'empêche pas!*
> *. . . houih! il danse bien!*[5]

The parody depends on the old European superstition about the Devil and the Jew both having a deformed foot, mixed in with the Grimm fairy tale about the Jew caught in the brambles. Although pricked painfully by the thorns, the Jew is forced to dance by the sound of a mischievous boy's violin. And the more the music plays, the better the Jew dances. In the context of an opera about a tormented Wandering Jew of the Ocean, Wagner obviously thought it was hilarious.

I do not want to dwell too much on Wagner's famously untrustworthy sense of humor. Let me just say that, to his annoyance, the audition with Scribe and Meyerbeer and the expected commission did not materialize. Not surprisingly, and not much later, he decided to write the libretto himself. He concocted another scenario, this time in German, converting Heine's merchant into a skipper and calling his daughter Anna.[6] Heine's name for the daughter, Katharina, probably did not have the right operatic resonance. A character called Anna, on the other hand, would have immediately reminded audiences at the time of Boieldieu's and Scribe's popular opera La dame blanche (The white lady), in which there is a character called Anna who is the white lady, even though the white lady is only meant to be a ghost. Or audiences might have thought of Marschner's well-known Hans Heiling, in which the heroine, Anna, finds herself married to the opera's spooky, supernatural protagonist, only to be saved in the end by the all-too-human hunter Conrad, whom she really loves. In Der fliegende Holländer, the exact opposite happens.

But the name "Anna" seems not to have pressed all the right operatic buttons either. Sometime during the early part of 1841 Wagner changed it to the more unusual sounding "Senta"—and I shall suggest a possible, if esoteric, reason for that in a minute. Now I would just like to note that Wagner also introduced two more characters—the Helmsman and Senta's nurse—and added the entire first act and the opening tableau of the second. In keeping with these new ideas he composed two more songs—the Helmsman's song and the Spinning Chorus—and according to his own account supposedly wrote the rest of the music in just seven weeks (again, note the number). Thus the work was no longer a "little opera in one act," as he had originally told Scribe, but a rather larger affair, which in his first autograph libretti he called a "romantic opera in three acts to be played in one" (Romantische Oper in einem Act u[nd] 3 Aufzügen).[7]

The projected "little opera" of May 1840 and the enlarged concept that emerged a year later are therefore not quite the same thing. Wagner expanded not only the outer aspect of the work—its physical scale—but also expanded its interior spaces, so to speak, where he could elaborate several motifs well beyond the restrictions imposed on the original project, not to say notions of opera current at the time. The Dutchman's nihilism and yearning for death; the quasi-Christian idea of redemption; Senta's preoccupation with dreams and folly or illusion (Wahn); the transformation of Senta's suitor into a hunter, whose humble profession and clumsy demeanor serve as a foil to her utopian release (in effect a love-death in the manner of Tristan): all these elements meant that by the time Wagner had finished the libretto of *Der fliegende Holländer* in 1841 he had included, at least in embryonic form, many of the major themes that dominate his later works.

THE FLYING SCOTSMAN AND A SKIRMISH
WITH PORNOGRAPHY

This is perhaps why my Scottish friends are always a bit taken aback when I tell them that the opera was originally set in Scotland. In the first manuscript libretto and orchestral score of the opera the place of the action is described as "the Scottish coast." Senta's fiancé is a huntsman called Georg instead of Erik. The name of her father is not Daland, but Donald, whose ship is manned by "Scottish" sailors. In the opening scene of the opera the ship drops anchor near a coastal village with the Scottish-sounding name of Holystrand. And Wagner's skipper greets the Dutchman in the third scene with the line *"Gastfreundschaft kennt der Schotte"* (literally, "The Scotsman knows hospitality").[8] In fact, as my late and much-missed colleague and fabulous Beethoven expert Alan Tyson once quipped when I told him this, "The opera has clearly been misnamed." Like the world's most famous steam locomotive and the old London King's Cross to Edinburgh express, it should of course be *The Flying Scotsman*.

But only two months before the Dresden premiere of *Holländer*, in January 1843, Wagner suddenly changed the location from Scotland to Norway. The decision caused him a lot of work. With a red pen, he went through the entire score, changing the names of some of the characters and adapting the stage directions. He also had to alter all the vocal scores and many of the cues in the orchestral parts already copied for the rehearsals. It was a huge job that added still more to the difficulties Wagner had in putting the opera into production, at least one of them caused by his liking for dubious jokes.

Right at the beginning of the opera, when Daland's ship drops anchor offshore from Sandwike, as the town is called in the Norwegian version, the tired Helmsman is put on watch and sings a song about his girlfriend, remarking ruefully that if it were not for the south wind he probably would not be able to see her again. "Ah, trusty south wind, blow some more," he sings, "my bonnie sweetheart's pining for me." He falls asleep. The Dutchman enters, sings his terrifying monologue, and the Helmsman wakes up. For comic relief Wagner has the Helmsman, still drunk with sleep and fantasizing about sex, mix up his original words: "Ah, my bonnie sweetheart, blow some more."[9]

The exclamation marks written in the orchestral parts suggest that the joke prompted such hilarity among the musicians that Wagner eventually had to drop the idea. But he did so only gradually: the phrase exists in the original version (the orchestral parts were written out in 1842, before the first performance took place) and intermittently in the revised versions from 1842 onward. By the time we get to Wagner's Collected Writings (1871) and the most-used score of the opera, edited by Felix Weingartner (1896), the line has been ironed out to "Ah, trusty south wind, blow some more, / my sweetheart's pining for me!" It is just another tiny example—one of many—of how Wagner's character, exuberant and rough in his early years, was later scrupulously ironed out and made more respectable through meticulous self-censorship.[10]

This later expurgated skirmish with pornography—by no means the last in Wagner's works—hardly explains why the change from Scotland to Norway was made at such a late stage. Were German opera-goers tired of Scotland? Did they prefer Scandinavian names like Sandwike and Erik, with those striking k's that make them look Norwegian? Or was Wagner simply disguising his debt to Heine and other composers like Boieldieu and Marschner? After all, Heine's merchant is a Scot, both Boieldieu's La dame blanche and Marschner's opera Der Vampyr are set in Scotland, and both operas have virile young men called George or Georg in love with the sexiest soprano in the cast.

TALES OF THE UNDEAD

Part of my point is that Senta's name is impervious to the geographical shift. So is the Dutchman's. Their situation reminds me in some ways of that memorable moment in the Marx Brothers' film Night at the Opera in which Harpo wreaks havoc with the backdrops in a performance of Verdi's Il trovatore so that the hapless tenor, Lasspari, has to sing his aria in wonderfully inappropriate environments, including two railroad cars, a fruit stand cart, and a battleship. The satire simply plays mercilessly on the abiding weakness of opera, which is that the emotional high voltage of the singing too often seems to bear scant relation to its surroundings. For entirely serious reasons, Wagner exploits the same flaw: it hardly matters where Senta and the Dutchman are singing. It could be Scotland or Norway—or, for that matter, Boston—because on one level these two characters are inveterate narcissistic loners, in love with each other's self-pity. Or, to put it slightly more positively: they are two people who will always be profoundly disconnected spiritually from wherever they are supposed to be.

They could be vampires. In folklore vampires can be of practically any nationality, and indeed such creatures have occurred in the folklore of practically every European culture. It is true that vampires in fiction and folklore are not always itinerants, mainly because they have to remain in their graves for at least part of the time during the day. (That could be hard if they were world travelers, even in today's jet age.) But in Kosovo-Metohija, in the former Yugoslavia, gypsies still believe that vampires wander far and wide around the globe, passing through many settlements, where they are bound one day to meet a wolf, be attacked, and be torn asunder.[11] And not far away from Kosovo-Metohija, if you look carefully at the map, is a moderately sized town called Senta, famous for the decisive military victory there in 1697 that made Austria the foremost power in central Europe. In the present context it is perhaps more important to note that Senta is right in the middle of the region where most vampire myths in folklore originated. Not Germany, not Norway, and not even Scotland, but the present-day Serbia-Montenegro and its borders with northwest Romania, better know to vampire fans as Transylvania: this is where Senta lies.

I have not got a shred of evidence that the famous heroine of *Der fliegende Holländer* is named after a town in the middle of vampire land, but anything of this sort is possible with Wagner, who to judge from numerous traces in his texts went out of his way to study folkloric traditions of all kinds in some detail. He is not very forthcoming about this in his writings, partly because his more noble-minded colleagues and patrons, notably Liszt, Ludwig II, Nietzsche, and Gobineau among others, had no real time for folk culture—*das Volkstümliche*—and merely dismissed this part of Wagner's intellectual makeup as yet another of his puzzling eccentricities.

Wagner gives the game away in his writings when he tries to explain the almost pathological self-exclusion of Senta in medical terms. "Senta is a very solid Nordic girl," he assures us. "But it has been observed how Norwegian girls have had feelings of such overwhelming force that they die of sudden cardiac arrest. Something like it probably is the case with the seemingly sickly and pale Senta." Let us just ignore the absurd reference to Norway. In any case, if Senta really has the alleged "Norwegian" heart condition, she is *really* sick, and not just seemingly so. What is interesting is the little word "pale" *(bleich)*—oddly repressed in later versions of this text[12]—which immediately brings the appearance of Senta into line with "the pale man" *(cet homme pâle / der bleiche Mann)* described in her ballad in both its French and German versions.

Marschner's vampire opera again served as a model. The story comes from the Lord Byron circle, which, like Bram Stoker later in the nineteenth century, seems to have reveled in ghoulish stories about the undead in preliterate societies. The plot is about an aristocrat, Lord Ruthven—a joking reference to Byron himself—who is really a vampire feeding on his female victims. One of them, Emmy, even sings a ballad to her mother about a picture of a "pale" man with a soulless expression. He is a vampire who sucks the blood of young women. Emmy also points out, anticipating her own fate, that anyone falling victim to him will herself become a "horrid vampire" *(grausiger Vampyr)*. In German the gender of vampire is masculine. According to folklore it can hardly be anything else, as most vampires of legend are male, except mothers who have died in childbirth. (Naturally I am discounting the countless lesbian vampires of more recent times.) Thus Emma sings: *"Nun geht sie selber, glaub es mir, / herum als grausiger Vampyr"* (Now she roams, I beg you hear / as horrid vampire far and near). Thus the irritating doggerel of Wilhelm August Wohlbrück's libretto, with the help of oversexed German nouns and adjectives, keeps the masculine gender of the noun "Vampyr" while managing to suggest that women who become vampires also become men. Or, to be linguistically pedantic—never a waste of time in this area of opera—the feminine pronoun "her" *(sie)* is made synonymous with the form of the adjective "horrid" *(grausiger)* that with its masculine ending describes the vampire unequivocally as male.

Wagner knew Marschner's opera well from his youth and even wrote some extra music for it.[13] He later claimed to find its contents repulsive, but that was just another diversionary tactic to conceal the fact that this modest piece of German *Schauerromantik* influenced him as much as it did. I am not aware that he spotted the hint of androgyny in Emma's ballad. But in his autobiographical texts he never fails to mention the legendary soprano Wilhelmine Schröder-Devrient, whose renditions of so-called trouser roles, such as Fidelio in Beethoven's opera and Romeo in Bellini's lyric tragedy *I Capuleti e i Montecchi*, made a profound impact on him. One of his main ambitions, he claimed, was to write an opera "worthy of Schröder-Devrient," and indeed it was Schröder-Devrient who first created the role of Senta.[14]. Interestingly, he described her during rehearsals as "pale and distracted" *(bleich und verstört)*. "[She] ate hardly anything and was in every way so unduly tense that I thought she could not escape a serious or even perhaps fatal illness."[15]

FEMALE SACRIFICE

From an early moment in his life Wagner was clearly attracted to images of androgyny in opera, and it would be nice to think that, coupled with the notion of two pale mutually blood-sucking vampires roaming the earth (either for real or in the fantasies of one of them), androgyny can tell us everything that we need to know about Senta. But, for a start, vampires in the folklore tradition are never pale. Unlike their fictional counterparts in novels and the movies, vampires in the Serbian tradition are commonly described as having faces that are florid, or of a healthy sunburned color, or just plain dark, which logically enough may be attributed to their habit of drinking blood. They also yearn to stay alive, which is why they drink the blood of others in the first place. What they are definitely *not* supposed to be doing is searching for death like Senta and the Dutchman.

The image of androgyny, too, whether one sees it as a shifting balance of masculine and feminine features in a single figure, or as a symbol of unity between a man and woman, is little more than a conveniently unstable notion that at any given moment can suggest a kind of benign two-way traffic between genders. The problem with Senta, however, is that she travels a one-way street. At the heart of her character are love and sacrifice, instinctive actions, random emotional excess, and hence a kind of soulless nonidentity, ironically not unlike the "pale" men she and her predecessor Emmy see in the portraits they describe. Stability of character is thrown to the winds—almost literally in the gale-infested crevices of Wagner's score—and fidelity to a man unto death alone can restore it. Only through the love of the Dutchman, in other words, does Senta exist at all.

This brings us to an important iconic aspect of Senta. In the first part of Goethe's *Faust*, Faust has a vision of "a pale, beautiful child" *(ein blasses, schönes Kind)*, whom he thinks resembles his adored Gretchen. The truth is that Gretchen's innocence is being destroyed by the skulduggery of Mephistopheles and Faust's willingness to go along with it, a process that is already implied in the famous scene in which Gretchen arranges flowers in front of a devotional image of the *Mater dolorosa* and begs the Virgin Mary for compassion for her own suffering *(Ach neige, /Du Schmerzenreiche . . .)*. The relevance of this to Wagner's Senta is suggested by two musical sketches, written side by side probably early in 1840, one with the heading "Gretchen" and the other with "Senta" followed by a question mark (ex. 1).[16] The first sketch is a theme for a projected symphony on the first part of Goethe's *Faust*, which Wagner planned in Paris in 1839–40 and never

Ex. 1. Sketch for the second movement of a planned symphony on Goethe's *Faust* (Nationalarchiv der Richard-Wagner-Stiftung, Bayreuth, A I d 2, verso).

finished. The second is an initial attempt to compose the plangent oboe melody, which occurs in the opera just at the moment when Senta leads her fiancé Erik to the picture of the Dutchman and asks him whether he, too, cannot feel the pain, the profound sorrow, afflicting the person in the image. Wagner later wrote in a letter to a colleague, "The second part of my *Faust* symphony would have had Gretchen as its subject, just as Faust was in the first movement. I already had a theme and the atmosphere for it in place;—then—I gave the whole thing up and—true to my nature—got on with the 'Flying Dutchman,' thereby freeing myself with the clear-cut definition of the drama from the fog of instrumental music."[17] It is possible that the G-minor melody, too, was originally intended for Gretchen, serving as a contrast to the naïve freshness of the first in D major, and after some hesitancy only later—hence the question mark—became associated with Senta. Touching naïveté and innocent suffering were clearly going to be the contrasting moods of the music.

When Wagner decided to abandon the idea of a symphony based on Goethe's *Faust*, he transferred the melancholic theme, probably with the *Mater dolorosa* scene in mind, to the appropriate moment in the opera where Senta likewise seems ready to take on the mantle of suffering. He had already set the Gretchen scene as a melodrama at the age of nineteen as part of his "Seven Compositions for Goethe's *Faust*"—proudly calling them "Op. 5"—and moreover in the same key of G minor with a similar atmosphere (ex. 2a).[18] True to his habit of reversing the meaning of his sources while retaining their iconic strength, Wagner's pale heroine in

(Gretchen steckt frische
Blumen in die Krüge.)

Ach neige,   du   Schmerzen - reiche,   dein

Ant - litz gnädig meiner Not!

Trans.: (Gretchen puts fresh flowers in the vases [in front of a devotional picture of the Mater
  dolorosa].)
  [spoken] Ah, let your face,
         you who are rich in pain,
         Look down kindly on my distress.

Ex. 2a. "Seven Compositions for Goethe's *Faust*" (1831): No. 7 Melodrama.

(Senta führt Erik dicht vor
das Bild und deutet darauf.)

Trans.: (Senta takes Erik close to the picture [of the Flying Dutchman] and points to it.)
  [sung] Do you feel the pain,
         The deep distress,
         In the look he casts down upon me?

Ex. 2b. *Der fliegende Holländer* (1840–41): No. 5 Duet, mm. 210–18.

Trans.: ERIK: You are so pale
Satan has ensnared you!
SENTA: Why are you so frightened?

Ex. 3. *Der fliegende Holländer* (1840–41): No. 5 Duet, mm. 187–241.

the opera does not ask for compassion from the sacred image of another woman, as in Goethe, but implores a man close to her to understand her compassion for the suffering enshrined in the portrait of another man (ex. 2b).

But if Gretchen's existence is in jeopardy, the threat to Senta's is just beginning, as Erik suddenly notices when he remarks, "You are so pale" *(Du bist so bleich)*. Indeed, the whole passage sounds like a demonized *Stabat Mater*. Senta is ensnared by Satan, Erik tells her with real insight, whereupon the orchestra suddenly hammers out a chord like a pack of yelping wolves (ex. 3). Senta's suffering has no supernatural excess about it: joy and indeed a kind of triumph supplant any tears she might shed for the Dutchman, as if the conviction that life does not exist were a reasonable and unshakeable certainty upon which the principle of fidelity unto death must rest for support.[19] Her double nature, the demonic and the saintly, are hardly ever clearer than at this crucial point. All at once, as we shall see in chapter 13, she is near the majestic, and at the same time twisted, character Kundry in *Parsifal*, whom Wagner once vividly described as a figure with eyes "darting like burning coals out of their sockets," but also with a look that can be "fixed and inert."[20] Or to put it another way: vampire and Madonna all in one.

THE DESIRE FOR *HEIMAT*

I still have not answered the question of why Wagner moved the action of *Der fliegende Holländer* from Scotland to Norway. One likely reason is that he wanted to heighten the autobiographical significance of the opera. Only a few weeks after the premiere he published his first excursion into the art of self-profile. It was a substantial essay called "Autobiographical Sketch" (February 1843) and contained a vivid account of a hazardous voyage along the Norwegian coast, which he had undertaken on his way to Paris shortly before beginning work on the opera. What could have been more effective than to give the work a similar atmosphere? "The voyage through the Norwegian reefs," he wrote, "made a wonderful impression on my imagination; the legend of the Flying Dutchman, which the sailors verified, took on a distinctive, strange coloring that only my sea adventures could have given it."[21]

But there may have been a still more cogent reason. In Boieldieu's *La dame blanche* and Marschner's *Der Vampyr*, Scotland is inhabited by aristocrats and fine people, whose wealth and natural authority over the less privileged are more or less taken for granted. The idea of moving *Der fliegende Holländer* from Scotland to Norway may have been one of the young Wagner's most brilliant autobiographical maneuvers. Given the superior background of some of the characters in the operas set in Scotland he took as his models, however, the opera's depiction of a northern rural community relatively unscathed by upper-class mores looked simply more convincing in a country without operatic associations suggesting the opposite. We do see in *Der fliegende Holländer* the presumably wealthy merchant Daland, yet even he is part of a *humble* community, one whose superstitions are integral to the existences of its inhabitants, who are practically untouched by modern decadence.

The kind of community presented in *Der fliegende Holländer* and the music its members like to sing bear a striking resemblance to the rural idyll of the north that Wagner described in detail in an essay on German music that he first published in Paris in 1840. This is nothing less than a primal scene of German music presented as a salutary counterexample to the suspect modern character of the French capital—an image drawing from several sources going back to the late eighteenth century that represent images of pedagogical fortitude, respect for the domestic and the sacred, modesty, glorification of the amateur, an intuitive sense of harmony, the need to make music in family surroundings, doing something for its own sake and not for profit, pristine inwardness, purity and depth of musical expression, and many other supposedly "German" traits.[22] This is one explanation of why the characters in this opera—and those in Wagner's later (controversial) portrayal in *Die Meistersinger von Nürnberg* (1862–67)—have a penchant for strophic song: "In truth the artistic construction of the chorale completely exemplifies the character of German art; the penchant of the people *[des Volkes]* for the lied is already manifest in short and popular chorale melodies, a number of which bear a striking resemblance with other profane, but always childishly pious, folk songs."[23]

This makes for instructive reading in the context of Senta's famous ballad at the center of *Der fliegende Holländer*, because we can see Wagner establishing at the time he was composing the opera the criterion of fidelity to folkloric origins that the strophic structure of the song expresses, including the enraptured, almost sacred quality of its refrain. Nor does it matter that this is Norway and not Germany. In this unalienated *Heimat* of the north, Wagner almost literally hands over to Senta a great literary and symphonic tradition, originally incorporated in his plans to write a multimovement symphony based on Goethe's *Faust*. Indeed, in her ballad she proves to be an intuitive master of German art and all that is essential about it: intense subjectivity, strong structure, and the ability to instruct the uninitiated. (The ballad does, after all, tell a powerful story about the Dutchman and his Faustian soul, the depth and detail of which Senta brings across to her naïve listeners with great effectiveness.) At her grandest, Senta is a symbol of that greatness, her very paleness embodying a spirit of understated musical authenticity, which, in contrast to the flushed decadence of French and Italian music, was destined, in Wagner's view, to spread its wings over the rest of the world.[24]

This by no means contradicts Senta's desire to escape the community she inhabits. In Wagner's way of thinking only her rootedness in folklore traditions and customs can assure her of redemption and make her worthy of assimilation to his symbolic order, in which the German spirit of the north reigns supreme. Her paleness is a sign of that rootedness. But it also carries traces of difference that made it hard for Wagner to contain her entirely within his own permissible ideological boundaries. His eloquent case for the essential nobility of German music and its hoped-for dominance over supposedly weaker, less pure cultures does not sit comfortably with her wanderings in dark regions of superstition and the occult. But this Senta, too, lives on—and long may she roam.

3. Wagner the Progressive

Another Look at Lohengrin

The critical star of *Lohengrin* has dimmed so much over the years that even Wagner's admirers sometimes find it hard to let it shine as brightly as it did at the height of the opera's popularity in the nineteenth and early twentieth centuries. The swan, one of the opera's central symbols, has become a kitsch icon, capable of selling anything from kettles to the Queen's favorite matches, but it is no longer quite the beautiful, enigmatic and sexually suggestive image it used to be. Harder to accept now, too, is the gullibility of the heroine Elsa. After falling in love with Lohengrin she is bartered with her consent in a marriage transaction that forbids her even to ask her groom's name and origin. Claude Lévi-Strauss has said that we no longer need to resort to the matrimonial vocabulary of Great Russia to see that in marriages like this the groom is the "merchant" and the bride the "merchandise" in a contract ensuring the continued existence of a male-dominated community.[1]

Stranger still are the medieval dualisms and theological mysteries of faith and redemption that nourish the plot of *Lohengrin*. Today they seem like distant relics, at least at first sight, but they probably looked just as odd to some observers in the context of the German idealism of the 1840s, when the opera was composed. Wagner probably sensed this himself, which may be one of the reasons for his occasional metamorphosis—albeit in private—into one of the opera's earliest critics. A few months after the successful premiere in Weimar (which, as a political refugee banned from Germany, he could not attend) he wrote to the literary scholar Adolf Stahr:

> There is a whole world between *Lohengrin* and my present plans. [Wagner had just started work on *Siegfried*.] What is so terribly embarrassing for us is to see a snake skin shed long ago dangled in front of us willy-nilly, as if one were still in it. If I could have everything my way,

Lohengrin—the libretto of which I wrote in 1845—would be long *forgotten* in favor of new works that prove, even to me, that I have made progress.[2]

Postwar generations have tended to agree. The former popularity of *Lohengrin* is suspect—it's considered fodder for the sentimental and old-fashioned perhaps, or a salutary reminder of the (supposedly) revisionist feudal ambitions of the old German middle class—while the daring modernity of Wagner's later works is admired and celebrated. During and immediately after the composition of *Lohengrin*, Wagner became enraptured with Young Hegelian ideas, devoured Feuerbach's critique of Christian belief (which threw a rather different light on the Christian symbolism of the opera), turned into a ferocious orator against the old feudal order in Germany, fought on the barricades in the 1849 Dresden Revolution, more or less gave up composing to write lengthy, socially critical tomes about the future of art, nearly jettisoned his marriage and "domesticity" (as he put it to Stahr), and began to develop a huge work that eventually became the *Ring*, in which myth and music were to combine in a utopian Artwork of the Future expressing profound insights into the world in ways no existing art form had ever done before. In other words, Wagner was telling Stahr that he had changed practically within the space of two years irreversibly into a modernist in the Young Hegelian mold who believed in correcting the mistakes of the past not by rejuvenating the old order, but by destroying it completely and creating something radically new in its place. That hardly sounded like the author of *Lohengrin*.

IMAGES OF INCEST AND SUPERSTITION

Wagner told Stahr in a suggestive phrase about the "twilight mist" *(Dämmerdunst)* lifting from him after *Lohengrin*, as if to say that he had experienced a kind of dawn banishing the dark magic and medieval miracle worship at the center of the opera from his mind for good.

That the situation was not quite as simple as this must have been clear to Wagner, who in his letter was actually taking issue (for diplomatic reasons only implicitly) with a recently published and highly influential article on *Lohengrin* by Franz Liszt. On Wagner's behalf Liszt had prepared and conducted the opera's first performance in Weimar on the 101st anniversary of Goethe's birth (28 August 1850) and taken great pains to ensure that the place and date would be seen to be highly symbolic. A growing nostalgia in Germany after the failed revolutions of 1848–49 for Weimar's former cultural glory, together with Wagner's burgeoning reputation as the new hope of German art, inevitably focused critical attention on the production. Also, the composer's enforced absence, and his status as a political exile with a price on his head, inevitably caught the lavish attention of the liberal intelligentsia and the press. Not surprisingly, the premiere turned out to be a major event that transformed Wagner virtually overnight from a provincial German kapellmeister into an international figure.

Liszt's sense of timing and uncanny knack for publicity did not desert him when he introduced *Lohengrin* to the world as an administrator and conductor. But Wagner was arguably less pleased with the high-flown language of his friend's essay on the opera (written in French and first published in German translation in April 1851), which at the start conjures up an undialectical, sentimental image of a premodern world unsullied by doubt in Christian belief. That alone could have hardly found favor with a recent convert to Feuerbach and admirer of the Hegelian Left. The constant implication of Liszt's argument is that, like the knight of the Grail, the opera is a marvelous wonder sent into a world that has "rejected miracles" and no longer "believes in divine origin or divine revelation." The pleasing sounds of the prelude, as if "reflected on a broad and calm stretch of water," can help us to grasp again the "indescribable power" of the secret of the Holy Grail. The opera shows us that what humanity needs is not yet more scientific endeavor, but an antidote to "the hate and envy that have befallen the men of invention and progress"—a cure for a civilization that is slowly being strangled by reason and lack of faith.[3]

Not to be outdone, Wagner decided in 1851 to make his view of *Lohengrin* known publicly as well. In his long autobiographical essay *A Communication to My Friends,* he dismissed the Christian imagery in the opera as "fortuitous" and argued ingeniously for a more fundamental view of the legend. He pleaded for a critical method that could reveal what is known in modern parlance as the "deep structure" of all myths that relate them to each other. The story of *The Flying Dutchman* is a reincarnation of the myth of the *Odyssey,* while the image of Odysseus yearning for an earthly woman, and escaping the clutches of Calypso and the attractiveness of Circe, has found its way in "enhanced" form into *Tannhäuser.*[4] Likewise, the relation of a supernatural being to a mortal in the myth of Zeus and Semele clearly relates it to the story of *Lohengrin,* though here Wagner was prepared to go even further than a comparison with the Greeks:

> A primal feature, repeated in manifold forms, permeates the legends of those nations who dwelt by the sea or by rivers that emptied into the sea: on the billows' azure mirror a stranger was seen to draw near, a

man of utmost grace and purest virtue who charmed and won each
heart by the irresistible spell that he wove; he was the fulfillment of
that desire which fills the yearning breast of him who dreamt of
happiness beyond the sea in a land he could not discern. The stranger
disappeared again, withdrawing over the ocean waves, as soon as he was
questioned about his innermost being.[5]

Passages like this, which reduce a complex web of tales and legends to a key
image of great emotional import, amply confirm Wagner's modern reputation, in Lévi-Strauss's words, as the "undeniable originator of the structural analysis of myth." If this is accepted, Lévi-Strauss continues, "it is a
profoundly significant fact that the analysis was made, in the first instance,
in music."[6]

In an exhaustive study of the Lohengrin legend published in 1911, Otto
Rank, a pupil and colleague of Sigmund Freud, came to the conclusion that the
truly astonishing prevalence of the same symbols in so many branches of the
myth must reflect, as Wagner had already suspected, primal feelings of awe-
some power. Indeed, Rank opened such a veritable can of psychoanalytical
worms in his detailed account of the anxieties and taboos hidden behind the
seemingly innocuous fairy-tale surface of *Lohengrin*, which even in a post-
Freudian era that has grown rather weary of the unconscious it is hard to
ignore. The hero's arrival on "the billows' azure mirror" is not surprisingly—
at least in Freudian terms—the birth out of the waters of the mother's womb,
and his departure a return into the underworld and the realm of death. The
forbidden question is the code of silence imposed on the child asking after the
secret of its own or its parents' origin. To pacify the child the right answer is
repressed and replaced by the fantasy of the stork, or, in many regions and
countries, the white swan, which pulls the newborn child out of the water in
a casket, and brings it to its parents, as if by a miracle.[7]

Rank also came to the conclusion that the forbidden question serves to
hide an incestuous relationship that is revealed and therefore proscribed the
moment the identity of the hero is known. The inevitable comparison with
the Oedipus myth turns *Lohengrin* in this scenario into a "rescue fantasy"
about the hero's "mother" that ends in her death.[8] (The strange coincidence
that Wagner's mother died when *Lohengrin* was just on the verge of completion did not go unnoticed by Rank.) Here Rank drew on Freud's theory
of the injured third party, which suggests that some men develop a subconscious need to save their mothers from the threat of the rival father, and in
order to relive the fantasy are instinctively drawn to women already attached to other men.[9] (Rank was also not slow to point out that Wagner's
famous adulterous love affairs, and the similar triangular situations in all

his stage works from *The Flying Dutchman* to *Parsifal,* follow a similar behavioral pattern.)

Friedrich von Telramund has formally renounced his claim on Elsa before the opera begins, but Rank had little trouble in showing that the attachment is still strong enough for Telramund to function, psychoanalytically speaking, as the evil father whom Lohengrin has to confront in order to save his surrogate mother, Elsa. Wagner took pains to change the sequence of events in the various versions of the legend in order to allow this traumatic confrontation to recur with increasing intensity, as in certain kinds of dreams that repeat a single theme in different contexts with greater clarity each time. Lohengrin easily wins his battle with Telramund on Elsa's behalf in the first act, but in the second he intervenes only just in time in a far more fraught situation between Elsa and Telramund, as Elsa's doubts about the forbidden question begin to surface. After Elsa decides on her wedding night in the third act to break the code of silence and to ask the question, Lohengrin kills Telramund at last, finally revealing his identity and origin in the concluding tableau over the dead body of his "father," and hence also revealing the real nature of the "incest" with the woman he set out to rescue.

DARK VISIONS

Wagner's prescient insight into the nature of myth allowed him to see *Lohengrin* paradoxically as a thoroughly modern work pointing to a utopian future precisely because it returns to the most fundamental origins of human feeling. Liszt was right nonetheless to stress the opera's culturally more specific traits, such as its obvious Christian symbolism and celebration of the medieval past, which Wagner's modernist posture at the time tended to obscure. (Rank dutifully follows Wagner, incidentally, in practically ignoring them too.) The final scene alone is liberally provided with Christian motifs. The dove that appears above Lohengrin's boat to pull it away when he withdraws over the ocean is an image that has strong associations with the Immaculate Conception. As the power of Lohengrin's prayer returns the swan to its original human form, a pagan symbol of miraculous birth is replaced by a specifically Christian one. Indeed, the very notion of the swan as a human being whose outer shape has been tragically altered touches on the idea central to Christian doctrine that only body and soul together can define an individual, and that rending the two asunder is the most terrible prospect anyone can face. Elsa is not only punished for answering the forbidden question by her parting from Lohengrin, whose true identity she has only just discovered, but also by the separation of her soul from her body before she slowly slips lifeless to the ground. (In the stage direction describing the death of Elsa, Wagner uses the poetic expression *entseelt,* which in the context can be taken to mean literally "deprived of a soul.")

The Christian symbols in *Lohengrin* are not a literal transposition of Christian dogma any more than are the liturgically inspired vocabulary and syntax in the poetry of Baudelaire, a famous admirer of the opera and its prelude in particular. Baudelaire was struck by the ethereal sound of the prelude, which gave him the sensation of weightlessness and strange visions of light.[10] The aspiration toward radiant light, however, is not fulfilled in the opera; nor is there the slightest sign of blissful release that marks the end of all Wagner's other major works—two reasons to concur with Peter Wapnewski's striking description of the opera as Wagner's "darkest tragedy."[11] Indeed, with the departure of Lohengrin and the death of Elsa, the ending is so equivocal and unusual for Wagner that it is legitimate to ask whether a sequel was planned that would provide the missing redemptive conclusion, and indeed whether that sequel turned out to be—unlikely as it sounds at first—*Der Ring des Nibelungen. Lohengrin* and the *Ring* bring several deep-seated traumas to the surface without covering them up, including incest in conflict with the moral imperatives of a crumbling social hierarchy, murderous struggles for power, and, as Morse Peckham pointed out in his book *Beyond the Tragic Vision,* the failure of leadership and the "impossibility of an adequate society."[12] One major difference, however, is the spectacular redemptive conclusion of *Götterdämmerung* that *Lohengrin* conspicuously lacks. It is not a major disparity, but rather a final resolution of tensions already emerging in the earlier work. And it took Wagner practically all of the twenty-five years he worked on the *Ring* to get it right, as we shall see later in this book.

THE SOUNDING OF THE NEW

Even when the critical star of *Lohengrin* shone at its brightest in the nineteenth and early twentieth centuries, the music of the opera was already suspect to any self-respecting champion of "progress," including at times, as we have seen, Wagner himself. Among the literati (e.g., Heinrich Mann, author of the novel *Man of Straw*) it was an easy target for caustic and amusing comment on reactionary middle-class mores that were enshrined in music with a disconcerting sentimental shimmer not out of place in the drawing rooms of the most conservative nineteenth-century households. Even Houston Stewart Chamberlain, normally the most stalwart evangelist of the Wagner cause in the *völkisch* circles of the Second Reich, described *Lohengrin* as a "moment of feebleness"[13] before Cosima Wagner's model production in Bayreuth (1894), conducted by Felix Mottl, made him change his mind. Other observers to this day, immersed in the advanced musical techniques of *Tristan und Isolde* or *Parsifal*, have found *Lohengrin* faintly obnoxious, or at least a puzzle.

The delicate position of *Lohengrin* in Wagner's musical development and the moral quicksands of its libretto made confusion inevitable from the start. The Dresden Uprising of 1849 had brought the composer fame as a revolutionary. As time passed, the label stuck less to his political than to his artistic beliefs, with the result that his first major theoretical works, published in the early 1850s, soon overshadowed *Lohengrin* as the more progressive aspect of his musical credo. The reaction to Wagner's London concerts in 1855 was typical. Readers of *Opera and Drama*, serialized in advance in *The Musical World*, were genuinely puzzled when Wagner conducted excerpts from *Lohengrin*. The critic of the *Morning Post*, William Howard Glover, praised Wagner's writings as "very original," but remarked that his music revealed "no epoch-making innovations."[14] The Bridal Chorus hardly sounded like the Artwork of the Future. And few could be expected to grasp the irony behind its huge success, especially when it was played at the royal wedding of Princess Victoria and Prince Frederick William of Prussia three years later. In its proper dramatic context an intimate masterpiece of sweet foreboding and a prelude to marital disaster, outside the opera house it gradually became a much-loved set piece at countless humbler weddings—a musical symbol of eternal faith in the institution of marriage.

The checkered history of *Lohengrin* is no less ambiguous than the work itself. In the first editions of the libretto and the full score Wagner called it a "romantic opera." Yet its atmosphere and certain aspects of its music suggest that it is closer to his later, more self-consciously modernist music dramas than it seems to be at first hearing. The spirit of the so-called classical period in the history of instrumental music is part of *Lohengrin*, too: the polyphonic orchestral writing much admired by Richard Strauss,[15] the close motivic relationships, and, above all, the neat, often uncomfortably schematic dramatic and musical symmetries are all evidence of Wagner's burgeoning ambition to raise the musical status of opera to the level of the great classical symphonists. The repeat of the Grail music in Lohengrin's narration in the third act in A major and the subsequent recapitulation in the parallel key of F$^\sharp$ minor of some of Ortrud's music from the second are two good examples. Indeed, both were originally conceived on an even grander scale before Wagner eventually put dramatic sense above abstract formal concerns and cut them down in the finished work.[16]

Musical details, too, are rarely observed accurately, usually because the composer's so-called progressive innovations are too often thought to consist merely of near-atonal chromaticism and irregular phrase structure. In fact the anti-chromatic moments of *Lohengrin* are sometimes the most striking and original (the opening of the prelude, for instance), and even the banal regular phrases of the Bridal Chorus can seem daring and ambivalent: as a phantasmagoria of marital bliss about to shatter, they actually presage a breakdown in human relations that is neither banal nor regular, at least in terms of the rigorous Victorian ethic of marriage the young Victoria and Frederick must have thought it reflected at their royal wedding in 1858. In a sense, *Lohengrin* is a contradiction in terms. Carl Dahlhaus has pointed out that it mixes genres that do not mix (fairy-tale opera and grand historical drama).[17] But still more paradoxically, its music can still sound strikingly new precisely where, according to conventional theory, it seems to have no modernist ambitions at all.

MUSIC ANALYSIS AND MUSICAL IMAGERY

It is often said that Wagner was uninterested in an analysis of his own music. Certainly his collected writings contain surprisingly few music examples: the journalist in him knew that most of his readers would find any technical discussion about music too remote from polemical debates about "true" German culture, politics, heroic myth, the demise of opera, and the future of music drama, subjects that were guaranteed to attract attention. But there are notable exceptions. His late essay *On the Application of Music to Drama*, published in 1879, is a rare attempt to focus on the processes behind his music with printed music examples rarely seen in Wagner's writings as a whole.[18] And several passages in his letters show that the question of what makes his music work, an analytical challenge that has since vexed generations of experts, also preoccupied him more than is generally acknowledged. Some of his most interesting remarks relate to the music of *Lohengrin* and prove that he saw it as a more significant musical landmark than did many of his admirers. In an undated letter (probably December 1851) to his colleague Theodor Uhlig, the arranger of the first vocal score of the opera, he wrote:

The business of the vocal score prompted me to take a quick look through the music of *Lohengrin* again. Since you sometimes write about these things, wouldn't you be interested in saying something about the network of themes [*das thematische Formgewebe*] and how, in the direction I've chosen to go, it must constantly create new forms? Among other things this occurred to me when I looked at the first scene of the second act. At the start of the second scene—the prelude with wind instruments accompanying Elsa's entrance on to the balcony—I noticed how in the seventh, eighth, and ninth bars accompanying Elsa's nocturnal appearance a motif is heard for the first time, which, fully formed, later undergoes spacious and broad development when Elsa moves in broad daylight and full brilliance toward the church. I clearly saw from this how my themes come into being always in context, and in keeping with the nature of a vivid image.[19]

Even a faithful follower like Uhlig may have balked at the idea of finding a thematic web in *Lohengrin*. Although without any knowledge of the music of the *Ring*, which was only begun in earnest two years later, Uhlig did know Wagner's ideas for the new kind of symphonic drama he was planning and already explaining in detail in writings that Uhlig was helping to prepare for publication. And what was already abundantly clear from these writings—mainly the three-hundred-odd-page treatise *Opera and Drama*, which finally appeared complete in 1852—was that Wagner was intending to write music on a far larger scale than he had ever attempted before, including large numbers of motifs, many with specific meanings (contrary to legend Wagner himself labeled some of them in his sketches)[20] entwined in a symphonic web spread over whole works from beginning to end.

Ever since, posterity has continued to understand Wagner's famous system of leitmotifs in terms of this method alone, without realizing—as Uhlig almost certainly did—that it was invented specifically for the *Ring*. The truth is that the method is qualitatively very different from the way motifs are used in *Lohengrin*, and different, too, from the methods he was to develop later in *Tristan, Die Meistersinger,* and *Parsifal,* not to mention the later parts of the *Ring* itself. Confusion about this important point was therefore grounded in Wagner's understandable wish to project his ideas about motif backward onto *Lohengrin* in order to make it seem like a logical precursor to the project he was currently working on—a self-invented myth that has persuaded countless commentators to privilege the issue of themes and motifs in the earlier work over more interesting aspects of the score. (There are only six motifs that recur regularly throughout *Lohengrin*, fewer than appear in the first scene of the *Ring* alone.)

To be fair, Wagner seems less obsessed by his "network of themes" in his informal letter to Uhlig than he does in his "official" writings. It is well to remember, perhaps, that he had still not heard *Lohengrin* in its entirety, let alone seen it in the theater, despite the fact that the rest of Europe's musical cognoscenti (who happened not to be revolutionary insurgents in Germany with warrants issued for their arrest) had had the opportunity of seeing the first full production under Liszt's direction in Weimar in the previous year. Astonishingly, he did not experience the entire opera in the theater until May 1861, thirteen years after he had finished it, in Vienna. While it steadily grew in popularity during the 1850s in German-speaking countries, all he could do in his Swiss refuge was to re-create its theatrical effect in his imagination—one explanation, perhaps, for the large number of surviving documents that attest to the extremely detailed personal care he took with its visual production.[21] And in his letter to Uhlig this may well be the reason for his acutely analytical approach to the music in terms of the opera's scenic realization. His "network of themes" that constantly creates "new forms" may at first sight be more applicable to the *Ring*. At the same time, it refers convincingly to the focusing of visual and orchestral images in *Lohengrin*, involving the vivid combination of immediate scenic impressions and local thematic ideas developed—somewhat paradoxically—on a large, almost quasi-symphonic, scale. It is, without doubt, one of the opera's most important achievements.

The history of opera is rich in examples of the literal musical representation of spectacular images on stage and also the not-so-literal depiction of characters' feelings deliberately hidden by those images, though real enough when translated into the "invisible" language of music. (Both aspects obviously anticipate with uncanny accuracy the power music was to have in the cinema.) Whether in the depiction of natural catastrophes, such as the avalanche in Cherubini's *Eliza*, or in the representation of telling and contradictory emotions, as in Gluck's *Iphigénie en Tauride*, where an unruly viola part betrays the true emotions behind Oreste's words "Le calme rentre dans mon coeur," composers have been unusually inventive in creating orchestral replicas of what audiences actually see, and also what they do not see but clearly sense behind the appearances presented to them.

A good example of the latter is the moment in the second act of *Lohengrin* when a seemingly distressed Ortrud, "powerless and pitiful" *(machtlos und elend)*, asks Elsa how she could possibly reward her for her sympathy. The agitated viola part in the accompaniment immediately betrays the skullduggery behind Ortrud's tactics, artfully deployed to gain Elsa's trust in a plot designed in the long term to ensure the downfall of Lohengrin.[22]

In one sense, it is a precise imitation of Gluck's technique. In another, its scenic presence at the very heart of the work after Ortrud's terrifying outburst "You gods profaned" *(Entweihte Götter)* is a telling and subtly positioned musical moment of great dramatic and structural consequence. The subtle tension between musical sound and visual action here is not, as in Gluck's opera, just a local event: using different musical means and different images, the tension increases almost imperceptibly as the action proceeds, until it breaks spectacularly into the open, first with Ortrud's interruption of the wedding procession leading into the church toward the end of the second act, and again in the third, when Elsa finally asks Lohengrin the forbidden question and destroys her relationship with him for good.

The more literal orchestral underlining of a "vivid image" in *Lohengrin*, too, was hardly an original innovation. Wagner's adaptation of the convention, however, permanently changed the scale and scope of the idea. The true originality of his so-called musical scene painting is the way it is used over long stretches to create a kaleidoscope of visual and acoustical images. The motif cited by Wagner in his letter to Uhlig in the seventh, eighth, and ninth measures of the second scene of the second act is introduced almost casually. Yet precisely for this reason its "spacious and bright development" more than nine hundred measures later in the second act has enormous suggestive power.[23] Wagner has smuggled the motif and its visual association into the listener's subconscious almost surreptitiously, rather like the seemingly insignificant mention in a novel by Proust of a character who turns out to be central to the narrative sixty pages later. Both the timbre and the simple outline of the motif are extended in their new context toward a musical depiction of Elsa's lonely procession in broad daylight toward the church: solo instruments are merged with ensemble textures, and just before the motif is taken up by the first and second violins, the music shifts unexpectedly toward the brighter key of F major. At its first appearance an idea without consequence, the motif becomes part of several delicately floating, chamber music–like textures, which, although they boast no adventurous harmonic or structural background, present an animated timbral landscape to the viewer expressing not just the onlooker's enraptured response to the innocent bride, but also, through notes also enchained by their stubbornly unchanging meter of four beats per measure, a sense that she is relentlessly processing toward her doom.

Soon after beginning the orchestration of *Lohengrin*, Wagner arranged Palestrina's *Stabat mater* for a performance he conducted himself in Dresden on 8 March 1848.[24] The two events perhaps have more to do with one another than is generally realized. Wagner added numerous dynamic markings to Palestrina's masterpiece, and he redistributed the voices into solo, half-choir, and full-choir groups in a way not unlike his treatment of instrumental lines in *Lohengrin*. At the beginning of the prelude, for instance, the Holy Grail—one of the most striking extramusical images in the opera—is re-created on a single chord of A major colored by the alternating superimposed sounds of, respectively, full violins, a third of the woodwinds, and four solo violins playing in their extreme upper register with harmonics. Not only are the overlapping instrumental "choirs" in the prelude reminiscent of Renaissance polyphony; the web of orchestral color itself is informed by its spirit.

This is especially clear when the prelude is compared with the "sunrise" in Félicien David's symphonic ode *Le Désert* (1844), to which it bears an uncanny resemblance. While David also chooses A major with high strings and solo woodwind, making effective use, too, of A-major and F$^\sharp$-minor chords in juxtaposition, Wagner combines this essentially static idea with greater differentiation of sound and strong horizontal lines that greatly enhance his highly suggestive acoustical metaphor Again, in the history of opera, the idea—in this case, the borrowing from church music to conjure up an atmosphere of the sacred in decidedly secular surroundings—was already not uncommon. Wagner would not have been Wagner, however, if he had not taken it several steps further. Richard Strauss and Theodor Adorno have already drawn attention to the imitation of the sound of the organ by the woodwinds as a way of allegorizing the poetic idea of the wedding and the archaic image of "an all-embracing cosmos confirmed by God."[25] On the surface it hardly sounds like a modernist idea. But the timbral inflections in the orchestration that result—a merging of entries and timbres into a seamless whole disguising the individual entries and sounds of the instruments involved, a bit like the combination of organ registers to create a composite timbre, in which the sound of each register on its own is no longer recognizable— was to become the rule in the music of Schoenberg and Alban Berg. Moreover, the suggestive instrumentation of the prelude permeates the orchestral style of the entire opera. It may be a metaphor (as Wagner himself described it) for the Holy Grail and its "descent from heaven escorted by a host of angels,"[26] which comes perilously close to the worst kind of musical religious kitsch. But on another level its sheer daring in setting up an ambitious architectural design over long periods of time stretching over the whole work set a new precedent for opera and purely instrumental music alike.

THE BEGINNING OF THE FUTURE

Apart from the prelude, which was written last, *Lohengrin* was the first of Wagner's operas to be composed through from beginning to end without regard for a conventional sequence of operatic "numbers." (Ernest Newman's statement that the third act was composed first and the second act last is not borne out by Wagner's sketches.)[27] The new technique added even more irony to the long-term success of *Lohengrin* as a series of set pieces performed outside the theater in concerts, weddings, drawing rooms, parks, health spas, and—perhaps least surprisingly—military parades.[28] And it certainly explains Wagner's reluctance to accept his publisher's demand for arrangements of "highlights" that could help to sell the opera, though he eventually agreed and personally put together nine of its "most attractive songs" for voice and piano, which quickly became a best seller.[29] Above all, the ambition to provide the music of the opera with greater continuity for dramatic reasons meant that Wagner confronted himself with a number of technical hurdles that help to account for its occasionally uneven quality, especially in the handling of the choruses.

Wagner decreed in *Opera and Drama* that the operatic chorus should vanish and be replaced by the orchestra. It was a Wagnerian law that Wagner himself disobeyed, but doubtless it is why the choruses in *Lohengrin* are traditionally regarded as the least interesting and most "reactionary" aspect of the work. Some are indeed overextended with conventional melodic lines made to bridge awkward gaps in the musical continuity. Yet Wagner's sketches prove that he took great pains to integrate them into the fabric of the whole work. On the rare occasions when the double male-voice chorus in act 2, "At this early hour, the call bids us assemble" *(In Früh'n versammelt uns der Ruf)*, is performed accurately and without cuts, its reputation as an operatic blockbuster pales before the subtlety of its individual lines. In a sense Wagner's choruses in *Lohengrin* are his second orchestra. They are alive with unusual sounds, and they are infused with a dramatic vitality easily transcending Wagner's later accusation that in opera the chorus can only play a conventional role as a poor relative of the main action.

Lohengrin is the first of Wagner's major works that he did not extensively revise. Parts of *Rienzi* were cut and modified even before its first performance; and largely for practical reasons different versions of it were performed with the composer's connivance well into the 1850s.[30] Both *The Flying Dutchman* and *Tannhäuser* were revised for a different reason. Cosima Wagner's diaries make it quite plain that *Zukunftsmusik* (Music of the Future)—a term Wagner hated but unwittingly encouraged through the stylization of himself as a musical progressive—played an important role in many attempts to make these operas conform to a later, more "official" style. In his final years Wagner expressed to Cosima his intention of thoroughly reworking the *Dutchman*,[31] and also famously said to her that "he still owes the world *Tannhäuser*," even after all the work he had done revising that opera over a period of at least thirty years.[32]

No such remark about *Lohengrin* has survived. He may have written a new introduction to the finale of act 1 when he conducted it in a concert in Dresden on 22 September 1848. (According to one witness, the performance was received with lukewarm applause and "lively opposition.")[33] And we know for certain from letters and other sources that he composed new transitions and endings for excerpts he conducted in Zurich and London in the 1850s and on a concert tour of Russia in 1863, most of which are lost. He conducted the opera several times and personally supervised two productions first given on 16 June 1867 in Munich and on 15 December 1875 in Vienna. Apart from minor cuts, he apparently altered nothing except some of the stage directions. The only substantial change he made was a cut in Lohengrin's narration in act 3, which he asked Liszt to carry out for the first performance.[34] This was not because he suddenly wanted to bring the opera up to date, however, but rather, as we have already seen, because he seriously miscalculated the dramatic effect of the old-fashioned formal symmetry he wanted to impose on the work.

In an open letter to Arigo Boito (1871), Wagner expressed dissatisfaction with performances of *Lohengrin* he had seen. Only once—in the 1867 Munich production—did he achieve an ideal performance of the work, "at least as far as its rhythmic-architectonic structure was concerned."[35] *Lohengrin* was his most popular work and the least understood. But his refusal to change hardly a note of it is surely a sign that it is closer to his later music dramas than is generally realized, and in a more profound sense than a superficial comparison of its motifs with the leitmotifs of the *Ring* can ever possibly demonstrate. Wagner wrote several times that his new path began with the composition of *The Flying Dutchman*. Careful listening and an informed view of the revisions in his early works, however, suggest that it is in *Lohengrin* where the Music of the Future really begins.

PART II

Der Ring des Nibelungen

4. Fairy Tale, Revolution, Prophecy

Preliminary Evening: Das Rheingold

Gods roam rivers and forests in the *Ring* to thwart their enemies. A handsome prince ensnared in the lair of a monstrous dragon kills the dragon and, with the help of a forest bird, braves a dangerous wall of fire to awaken a beautiful princess on the top of a mountain. Ugly dwarves and toadlike creatures infest the tale with evil. Two lumbering giants manage to set the whole amazing story in motion, one brutally battering the other to death. No magic carpets are in sight. There are lots of thrilling rides, though, including a descent through the earth to a terrifying underground kingdom and a fantastic journey on horseback through storm-tossed clouds. Wondrous objects are on display. The magic hood transforms its wearer into any shape its wearer desires. The hero's sword can kill the mightiest of dragons and penetrate any fire or thicket. And the magic ring itself, from which the cycle of dramas takes its name, empowers its owner to rule the world.

One of the Rhine maidens tells us in the opening scene that the only person who can forge the mighty ring is someone who has first renounced love—a proviso that immediately shows that the *Ring* is far from being just another fairy tale. Anyone tempted to see it as a cross between Snow White and Sleeping Beauty in mid-nineteenth-century garb—a sort of Disneyland before the fact—is likely to agree with the German Board of Film Censors, which routinely places a notice on video recordings of the *Ring* to the effect that the cycle is suitable viewing for everyone "over the age of six." It is probably incautious advice. As always children love the Punch and Judy violence, one giant bludgeoning the other to death, or the hero suddenly murdering an evil dwarf with the magic sword simply because he finds him revolting. Translate this into an allegory of the underlying anarchy of modern society, a war of all against all that legal order can barely resolve, let alone prevent, and children are likely to be baffled. Not that sensitive parents would want it otherwise.

The stark truth is that *The Ring of the Nibelung* was intended from the start as an onslaught on the bourgeois-capitalist order, which for well over two centuries, as Wagner and others saw it in the 1840s, had failed to heal the wounds it had inflicted on society. The social system that had prevented the birth of a world based on true justice and love had to be attacked with every means available. For Wagner that did not mean cynical or destructive means, but rather a radical examination, in essay and dramatic form, of prevailing middle-class institutions and values. He read widely, refusing to ignore even the most cobweb-ridden corners of German academic writing on medieval German and Scandinavian sources. And he devoured modern polemical works on philosophy and politics, not to mention controversial books on religion that still count today among the most eloquent attacks on Christianity ever written. The dictum of Bruno Bauer (a prominent German intellectual of the 1840s) that God was the "bailiff" of a "hell composed of a hatred for humanity"[1] is certain to have come to Wagner's attention, as did Feuerbach's *Essence of Christianity*, by far the most influential treatise on religion in the period. Feuerbach agreed with Bauer's dictum, but he also believed in the reversal of humanity's projection of its instinct for justice and love onto God—a projection that in his (and Karl Marx's) view was a misguided draining away of spiritual energy into a fictitious, objectified channel, and one of the main reasons for the desolation of modern living. Feuerbach's insistence that life must show God its back and return to humanity is essentially the idea behind Alberich's curse on love at the beginning of the *Ring* and Brünnhilde's monologue at its end, which returns love to the orbit of human aspiration and feeling.

Wagner also read the writings of the French socialist thinker Proudhon (Cosima Wagner's diaries attest that he was enthusiastic about them to the end of his life) and many others in which the curse of capital and the resulting objectification of human labor are discussed. There is no evidence that Wagner read Karl Marx, though he may have heard about his ideas from the radical political figure Michael Bakunin, whom he certainly did know. In view of his enthusiastic agreement with other like-minded thinkers, however, it is not going too far to suggest, as the historian Mark Berry has said, that he would have wholeheartedly agreed with Marx's description of capital as the "visible god-head, the transformation of all human qualities into their opposites."[2] Indeed, the first scene of *Das Rheingold*, in which the Nibelung dwarf Alberich, after renouncing love, the most tender human quality of all, snatches the gold and goes on to build his vast industrial empire in Nibelheim, is undoubtedly a vivid dramatization of this very idea.

The *Ring* began in the late 1840s as an allegorical comment on social unrest. As Wagner expanded the project in the early 1850s, it soon turned into a parable of human destiny dominated by riddles and emotional conflict that dissolved politics into philosophical poetry, as it were, and reached far beyond the Revolution of 1848–49 that first inspired it. This is not to say, as many still do, that Wagner had a political change of heart. We only need to read his letters to see that he seldom stopped believing in his particular brand of revolutionary idealism, even though he was forced, for the sake of sheer survival, to repudiate some of it in public. His beliefs had been part of a utopian quest for a new kind of theater even before the 1848–49 Revolution. Wagner himself suggests in his autobiographical essay *A Communication to My Friends* (1851) that composing his previous work, *Lohengrin*, had already made it clear to him that a new form of musical drama had to prevail, a form that, clouded by paradox and contradiction as it might appear to be, was far more effective than any written social comment ever could be in addressing strong feelings about the need for revolution and change.[3] (Not that Wagner was incapable of hard-nosed political analysis. The sharp and extremely detailed critique of the Dresden Court Theater he wrote in 1848, for instance, raises many issues about the erosion of standards by business interests and the incompetence of unqualified heads of artistic institutions, issues that are perhaps even more relevant at the start of the twenty-first century than they were in the mid-nineteenth.)[4]

In a world liberated by global communications, Wagner's utopian socialism (like his notorious anti-Semitism) is often greeted with a skeptical shrug, if not outright disbelief. But many of the impasses and dangers of middle-class values he predicted and warned against in the *Ring* have hardly failed to materialize. The cold fire of calculating reason represented by Loge has indeed won out in a management-obsessed world demonized by objectification (the obsession with news, for instance) and by what Wagner and his socialist *confrères* in the 1840s would have almost certainly regarded as the fatal isolation of Internet mania and mobile phone conversations on windy pavements. Morse Peckham suggested long ago, too, that what Wagner meant by the creation of Wotan, standing as he does at the crossroads of love and power in the *Ring*, was that society's problems hinge to a large extent on the imperviousness of the natural world to morality.[5] Or, to put it another way: the more Wotan tries to harness the power of imagination and natural energy through the self-imposition of knowledge and law, the more this need for social order, love, and freedom founders when confronted with the amorality of instinct and survival. Indeed, Wotan himself resorts to violence when in desperation he brutally tears the ring from Alberich's finger. And he is ready to do so precisely because he feels unrestricted by contractual agreement. All of a sudden, in the name of power, law and lawlessness become virtually the same.

The predicament is suggested right at the start. The prelude to *Das Rheingold* is a powerfully suggestive musical idea with roots in the instrumental pastorale of the seventeenth and eighteenth centuries. Wagner adopted some of the devices of the pastoral genre—the drone bass, the lilting 6/8 meter, triadic harmony—and stretched them out, so to speak, into a ritualistic, static musical allegory that gives the listener a sense of returning back to a state of pristine innocence. The choice of E♭, too, forges a conscious musical link with the Norns at the start of the fourth drama in the cycle, *Götterdämmerung* who, for the first time in the *Ring*, give a retrospective account of Wotan and the World Ash Tree that puts the start of the whole cycle in a different light. Before the cycle begins, Wotan has violated the tree in order to gain wisdom and to wrest from it his spear, on which he carves his runes of world governance. He has sacrificed an eye and the tree has withered. But how can he justify any responsible rule of the world if it is based on a violent act? The more he searches for an answer the more he is drawn into a paradox of his own making that will cause him to fail in reconciling the conflict.

Thus the prelude to *Das Rheingold* is not quite what it seems. As the curtain rises, the serene harmony of the E♭-major chord gradually becomes a restless accompaniment to the troubled image on the bed of the Rhine. Indeed, the "swirling waters" and "wild craggy confusion" Wagner requires in the stage picture may be interpreted without too much special pleading as symbols of the cruelly insoluble dilemma that pervades Wotan's story from the start. In retrospect, the music of the prelude is mere illusion—a fitting start to a highly charged drama of feelings and ideas in which, under the surface, the irony is desperate and the action uncompromisingly violent.

Wagner refused to hide the brutalities in pagan myth. He also knew that for most modern audiences the gods and heroes in the *Ring* are remote and difficult to understand. *Das Rheingold* can be exciting drama, but it also has something didactic about it: it is a kind of mythological *Lehrstück*, or "teaching piece," with more than its fair share of bureaucratic advice and gnomic prophecies. In the unintentional comedy scene (as Stravinsky called it), in which Wotan refuses to pay the giants for building Valhalla, Fasolt pointedly reminds Wotan (though he hardly needs reminding) that his power is limited by legal contract. Loge tells the gods all they want to know about Alberich and the gold (though he is really instructing the audience about the workings of the myth), and Erda tries in vain to teach Wotan how to look into the future of the world. "All things that are, perish," she tells him, adding unhelpfully, "For the gods, a somber day will dawn/darken."[6] Loge's own prediction is typically brisk and to the point. The gods, he confides knowingly to the audience, "are hastening toward their end."

The metaphors and prophecies in *Das Rheingold* are a kind of blueprint for the mythical discourse in the rest of the *Ring* and help to build up the sense of inevitable end that colors the story of Wotan throughout the cycle. Wagner is also careful to introduce the audience to the different worlds of his myth. Like the prelude, they are never quite what they seem. Nature is allegedly "goodness and truth" (the Rhine maidens), but it can be scheming (Loge) and subtly double-edged (Erda). Society is "false and base" (to quote the Rhine maidens again), though it can have moments of great tenderness. And despite the colorful magic and childlike directness of the fairy-tale world—for many adults the most problematic level in the *Ring*— it is a savage primitive state where sadistic coercion (Alberich/Mime), brutal murder (Fafner/Fasolt), and the survival of the strong and cunning prevail.

Eero Tarasti has pointed out that each level of *Das Rheingold* has a distinct set of characters who can exist on two levels at once (the gods, for instance, are both part of society and personifications of nature) and move from one level to another.[7] This is the reason for the memorable orchestral transitions and "journeys," and it explains, often better than do the mechanics of the plot, some strange moments in the action. The ransoming of Freia for instance—usually judged to be a cumbersome and rather bureaucratic affair—is really the most significant event in *Das Rheingold* apart from Alberich's robbery of the gold. Up to the moment of Freia's departure the action takes place in a "timeless" world of nature and gods, but as soon as Fafner announces to Wotan that the Giants will take her away and keep her "until evening," the passing of real time begins to take effect. The golden apples wither and the gods age. Loge intimates to the gods (and the audience) that they are being forced to abandon nature ("the fruit droops and dies," he tells them) and to move onto a social plane where, like other mortals, they will grow "old and gray." At this point the tragic conflict between the natural and social worlds—the central focus of the entire *Ring* cycle—makes itself felt for the first time. From here onward Wagner fills the plot of *Das Rheingold* with events that literally mark out time like a clock: the journeys to and from Nibelheim, Alberich's sequence of disguises using the Tarnhelm, the laborious dragging of the gold onto the stage by the Nibelungs, and the strangely bureaucratic ritual of the piling up of the gold in front of Freia. Wotan agrees to give up the ring and let Freia return. The gods are freed from the tyranny of time and allowed to reenter the ahistorical realm of nature where Donner's thundercloud bursts to reveal the rainbow bridge to Valhalla.

Das Rheingold begins and ends with a nature myth. *Götterdämmerung*, the last work of the cycle, also frames the "historical" time of its central action (the social world of the Gibichungs) with a "timeless" prologue and a final scene that banishes history to celebrate the power of the natural elements. The parallel reinforces the already rather mechanical symmetries in Wagner's tale. But it is quite deliberate—and so are the differences. The three Norns at the beginning of *Götterdämmerung* are foreshadowed by the three Rhine maidens at the start of *Das Rheingold*. But the Norns begin their song in the minor version of the Rhine maidens' key (E♭) and with the heavier burden of a conflict that is about to reach its breaking point. The social struggle at the center of *Das Rheingold*—in which Wotan, with the help of the rational Loge, tricks Alberich into submission and defeat—is turned on its head in *Götterdämmerung* by Alberich's son Hagen, who, with the help of the ingenuous Gunther, deceives Siegfried and kills him. Both heroes go on journeys between the worlds of society and fairy tale, except that they go in reverse directions and between radically different kinds of worlds. Wotan's descent from the society of the gods into the bowels of the earth in Nibelheim in *Das Rheingold* is nearly the exact opposite of Siegfried's journey up the Rhine in *Götterdämmerung*, from the fairy-tale romance on Brünnhilde's rock to the hall of the gods' enemies, the Gibichungs. Similarly, Wotan's decision in *Das Rheingold* to heed the advice of a representative of nature (Erda) that he should part with the ring is reversed in *Götterdämmerung* when Siegfried decides to ignore the warning from the natural world (the Rhine maidens) and keeps the prize.

Perhaps the most striking parallel is between the last scenes. The triumphant yet decidedly hollow music that accompanies the gods into Valhalla at the end of *Das Rheingold* tells the audience that the story is still incomplete. Plaintive cries from the invisible Rhine daughters sully the triumphant march of the gods over the rainbow bridge into Valhalla—a confrontation between nature and society that is a reverse image of their reconciliation, through Siegfried's death, at the end of *Götterdämmerung*. (The symmetry is suggested, too, by the spectacular orchestral effects and the key of D♭ major common to both scenes.) The parallel inspired one of Wagner's best ideas: the last-minute appearance in *Das Rheingold* of the heroic "sword" motif in the orchestra just before Wotan greets Valhalla, as if it were announcing "a new deed to be accomplished in the future."[8] At the center of a continuing conflict between nature and society that has only been momentarily subdued by Wotan's decision to relinquish the ring (as Loge's cynical comments make clear), the motif emerges in the presence of the wrong hero like a lesson and a prophecy. The true hero of the story alone can properly resolve the conflict, it seems to say, and only by the end of the tale will he have succeeded in completing his task.

5. Symphonic Mastery or Moral Anarchy?

First Day: Die Walküre

The great writer on music Donald Francis Tovey once claimed, with some justification, that the enormous power of Wagner's music made him, by an odd paradox, a dramatist for listeners who are not habitual theatergoers. Tovey was well known as a vociferous opponent of Wagner extracts in the concert hall (by which he meant short arrangements such as the Ride of the Valkyries), though curiously he had no objection to whole scenes or acts performed with a full complement of singers. Audiences listening to these larger stretches of music away from the theater might even gain from the lack of a theatrical context, he wrote, finding themselves free at last from the aesthetic discomforts that are inseparable from all efforts to present Wagner on stage.[1]

Tovey's words are still music to the ears of those who react negatively to the (for many parlous) current state of Wagner production. Yet performances and judgments of Wagner's music at some distance, or even completely apart, from its full theatrical presentation will probably always raise more intriguing questions than they answer. Tovey rightly cites the case of Brahms (by no means the anti-Wagnerian most of his friends wished him to be), who liked his Wagner dramas one act at a time, placed at a distance from their dramatic content so that he could better savor their purely symphonic coherence. Wagner himself conducted the first-ever public performances of The Ride of the Valkyries and Wotan's Farewell from *Die Walküre* in a concert in Vienna on 26 December 26 1862, with detailed program notes about their scenic and dramatic contexts. The success of the extracts was enormous, despite the fact that the music, and Wagner's vivid notes, could only give a sketchy idea of their origin in the *Ring*, the music of which at the time was incomplete, and even as a libretto was unknown to most in the audience. (Wagner did not finish the music of the *Ring* until

1874, and the only published libretto available at the time of the Vienna concert was a private edition limited to only fifty copies.)

It seems surprising today, given the current rapid turnover of new music, that the Vienna concert was the first time any music from the *Ring* had been heard in public. Wagner had already been working on it seriously for nine years and knew that large chunks of it would be a success in the concert hall. So why had he not let some of it be heard before? The answer is partly circumstantial—Wagner was in exile during the 1850s and heavily in debt most of the time—but mainly ideological. Wagner simply did not want the seamlessness of his dramas, the burning musical arcs that span hours in the theater in the name of a utopian future for humanity, to be sullied by the practice of presenting mere highlights in concert form. After the first performance of the whole of *Die Walküre* in Munich on 26 June 1870, demands for concert performances of extracts from it were so great that this time Wagner felt compelled to explain his objections to them in public, even though he had encouraged the practice in the first place by personally conducting the Vienna concert some years before. By any standards the Munich world premiere of *Die Walküre* was a triumph, and even the most hostile of critics described it as a work of "gigantic talent."[2] Brahms, Liszt, Joachim, and Saint-Saëns, as well as many other musical luminaries in Europe, were all present, with the exception of Wagner himself, who had pointedly stayed away because King Ludwig II had ordered the performance to take place against his wishes. Indeed, Wagner continued to insist long afterward that only he could solve the problems of producing the work: "The strange success of the Munich performances of *Die Walküre*—with which I had nothing to do—showed me how incorrectly my work had so far been understood. If it had been properly understood it would not have occurred to anyone to ask me for permission to perform extracts from it in the concert hall."[3]

But as Wagner's most outstanding biographer, Ernest Newman, wryly noted, to say that *Die Walküre* had succeeded for the wrong reasons was to admit the fact of its success.[4] Wagner's zealous idealism, especially his argument that *Die Walküre* had been misunderstood because it had been performed outside the context of the complete *Ring* and was hence still vulnerable to exploitation as a series of "operatic" or "purely musical" numbers divorced from any serious dramatic meaning, paled before the enthusiasm that greeted the work. Indeed, far from ruining the prospects of Wagner's own production, the Munich premiere helped to generate so much interest in the *Ring* project and the building of a special festival theater for it in Bayreuth that the performance of the full cycle there, which eventually took place in 1876, almost seemed like a fact of history before it had actually happened.

The startling disparity between unstinting admiration for Wagner's music and skepticism about his dramatic ideas has arisen too frequently in the history of his fame for it simply to be described as a series of misunderstandings. Some of the greatest Wagnerians of the nineteenth century, including Baudelaire and Nietzsche, became immediate converts to Wagner's cause merely by hearing excerpts of his music in the concert hall. Not that they interpreted that cause in ways that were anything other than strikingly divergent from Wagner's own understanding of it. Baudelaire went so far as to say that the musical extracts he heard in the concert hall had a self-explanatory quality about them that made the larger works perfectly intelligible even to those who had no knowledge of their libretti.[5] It was hardly flawless logic, but in putting it that way Baudelaire was perhaps already suggesting that the sheer imaginative power of Wagner's music— its aura, so to speak—can transport listeners into their own wondrous, secretive worlds that make sense precisely because they have little to do with some distracting stage "business." A famous anecdote about the composer Anton Bruckner puts the point more bluntly. After seeing *Die Walküre* in the theater for the first time, Bruckner is said to have rounded off his enthusiastic comments on the symphonic breadth, the fabulous orchestration, the motivic inventiveness, the harmonic ingenuity, and not least the superb formal organization of Wagner's music with the irritable question: "Why *do* they burn Brünnhilde at the end?"[6]

The critical reaction to the first performance of *Die Walküre* in Bayreuth on 14 August 1876—this time as part of a staging of the entire *Ring*—was equally enthusiastic about Wagner's musical score, but, doubtless because it was being seen in the context of the cycle as a whole, critics were more reserved about its dramatic content. As usual, the most interesting comments came from those who refused to idolize him, and even eventually rejected him, yet still retained some critical respect for what he was trying to do. Max Kalbeck, an admirer of Brahms and eventually his official biographer, noted with approval Wagner's efforts consciously to overcome the limitations of the operatic medium with a "speaking orchestra" in which highly refined instrumentation and the huge expressive power of the composer's orchestral melodies compensated for the inability of sung drama to clarify dialectical and ironic moments in the text. But while Kalbeck admired the command of form and sensual expression in Wagner's music, he pointedly disapproved of its opposite in the drama itself. On the first act of *Die Walküre* he wrote, "Once the fleeting intoxication of the senses subsides, moral scruples start assembling in a long queue to claim their rights. In terms of its effect, the whole first act can be put beside the most sublime creations the human mind and art are capable of producing. Beautiful and moving as it is, however, its ethical anarchy is outrageous and provocative, a slap in the face for all religious feeling."[7]

Kalbeck goes on to say that it is no use claiming (as Wagner's admirers do) that other authors treat similar situations in the same way. Oedipus sleeps with his mother, but meets his dark fate unknowingly, without having the faintest idea of his guilt. He perishes as a tragic hero, and pays for the crime he committed in all innocence in such an appalling way that we come into conflict not with the hero, but with the powers that entwined him without his knowledge in a labyrinth of guilt. Wagner's intention is quite different. Wotan's children pursue their culpable passion knowingly and go to their destruction with "seeing eyes."

Biographer in the making as he was, Kalbeck could well have had in mind something of the kind he would never have to deal with when he eventually came to write his famous life of Brahms: Wagner's scandalous affair with Mathilde Wesendonck. Whether they slept with one another or not— for a number of reasons this is one of the central questions of Wagner biography, though we shall probably never know the answer for certain (see chapter 11)—their adulterous "affair" was an open secret in 1876, the obvious inspiration behind *Tristan und Isolde*, and also (supposedly) the external stimulus for the startling change from the remote world of *Das Rheingold* to the more human, glowing colors of *Die Walküre*. Later, Ernest Newman even went as far as saying that "we must credit her [Mathilde Wesendonck] with much of the music of *Die Walküre*," adding that "during the composition of the first act . . . [Wagner] constantly saw himself and her in his Siegmund and Sieglinde." Certainly Newman was right to point out that Wagner inserted into the composition sketch of the first act no fewer than seventeen coded messages to her. At the moment when Siegmund and Sieglinde "gaze raptly into each other's eyes with the utmost emotion," to cite one example, Wagner added "L.d.m.M??" (*Liebst du mich, Mathilde??*, or Do you love me, Mathilde??).[8]

Kalbeck was right in the sense that Wagner really did deliberately treat his self-created myth in a way completely different than his ancient forebears did. At the same time, Kalbeck was blissfully unaware of the Hegelian Left background of the *Ring* and the intellectual ferment of the 1840s that not only formed Wagner's ideas about the nature of community and the future of music, but also, in a radically different way, Marx's and Engels's *Communist Manifesto* and the dictatorship of the proletariat. In other words, Kalbeck's prim defense of conventional middle-class ethics missed the point entirely.

"If the term *Kultur*-Bolshevist had existed in Wagner's day," Thomas Mann said in a lecture on the *Ring* delivered in 1937, "[cultivated middle-class Germans] would undoubtedly have applied it to him."[9] It is hard to imagine Kalbeck, who remained entrenched in conservative music criticism to the end of his days, ever understanding the import of that striking statement, even though he lived long enough to be aware of the Russian Revolution and its immediate aftermath. (He died in 1921.) Even today the *Ring* has been swathed in so much cultural cotton wool and doubtlessly genuine, if intellectually naïve, panegyrics about the truly stunning qualities of Wagner's music that it is still sometimes difficult to see the point of Mann's remark. The "planetary success" (Mann again) accorded to the work by an international public may have made it a source of endless pleasure for the nerves and intellects of modern audiences, who are perhaps not as unlike audiences in Wagner's own time as we sometimes like to think. Even given the composer's blatantly political interests, however, it seems harder than ever now to take the *Ring* seriously as political drama on a par with the great plays of Shakespeare or Schiller, with whom Wagner liked to be compared. Claims on it by politicians of all ideological shades, including the very darkest, have not helped. In the Wagner anniversary year 1933 alone, Soviet commissar Anatoly Lunacharsky and Nazi propaganda minister Joseph Goebbels both saw it as a work exemplifying their idea of "revolution."[10] Indeed, the sum effect of political turf wars over the *Ring* has probably been its reduction in the eyes and ears of many to a meaningless and ugly surrealism. The writer Susan Hill, often forced as a child to go with her parents to hear the whole thing, which of course meant that she had to pretend to like it as well, has said frankly that it now reminds her of the kitchen scene in *Alice in Wonderland*, "where everyone is throwing pots and pans at everyone else, the baby is yelling at the top of its voice, the Duchess is screaming and there seems no good reason why it should ever end."[11]

Die Walküre, like the kitchen scene in *Alice*, can indeed be seen as an allegory of the underlying moral anarchy of modern society and its outwardly stable family structures. Wagner was a *Kultur*-Bolshevist before his time in the sense that he saw the *Ring* project from the start as a frontal attack on prevailing middle-class institutions and values, albeit with consequences different than those envisaged by Marxist philosophy. This has led to the criticism that he gave his cycle of four dramas a social and ethical dimension of such weight that it raised the stakes too high in terms of what a work of art—especially one that relies heavily on the notoriously elusive art of music—can be expected to deliver. When one is confronted with a work like *Die Walküre,* however, the argument is far from convincing. Not only did Wagner's musical inspiration blossom forth in this work as never before (he confessed as much himself), but he also created a powerful piece of theater that, despite its mythological paraphernalia, outdoes even Ibsen in showing how middle-class life has become enmeshed in a social order failing for well over two centuries to heal the wounds it has inflicted on society. Even if we have to accept now that aspects of Wagner's allegory are stilted, and in the nineteenth century they perhaps already were, there is no denying that the magnificence of this "terrible tragedy," as Wagner described it,[12] is due in no small measure to its ambition as social drama.

Die Walküre has always been by far the most popular work in the *Ring,* and, like the Vienna concert in 1862, when Wagner first introduced some of its music to the world, it has a profound effect on modern audiences. Its wonderful score sets alight not only a stirring adventure tale with all the usual ingredients—male rivalry, passionate love, adultery, the thrill of the chase, crime and punishment—but also a tragic family drama to which practically everyone can relate. One perceptive commentator, Robert Raphael, has even been tempted to describe it as "the horror of parenthood."[13] Wagner himself originally thought of calling it *Siegmund and Sieglind: The Punishment of the Valkyrie,*[14] a clumsier title than the one he eventually gave it, but a more accurate one in the sense that it clearly points to the fact that the drama is essentially about Wotan's children, who with "seeing eyes" defy the sanctity of parenthood by challenging his attempts to exploit them for his own ends. The startling emotional clarity of the final scene between Wotan and Brünnhilde in the third act is as powerful and relevant today as it was in the nineteenth century, at least in part because the cycle of deep affection between father and daughter, including the daughter's rebellion against the full abdication of the female subject to the father, and her subsequent punishment in the father's name, is still part of countless family histories.

The tragic paradoxes of *Die Walküre* are drawn from Greek myth and Shakespeare (particularly *King Lear*), but they also have a real basis in the mid-nineteenth-century idea that family relations inevitably reflect the bourgeois-capitalist system in which they are situated. Two barren marriages (Sieglind and Hunding, as well as Fricka and Wotan), incest between brother and sister (Sieglinde and Siegmund), and filicide by proxy (Wotan lets Hunding kill Siegmund) all contribute to the important idea that any attempt to escape family life with immoral acts directed against it (and hence the prevailing social order as well) only leads to tighter imprisonment within its moral code. *Die Walküre* shows the first calamitous effects of the conundrum within the orbit of human aspiration and feeling. It is not, as Brahms's biographer Max Kalbeck claimed, a perversion of Greek tragedy, but something entirely different, deliberately poised, albeit precariously, between supreme beauty and musical mastery on the one hand and, on the other, at the most intimate level, the tragic modern conflict of human beings in a disenchanted world.

6. Siegfried Hero

Second Day: Siegfried

At the end of the Walt Disney animated film version of *Beauty and the Beast*, the hero emerges from the skin of an ugly animal redeemed by the love of a faithful woman. The hero has long brownish-blond hair and a muscular body. His radiant blue eyes shine forth, and the swirl of his handsome torso as he emerges from his animal "other" gives the sign to the amazed onlookers—including his adoring savior, now miraculously turned into a beautiful princess—for dance and song. Transformed by the faith of his bride into an erotic ideal of youth and strength, he sets everyone free from the plague of past transgressions and the curse of darkness.

Disney's beast-cum-hero is also intelligent. The film stresses his vast library and a learning that is disconsolate because it has been won in the absence of true love. What is clear from the start is that his outer ugliness and uncouth ways belie his inner warmth and vast font of knowledge. He is the ideal modern hero: he has a murky past and less-than-elegant manners, perhaps, but he is always one step ahead of everyone, with a superior mind and huge warmth of character that will eventually, with a faithful woman at his side, carry humanity aggressively into a blazing future.

Wagner's Siegfried, by comparison, is often greeted by modern audiences with large doses of skepticism. Intelligent he definitely is not, and he celebrates his lack of intellect almost from the start. He has no history to speak of and scarcely knows who he is, let alone anything about sex. At the outset he looks naturally strong, with a powerful physique (the current stock of capable Wagnerian tenors permitting). And there is no doubt that when he comes face to face with the sleepy old dragon in the second act, he will be able to dispatch his animal "other" with almost alarming insouciance, unlike Disney's hero, who has a protracted emotional struggle getting rid of his.

61

Already in the first scene of the opera Siegfried's overbearing manner is loutish, an unsettling reincarnation of nineteenth-century hubris. Indeed, for many embroiled in the turbulence of modern life, he represents an appalling moral void that looks suspiciously like part of an unsettling drawing-board version of the hero figure first celebrated by fascist movements in the twentieth century. Disney's beast-hero is not without some of these traits as well, though despite the modern spin and unobtrusive reliance on nineteenth-century heroic archetypes, his story at first sight seems as fresh and delightful as ever. It was the sheer charm of *Siegfried*, too, that impressed even Wagner's most skeptical critics when it first appeared in public at the first complete performance of the *Ring* cycle in Bayreuth in 1876. "It shows all the characteristic qualities of the poet composer," the critic Paul Lindau wrote, expressing genuine surprise, "with a clarity and sharpness as none of the other musical dramas do."[1] Here was the composer who, at his best, could conjure sounds never before heard from the orchestra, who combined song with expressive instrumental writing to touch, through his hero, the deepest and most wonderful feelings in his audience, and who with breathtaking obstinacy never bothered to ask his listeners if they actually minded being taken to the limits of their endurance. This positive tone, surprising from a critic not usually that well disposed toward Wagner, was echoed by the composer's most prestigious opponent in the press, Eduard Hanslick, who was astonished to discover the "freshness" of tone, the realism, and the natural boyishness of the hero in the first two acts, speaking of him as a welcome contrast to the "stilted" character of the previous dramas, despite the questionable "brutality" of his forging songs.[2]

The small question marks in this sympathetic reception of *Siegfried*, however, have grown larger over the years. In particular, the apparent brutishness of the hero was felt by many even in the nineteenth century to travel too far beyond civilized moral boundaries, let alone the permissible limits of artistic expression. Some of the doubts admittedly had less to do with the work itself than with a lack of subtlety and insight that became all too apparent in the earliest performances and interpretations of it—a development in the history of *Siegfried* that Wagner himself predicted. This was one reason why Heinrich Porges, in his eyewitness account of the stage rehearsals for the first *Ring*, which was especially commissioned from him and personally vetted by Wagner, went out of his way to stress that "Siegfried should not create the impression of a character drawn with the conscious intention of violating the standards of civilized society; everything he says and does—even the rather crude aspects of his genuine boyishness—must be presented as the natural expression of an essentially heroic personality who has not yet found an object in life worthy of his superabundant strength."[3] The dubious policing of Siegfried's character was already too late. His boyishness may be genuine, and doubtless adolescent insecurity lies somewhere beneath his outer confidence (the teenager, for instance, is desperate to know where he comes from and who his parents are). But Siegfried the iconoclastic hero is evident from the start. He is a rebel against the status quo, a reckless forger of a magic sword and ransacker of a dragon's cave. In Christian terms he is, in Eric Bentley's words, "an unregenerate pagan devoid of compassion" who treats his mentor, Mime, as roughly as his anvil: he is a crude emanation of vital energy.[4]

Porges's description of the "essentially heroic" figure yet to find an object "worthy of his superabundant strength" is chilling as well. Hitler's letter to Wagner's son, Siegfried, written in Landsberg prison in 1924 after an early local election victory of the Nazi party in Bayreuth, says it all. "I owe my people not so much words as deeds," Hitler wrote, seven years before he eventually came to power. "I was filled with proud joy when I heard of the victory of the *Volk*—above all in the city where the sword of ideas with which we are fighting today was first forged by the Master."[5]

The heroic figure of Siegfried is in an especially precarious position in the richly embroidered allegory of the *Ring*. Essentially, heroic personalities may have long ago been relegated to the comic strip and remaindered in the industrialized fairy tale of the Walt Disney film factory, but Wagner's hero is still often seen (not without reason) as an oversized replica of a naïve and outmoded blond-beast primitive that anyone aware of the pervasive *völkisch* history of the archetype prefers to reject as one of the parts of the nineteenth- and early-twentieth-century imagination least relevant to their own concerns. Accordingly, the course of German history since 1876 has prompted many to interpret Siegfried less as the hero of a romantic dream of nature with murmuring forests and exotic creatures than as a nightmarish figure with a leading role in an epic that turned tragically into a self-fulfilling prophecy—a fair-headed, protofascist superman marching to the tune of the will to power toward catastrophe and the inevitable destruction of the German Reich.

But this rather lurid scenario hardly offers much insight into the complexities of this apparently steeliest of Wagnerian heroes and what he is supposed to represent. In fact, the figure of Siegfried is a daring mixture of the comic and the heroic (a mixture that Wagner took from Fouqué's *The Hero of the North*) with added ingredients taken from ancient myths about the sun. Not least Siegfried is intended as an analogy with the 1848–49 Revolution and its aftermath; he is, as Thomas Mann put it, a "harlequin, god of light, and anarchist social revolutionary, all in the same person."[6] And, like the hero in *Beauty and the Beast*, he takes part in a fairy-tale world, the savagery and brutality of which Wagner refused to cover up in a far more modern way than Disney would have ever dared.

Given its roots in popular fiction, *Siegfried* should be one of Wagner's most popular operas. The story is not difficult to grasp, with its deliberate borrowings from attractive fairy tales like *Sleeping Beauty* and Grimm's *The Boy Who Left Home to Learn Fear*. Wagner himself said that even those in the audience without the slightest knowledge of the story would be able to learn it easily from any performance of the opera because they would be "like children getting to know it in a fairy-tale."[7] The work contains well-known concert numbers such as the Forging Songs and the Forest Murmurs. Some of its themes are well known from the *Siegfried Idyll*, the justly famous and wonderfully allusive work Wagner wrote for his wife Cosima in 1870. And there has been no shortage of literature about it, including Bernard Shaw's vivid account in *The Perfect Wagnerite* that entertainingly (and mistakenly) equates Siegfried with the anarchist Bakunin, with whom Wagner stood on the barricades of the Dresden Revolution of 1849.[8]

On closer examination the story of the rough-and-ready, disconcertingly stupid boy of the woods who confronts evil with his innate superpower, effortlessly kills a dragon and one of his enemies (Mime) as if it were simply "natural" justice, and gets his woman in the end in predictable comic-book fashion is actually a far from simple allegory of social change that borrows heavily from several myths and the genres of popular fiction. At the same time, the allegory focuses on a number of concrete ideas; and Wagner's works do involve ideas and not belief, as Susan Sontag has rightly said.[9] First of all, it is crucial that Siegfried should be a hero of "nature." His purpose is that of "the artist of the future" to lead humanity, the "people," back to the heart of "nature." He is the antidote to a divisive Alexandrine culture and the embodiment of one fundamental idea. Greek antiquity represents the long-lost ideal of a close alliance of culture and community that has been rent asunder by the power interests of industry, state, and church. The task of the hero, the "artist of the future," is therefore to restore the vanished harmony of art and community (allegedly) known to the Greeks. And he is to do this by moving "modern" consciousness, focused as it is on money and competition, away from its center of interest with an aesthetically renewed mythology that could once again open it to the experience of the archaic. The goal of humanity, the restoration of a lost sense of unity, is directed both forward and toward a distant point in the past: the future of man is to become at the same time his "fundamental origin" *(Ursprung)*.[10]

It all sounds at first like the *éclat triomphale* of the composers of the French Revolution that Beethoven adopted in some of his symphonies: the end-directed striving for a brilliant conclusion in the brightest musical colors and rhythms that emulates the vision of a utopian future for mankind. This is why each act of *Siegfried* moves in an upward curve from darkness to light, from a minor key and sinister orchestration toward a blaze of color in the major. From the dominants of B$^\flat$ and F minor to D and E major in acts 1 and 2, respectively, and from G minor to a glorious C major in the final act, the musical curve each time moves higher and higher. An ever-widening network of symphonic motifs is meant to guarantee the unity of this magnificent formal arch, until the hero in the third act seems literally to traverse the curve himself by climbing up through the flames "to the peak" (according to Wagner's stage direction) to reach the loftiest plane of all, where he finds Brünnhilde. No one who has actually read Wagner's writings and absorbed their basic idea can fail to sense in the smallest details as well as in the larger forms of the music in *Siegfried* an allegory of the movement from the "dark ages" to the bright light of the future, the leading back to the "fundamental" feelings of the ancients and hence to man's "natural" condition, the striving for "perfection," and—last but not least—the reason why the work makes such nearly unattainable demands on the singer in the main role.

But seen in the context of the entire *Ring*, the hero Siegfried is already light-years away from the early revolutionary optimism of the French. And he always was, right from the moment during the 1848–49 Revolution when Wagner first invented him. He is so hedged about with opposites and contradictions that his development as a character is well-nigh impossible. It was again Eric Bentley who first pointed out that while Siegfried speaks of life, light, day, and creation, others speak of death, darkness, night, and annihilation.[11] At one point the Wanderer refers to Siegfried's imminent arrival like this: "in gladness, the god gives way to the eternally young." Wagner said of this passage that it should sound "like the proclamation of a new religion."[12] "Siegfried," he wrote, "is the man of the future whom we have wanted and desired but who cannot be made by us and who must create himself through our annihilation."[13] But this is contradicted by the continuation of the *Ring* itself: Siegfried is the one who is annihilated, and we, the audience, are offered renewal for the future by the music at the very end of *Götterdämmerung*, the most valuable quality of which, as Shaw rightly noted, is its "gushing effect."[14] If our Nordic superman is the man of the future who leads us with phenomenal strength into a new age of light and social harmony, why is he doomed?

The simple answer is that despite the brilliant visions of a future social utopia that flash past in *Siegfried*—not to mention the fake happy ending of *Götterdämmerung*, the almost Disney-like artificiality of which Shaw's icy critical gaze immediately recognized—Wagner intended the whole *Ring* project from the start as a profoundly pessimistic comment on the human condition. The boyish playfulness of the hero only makes matters worse. Indeed, Wagner himself grew weary of the almost overbearingly optimistic sense in *Siegfried* of successfully (and endlessly) overcoming the immediate past and returning to a pristine state of consciousness—a process that is reflected in his notorious agendas about the "end" of opera, the symphony, art as commerce, and even in the very philosophy that he inherited from the so-called Young Hegelians like Ludwig Feuerbach and Bruno Bauer. In 1856 he wrote to his benefactor Otto Wesendonck, "I am no longer attuned to *Siegfried*, and my musical sensibility already roams far beyond it to where my mood belongs—to the realm of melancholy."[15] The following year he finished composing the second act (though not its orchestration), packed away his Young Hegelian idealism, stopped his hero in his tracks on his way to the "new age," and went on to write *Tristan und Isolde* and *Die Meistersinger von Nürnberg*.

It is reasonable to explain Wagner's decision to leave his favorite hero stranded in a beautiful forest at the end of act 2 of *Siegfried* with the argument that he was beginning to have both philosophical and musical doubts about him. The thought that he now had to set to music the crucial confrontation at the center of the last act (the sharp blade of the hero's sword brutally cuts through the Wanderer's spear, the symbol of the latter's bondage to the past) could have persuaded him that he had overstated the Young Hegelian case against history. And there can be no doubt, as I explain in more detail in chapter 16, that when he set the work aside in 1857 he was beginning to question a main premise behind his system of ideas concerning the value of the "new" in radically breaking with the past. Here it is enough to say that it gradually began to dawn on Wagner that the belief he once entertained in the radically new as a central category of the modern could only lead to a suffocating purity, an ever-tightening circle of endless renewal and meaningless repetition. For a former advocate of revolutionary change who had actually been on the barricades in Dresden in 1849 alongside Bakunin, it was just about the most pessimistic thing he could imagine.

Another reason he interrupted work on *Siegfried* in 1857 was an economic one: without a publisher or a theater who would even begin to contemplate the prospect of taking on the *Ring,* he was forced into moving on to another work, *Tristan und Isolde,* which he fondly thought would be easier to perform and bring him some money. In the long run the dire economic circumstances that forced Wagner to take this step were not a catastrophe, but rather a stroke of good luck. After finishing *Tristan,* and after that *Die Meistersinger,* he returned to his abandoned hero after an interval of twelve years and began composing the third act of *Siegfried* with a vastly enriched musical language that he had developed while composing those two profoundly pessimistic works. The doomed trajectory of his favorite hero was now musically assured. The stratospheric violins in unison that accompany Siegfried just before his meeting with Brünnhilde underscores still more emphatically Wagner's original metaphor of upward movement into the rarified heights of German idealism. Yet the wonderfully luminous counterpoint and sheer harmonic invention that suddenly confront the listener in the third act of *Siegfried* now convey a much truer sense of the tragedy that lies behind the hero's ecstatic discovery of himself and his feelings of love. The sheer symphonic sweep of the final act (which is much less palpable in the first two) drives Siegfried toward one of the most complex endings in all of Wagner—a deliriously happy conclusion in an emphatic C major in which, on the brink of disaster, he sings with his newly awakened princess of "laughing death" *(lachender Tod).*

7. Finishing the End

Third Day: Götterdämmerung

The *Ring* has been produced and "explained" in so many contradictory ways that it probably counts as the most ingratiating work ever written for the operatic stage. Whether one thinks of Bernard Shaw's matter-of-fact socialist view of it or the dreamy Christian-Catholic commentary by the young Paul Claudel (not to mention sharply divergent interpretations in more recent times), the skeptic may wonder whether the *Ring* can mean anything at all.[1] Shaw would have been delighted to read in Cosima's diaries that Wagner, on a journey up the Thames, described the City of London as "Alberich's dream come true—Nibelheim, world domination, activity, work, everywhere the oppressive feeling of steam and fog" (27 May 1877). And Claudel must have been intrigued by parts of Wagner's writings that have a direct bearing on seemingly Christian references in the *Ring*—the abstruse connection between the Holy Grail and Fafner's Hoard outlined in the essay *The Wibelungs* (1848–49), for instance, or the trenchant analysis of the religious basis of myth in the treatise *Opera and Drama* (1851–52).

Virtually any opinion about the *Ring* can be supported by Wagner himself, who once summed up his all-encompassing view of it by bragging that it contains "the very essence and significance of the world in all its possible phases." Wagner, as Shaw said, can be quoted against himself almost without limit.[2] Yet the more he tried to explain his own work, the more he was aware that to interpret the *Ring* coherently is to venture onto a slippery precipice. "We must learn to *die*," he wrote emphatically in a letter to his former colleague and fellow revolutionary August Röckel, "and *to die* in the fullest sense of the word; fear of the end is the source of all lovelessness."[3] This key sentence about the *Ring*'s "meaning" was really not much more than a Feuerbach-like homily on the nature of love mixed with the old cliché that heroes' lives, in order to be successful, must be untarnished by the fear of death. In any case, two years later Wagner changed his mind. After reading Schopenhauer, he solemnly announced to Röckel in 1856 that he now saw "love" as an "utterly and completely devastating" *(gründlich und verheerend)* part of the *Ring*.[4] Indeed, in his opinion the revolution was so complete that he had to provide the cycle with yet another new ending. In 1856 it was already the third.[5]

Wagner's difficulties in coming to terms with the *Ring* (at least in his letters and according to Cosima's diaries) are no more obvious than in his comments on *Götterdämmerung*. "The gods' downfall is not the result of points in a contract," he complained to the literal-minded Röckel, "for which one would need only the services of a legally qualified politician acting as a lawyer; no, the necessity of this downfall," he added vaguely, "arises from our innermost feelings." Nor was the significance of the ending the only part of *Götterdämmerung* he found hard to elucidate. Explaining to Röckel why Brünnhilde yields so quickly to Siegfried in the first act, he wrote desperately, "You feel that something 'inexpressible' is happening here, so it is very wrong of you to ask me to speak out on the subject!" Years later, when at last he was able to compose the music, the work at times seemed to be quite alien. Not only was the logic of the action as awkward to justify as ever, but the text had also gone cold on him. The scene between Waltraute and Brünnhilde in the first act, Cosima wrote in her diaries, "he finds 'utterly incomprehensible,' so completely did he forget it" (20 June 1871).

Wagner's perplexed reactions are a striking contrast to the brash certainties of some of his admirers, including Shaw, who was the first to present a seemingly watertight case against *Götterdämmerung* that makes critical capital out of its creator's confusion. On the surface Shaw's main complaint seems to be about the "outbreak of the old operatic Adam" in Wagner.[6] Certainly the libretto of *Götterdämmerung*—first written in 1848 as *Siegfrieds Tod* (Siegfried's death) and revised in 1852—has more than a few remnants of the "number" opera Wagner was at pains to discredit, including the choral tableau of the Vassals scene; the conspiratorial vengeance trio in the second act, which Shaw mischievously likened to the trio of the three conspirators in Verdi's *Un ballo in maschera;*[7] and the cataclysmic eruption of the natural elements at the end borrowed from French opera (more on this later). Wagner himself told his assistant Heinrich Porges during rehearsals for the first performance in 1876 that the scene between Gutrune, Hagen, and Siegfried in the second act is a "very detailed dialogue," "a kind of animated conversation on the stage, to be performed wholly in the style of comic opera."[8] He had not even bothered to tamper with the operatic formulas in the 1852 revision, despite having only just consigned "opera" and all its attendant vices to the rubbish heap of history in *Opera and Drama*. As Shaw knew, Wagner the theorist and Wagner the practical man of the theater were not always one and the same.

What really disturbed Shaw was his feeling that by the time Wagner began to compose *Götterdämmerung* he had come such a long way, artistically and intellectually, since writing the libretto that the music no longer rang true. "There is not a bar in the work," he wrote, "which moves us as the same themes move us in The Valkyrie. . . . When Wagner first sketched Night Falls on The Gods he was 35. When he finished the score . . . he had turned 60. No wonder he had lost his old grip of it and left it behind him."[9]

We know from Cosima's diaries that Shaw was partly right. Busy with the music of the second act on 28 July 1871, Wagner is quoted as saying, "I curse this composing, this grind I am involved in. . . . This *Nibelungen* writing should have been finished long ago." And about the third act, Cosima writes, "R. is very tired of composing. . . . [O]n the arrival of Siegfried's corpse he could in fact just write in the score, 'see *Tristan*, Act III'" (17 March 1872). Nor are these isolated examples. He has "no desire to write another note of his *Nibelungen*" (2 November 1869); he speaks of "losing the urge" to compose (24 November 1870); he "girds himself for composition" (20 June 1871), and he even doubts his skill: "I am now sketching a big aria for Hagen. . . . It is incredible what a bungler I am. . . . Mendelssohn would raise his hands in horror if he ever saw me composing" (23 June 1871).

For Shaw it was simply historical bad luck that *Götterdämmerung* had to wait for more than two decades before Wagner, who had allegedly long since reneged on the spirit of the 1848–49 Revolution, could finish it. "Siegfried did not arrive, and Bismarck did. . . . Alberich had got the ring back again, and was marrying into the best Valhalla families with it."[10] But the witty image of the once passionate revolutionary who no longer believed in his own allegory and was therefore unable to find the right music for it is belied by Wagner's score. Indeed, in retrospect it seems like an astonishingly happy chance of history that Wagner (leaving moments of doubt aside) composed *Götterdämmerung* when he did. He said to Cosima that after *Die Walküre* and the first two acts of *Siegfried*, "you can understand that I felt the need . . . to write *Tristan*" (6 March 1870). Before returning to the *Ring* he went on to finish *Die Meistersinger von Nürnberg* as well, and his music gained so much in power and sophistication as a result that it is difficult to imagine how he would have done justice to the daunting scale of the cycle's grand conclusion had he composed it any earlier. The sheer richness of harmonic detail, the ever-resourceful transformation of motifs, and the vitality of orchestral invention worthy of Strauss or Mahler:

this was not the work of someone whose head had been turned by the outcome of the Franco-Prussian War and who had allowed the *Ring* allegory—as Shaw put it—to "collapse."[11]

Wagner's conceptual and practical difficulties with *Götterdämmerung* were due not simply to the passage of time and his growing estrangement from an old libretto, but also to an aspect of the work that had been there from the start: its negative dramatic structure. We only need to imagine the 1848 libretto to guess the nature of the problem. The action begins in the Hall of the Gibichungs (the prologue and the other *Ring* dramas were not written yet), which means that Siegfried and Brünnhilde are not seen together as lovers at all. The antihero Alberich does not confront his great antipode Wotan or rob the gold from the Rhine maidens: he simply tells Hagen at the beginning of the second act that he has stolen it. As in the final version, Siegfried does abduct Brünnhilde in the first act, and she does (unjustly) accuse Siegfried of rape and plot his murder in the second. But if the hero and heroine are only shown together as implacable enemies, the sudden happy end, which in the 1848 version includes a fleeting image of Brünnhilde on horseback reconciled with a Siegfried especially resurrected for the purpose, hardly looks convincing. Moreover, Alberich is deprived of the chance of actually committing his primal crime in front of the audience—the rending asunder of nature and society that Siegfried ultimately reverses by sacrificing his life, and on which the full force of the drama depends.

To be effective, the bleak dramaturgy of the 1848 version not only needed the characters' epic narrative of past events to set it in relief, but it needed sharp physical contrasts on stage as well. Wagner's solution was to give *Siegfrieds Tod* a prologue, to expand it into the whole *Ring* cycle, and then later to revise it again in light of the three new preceding dramas he had written in the meantime.[12] But the negative images and drastic reversals remained. Wagner even completely rewrote two key scenes in order to reinforce them. In the revised version, the Norns now speak of Wotan desecrating the World Ash Tree to make a shaft for his spear, and of the breaking of the spear by Siegfried. (Wagner added this last event to the final version of *Siegfried* as well; curiously, it is not present in the first version of that work either.) They also speak of Wotan sitting with shattered spear in hand waiting for the end, ordering his heroes to fell the withered tree and pile the logs around Valhalla, which at the end of the drama Loge will set alight.

In another scene Brünnhilde hears the same story from Waltraute, and one of the reasons for the reiteration is that Wagner wanted to further strengthen the imagery of the resigned god and the spear so that they not only recall earlier parts of the cycle, but also act as the reverse of a central image in *Götterdämmerung* itself. At the end of *Die Walküre* Wotan announces that only the hero unafraid "of the tip of my spear" *(meines Speeres Spitze)* shall penetrate the fire surrounding Brünnhilde's rock. When Siegfried decides in *Götterdämmerung* to swear a fatal oath on the tip of Hagen's spear, Hagen deliberately mimics Wotan's words; and after Siegfried unwittingly betrays the oath in the third act, Hagen uses the weapon to kill him. Originally a prophecy of Siegfried's heroic deeds, the same words and the same symbol come to foretell, and to be instrumental in, his death on trumped-up grounds of perjury.

Left over from the original version are some alarming changes of personality and stagy effects (Shaw rightly abhorred them) that are still hard to take, even if in the context of the entire *Ring* they are easier to understand. No number of magic potions and rebarbative oath takings can make us really believe Siegfried's selective amnesia about Brünnhilde until we realize that he has left behind the world of Sleeping Beauty and Grimms' fairy tales in *Siegfried* and entered an almost Shakespearean world of human treachery and bloody intrigue in the Hall of the Gibichungs. On this level of the epic, the evil surroundings seem to infiltrate his character and turn him into his own opposite by a kind of mythological osmosis. Brünnhilde—after Wotan the most ubiquitous "traveler" in the *Ring*—escapes elegantly enough from Wotan's sphere of influence in *Die Walküre* (so much so that she can dictate the terms of her own punishment) and effortlessly turns into a fairy-tale princess in *Siegfried*.

But when she is confronted with the "false" Siegfried in *Götterdämmerung,* the sight of the powerless heroine still wearing the all-powerful ring is scarcely credible. So, too, is her schizophrenic leap into the character of an evil, scheming villainess who helps the Gibichungs to plot Siegfried's downfall—that is, until we realize that this is yet another of Wagner's fearful symmetries. Having been forced by a reluctant Wotan to leave the gods, but at least having done so on her own terms, she is now forced by a determined Siegfried to journey back to the gods' enemies, and according to their conditions.

It can be argued against Shaw that these punctiliously dialectical structures in the expanded *Ring* are actually set into welcome relief in *Götterdämmerung* by the messier methods of opera. Wagner's sometimes near-fatal passion for binary opposites, stemming in part from his interest in German idealistic philosophy, was throughout his career nearly always saved from leading to certain theatrical disaster with timely injections of down-to-earth operatic practice. Shaw insists that the trajectories of

Wagner's libretti and his music had to be the same, and that when they were not, aesthetic and ideological failure inevitably ensued. But Wagner's music during the course of his life became radically distant from grand opera, while his libretti at the same time remained forever indebted to its management of large-scale effect and intimate passion. The disparity was a guarantor of success, not a disaster.

This perhaps explains the striking similarity between Shaw's critical method and that of Heinrich Heine, who also did not hesitate to see a politically inspired allegory in a work like Meyerbeer's *Robert le diable* (Robert the Devil), which enjoyed a fabulously kitsch-laden libretto by Eugène Scribe and Germain Delavigne, ensuring its success from the start in the heady atmosphere of 1831 post-revolutionary Paris. In some ways Shaw's and Heine's critical method simply reflects the gallimaufry that at the time usually passed for a successful grand opera libretto. In the jumble of Wagner's allegory, Shaw picked out Siegfried both as the political revolutionary Bakunin (with whom Wagner was indeed associated during the Dresden Revolution) and as a Protestant unwittingly giving way to Bismarck in the guise of the evil reactionary Alberich. Similarly, Heine saw Robert as Louis Philippe, the so-called Citizen King of France from 1830 to 1848, who was the son of the notorious Duke of Orléans, known as Philippe Egalité, and of a princess who was as pious as the daughter Penthièvers.[13] Robert, according to Heine, thus embodied the spirit both of his father, the incarnation of evil and the revolution, and of his mother, the incarnation of good and the *ancien régime*. The allegorical syncretism in the libretti set by Meyerbeer and Wagner, in other words, found its match in critical responses from Heine and Shaw that were equally as alluring and provocative.

Only in the 1922 preface to the fourth edition of *The Perfect Wagnerite* did Shaw admit that historical events culminating in the disaster of the First World War had vindicated the calculated ambivalence in Wagner's allegory.[14] It is true that in grand opera—the tradition that left perhaps its deepest imprint on Wagner's works—the heroes are maddeningly indecisive about their class allegiances. Masaniello in Auber's *La muette de Portici* (The mute girl of Portici), first performed in 1828 (also with a libretto by Scribe and Delavigne), offered a prescient image of the social rebel that was to emerge in the 1830 Revolution, despite the setting of the opera in Naples and Portici in 1647. Masaniello bravely leads a rebellion against the status quo but saves the lives of his royal superiors, and is killed by his own men as a consequence. And in the contest for best equivocal hero stands no less a figure than Wotan, who is inclined to appear either as guiltless, basking in his own magnificence, or as disconsolate, desperately in need of being relieved of his guilty past.

Intended no doubt in part to thrill and at the same time pacify the audience, the presentation of the natural elements in many grand operas seems swiftly to resolve the conundrum at the end, but without actually doing so. Valhalla is consumed by fire and Hagen is pulled down by the Rhine maidens into the depths of the Rhine; Vesuvius conveniently erupts in *La muette*; and shortly before the final tableau of *Robert le diable*, Robert's father and tempter, the devil Bertram, is swallowed up by the earth. Yet simultaneously a celebration of the status quo is in order. In the original 1848 libretto of *Götterdämmerung*, Wotan, the invisible reigning god, is acclaimed by the men and women surrounded by the flames of Siegfried's and Brünnhilde's funeral pyre just as the hero of *Robert le diable* is led to his princess in the nave of a cathedral, accompanied by a chorus of angels and earthly celebrants, or, in Heine's caustic words, "in the bosom of the church surrounded by the humming of clerics and clouded in incense."[15]

In a chapter called "Why He Changed His Mind" added to the first German edition of *The Perfect Wagnerite*, Shaw claimed that Wagner had set his original enthusiasm for the 1849 Dresden Revolution "to his own greatest music," only to deride it twenty years later in the expanded *Ring* "to the music of Rossini."[16] All that actually happened was that Wagner had created four dramas instead of one, dramas that shifted the emphasis from the heroic optimism of Siegfried toward the tragic resignation of Wotan. And contrary to what has been suggested by Shaw and others after him, including Kurt Hildebrandt and Carl Dahlhaus, there was no need for him to wait for the infamous day of Louis Napoleon's coup d'état in Paris in 1851, when the revolution finally collapsed, before "changing his mind." In Heine's terms, the vacillation between the desire for revolution and the "end," the realization of the evil it can unleash, and the calming sense of some kind of retrenchment pervading the endings of works like *La muette de Portici* and *Robert le diable* are also a constituent part of the ending of the *Ring*. The librettists of grand opera, in other words, had already provided Wagner with a model for just such a volte-face.

Wagner made good use of the highly calculated ambivalence he inherited from grand opera, however, by creating two heroes instead of one—one on each side of the political divide—a maneuver that at least tried to turn inspired kitsch into something more challenging. Siegfried sacrifices his life in the name of a new social order while Wotan, in effect the representative of the *juste milieu*, moves in a gray area between absolute power and the inability to rule. And the combination allowed a riddle-infested shadow to fall over the end of the *Ring* that has held generations of audiences and scholars in thrall ever since.

The only other work that features nearly such a controversial presentation of the mythical revolutionary ethos of the nineteenth century as a conflict between two blood-related yet politically opposed figures is Verdi's *Don Carlos*, first performed in 1865. The tense relationship between Don Carlos, the hero of freedom, and his father King Philip, the tragically indecisive ruler who eventually sides with the reactionary Catholic Church demanding the death of his own son, comes to its climax in a concluding scene not unlike the end of the *Ring* in the way the obviously contemporary political allusions of the action are positioned and realized. Indeed, it was widely believed at the time, as Georges Bizet put it in a letter to his composer friend Louis Lacombe, that "Verdi is no longer an Italian. He is imitating Wagner."[17] Bizet was probably thinking of *Lohengrin*, then one of Wagner's best-known operas, which at its end, with the appearance of Lohengrin's successor Gottfried, already contains the seeds of the idea of the failed leader in a strife-torn struggle for redemption, followed by a younger heroic figure who is destined to achieve something that the older hero never could. Both Verdi and Wagner were interested at the ends of *Don Carlos* and *Götterdämmerung*, too, in avoiding the dully recurring image, familiar from grand opera, of the lone and haplessly divided hero.

It therefore makes sense to take a more exact look at this rare moment when the two operatic giants of the mid-nineteenth century, who had nothing to do with each other during their eventful lives, are closer than they normally seem. I shall do that in the next chapter in the context of Walter Benjamin's theory of seventeenth-century baroque drama. Indeed, the comparison with Verdi shows that Wagner was more focused about *Götterdämmerung* and its long-term implications than Shaw originally imagined. Finishing the end was a notable feat against the odds. The vast project of the *Ring* was intended from the start as a striking utterance about the condition of humanity. After many interruptions and serious doubts about his ability to complete the composition of it, Wagner seems to have grasped its full implications in musical terms only at the very last minute.

PART III

The Elusiveness of Tragedy

8. *Don Carlos* and *Götterdämmerung*

Two Operatic Endings and Walter
Benjamin's Trauerspiel

DISCONSOLATE WORLD HISTORY

Walter Benjamin's book *Origin of the German Mourning Play (Ursprung des deutschen Trauerspiels)* was researched and written between 1919 and 1925. Benjamin submitted it to the University of Frankfurt am Main as his postdoctoral thesis, only to have it gently suggested to him in a letter dated 27 July 1925 from the dean of the Faculty of Philosophy, Professor Franz Schultz, that he should withdraw it.[1] Legend has it that the Frankfurt professors did not understand a word of it. But some little-known contemporary reviews of its publication in 1928 and its immediate influence on others, most notably Adorno in his Kierkegaard book of 1933, show that its message was clearly understood at the time.[2]

Benjamin's failed postdoctoral thesis is an esoteric study of German baroque drama, an attempt to revaluate the once despised literary art of the German seventeenth century. As Charles Rosen says in a more recent and justly famous review of the English translation,[3] it is also "a sustained attack on almost all the forms of criticism and literary study that were practiced in the university—and that are still practiced today."[4] My initial reading of this difficult book is influenced by Rosen's, though I want to continue my analysis into areas he does not discuss. Also, given the few derogatory words devoted to opera in his book on the mourning play,[5] Benjamin would doubtless have put Verdi's *Don Carlos* and Wagner's *Götterdämmerung*—the two nineteenth-century operas aspiring to the condition of the tragic on which this chapter focuses—low on his list of intellectual priorities. At the risk of reading him too much against the grain, I nevertheless want to look at the endings of these operas in the light of his theories.

For Benjamin, classical tragedy and the baroque mourning play are not only separated by time; they are also entirely different. He therefore rejects the view, current in the 1920s, that plays by baroque dramatists such as Andreas Gryphius and Daniel Caspers von Lohenstein were barbarous and pedantic imitations of Greek tragedy. He also dismisses contemporary baroque theorists, who tried to give dignity to the plays by misleadingly claiming that they fulfilled the requirements for tragedy laid down by Aristotle. Instead, Benjamin distinguishes tragedy from *Trauerspiel*, describing them as two distinct genres in terms of three main categories that are also central to nineteenth-century operas that aspire to the condition of the tragic: history, myth, and social hierarchy. On the content of the mourning play of the baroque, Benjamin writes, "Historical life, as it was conceived at that time, is its content, its true object. In this it is different from tragedy. For the object of tragedy is not history, but myth, and the tragic stature of the *dramatis personae* does not derive from rank—the absolute monarchy—but from the pre-historic epoch of their existence—the past age of heroes."[6]

As Rosen says, the relation of the plays "to the theological outlook of the German seventeenth century, in particular to the devaluation of everyday life in the Lutheran opposition to the Counter Reformation (most of the German playwrights were Lutheran),"[7] is also a subject that interests Benjamin. The rigorous morality of Lutheran teaching, Benjamin insists, influenced civic life and made it a testing ground, though one that was only indirectly religious. It instilled into the people a strict sense of duty and obedience, "but in its great men it produced melancholy."[8] Rosen then goes on to say that this melancholy, according to Benjamin, is alien to Greek tragedy.[9] For admirers of Aeschylus and Sophocles, the claim may look overwrought, and indeed Benjamin's point is not so much that melancholy was alien to the Greeks, but rather that the grief of the mourning plays sprang from the melancholy of the great men of the seventeenth century. That melancholy, in turn, in ways unfamiliar to the ancient tragedians, is entwined in the plays with politics and theology: "The antithesis between the power of the ruler and his capacity to rule led to a feature peculiar to the *Trauerspiel* which . . . can be illuminated only against the background of a theory of sovereignty. This is the indecisiveness of the tyrant. The prince, who is responsible for making the decision to proclaim the state of emergency, reveals, at the first opportunity, that he is almost incapable of making a decision."[10] The enduring fascination of the tyrant is rooted in the conflict between the impotence and depravity of his person, on the one hand, and, on the other, the extent to which the age was convinced of the sacrosanct powers of his role: "It was therefore quite impossible to derive an easy moral satisfaction ... from the tyrant's end. For if the tyrant falls, not simply in his own name, as an individual, but as a ruler and in the name of mankind and history, then his fall has the quality of a judgment, in which the subject too is implicated."[11]

Politics and theology are also implicated in the conception of history in the *Trauerspiel* as catastrophe. Benjamin speaks of the heroic sense of time in the mourning play that is, so to speak, frozen. This freezing of time is antihistorical in the sense that it signifies the need to bring history to an end in a world drained of a historical dynamic. For the baroque dramatist, Benjamin writes, chronological movement is grasped and analyzed in a spatial image. Indeed, his *Trauerspiel* book has been not incorrectly described as an account of what it means to convert time into space filled with what he calls an awareness of the "disconsolate chronicle of world-history."[12] However, this is not, as far as I can see, an attempt to define the genre in terms of its effect. In the book Benjamin rails often enough against critics who like to see tragedy in terms of catharsis and what Nietzsche's critic Wilamowitz-Moellendorf rather nicely described as "the unfortunate pair, fear and pity."[13] Benjamin prefers rather to describe the genre in terms of materialist metaphors that one can see and touch—old relics, fragments, ruins—in which a discontinuity of meaning and image rejects the false appearance of artistic unity.

REDEFINING THEORIES OF THE SYMBOL AND ALLEGORY

Benjamin clearly is not just talking about German baroque drama. The book has a wide range of reference, almost as if Benjamin, like the baroque dramatists themselves, deliberately chose a dead object in order to extract out of it something of enormous and vital consequence for his own time. It is obvious that he deliberately (and wildly) oversteps the material he presents to outline a critical method that reflects his own pessimism—a theory of catastrophe in a real world in which one no longer waits for the moment when the Messiah will appear to effect even small changes.

Benjamin's book is also clearly relevant to the intellectual world of romanticism. The discussion of allegory in the last part shows that he was concerned with romantic theories of the symbol and not just with the allegorical elements in baroque drama. What he wants to do, he says, is to create a philosophical basis for the study of allegory as a whole.[14] And central to this project is a new definition of the borderline between symbol and allegory. Benjamin objects to the view of the romantics, who approved of the simultaneous presence in the symbol of the general and the particular. The romantics saw allegory on the one hand as seeking access to the general through the particular, and as such artistically less worthy, since its expressive power is exhausted once its meaning has been revealed. Due to its self-referential properties and ability to fuse contraries, the symbol, in contrast, can express the inexpressible and open up an infinity of meaning that allegory cannot.

Benjamin calls this definition destructive because it has repressed a genuine, theological notion of the symbol: "The unity of the material and the transcendental object, which constitutes the paradox of the theological symbol," he writes, "is distorted into a relationship between appearance and essence."[15] As a symbolic construct, according to the romantics, the beautiful is supposed to merge with the divine in an unbroken whole. The heart of the ethical subject gets lost in the beautiful soul, with the result that both classical and romantic thinkers, by turning the symbol into an absolute while rejecting the category of allegory, misjudged both forms of expression. Only two scholars, Friedrich Creuzer and Joseph Görres, had an inkling of the true state of affairs—Creuzer when he introduces the notion of time into differentiating the two categories, and Görres when he associated symbol with movement, and allegory with the notion of dogged perseverance (*Beharrlichkeit*).[16]

Benjamin's own way of contrasting the concepts goes something like this:

> Whereas in the symbol the transfigured face of nature in the light of redemption appears fleetingly with the transfiguration of decline, in allegory the observer is confronted with the *facies hippocratia* of history as a petrified, primordial landscape. Everything about history that, from the very beginning, has been untimely, sorrowful, unsuccessful, is expressed in a face—or rather in a death's head. And although such a thing lacks all "symbolic" freedom of expression, all classical proportion, all humanity—nevertheless, this is the form in which man's subjection to nature is most obvious. . . . This is the heart of the allegorical way of seeing, of the baroque, secular explanation of history as the Passion of the world; it is significant only in the stages of its decline.[17]

Benjamin is not just berating the romantics for refusing to formulate a theory of allegory. They spurned allegory in favor of a more impressive theory of the symbol. But they actually indulged wholesale themselves in allegorical forms and techniques, sometimes borrowing from the baroque, while under the mistaken impression that they were nobly trying to revive the spirit of classical tragedy. Benjamin rightly points out that no one struggled more than Schiller did to re-create the pathos of antiquity in subjects rooted in political history—subjects with no connection to tragic myth. And the same can be said about Wagner, who took Schiller as a model here. In an early enthusiastic review of Bellini's *Norma*, written in 1837, Wagner was already suggesting, borrowing an idea from Schiller, that a work like *Norma* could lead to a revival through the medium of opera of "the demeanor of Greek tragedy,"[18] a prescient remark in view of a similar faith he later place in the *Ring*. But Wagner's passion for allegory—a passion he never really discussed—led him to drench his stage works with Christian images and clear references to modern social and philosophical ideas that bear no relation to Greek tragedy whatsoever, even though—and this may be what Wagner meant by the word "demeanor"—they aspired to its ambition.

Benjamin claims that the technique of romanticism leads in a number of respects into the realm of emblematics and allegory, though he preferred to present the relationship with another image from the baroque. Here is the famous passage from his book again:

> In its fully developed, baroque, form allegory brings with it its own court; the profusion of emblems is grouped around a figural centre, which, as opposed to the approximate descriptions of concepts, allegories do not lack. The emblems seem to be arranged in an arbitrary way: *The confused "court"*—the title of a Spanish *Trauerspiel*—could be considered as the model of allegory. This court is subject to the law of "dispersal" and "collectedness." Things are assembled according to their significance; indifference to their existence would allow them to be dispersed again. The disorder of the allegorical scenery presents the opposite of the elegant boudoir. In the dialectic of this form of expression the fanaticism of the process of collection is balanced by the slackness with which the objects are arranged.[19]

In the wider context of Benjamin's theory of melancholy, the allegorical technique becomes part and parcel of the view that life is an illusion that, when dissipated, reveals nothing. Elsewhere, Benjamin cites Schopenhauer both critically and admiringly to support the idea. Indeed, Schopenhauer's insights into the differences between Greek and modern tragedy are central to Benjamin's own thesis. Schopenhauer believed that the tendency to the sublime in modern, as opposed to ancient, tragedy was the dawning of Christian resignation and renunciation: "the tragic heroes of the ancients show resolute and stoical subjection under the unavoidable blows of fate; the Christian tragedy, on the other hand, shows the giving up of the whole will to live, cheerful abandonment of the world in the consciousness of its worthlessness and vanity."[20]

Following Schopenhauer, Benjamin insists, recklessly perhaps, that the knowledge that the world and life can afford us no true satisfaction is the essential, indeed the exclusive, characteristic of seventeenth-century allegory. This is the true significance of its discontinuities, he claims, its unresolvable discrepancies between meaning on the one hand and visual signs and images on the other.

OPERA AND THE "DOWNFALL" OF THE *TRAUERSPIEL*

One of the weaknesses of Benjamin's *Trauerspiel* book is that it is reluctant to investigate the role of music. In the chapter on allegory Benjamin does point to the lesson to be learned from the musical philosophy of romantic writers: "Music—by virtue of its own essence . . . is something with which the allegorical drama is intimately familiar. This, at least, is the lesson to be derived from the music philosophy of the romantic writers, who have an elective affinity with the baroque."[21]

Benjamin is interested in a non-Hegelian view of the romantics that stresses their open-ended diversity, rather than some preordained goal. But in chiding opera for its "self-indulgent delight in sheer sound"[22] and accusing opera of participating in the downfall of the *Trauerspiel* because it can encounter no resistance, no obstacle to meaning, he seems to be verging on a quasi-Hegelian view of music as an expression of feeling or *Empfindung*, but one that can never enter a structure of reflection that gives it objective validity.[23]

Hegel's view of music was in many ways similar to Kant's and some of Kant's contemporaries, including those prepared to reflect on the connection between music and tragedy. In 1797 Goethe recommended Mozart's *Don Giovanni* to Schiller as proof of Schiller's belief that opera was the genre that could revive the *Trauerspiel* out of the spirit of antique tragedy.[24] Schiller's view of music in opera was dialectical, though hardly much different from Hegel's. On the one hand, Schiller regarded music in opera as an accompaniment that can distance an audience from "the miraculous [on stage] that is all of a sudden just tolerated" *(das Wunderbare, welches hier einmal geduldet wird)*. On the other hand, he saw music, precisely because of its indifference to concepts, as a means of making an audience more receptive to the pathos of the tragic through its sensuousness and harmonic allure.[25]

Instead of confining the role of the music in *Don Giovanni* to a catalyst of tragic effect, however, a close study of Mozart's manipulation of musical style in the opera can uncover an allegorical layer that, on the contrary, turns out to be central. The fragment of stiff, aristocratic-sounding baroque music, with its sharp dotted rhythms, that occurs when the tyrant Don Giovanni bravely affirms his negative philosophy in the face of death—at the words "I am firm of heart: I have no fear" *(Ho fermo il core in petto: non ho timor)*—transforms him at a stroke into a martyr. The historical dimension the music injects into Giovanni's role as a noble—a class in 1787 clearly perceived to be under threat—clarifies Giovanni's sudden readiness to accept death. He becomes, as it were, a sacrifice on the altar of social progress. As in the baroque *Trauerspiel*, the tyrant-drama and the martyr-drama imply each other as the reverse images of the same form. The sound of the trombones and its quasi-Christian association with the Last Days underscores the duality of the image as the tyrant descends to Hell, not as an individual, but as a noble in the name of history, a martyr whose fall is played out as a judgment, in which those dependent on Giovanni are also implicated. Hence the controversial last scene of the opera—expurgated in the nineteenth century, when one was not allowed to think about such things—during which, albeit in deceptively comic mode, each character has to justify their reaction to the demise of an individual who secretly reflected their own investment in a society that they now reluctantly have to realize is a relic of the past.

SORROWS OF THE EARTH

Schiller's enthusiasm for *Don Giovanni* and its Counter-Reformation imagery was shared by the nineteenth century, and it has left its traces in several operatic works, including Verdi's *Don Carlos*, which had a French libretto in five acts by Joseph Méry and Camille du Locle, and was later revised into four acts in French before being translated into Italian and becoming known to the world as *Don Carlo*. It has often been remarked that Verdi took some time to sympathize seriously with Schiller's dramatic ideals. But after *I Masnadieri* and *Luisa Miller*, both based on Schiller, he seems to have taken the tragic potential of Schiller's *Don Carlos* on board from the start, fully aware of its complexities and the difficulties of realizing it in music. The first sign of this was Verdi's insistence, after receiving an initial synopsis in 1865, that two dialogues should be included—one between the despotic King Philip and the Inquisitor, the violently dogmatic representative of the Roman Catholic Church, and another between Philip and his liberal counterpart, the Marquis of Posa.[26] Verdi sensed that the core of the drama lay in the grief of the ruler, a grief springing from the antithesis between his formidable power and his questionable capacity to rule. In the Philip/Posa dialogue in act 2, the politically innovative Posa presents Philip with the possibility of freeing Flanders, a decision Philip deflects by confiding in Posa the melancholy of his loveless marriage. In the other dialogue, which occurs in act 4, the Inquisitor asks almost at once what action Philip has taken against his rebellious son, Don Carlos. "All . . . or nothing!" *(Tout . . . ou rien!)* is Philip's enigmatic reply, revealing at once in this remarkable scene not just the collusion of State and Church, but, far more importantly, the tyrant king's indecisiveness and his own equivocal view of his function as sovereign.

Verdi also accepted, at least at the start, that the object of Schiller's *Don Carlos* is not history in the literal sense—most of the historical facts are hopelessly skewed—but history viewed through a magnifying glass, as it were, which deliberately enlarges, and at the same time distorts, certain of its most important events in order to turn it into something more akin to allegory and myth. Verdi found the idea less sympathetic when he came to revise the opera, but soon after the death of Meyerbeer in 1864, he clearly relished the prospect of moving toward a more allegorical mode of writing that does not demand continuity and concision in quite the same degree as dramatic realism and melodrama do. He had already done so in the case of *Il trovatore*. Indeed, like *Il trovatore* and also Schiller's original text, the opera quickly took on the contours of a sprawling melancholic drama of the baroque moving inexorably, in fits and starts, toward its finish, which explores the human soul in slow motion and at the same time allows for sudden and swift changes of direction in the action as well.

It is well known that the sheer scale of *Don Carlos* was a problem from the beginning, but it is not usually appreciated why the almost saturnine slowness of parts of the action was so crucial to the authors' original idea. Politics and religion are implicated, as Benjamin puts it in the context of the baroque mourning plays, in a concept of history as catastrophe that is grasped not so much in terms of chronological movement but as a spatial image. Indeed, not just the individual parts, but the whole of the vast historical panorama of *Don Carlos*, can be seen as a circular space in which, as one of the reviewers of the first performance put it, "the "denouement . . . returns the action to its point of departure" *(le dénouement . . . fait revenir l'action à son point de depart).*[27]

At the start of the original version, time seems to be literally frozen and turned into a sorrow-laden space as we see the woodcutters, their wives, and their children struggling with cold and hardship in the Forest of Fontainebleau in the depth of winter.[28] The opera finishes after the longest possible journey through contrasted explorations of melancholy in a similarly enclosed space with what amounts to an expression of hope that this sorrowful history will give way to an eternal future of happiness. That hope, however, is precariously poised. Don Carlos, about to be sacrificed as a martyr in the name of liberal progress, is suddenly embraced by King Philip's deceased father, Emperor Charles V, who emerges from his tomb disguised as a monk. They are protected by God's presence in the cloister of Saint-Just, the emperor tells Carlos, and Carlos can therefore hope to find in God the peace for which his heart yearns. In the language of *Don Carlos*, God is nothing less than a coded word for a utopian world where life is better, or, as Elisabeth and Don Carlos put it in their final duet, "where the future will ring the first hour" *(où l'avenir sans fin sonne la première heure).* But the alarming brevity of the opera's final image, and Charles V's words "the sorrows of the earth will still follow us into this place" *(les douleurs de la terre nous suivent encor dans ce lieu),* also convey the disconcerting message that this hope is fragile and that the sorrows of the world are in pursuit of those in the very place they have chosen to escape from them. In spite of the sudden spectacle of salvation for Carlos, therefore, the ending is laden with a pessimistic sentiment that brings it closer to the beginning of the opera than it first appears to be.

This is suggested, too, by even a cursory look at some telling details in the score. Verdi took a standard rhetorical device for the expression of sorrow—a semitone figure falling onto the fifth of the scale with the accent on the first note[29]—and ingeniously manipulated it to create a nearly motionless acoustical image of melancholy. The fifth degree is approached by a semitone from beneath instead of above (A♮ to B♭), and the two notes are sounded together as a repeated acciaccatura. The little fragment feels like a frozen object in sound: indeed, nothing could be more apt at the very start of the opera in the original version (ex. 4a). The fragment wends its way through the score in several guises, including the chanting of the monks at the opening of the second act, where it appears this time as A and A♯ inside the slow succession of a chord changing from minor to major (ex. 4b). The fragment is eventually transformed into its more familiar (5)–6–5 (minor) appoggiatura form (marked x in Example 4c) in Philip's anguished monologue at the start of act 4.

In the opera's final moments both forms of the figure are developed. The acciaccatura opens the duet between Carlos and Elisabeth (ex. 5, mm. 1–34) and is prominent at several places after that. Indeed, after Elisabeth's words

Ex. 4a. *Don Carlos,* original Paris version 1867, Prelude to act 1.

Ex. 4b. *Don Carlos,* Paris version 1867, act 2, scene 1.

that lie at the heart of this operatic mourning—"They are the tears of the soul" *(Ce sont les pleurs de l'âme)*—both this and the appoggiatura form of the figure are sounded simultaneously in a remarkable passage that surely represents the meaning of these sorrowful words in strictly instrumental terms (ex. 5, mm. 123–26). More importantly, the figure of sorrow in its ascending form, elongated and hence no longer an acciaccatura, is sounded three times at the very end of the opera, as if the sorrow it represents, and the cause of that sorrow, remain unassuaged and unresolved (mm. 261–63).

Verdi was initially enthusiastic about this ending, but in later years he became more critical of it on account of its lack of historical verisimilitude.[30]

Ex. 4c. *Don Carlos*, Paris version 1867, act 4, scene 1.

Many of the reviewers of the premiere had been sent unsolicited copies of Louis-Prosper Gachard's history *Don Carlos et Philippe II* (1863) by its publisher, Michel Lévy, an event that had already prompted them to remark with similar bemusement on the large gap in *Don Carlos* between histori- cal fact and "poetic fiction" *(la fiction poétique)*.[31] Verdi's skepticism about the gap grew significantly only much later, when he was preoccupied with extensive revisions of the opera. That skepticism had aesthetic consequences that have never been properly assessed, though there has been no shortage of resourceful archival work to quantify the changes he made. There have been murmurs of approval about the results. On the excision of Carlos's summary trial by Philip and the Inquisitor in the finale, for instance, Julian Budden regards the removal of this ritual judgment as "welcome" because it is "artificial in its context; it makes far too steep a descent from the high spirituality of the previous duet, and in any case Verdi had done the same thing very much better in the fourth act of Aida."[32]

Ex. 5. *Don Carlos*, Paris version 1867, act 5, Duet and Finale.

But no part of *Don Carlos* was ever really comparable with *Aida*. Alone the excision of the judgment scene in the final moments of the revised version shows that Verdi was not so much afraid of an invidious comparison with *Aida;* rather, he was keen to downplay a feature of the original it had inherited from the baroque that was at odds with the immediacy and urgency of melodrama in the *grand opéra* mode. Without the confrontation between Carlos and his two oppressors, the sense of the tyrant-drama and the martyr-drama as reverse images of each other, a strong feature of the opera in its original form, and, as in *Don Giovanni,* familiar from Counter-Reformation drama, is considerably weakened. The unruly close of the revised 1884 and 1886 versions, too, has nothing of the careful poise of the original (ex. 6). The judgment is summarily replaced by a brief rapid passage, the monks do not announce that Charles V is "nothing but ashes and dust" *(n'est plus que cendre et que poussière),* and the motif of sorrow, briefly audible, is swallowed up in a hectic rush for the end.[33]

The appearance of Charles V at the end of all the versions is an invention of the authors of *Don Carlos.* It has been roundly criticized by literal-minded critics as absurd and an insult to Schiller, which may be because it has mainly been judged from the familiar 1884 and 1886 revisions rather than from the original, in which the allegory is given more weight. The real reason, I suspect, has more to do with a fundamental misunderstanding of the nature of the image the authors originally wanted. Coming straight after the judgment of Carlos by Philip and the Inquisitor in the early versions, the image underlines with a vengeance the difference pointed out by Schopenhauer between the tragic heroes' stubborn subjection to fate in ancient tragedy and the resignation at the heart of the Christian *Trauerspiel.* In contrast to the tough stance of the Greek heroes, the protagonists of the *Trauerspiel* celebrate the hope for a happy departure from the world in the sure knowledge of the worthlessness of history, with the added luxury in *Don Carlos* of a gong stroke and a kind of Bengal lighting effect. The allegorical spectacle was admittedly given short shrift in the later versions. In the original, however, it conveys much more the sense that the material objects of the mantle and crown adorning the revived body of Charles V— described as "extremely opulent" *(ricchissimi)* in 1867, but not in 1884 and 1886[34]—carry the weight of history. The petrified images of the mantle and crown decorating the emperor's body and the monks' words about "ashes and dust" in the original version therefore confront their audience in no uncertain terms with history's *facies hippocratica*—the pallor of death— which seems to express both a hope for a release from that history and everything that is sorrowful about it.

Ex. 6. *Don Carlos,* ending of the revised 1884 version.

The revision of the ending therefore raises the question of whether Verdi's changes of mind about all of *Don Carlos* were simply workmanlike refurbishments of an awkwardly constructed opera, or instead a retrenchment. While his overhauling of the opera's structure is generally accepted as an attempt to sharpen its scenic and musical cogency, further critical appraisal of his revisions may well come to the conclusion that what he really did was to beat a retreat from the daring allegorical moments of the original back to the tried-and-true effects of melodrama. Perhaps on further reflection the original five-act *Don Carlos* and its subsequent revisions and compression into four will even come to be regarded not so much as distinct versions of a single opera, but rather as distinct operas in which a single subject is seen from significantly different points of view.

MOTIVIC ALLEGORY AND HISTORY AS WORLD PASSION

If Verdi moved back from *Trauerspiel* to grand operatic melodrama in revising *Don Carlos*, Wagner did the opposite while composing the ending of *Götterdämmerung*, and indeed he seems to have been able to assemble the baroquelike imagery of its ending in full only at the very last minute. At an early stage in the opera's genesis, Wagner called *Götterdämmerung*—one of the most astonishing of his dramatic creations—"A grand heroic opera" *(Eine große heroische Oper)*, clearly relating it to the Meyerbeerian mode of grand operatic melodrama. But only two years later he changed his mind and called it "A tragedy" *(Eine tragödie).*[35]

As we saw in chapter 1, Wagner claimed in his autobiographical writings to have preceded work on the *Ring* with a tortuous debate with himself about the choice of history or myth as the focus of his future music drama. He says he definitely came down in favor of myth, as if to prove that what he eventually did was to write something akin to Greek tragedy. It is not hard to prove that far from simply choosing myth over history, he actually blended the two.[36] Nowhere is this more obvious than in his literary labors of 1848 and 1849: socialist ideas about love, power, and property wander from one subject to the next almost oblivious of their historical or mythical context. Wibelungs are Nibelungs. The Grail is the Hoard. Friedrich I is Siegfried. Siegfried is Christ. Was it to be Wieland or Achilles? For a time the precise vehicle of Wagner's ideas hardly seemed to matter.[37]

After much vacillation worthy of the heroes he was thinking about, Wagner finally settled on the Siegfried legend, mainly because the disparate sources associated with it gave him the most spacious platform on which to create his theater of ideas about love, power, property, nature, religion, and the possibility of social change—a theater of ideas that were to be expressed in provocatively vivid and sensual fashion. The sources also provided endless possibilities for allegory. In this labyrinth of images and ancient tales, its heroes, heroines, villains, and even stage props imbued with "fate" such as the ring and the spear could be treated much as if they were disparate emblems gathering and dispersing around a figural center like Benjamin's "confused court," the name of the Spanish *Trauerspiel* that was for him the model of allegory, as we saw above. Wagner's method even extended to the overcoming of "opera" itself. In contrast to the symphonic seamlessness of the first three parts of the *Ring*, the operatic remnants in *Götterdämmerung*, for which Bernard Shaw reserved his deadliest scorn, are not so much the accidental leftovers from Wagner's pre-1849 operatic past as allegorical relics in their own right, essential to the logic of dramatic reversal in the last part of the cycle. Indeed, one of the most operatic features of *Götterdämmerung*—the empty space created by the fact that the characters merely "invoke" the gods as if they were taking part in a conventional *opera seria*—turns out to be the greatest reversal of all and the dynamic core of the allegory. Very much present in the first parts of the *Ring*, the gods are suddenly physically absent in *Götterdämmerung*, yet at the same time more central to the drama than ever before.

The scenic terrain of the *Ring*, too, with its giants and fire-breathing dragon, storms, forest, rivers, and clouds resembles the breathtaking visual ambition of baroque theater. And certainly the problem for a vitalist like Shaw was that, despite the *Ring*'s outward heroics, its allegorical vision of human existence is pervaded by melancholy and provided with an apparatus capable of expressing it. The ending is not so much a text sung by a supposedly redemptive heroine, but instead the musical setting of a predominantly melancholic *scene*—and a scene with enough fire, water, animals, crowds, gods, and falling debris in it to rival the most ambitious theatrical extravaganza of the seventeenth century. The music acts as a kind of negative electrode that finally completes a highly charged circuit built up by previous parts of the *Ring*. It also reflects the inspired disorder of the allegory with a tension similar to Benjamin's "confused court": the daring contrast between Wagner's near fanaticism in gathering together salient motifs in the *Ring* with the meanings that have accrued to them during the course of the cycle still intact on the one hand, and the slackness of their formal arrangement on the other.

In the music of *Götterdämmerung* generally, many motifs are closely tied to meanings while others are relatively indifferent to them—a calculated inconsistency that was one of the fruits of writing *Tristan* and *Die Meistersinger.* In the opening Norns scene the Valhalla and spear motifs (to name only two) are used very precisely. But it is hardly obvious, except in the widest sense, why the scene should begin with a recollection of Brünnhilde's awakening in the remote key of C♭ minor, only to be followed soon after by a fragment of her "magic sleep" motif at the third Norn's "Why aren't we spinning and singing?" *(Was spinnen und singen wir nicht?),* unless we accept the unlikely proposition that Brünnhilde has succumbed to a sudden and inexplicable bout of narcolepsy. Quite apart from the odd chronology, the Norns in any case are more interested in Wotan and his broken spear than in Brünnhilde, whose name they utter just once, and then only in passing. Yet it is precisely this contrast between the almost pedantic local appeal to musical memory and the more generalized (and magnificent) symphonic distortion of familiar material that registers the peculiar tension and propels the terrific forward sweep of *Götterdämmerung* in virtually every scene— and especially the last.

As *Götterdämmerung* progresses toward the hero's death and its aftermath, the score adopts the character of allegory with mounting persistence. Wagner's allegorical system, in which configurations of death, though saturated with history, strive for an eternal space, seem increasingly to resist development and closure. This is nowhere more apparent than at that moment of quasi-resurrection when Siegfried is brought back momentarily from the dead, only to have his happiness and strength of existence in death reaffirmed. When Hagen lunges for the ring on the dead Siegfried's hand in the final scene, the hand raises itself threateningly, Gutrune shrieks in horror, and the symphonic impetus of the music seems to shrink as two key musical icons are placed stiffly side by side. The so-called sword motif and the descending motif over a 6/3 D-major chord in *Das Rheingold,* which accompany Erda's words to Wotan "A dark day dawns for the gods" *(Ein düstrer Tag dämmert den Göttern)*—a phrase from which *Götterdämmerung* obviously gets its name—appear practically in their original form, undeveloped, with similar orchestration (trumpet and strings), in the latter case at the original pitch. Brünnhilde strides firmly into the foreground to take over; but it is the hero's momentary re-death, as it were, a brilliantly calculated moment of stasis in the action, that has actually given the situation new life.

The conflict between symphonic development and the increasingly petrified landscape of Wagner's allegorical motifs is sharpest in the cycle's closing moments. Sometime after the *Ring* had been completed, Cosima wrote in her diaries, "[Richard] takes a looks at the ending of *Götterdämmerung* and vows that he'll never do anything as complicated as that ever again" (25 November 1880). Looking at Wagner's sketches, it is not hard to see why. The first draft of the ending, in its final form one of the greatest moments in musical theater, is perhaps one of the most disconcerting documents in the Bayreuth archives.[38] If one takes an uncharitable view of musical composition, it could have been written by a roughly trained university student doing a paper in tonal composition. And indeed there is no better proof than the difficult journey from this to the magnificent final version of Thomas Mann's remark about Wagner's dilettante traits, which, he claimed, were raised miraculously with enormous effort to the level of genius.[39]

Yet, despite its obvious clumsiness, the sketch promises something highly original and unorthodox: the usurping of quasi-symphonic development by motivic allegory. In the final phase of the score, beginning with the announcement of the Rhine maidens motif, with the so-called redemption through love motif soaring high above it, Wagner arranged the music in an almost distracted manner, vaguely adjacent, but not necessarily directly related, to the tonal center $D^\flat$. It is important to remember that Wagner understood the so-called redemption through love motif (the label is an invention of Wolzogen's) as the "glorification of Brünnhilde," and moreover as a motif, as he put it to Cosima, "which at the end of the work is taken up, so to speak, by everyone,"[40] presumably meaning the wider community represented by the silent chorus on stage. It is important because a key idea behind the allegorical musical scenery at the end of the *Ring* is the sound of both a Brünnhilde and a Siegfried motif gathered around the figural center of an image devoted to the gods. According to the original context of the image, as Waltraute describes it to Brünnhilde in Act I, Wotan is at its center: silent, disconsolate, and still clutching the shattered fragments of his spear, not unlike the melancholic rulers of the German baroque dramas holding the sorrowful history of the world in their hands like a scepter.

This powerful image of the once all-powerful gods, however, appeared in Wagner's sketches only at a very late stage. Waltraute's description of them in the stage direction in the concluding moments of the *Ring* is not to be found in any draft of the libretto; nor is it in any version published prior to the completion of the score. It is not even contained in the text that Wagner published in his collected writings in 1873, a year after the composition sketch of *Götterdämmerung* was completed.[41] We are thus faced with a remarkable probability: only while recomposing the music of the ending of the *Ring* sometime between April and July 1872 (the period in which the full second draft of the music was finally completed) does Wagner seem to have introduced the image of the gods and their indecisive and resigned ruler—the very image that brings the whole sprawling allegory of the *Ring* to its magnificent climax. For once, Wagner's somewhat enigmatic description of his music dramas as "deeds of music made visible"[42] seems perfectly appropriate.

In the first sketch, Wagner made an awkward attempt to develop the Brünnhilde motif in counterpoint with an elongated form of the Valhalla motif until it arrived at an announcement of the Siegfried motif in F major and minor (ex. 7). The advantage of this was that at this pitch level the last note of the motif, $D^{\flat}$, could simply link directly to the final statement of the Brünnhilde motif in $D^{\flat}$ major, the key associated with Valhalla. As Valhalla goes up in flames, the music then resonates with the transposed quasi-ecclesiastical plagal movement in the final part of the original Valhalla motif. With the motifs arranged in this way, there is no clearly defined cadence that establishes $D^{\flat}$ as tonic. Indeed, the tonal slackness of the arrangement is in sharp contrast to the obvious fanatical collection of meaning as Wagner tries to group the musical emblems together.

The second version is hardly much better (ex. 8). Wagner attempts to enrich its meaning yet again with a sequence of falling thirds. The end of the Valhalla motif now sounds as a perfect cadence on $D^{\flat}$, while the all-important plagal effect is reserved for the Siegfried motif, this time transposed to $D^{\flat}$ major and minor so that its last note is $B^{\flat\flat}$. The end of the Siegfried motif then sounds together with a perfunctory final statement of the Brünnhilde motif over a $G^{\flat}$-minor chord that eventually moves to the tonic—an extraordinarily gauche attempt at a final plagal cadence that sounds even worse than it did in the first version.

The important aspect of this second attempt is that the Valhalla motif has been transformed into a crude transposed version of Waltraute's music from her scene with Brünnhilde in the first act of *Götterdämmerung* in the measures immediately preceding her description of the sorrowful Wotan that begins with the words "So he sits, saying nothing" *(So sitzt er, sagt kein Wort)*. In skeleton form, this music was introduced into the second sketch of the ending (ex. 8, mm. 1–8), and a scenic direction in the spirit of Waltraute's description relating to all of the gods was added, duly appearing eventually in the printed score. The introduction of this wonderful idea at the last minute led to an equally wonderful paradox in the final version (ex. 9, mm. 1–10): the more Wagner reverted to the original shape of Waltraute's music describing the once illustrious hall of gods and heroes, virtually unmodified except for its orchestration, the

So geschehen und geschlossen / am Tage, da mir vor / 7 Jahren mein Loldchen [Isolde Wagner] geboren surde / 10 April 1872. / RW

Ex. 7. *Götterdämmerung,* first draft of the ending (Nationalarchiv der Richard-Wagner-Stiftung Bayreuth, A III f 1, fol. 71r/72v).

more this literal, nondevelopmental return to music previously heard lent to the ending a brilliant and grand sense of forward cumulative motion.

Logically enough, according to Wagner's allegorical vision, the only other significant motif introduced at this late stage was Erda's descending motif over a 6/3 D-major chord from *Das Rheingold* (ex. 9, mm. 12–13), previously heard at Siegfried's "re-death" earlier in the final scene. Once again the visual image is enough to recall the meaning of Erda's fateful words to Wotan, this time even more sharply as Valhalla is enveloped in flames. Thus the motif

Ex. 8. *Götterdämmerung,* second draft of the ending (Nationalarchiv der Richard-Wagner-Stiftung Bayreuth, A III f 1, fol. 72v).

sounds as a logical consequence of Waltraute's memory of the sorrowful Wotan, magnificently recalled by the orchestra in the previous few measures. Still at exactly the same pitch it was in *Das Rheingold,* Erda's music makes present not only her prophecy of the "dark day" that will befall the gods, now actually seeming to dawn as the motif sounds again, but also Wotan's indecision about the ring that set the whole catastrophe in motion in the first place.

THE RESISTANCE OF CRITICAL THEORY TO OPERA

Adorno saw the contradiction between the rigid countenance of Wagner's motifs and the symphonic ambition of his music as a negative moment.[43] On the contrary, this is the heart of Wagner's allegorical way of seeing and hearing. At the end of *Götterdämmerung* the observer is once again confronted with the pallor of death—the *facies hippocratia*—the petrified primordial

Ex. 9. *Götterdämmerung*, ending (skeleton reduction) in the finished version (22 July 1872).

landscape where the weight of history, carried by Waltraute's musical description of Wotan's state of mind, appears untimely, unsuccessful, and laden with melancholy. Wagner's allegory may lack all symbolic freedom of expression, all classical proportion, even all humanity. But behind the glittering flames and the healing balm of the Brünnhilde motif, the secular explanation of history as World Passion is frozen musically into an allegorical form, which, precisely because of its sepulchral repose, can pose the enigmatic question of the nature of human existence it does.

In his book on Alban Berg, Adorno points out that Benjamin was uninterested in music, and even showed clear animosity toward musicians in his youth.[44] This did not stop Benjamin from attending the premiere of Berg's *Wozzeck*, or prevent him from making some perceptive remarks to Adorno about the way Berg had stylized his music to bridge the large historical gap between the opera and Büchner's original play. Adorno was quick to let the world know that he did not share Hegel's unwillingness to admit music to the realms of "higher criticism." He used Hegelian methods to place music at the center of his philosophy, and there is no doubt that his ambitious aim not only to salvage music from the musicologist,[45] but also to place it center stage in the debate about modernity, is of the first importance.

Adorno's music criticism, however, is full of difficulties, including his normative view of musical material that reduces music to a goal-oriented trajectory through history, one reliant on only a few technical categories. Another is his view of music analysis: Adorno assumes that for music to be meaningful, it must be amenable to technical analysis that necessarily reveals its object as a progressive dynamic moment in an evolution of Western music that posits middle-period Beethoven as its ideal. Indeed, Adorno's failure of critical nerve at key moments in his writings on nineteenth-century opera, especially in his Wagner book, is symptomatic of his reluctance to see truth in music that falls outside the historically significant development of musical material as he sees it. Is there more to be said about nineteenth-century operas that aspire to the condition of tragedy keeping Benjamin's concept of *Trauerspiel* and his theory of melancholy in mind? I think that there is, despite the irony that it is Benjamin, the critical theorist most resistant to music and opera, who seems to have shown the way forward in the difficult task of decoding their disconsolate message.

9.   Wagner's Greeks, and Wieland's Too

At the core of Benjamin's critique of the theory of tragedy is a reappraisal of the Greek view of tragedy in contrast with a modern Christian concept of it, albeit seen from the point of view of the political left of the 1920s. At the opposite end of the political spectrum, from the late twentieth century onward, the debate about the Greeks in relation to Wagner has been strongly influenced by three lectures, first given at the Bayreuth Festival between 1962 and 1964, by the conservative German classicist Wolfgang Schadewaldt.[1] Because the earlier path-breaking work on the subject by scholars such as Wolfgang Golther[2] and Robert Petsch,[3] in the early part of the twentieth century, had long since been forgotten by the 1960s, much of what Schadewaldt had to say to his Bayreuth audience was new to them. His approach was straightforwardly taxonomic, starting with a description of Wagner's early interest in the Greeks largely based on an uncritical acceptance of his autobiography, *Mein Leben*. This was perhaps a little unwise, if only because Wagner's account is for cogent reasons inflected theatrically to give a sense of his intense war against philistinism, with which he was faced at the time. His autobiography, for example, includes the tall tale that on his transfer at the age of fifteen from the Dresden Kreuzschule to Leipzig's Nikolaischule, he was put back a year, despite having already translated into German twelve books of Homer from the original Greek. Wagner, by his own admission later in *Mein Leben*, never learned Greek properly, though in the end it hardly mattered.[4]

Schadewaldt vividly describes Wagner's growing interest in the Greeks through the early part of his adult life, including his engagement with (in addition to Homer and Aeschylus) Sophocles, Euripides, Aristophanes, and Plato. And we hear about the influence not just of the Greek playwrights, but also of contemporary historians of classical antiquity in the first half of the nineteenth century, such as Boeckh, Otfried Müller, Welcker, and Droysen, who at the time were all in the process of elaborating a new and highly stratified image of classical Greece, contrasting sharply with the eighteenth-century tradition. We hear about a so-called Greek archetype, referring to Wagner's belief, many years before Lévi-Strauss, in an essentialist approach to myth, his own self-constructed myths included. And we also hear about Wagner's—and the reader also assumes Schadewaldt's—notorious anti-model, the performance in Potsdam of Sophocles' *Antigone,* with music by Mendelssohn, in 1842 at the behest of Friedrich Wilhelm IV of Prussia. Schadewaldt accurately described Wagner's belief in the fundamental untruth of this revival, though he left aside the strong anti-Semitic sentiment behind it.

Schadewaldt's third lecture is simply called a "supplement" and deals with a number of general points concerning the influence of the Greeks on *Parsifal, Tristan,* and *Die Meistersinger.* Most of these are straightforward questions based on simple comparisons: for example, is Hans Sachs in *Die Meistersinger* based on Socrates? Schadewaldt claimed that he was, and naturally the Wagner industry has periodically gone into overdrive ever since to find support for this dubious assertion, or simply to reject it. More seriously, in the closing stages of the lecture, Schadewaldt concludes with a grand statement that should have kept everyone busy. It is not so much terror or fear or catharsis that makes the tragic effect of Wagner's dramas among the most powerful in all of theater, but compassion—*Mitleid.* The claim deliberately begged many questions about the nature of tragedy, and Wagner's ambition to write one in the spirit of the Greeks. It also raised the issue, perhaps unwittingly, of whether Wagner ever succeeded in writing a tragedy in the Greek spirit at all, given his preoccupation with quasi-Christian categories like compassion and redemption that seem quite foreign to it.

THE LOVE AFFAIR WITH NEO-HELLENISM

Schadewaldt adroitly avoids the awkward issue of whether the music dramas attain the status of the tragic by describing Wagner's lifelong enthusiasm for the Greeks but failing to enter into its complexities and changing political character. Plunging into a study of the Greeks, Wagner wrote of his early years, was "the one and only way . . . to gain a breath of freedom" from a life dominated by "upsetting tasks." And Greek antiquity was the province out of which the "ideal" of his "artistic vision" developed.[5] These comments suggest that, from the start of his career, Wagner was in thrall to the idea of the Greeks as the pristine source of a lost culture—an ideal of fundamental origins projected onto the utopian future of a society encumbered by alienated living and a lack of spiritual freedom.

This reading of two tiny phrases plucked from Wagner's many published words on the Greeks may look heavy-handed. But the weakness of the several existing discussions of his relationship to the Greeks, many of them influenced by Schadewaldt, is that the larger context of his love affair with neo-Hellenism in the German Idealist tradition is presented only in atrophied form, or neglected altogether. Hugh Lloyd-Jones acknowledged Schadewaldt's influence at the end of his own interesting essay on Wagner and the Greeks, but he immediately qualified it by remarking that his German colleague's attitude was "more reverential" than his, adding a bit cheekily, though significantly, that his own piece "was not written for Bayreuth."[6]

Lloyd-Jones clearly sensed a problem. Schadewaldt was of course sophisticated enough to know that talking about Wagner and the Greeks can be like talking about chalk and cheese. Toward the end of his first lecture he writes that "we should guard ourselves against the exaggerated and historically unjustified assertion that Wagner's music drama represents a revival of Greek tragedy." Yet he is also prepared to downplay the difference by treating the relationship between Wagner and the Greeks metaphorically. Thus Wagner " 'turned toward the Elysian fields' in order to project the image of the modern individual onto the broad horizon of forces, figures, mythical fates, and world events. [He] lets the image of the modern individual, which unites features of Ulysses and Prometheus, confront its own sense of tragedy in an enormous magnifying glass as it were."[7] Wagner, it seems, can reach out and shake hands with Homer and Aeschylus over the ages after all.

Lloyd-Jones is more unequivocal. He finds "something profoundly alien to the spirit of an ancient tragedy" in the *Ring*, and frankly admits that Wagner "is not a true tragedian. Nor is the theodicy of the *Ring* significantly like a Greek theodicy."[8] There are other questions, too, simmering under the surface of Schadewaldt's text. How could Wagner be so enthusiastic about Greek culture, to the extent of incorporating specific situations in ancient tragedy and allusions to Greek literature in his own works, yet at the same time seem so distant from it? And why did Bayreuth in the 1960s need a "reverential" view of the subject when the climate of opinion there had already been influenced by the positive skepticism of Wieland Wagner? Wieland's skepticism, after all, was deemed quite radical at the time: it was directed not only toward his grandfather's problematic advocacy of German supremacy in his prose works, but also toward the creative fallout from the rebarbative idea of German dominance in the works themselves.

GREEK CULTURE AND GERMAN IDEALISM

It is not hard to see in the phrases from Wagner's writings about the Greeks a central thread of German speculative philosophy—or at least some of its loose ends—which was spun out in a variety of ways by many intellectuals of Wagner's generation and before. Schiller's *On the Aesthetic Education of Man* (1795) is probably the clearest statement of the idea that the educated citizen living among the fragments of modern life, despite advances in legal reform and scientific knowledge, is still in need of meaningful aesthetic experience that could lead to a conscious unification of culture that the Greeks seemed to have created quite naturally. Schiller was not suggesting that modern citizens should become Greeks, but rather that the Greeks were a prelapsarian moment of cultural immediacy that we moderns, in our own way, should seek to regain.

In a nationalist corner of German Idealism, Fichte posited a unified Germany as an a priori category in his *Addresses to the German Nation* (1808) and presented German as the only remaining primordial language in touch with nature. Here, too, Fichte's model was the supposed purity of Greek culture, in particular its roots in a "natural" congruence of language and nation, and—for nationalists of Fichte's generation, at any rate—its unblemished racial character. (The heady influence of Fichte's ideas on German thought and practice in the nineteenth century, incidentally, is perhaps the reason why the issue of language and nation, in which Wagner played a not insignificant role, and for which classical studies provided a formidable example, gradually came to be defined in terms of ethnic categories rather than the broader historical agenda of Schiller's and Humboldt's liberal humanism.)

In Wagner's time, the German Idealists' view of Greek culture as an ideal of perfection was essentially a moral category, but one at the core of politically very diverse visions of the future. Wagner, who was never less than an omnivorous consumer of current ideas, occupied equally diverse positions in the debate, which is why his view of the Greeks can take on disconcertingly different forms. Early in his life, as Schadewaldt points out, he identified with the Greeks in the name of the liberal humanism enshrined in the education in philology he received from his teachers, and especially his uncle Adolf, who was a scholar of considerable local repute. Schadewaldt does not make it quite clear, however, that in the years leading up to the Dresden Revolution of 1849 Wagner's attitude toward the Greeks became more left-wing and simultaneously more racist. Now the Greeks were placed in the service of a quasi-Hegelian merry-go-round of ideas, which were presented with numbing length in his essays *Art and Revolution* (1849) and *Opera and Drama* (1852). These works dogmatically asserted that the preservation *and* the annulment of Greek culture were part of an essential stage in the dialectical progress of history toward the "purely human" and the so-called Artwork of the Future, which did not, however, include the Jews or the French.

Roughly speaking, there was also a third, much more decisively nationalist phase in Wagner's political thinking (and, not surprisingly, an even more embarrassingly blatant anti-Semitic and anti-French one), which he expounded in a long series of essays collectively published in the 1860s under the title *German Art and German Politics*. His view of the Greeks played a significant role here, too, even though he seemed at first to be returning to his earlier undialectical thinking with a simple proposal of marriage between the Greek ideal and the German spirit.[9] The idea is not dissimilar to the wedding of Helen and Faust in the second part of Goethe's *Faust*. But in fact it is saturated with racial prejudice that places it at a considerable distance from what Schadewaldt himself described in his third lecture as Goethe's "straightforwardly naïve embrace of the Greeks" *(unmittelbar naives Ergreifen der Griechen)*.[10]

In brief, the threads of this last, highly idiosyncratic and far from naïve phase of Wagner's neo-Hellenism, in which Schadewaldt appears to take no interest, can be disentangled as follows. The Greeks gave birth to art; but what has been long overdue among the modern races is the rebirth of this true spirit of art, the original vitality of which, in a Fichtean twist, only the German race, returning to its primordial "natural" language and cleansed of all Jewish and French influence, is capable of embodying. The guarantee of the Wagnerian Artwork of the Future is therefore threefold: it will ennoble the individual through a heroic dramatic art based in part on the Greek ideal and borne on the wings of German music; it will stipulate the creation of a purified and hence unified culture of the kind once supposedly possessed by the Greeks; and it will guarantee to underwrite the integration of the German race, not with debilitating criticism or scientific reasoning, but with a mystical belief in the supremacy of the racially pure but as-yet-to-be-created German nation-state. Above all, this belief is to be succored by the experience of the Wagnerian work of art "dedicated to trust in the German spirit" (a part of the wording at the head of the first printed scores of the *Ring*) in a building dedicated in turn to its performance. This plan in particular is intended as a modern reincarnation of an ancient rite: just as Greek tragedy was celebrated communally at the Theater of Dionysos in Athens, or that in Epidaurus, so the German people are to celebrate the Wagner drama in a special place. For the Greek, or for the German, the uplifting experience of the tragedy was, or is to be, a reflection of unified nationhood and enduring spiritual vitality.

In other words, the Greeks—homogenized, idealized, unified, purified, communalized, culturally deified—finally became the principal touchstone of Wagner's utopian fatherland of the future. Wagner set out this mission clearly enough in his writings, and denial of its existence invariably comes from those who have not read them. Nor is it just the benefit of hindsight that gives them at times an air of fascist rodomontade. Ernest Newman was probably right when he surmised that King Ludwig II (who, in any case, did not share Wagner's anti-Semitic views) had the publication of *German Art and German Politics* suspended because of its vicious polemics against the French.[11] And Wagner's visceral attacks on the Jews were hardly greeted with equanimity either, even though many of his contemporaries, aware of his greatness as an artist, were prepared to overlook them.

ESCAPING HISTORY WITH THE GREEKS

In the aftermath of the Second World War, when memories of Hitler's patronage of Bayreuth were still fresh, history finally took its toll on the dramas themselves, which in Germany began to look as if they would be sullied forever by Wagner's political obsessions. Holding on firmly to the idea that there was still a core of humanity in the works, Wieland Wagner set about "clearing out the attic," as he put it, to find out where it was. One of the first steps he took in removing the bric-a-brac was his 1952 Bayreuth production of the *Ring*, which Frederic Spotts has memorably described as "a penance by Bayreuth for its honored place in the Third Reich."[12] The Germanic heroic epic vanished, and in its place the astonished (not to say, in part, infuriated) audience witnessed a "timeless" tragedy in the manner of Aeschylus. The Nordic gods looked like Greek sculptures, and Wotan and Siegfried behaved as if they were Zeus and Heracles, while Brünnhilde's conflict with Wotan resembled Antigone's with Creon. The principal stage feature, too, was a disc that consciously re-created the *orchéstra* of the Greek theater. The drama was played without a stage curtain, which gave the audience the exciting impression that they were participating in the action unfolding before them. In the Greek theater there was no double proscenium arch and no "phantasmal sounding music from the 'mystic gulf', like vapors rising from the holy womb of Gaia beneath the Pythia's seat."[13] In short, there was not the palpable distance between the audience and the players as there is in Bayreuth. Indeed, the difference is so fundamental that it is hard to agree with Schadewaldt's assertion that Wagner "captured with great perspicuity the ancient Greek *théatron*."[14] In creating an illusion of direct involvement with the drama, almost as if the "mystic gulf" of the sunken orchestra no longer existed, however, Wieland would probably have agreed with Schadewaldt, if only because the idea of a *Ring* purified of any association with the appalling inhumanity of the events for which Bayreuth in the Third Reich acted as a prestigious showcase was at the time more important to him politically than any quibble about historical verisimilitude.

Wieland's recourse to the Greeks in the "de-Germanification" of his grandfather's works came to a climax in his 1958 Bayreuth production of *Lohengrin*, generally considered to be one of his finest. This was the moment when he realized the full import of the fact that Wagner had been reading Aeschylus when he composed the opera. And it was in the wake of the success of this production that he invited to Bayreuth Schadewaldt, whose first lecture duly appeared in the program book for the *Lohengrin* performances in 1962. It is not clear whether Wieland was aware of his guest speaker's earlier sympathies with National Socialism. As a young academic Schadewaldt had played a not insignificant role in the notorious election of Heidegger to the rectorship of Freiburg University in 1933,[15] and his continued prestige with the Nazi hierarchy until the end of the war is proved by the appearance of his work in several publications maintaining (for instance) that "the awakening of the racial instinct of our people allows us to feel our affinity in blood and kind to both peoples of the Graeco-Roman world."[16] In a way, it is irrelevant whether Wieland was aware of this or not, since in any case he quite openly regarded himself as compromised (if not more so than Schadewaldt) in view of the support he had willingly received as a young man from Hitler himself.[17] The irony can hardly be overlooked, however, that in their endeavor to expunge the problematic past of Wagner's dramas, as well as their own, Wieland and Schadewaldt both resorted to a similarly sanitized view of the Greeks that Wagner himself had exploited to gain credence for the idea of German supremacy in the first place.

"No, we do not want to be Greeks again," Wagner declared after the 1848–49 Revolution, but only because the historical distance from the Greeks had taught the German people not to make the same mistakes. "What the Greeks did not know, and the precise reason they had to go to their ruin, is what we do know."[18] And what the ancients did not know, according to Wagner, was the meaning of history and the efficacy of revolution. A reversal of their fate is therefore in order: the destruction of their "timeless" myth through a lack of historical awareness can now become the re-creation of that myth in a new form that will be indestructible for all time, provided that the people for whom it is intended remain active in the name of their historical destiny. Thus for Wagner, there is no longer a place in modern tragedy for the Greek hero who valiantly subjects himself to the inevitable blows of fate. But there *is* room for the hero whose primal strength is conditioned by the melancholy history of those around him and nourished by his instinctive ambition to overcome that history with great deeds, whatever the cost.

Schadewaldt was therefore right to stress Wagner's awareness of the historical distance that separated him from the Greeks. This is not the same thing, however, as saying that Wagner recognized that one of the main differences between himself and the Greeks was the idea of history itself, almost as if he regretted that the ancient tragedians had never read the complete works of Hegel. As a consequence, and contrary to what he himself expected, his new tragedies in which "the free, strong, and beautiful individual will celebrate the joy and pain of his love . . . free from all convention and etiquette"[19] today look less like "timeless" myths than historical allegories in mythic guise about the tenacious illusions of modernity and in particular about the tragedy of German nationhood.

This is not quite what Wieland Wagner meant when he spoke of "clearing out the attic." Indeed, Schadewaldt played a small, though by no means unimportant, role in helping Wieland perpetuate the myth that Wagner's dramas could be seen through the lens of the Greeks as having their origin in the more problematic nationalist corners of German Idealism greatly diminished and cleansed of their immediate past in prewar Bayreuth. Once cumbersome beings in the service of German nationalist ideology, Wagner's dramas shed their skins, so to speak, to metamorphose into creatures of sublime beauty and universal truth. In Wieland's hands, they essentially became works without a palpable history, despite the clamor in the wings, which can still be heard, that they are nothing of the sort.

PART IV

Tristan und Isolde

10. Dangerous Fascinations

Tristan und Isolde was composed quickly between 1857 and 1859, when, as Wagner often later intimated to friends, every fiber, every nerve in his body, was tingling and alive. Its tale of illicit sexual attraction, not to mention the orgasmic voluptuousness of its music, have held the Western world in thrall ever since. Bernard Shaw once observed that Wagner retraced "poetic love" to its "alleged origin in sexual passion, the emotional phenomena of which he has expressed in music with a frankness and forcible naturalness that would have possibly scandalized Shelley."[1] By that Shaw meant that Wagner's translation of the emotions that accompany the union of a pair of lovers into music, in the first act of *Die Walküre* and especially the whole of *Tristan und Isolde*, posed a moral as well as a musical challenge for nineteenth-century audiences that went far beyond the notion of tragedy inherited from the Greeks and its emphasis on a communal celebration of human concerns. One small historical detail illustrating the point is the fact that Duchess Sophie of Bavaria was not allowed to attend the first performance of *Tristan* in Munich in 1865 out of moral considerations, even though she was a mature twenty-year-old woman who had recently married Duke Carl Theodor, a relative of King Ludwig II of Bavaria.[2]

Wagner's need to present unquenchable yearning and sexual passion in a convincing way led him to widen the scope of his musical resources so drastically that *Tristan* almost inevitably became one of the most important and revered musical works of the nineteenth and early twentieth centuries. In 1878 Cosima Wagner wrote in her famous diaries that Wagner spoke of his need at the time he was writing *Tristan* "to push himself to the limit musically" (December 11), strongly implying that his need to escape the constricted leitmotif system of the *Ring* led him to write it in the first place. As a result, he left his favorite hero alone in the forest at the end of the second act of *Siegfried* and did not touch the music of the *Ring* again for another twelve years. Certainly the expansion of harmonic possibilities in the very first chord of the Prelude to *Tristan* (the so-called Tristan chord is by far the most widely analyzed collection of four notes in Western music) and the sheer freedom and invention in the handling of individual chromatic lines mean that it is quite justifiable to speak of the music of the opera as a harbinger of the new music of the twentieth century. (*Tristan* is never actually atonal, though it energizes the tonal system from within to near the breaking point.)

Composers have frequently acknowledged and parodied the modernist ambition of *Tristan* by using its opening phrase in their own works; this includes Wagner himself, who was the first to cite it with irony.[3] In act 3 of *Die Meistersinger von Nürnberg*, the stage work he wrote after *Tristan*, we hear the chord and the harmonic progression around it at Hans Sachs's words to Eva, "My child, I know a sad tale of Tristan and Isolde" *(Mein Kind, von Tristan und Isolde kenn' ich ein traurig Stück)*. The historical Sachs of the sixteenth century really did write a piece about Tristan and Isolde, though the point the character in Wagner's opera is making is that he feels similar to the cuckolded King Marke in *Tristan*, an older man unable to possess a younger woman (Eva) and forced to give her up to a favored younger colleague. The harmonic progression sounds startlingly like it does in *Tristan*, except that the hints of resignation in the dramatic situation this time suggest a different purpose, almost as if Wagner were saying, "it will surely be hard for music to go any further than I have already taken it in *Tristan*."

Most later composers of any stature disagreed entirely, including Alban Berg, who invented perhaps the subtlest, most fascinating quotation and transformation of the *Tristan* opening in the final movement of his *Lyric Suite* for string quartet—fascinating because it recalls not just the musically avant-garde aspect of *Tristan*, but also the work's dangerous erotic raison d'être. Berg blended the chord into a highly structured movement based on his idiosyncratic application of Arnold Schoenberg's serial method, and in such a way that it can be explained, as Berg himself pointed out, in terms of the working of the twelve-note row.[4] At the same time, it was intended as part of a secret program referring to his affair with Hanna Fuchs-Robettin, the sister of Franz Werfel and wife of a rich industrialist (a fact Berg did not want to be made public).[5] The parallel with Wagner's infatuation with Mathilde Wesendonck, one of the inspirations behind *Tristan* and also the wife of a wealthy businessman, is obviously not a coincidence.

Another irony of the Wagner citation in the *Lyric Suite*, which was almost certainly not lost on Berg, was that Schoenberg had invented "the dry mathematics of the atonal system" (as one of his critics put it) precisely in order to, among other things, escape the sensual and intellectual force of *Tristan*. Indeed, an entire generation of musicians and literary figures had succumbed to that force and been unable or unwilling to free themselves from it. Friedrich Nietzsche, even after he had turned against Wagner, called *Tristan* the "voluptuousness of hell," adding that "the world is poor for him who has never been sick enough" to experience it.[6] The seemingly perverse inversion of conventional morality was merely Nietzsche's way of summing up the extremes of aestheticism and *décadence* (Nietzsche deliberately used the French word) with *Tristan* at their center—extremes that by the end of the nineteenth century had long since replaced official religion as the focus of intellectual and subjective experience.

And into the first two decades of the twentieth century the cult continued to flourish, this time in music with works like Richard Strauss's *Elektra* (first performed in 1909) and Schoenberg's *Erwartung* (composed in 1909). Both one-act operas are daring experiments in, respectively, advanced tonality and nonserial atonality, and both undoubtedly have their origin in the bold harmonic world of *Tristan*. But they also intensify the more scandalous traits of Wagner's opera that Nietzsche likened to the effects of a drug: the dissolving of worldly boundaries, the celebration of the dark corners of human existence, the retreat into sickness, and the death-devoted rebellion against existence itself, whether in the public or private spheres. These are the aspects of *Tristan* reflected in Strauss's and Schoenberg's operas, both of whose protagonists, like Isolde, are women searching frantically, often in dreamlike states of being, for ways out of the world into a condition of untrammeled subjectivity or, as some would say, pure insanity.

If Schoenberg managed to "escape" the tentacles of Wagner's *Tristan* in his more astringent serial works, Strauss remained faithful to its legacy to the end of his life. He is said to have uttered on his deathbed the phrase "Greet the world for me" *(Grüß' mir die Welt)* in the presence of his friend and colleague, the opera producer Rudolf Hartmann.[7] Neither of them could remember the exact origin of the words: they were something so familiar, so ingrained in Strauss's being, that it was no longer possible without conscious effort to identify where they had come from. The line is Isolde's to her confidante Brangäne in the first act of *Tristan*, in which she thinks she is going to die after taking the "death" potion with Tristan. Unknown to Isolde, Brangäne then exchanges the vials and gives Tristan and Isolde the "love" potion instead, with the result that they live on for another two acts to sing some of the most astonishing music ever written for the operatic stage. Whether Strauss was aware of it or not, the irony of his less-than-exact recollection of where

Isolde's words had come from was that he, too, had lived on after a point of crisis, which this time was the cultural pessimism that had begun to descend on many leading artists just before the outbreak of the First World War. And he had lived on to create music that remained faithful to the exquisite passions of *Tristan*, its yearnings, melancholies, lusts for sensuality, and, last but not least, the graphic presentations of sexually driven emotion that we find, for example, in the last act of *Arabella*, his final collaboration with Hugo von Hofmannsthal.

But at the time of Strauss's death in 1949, the radical, nihilistic daring at the core of *Tristan* that had continued to fascinate the long nineteenth century right up to 1914 was, like his remembrance of Isolde's words, only a distant memory—and, indeed, perhaps it always had been. Referring to the dying embers of his life, Strauss told his daughter-in-law at the time, "I composed it all in *Tod und Verklärung* (Death and Transfiguration) sixty years ago. This is just like that."[8] It was yet another reference on his deathbed to *Tristan*, albeit an indirect one in the sense that it referred to a symphonic poem he had composed many years before, in 1888–89, a work that had been strongly influenced not only by the symphonic ambition behind Wagner's opera, but also by the metaphysics of death and transfiguration enshrined in Isolde's final soliloquy. But highly original as the symphonic poem is, not even this music could ever match the original intensity and sheer musical daring of Wagner's opera, as Strauss himself knew. At almost exactly the same time *Tod und Verklärung* was being composed, Nietzsche announced in *Ecce Homo* (1888) that "I still today seek a work of a dangerous fascination, of a sweet and shuddery infinity equal to that of *Tristan*."[9] Indeed, since *Tristan* was first put before its astonished audiences in Munich in 1865, nothing quite like it has ever been heard again, despite the many distinguished composers who have tried to emulate it. To this day it is a work about which we can safely say that without it Western music since the nineteenth century would have taken a different course. Not even Wagner's most implacable enemies could afford to ignore it; but neither have his many friends, especially those who prepared the way for what we understand today as modern music, ever been able to recapture entirely the power of its radical spirit.

11. Public and Private Life

Reflections on the Genesis of
Tristan und Isolde *and the*
Wesendonck Lieder

ABANDONING THE MONUMENT TO LOVE

The fact that *Tristan und Isolde* had deep personal roots is now an ineradicable part of its history. Wagner first conceived it in 1854, at a time when he was almost wholly dependent on the patronage of a rich Swiss businessman, Otto Wesendonck, who not only advanced large sums of money to pay off his debts, but also provided him with a house close to his imposing estate in Zurich. The house was promptly named "Asyl" by its grateful and impecunious recipient, then still a political refugee from Germany with a price on his head. Wagner responded, practically from the start of their acquaintance in 1852, by falling head-over-heels in love with Otto's attractive wife, Mathilde Wesendonck, who seems to have reciprocated with genuine affection that stretched, but cautiously did not overstep, the limits of upper-middle-class decorum. For his part, Wagner was smitten, his love for his patron's wife inevitably coming into painful conflict with his genuine loyalty and gratitude to his patron—a conflict similar, as biographers never fail to point out, to that between Tristan's passion for Isolde and his loyalty to his protector King Marke.

The situation left an indelible mark on the conception of *Tristan*, though at first Wagner only hinted at the disconcerting nihilism that was to become a major part of the final work. In a famous letter to Liszt from December 1854, he wrote:

> Since I have never enjoyed in life the actual happiness of love, I want
> to erect another monument to this most beautiful of all dreams, in
> which, from beginning to end, this love is going to satisfy its hunger
> properly for once. I have worked out a *Tristan und Isolde* in my
> head—the simplest and at the same time most full-blooded musical

conception. Then I'll cover myself over with the "black flag" flying at the end so I can—die.[1]

Wagner's mention of the black flag—a detail of the Tristan legend that was among the first to catch his attention—suggests that he originally had a different idea of the opera's outcome. His wrapping the black flag in ironic quotation marks, too, spoke volumes. In the legend, Tristan lies sick and incurable in the care of his wife, Isolde of the White Hands, while they await the arrival by ship of another Isolde, the Irish princess and wife of King Marke, whom Tristan secretly loves and whose powers alone can heal his wound. If the ship is flying a white flag, Isolde is on board; if the flag is black, she is not. As the ship comes into view, it is flying a white flag, whereupon Isolde of the White Hands, jealous of her husband's dependence on King Marke's wife, tells him the flag is black. Mistakenly believing that he will never again see the Isolde he really desires, Tristan dies of grief. To Liszt, fully aware of his friend's tangled emotional and financial state, the coded message could not have been clearer: the beautiful dream of love, beyond the pale of a loveless marriage with my wife Minna, to whom I, Richard Wagner, am ethically and legally bound, can at least be conjured up in a work of art, even though I will never enjoy the sight of the white flag, concealed forever from me by the public bond to my lawful spouse.

The subsequent development of *Tristan und Isolde* in Wagner's imagination gradually transformed the shadowy dilemma of his unhappy marriage and its petty jealousies into a wider examination of the tragedy of the human self as he saw it. The "beautiful dream of love," in other words, developed into a conundrum far beyond the confines of Wagner's private world: how can some of the most beautiful and ecstatic love music ever written exist alongside a nightmare of delusion and its resolution in death? The trivial modern phrase "to die for," used to express the succumbing to culinary bliss, suddenly became appallingly literal. In the summer of 1856 Wagner wrote to August Röckel for the first time about the subject of *Tristan und Isolde*—a not insignificant fact in light of their serious intellectual companionship dating from the 1840s and their participation in the 1849 Dresden Revolution. He talked of a concept "in my head," describing it with a single starkly worded phrase: "love as terrible torment" *(die Liebe als furchtbare Qual)*.[2] Egon Voss has rightly said that the phrase, and those like it in prose sketches for the opera written down shortly after this letter, leave no doubt that the conception of the opera had altered significantly.[3] Gone were the black/white flag and the jealousies of the rival Isoldes, and nowhere was there mention of "the beautiful dream of love." What remained was a full-blooded musical conception, now saturated with an erotic hunger that could no longer be satisfied any more than it could be naïvely portrayed as a monument to a fulfilling erotic relationship permanently denied to its author. *Tristan* had changed from a relatively straightforward story of imagined love tragically compromised by jealousy into a desolate near-metaphysical exploration of the anguish of being-in-the-world brought about by the fatal intoxication of exquisite passion.

THE *TRISTAN* FACTORY

It has long been known, but seldom properly acknowledged, that Wagner's original intention was to turn *Tristan und Isolde* into an easily performable work that all opera houses would be eager to produce. As always, Wagner urgently needed money. In 1856, when his contract negotiations with the firm of Breitkopf & Härtel to publish *Der Ring des Nibelungen* were about to fall through, he wrote to Liszt that if this were to happen (as indeed it did), he "would have no alternative but to give up the *Nibelungen* and instead to start planning a simple work—like *Tristan*—that would give me the advantage of getting opera houses to produce it quickly and thereby earning myself some money."[4] By September 1857, full of hope but under the pressure of ever-increasing financial worries, which were only partly assuaged by the generosity of the Wesendoncks, he was able to announce to Breitkopf & Härtel:

> I am about to begin the musical composition of *Tristan und Isolde*—this will be the title of my new work—the libretto of which I have already finished. Among other things, I have taken this subject to heart because it presents almost no difficulties for the scenery and the chorus. Practically the only demanding task will be to find a good pair of singers for the main parts, which means that I shall possibly easily get a good first performance and the chance of distributing it to the theaters very quickly, unimpeded by any obstacles.[5]

We know now that *Tristan und Isolde* later met with rejection because it was reputedly unperformable. Originally conceived as an opera that was to be relatively undemanding of its performers, it ended up being one of the most difficult works of the nineteenth century—a challenge to precisely the same circumstances of the opera business that had originally forced Wagner to conceive it as a "simple work."

On 4 January 1858, Wagner, who according to Hans von Bülow was in "dire financial straits,"[6] made the following offer to his publishers:

Some Signposts to the Genesis of the Orchestral Score of *Tristan und Isolde*

	Composition sketch	Orchestral sketch (particell)	Full score	Simultaneous production of the printed score B = Breitkopf & Härtel
Act 1 Beginning	1 October 1857	5 November 1857	6 February 1858	27 February 1858: contract sent to B. 15 March 1858: B. sends trial proof sheets to W.
Act 1 End	31 December 1857	13 January 1858. W. writes at the end, " never has anything been composed like *this*."	3 April 1858	5 May 1858: W. receives 40 pages to proofread. 20 November 1858: W. receives final proof of act 1 ending.
Act 2 Beginning	4 May 1858	5 July 1858	Toward the end of 1858	24 January 1859: W. sends B. "a part of act 2."
Act 2 End	1 July 1858	9 March 1859	18 March 1859	17 March 1859: W. demands 100 louis d'or from B. 19 July 1859: B. sends W. proofs of first part of act 2.
Act 3 Beginning	9 April 1859	1 May 1859	April–May 1859	31 August 1859: W. sends proofs of act 2 to B. 5 June 1859: W. sends B. first part of act 3. 21 June 1859: B. acknowledges receipt of pp. 255–74 of manuscript full score.
Act 3 End	16 July 1859	19 July 1859	6 August 1859	7 August 1859: B. receives the "last installment" of the manuscript full score. W. receives the rest of his honorarium. 14 December 1859: B. receives final corrected proof of act 3. 13 January 1860: B. sends printed score to W.

I propose a fee for the score of *Tristan* of six hundred louis d'or, or twelve thousand francs. I must insist, however, that it be paid to me in full, and in cash, by the time the score is finished. I suggest that each time I deliver the full score of one of the three acts, I receive a third of the total fee, i.e., four thousand francs. For the production of the score we still have to decide the following. The score will be engraved, and the engraving is to begin immediately after I have sent in the manuscript. This can be arranged so that when I've finished the manuscript, the engraving will be finished shortly thereafter.[7]

Breitkopf & Härtel made a counteroffer of two hundred louis d'or to be paid in two installments on completion of the first and third acts. Wagner accepted without demur: it was still a not inconsiderable sum, and on top of it he eventually received, at his insistence, an advance payment of another hundred louis d'or after finishing the second act on the strength of future royalties.[8]

Wagner's urgent need for cash led to a rigorous rationalization of the composition of *Tristan* that stood in stark contrast to the work's stubborn individualism and the almost flamboyant aura of erotic excess that surrounds it. To make sure he had a regular income, he suggested an arrangement rather like a factory assembly line that enabled him to work simultaneously on the opera's composition and its publication. As the dates of the genesis of *Tristan* make clear (see table), the score was not put into print once the whole work was finished, but during work on the composition sketches, the detailed sketches of the orchestration, and the manuscript full score itself.[9] This meant that while Wagner was correcting the proofs of the first act, he was still busy composing the second; and similarly, while correcting the proofs of the second act, he was still working on the third. Some of his instructions to his publisher are almost reminiscent of assembly-line conditions. He wrote to Härtel, "Please be so good as to inform me exactly how much of my manuscript the engraver gets through daily or weekly; I'll then adapt accordingly and keep in step with him, though I'll always try to give him a bit extra as well."[10] As a result, Wagner had to send off pages of the manuscript score of the third act before he had even finished writing down the rest of the act in his outline composition sketches, thereby denying himself the possibility of revising what he had already composed.

Anyone who wants to see the sketches and score of *Tristan* as "gifts of heaven"[11] will probably take refuge in the idea that Wagner already had the entire work in his head before he wrote it down. But the composition sketches, although they are generally fluent, show that he was often not at all clear how the music should continue after sending what he had just finished off to the printer.[12] His sense of form was always one that groped its way forward. In this respect Wagner was unlike Beethoven, who—in the sketches of the Sixth Symphony, for instance—was in the habit of going back to music he thought he had finished and changing it significantly in order to create, retrospectively, the right balance in accordance with a long-range perspective of formal coherence.

What is exciting about the music of *Tristan* is that it presents a bold antithesis to the classical idea of sonata form. Only Isolde's famous final scene in the opera could possibly qualify as a "classically" inspired passage, as it is an obvious reengagement with music previously heard in her passionate duet with Tristan in the second act. But the repetition of sections of the duet in the final scene is both too exact, in the sense that the passages have been lifted out of their original musical context and placed in new ones without significant change, and too radically different, because of large cuts in the original statement of the music and a halving of its note values. Isolde's *Liebestod* may count as a recapitulation of sorts, but hardly in the sense that Haydn, Mozart, and Beethoven understood the process.[13] It seems more like a foreshortened memory of something that needs to be resolved, yet at the same time renounced, obliterated. In a sense, while writing *Tristan* Wagner resembled Orpheus in that he was not allowed to look back. The music constantly presses forward in search of formal possibilities that seem permanently open-ended—a radical aspect of the opera that had an even greater influence on modern music (Pierre Boulez's preoccupation with permanently evolving, nonrepetitive forms, for instance) than its much-vaunted chromaticism.

In the midst of his *Tristan* factory, Wagner himself clearly suspected that the work was destined to change music history forever: "The process of correcting the proofs of the second act, while I was simultaneously in the throes of composing the ecstasies of the third act, had the strangest, even uncanny, effect on me; for it was in just those first scenes of this act [i.e., the third] that I realized with complete clarity that I had written the most audacious and original work of my life."[14]

THE ULTIMATE PRIVATE ART

In apparent contrast to the purposeful rationality behind the genesis of *Tristan,* the *Wesendonck Lieder* were not composed in any particular order. Indeed, Wagner changed their order twice before settling on a final one for publication in 1862, and then only because he was practically forced to publish them to pay off yet more debts.[15] In other words, he neither conceived the lieder as a cycle, nor did he at first want them printed and dragged into public view. This tends to support the generally accepted rationale for their existence as expressions of an adulterous passion that Wagner was at pains to keep private. Voss claims that Wagner wrote the *Wesendonck Lieder* as "an artistic reaction against the apparent impossibility of consummating [his] love or, as far as Mathilde Wesendonck was concerned, as the symbolic expression of a mutual feeling that could not be displayed openly."[16] But no conclusive evidence exists that Mathilde Wesendonck felt the same way about Wagner as he felt about her. Elsewhere Voss raises the perfectly legitimate question of why Otto Wesendonck, after the "threat" to his marriage had come into the open, continued his support of the composer on such a lavish scale.[17] The answer is surely that as a successful businessman with a realistic perception of human relations, he knew the crucial difference between flirting and a deep-seated mutual erotic attraction that really would have endangered his marriage.

Wagner's own description of two of the songs—"Im Treibhaus" and "Träume"—each as a "study for *Tristan und Isolde*"[18] suggests they had a wider purpose in relation to the composition of the opera than just his relationship with the author of their texts. ("Träume" formed the basis of the second act love duet's centerpiece "O sink' hernieder" and "Im Treibhaus" was transformed into the bleak opening of the third act.) After all, Wagner was not in the habit of writing lieder at this stage in his career, which immediately suggests that there must have been a cogent artistic reason for his sudden decision to spend valuable time on them that could have been devoted to *Tristan*.

What I am suggesting is that all the *Wesendonck Lieder* had a wider creative connection with *Tristan* not limited to the two songs actually used in the larger work. In abstract terms the link is about style, expressive manner, and gesture. But it is also about exploring an *idea* of the lied (almost by definition a diminutive art form on a private scale) that was just as central to the conception of *Tristan* as its larger symphonic ambition. Indeed, the work's many expressive subtleties are a result of this paradox.

Thoughts lavished on art song in Wagner's time also made it inseparable from the aesthetics of *Tristan*. As Liszt put it in 1855 in a seminal article on the lieder of Robert Franz in the *Neue Zeitschrift für Musik*, "the lied is poetically and musically a product wedded exclusively to the Germanic muse like the words *Sehnsucht* [intense longing] and *Gemüth* [roughly, mind as a state of feeling] . . . which belong only to the German language and remain untranslatable."[19] Fortunately Liszt's slightly alarming nationalist sentiments pale before his reflections on the lied's aesthetic and psychological significance. As an avid reader of the *Neue Zeitschrift*, Wagner was almost certainly acquainted with them and—surely not entirely coincidentally—just before beginning in earnest with the composition of *Tristan*, he invited Robert Franz to the Wesendonck estate in Zurich in order to get to know his songs more intimately. His reaction was indifferent and (probably) not lacking in jealousy, which does not mean that he rejected Liszt's ideas, or that his ambition to write such lieder himself lessened.[20]

According to Liszt, with Robert Franz the lied enters a "new phase"; he is a "psychical colorist"; his lieder are mostly "moods that are deeply self-absorbed" *(Stimmungen, die sich in sich vertiefen)* and "seldom strive dramatically beyond their limits"; his lyricism has "much of a feminine sensitivity" about it; "pain" *(Schmerz)* is transformed in his lieder almost before our very eyes into "a feeling of blissful dying away" *(ein Gefühl seligen Sichverlierens)*; modulation determines feeling much more than melody; "subsidiary modulations" *(Nebenmodulationen)* surge into "the smallest, most secret layers of feeling." Finally, he is endlessly inventive in the way he avoids closing cadences in the vocal parts so that the music can press forward toward the end with the "reverberating reinforcement" *(nachhallendes Bekräftigen)* of the accompaniment.[21]

The litany of poetic and musical metaphor seems better suited now to the *Wesendonck Lieder*, and, by extension, to *Tristan*, than it does to the restricted expressive range of Franz's music. To put it another way: the serious exploration of the German lied and its expressive possibilities in the *Wesendonck Lieder* served as a vessel through which essential parts of *Tristan* had to pass. Alone, the tension between the private character of the lied and the public face of opera greatly helped to define the opera's sound-world. Its static self-absorbed moods are sharply contrasted with active high drama, and the blissful dying away of some of its music is almost fiercely at odds with the symphonic momentum of its motifs. Last but certainly not least, extrovert melody brutally awakens intimate modulations of the most painful moments of confusion and self-examination that show how the smallest, most secret layers of feeling are constantly vulnerable to public, often violent, action.

Perhaps most importantly, Wagner wanted to explore the nature of the lied to find exactly the right mood of quietist renunciation in *Tristan*—the wishing-to-be-apart-from-the-world inspired by Schopenhauer that found its equivalent in the famous romantic image, enshrined in the lied since the days of Goethe, of the poet accompanying himself on the lyre, losing himself in improvised song. "His tender way of feeling," Liszt enthused about Robert Franz, "and his fine, penetrating spirit (a spirit that nonetheless hates every noise, every pandemonium) hold him closed within himself, as if he were afraid of every exchange of opinion that could end in bitterness, as if to avoid every battle in which the strings of his lyre could be plucked too hastily and produce sounds that are less than pure, harmonically rich, and tender."[22]

Liszt thus defined the lied as the artistic expression of the (male) individual deeply absorbed in his own being, the ultimate private art. On one level, indeed, the genesis of the *Wesendonck Lieder* shows a similar disconcerting narcissism: Wagner gradually shrouded the lieder and his letters to Mathilde Wesendonck in total self-absorption to such an extent that he subtly began to erase all trace of her. The title page of the first publication of the lieder— *Five Poems for Woman's Voice Set to Music by Richard Wagner*—omitted her name altogether, with the result that for most of the nineteenth century the texts were widely assumed to be by Wagner. [23] The lieder also reveal the saturnine state of mind that led to the unforgettable sound-world of *Tristan*—the lonely individual, talking on his own, searching for intimacy, and insisting on "pure" love in the abstract, but discovering it only in music of striking melancholic intensity. Indeed, Wagner himself practically came to the same conclusion. Cosima Wagner reports in a memorable moment in her diaries that the arrival of an edition of the *Wesendonck Lieder* arranged for violin and piano prompted him to remark, "With my so-called love affairs it was just as with my [first] marriage; Minna married me when I was in a very wretched position . . . but at the same time I was quite without influence over her. And thus it was, too, with the other relationships; it all belonged somewhere else. . . . I just spoke in monologues."[24]

THE FLIGHT INTO THE PUBLIC REALM

The view of *Tristan und Isolde* as both industrial product and isolationist experiment in musical intimacy says at least two things. First, only six months separated the completion of the manuscript score and the publication of the full score in January 1860, the fastest turnaround for any of Wagner's major works. Indeed, the speed with which Wagner and his publishers managed to get the opera into print is a sign that it was intended from the start as an emphatically public work. The fact that it was the first of Wagner's stage works to be properly engraved in full score—no mean undertaking for something so lengthy and complex—also strengthens the point. Forget the myth about the former revolutionary, now resigned, full of renunciation, wrestling with his inner demon, and suffering from a bad case of withdrawal from life. *Tristan* clearly represents a flight from the private into the public realm, not the reverse.

Second, Wagner's letters to his publisher about money and the flight into pure imagination that led him to distance himself from Mathilde Wesendonck hint at a desertion of feeling and a collapse into abstract social relations that seem to be not only bizarrely at odds, but also more subtly in tune, with the hot-house aestheticism of *Tristan*. When Wagner wrote to Liszt on New Year's Eve in 1858—"My Franz, when you see the second act of *Tristan* you will have to admit that I need a lot of money. . . . Send your Dante [Symphony] and your [Graner] Mass! But first money!"[25]—he was consciously lifting the veil off a reality he knew was only superficially protected by fantasies of material and spiritual wealth. Indeed, the letter led to a serious rift between Wagner and Liszt, from which their relationship never completely recovered. Liszt wrote back sharply: "As the Dante Symphony and the Mass do not count as bank shares, it will be superfluous to send them to Venice. I regard as no less superfluous the receipt from there of any more emergency telegrams and wounding letters.—In earnest, truest devotion, I remain your F. Liszt."[26]

No wonder Liszt was disconcerted. He had received the first act of *Tristan* on 26 December and gushed to Wagner in an immediate letter of thanks about how the "heavenly Christmas present" had put "the entire children's world of Christmas trees decorated with golden fruits and gleaming presents" into the shade. "Away with all the cares and toils of the real world," he continued, "there [in *Tristan*] one can cry and let oneself go again."[27] Wagner's answer to this particular piece of Lisztian wishful thinking was simple: "You are replying," he wrote, "with too much pathos,"[28] almost as if he were snapping someone on a psychiatrist's couch out of a moment of tearful self-pity. The notion that his preoccupation with myth preempted many of Freud's insights into the human psyche is laid down in tablets of stone in modernist lore. His bracing remark to Liszt, however, suggests that he may well have dismissed modern psychoanalysis as so much humbug designed specifically to assuage essentially cold hearts protected by their wealth from life's realities. Certainly the stark contrast at the time between Wagner's impecunious circumstances and Liszt's socially and financially secure position seems to have sharpened the insight of the composer of *Tristan* into the bleak actuality of modern social relations. The sumptuous sounds of the work may act as a sop to the emotional discomforts of an outwardly comfortable life; but behind them, Wagner is suggesting, lies a bleak truth about human existence, which, from the safe, economically well-upholstered vantage point of the successful bourgeois, no one ever dares fully to acknowledge.

Paradoxically, the sheer intensity of feeling Wagner was putting into *Tristan* also demanded a less intimate audience—recipients at a safe distance unlikely to jeopardize further an emotional space already functioning at dangerous levels. The result was Wagner's eagerness to make it public as quickly as possible and with as many rational and neutral means he could muster. Wagner's famous remarks to Mathilde Wesendonck about the supposed threat to the public's mental health posed by *Tristan* can therefore be read a bit differently: "This *Tristan* is turning into something *terrible!* This last act!!!—I fear the opera will be banned—unless the whole thing is parodied by bad performances—: only mediocre performances can save me! Perfectly *good* ones are bound to drive people mad,—I can't imagine it otherwise. That's just how far I've had to go. Oh woe! I've just been in the thick of it! Adieu!"[29]

It is almost as if Wagner regarded his future *Tristan* audience as total strangers in whom he would find it easier to confide than those closer to him—the audience as the "big Other itself," the neutral receptacle for Wagner's secrets, as a post-Lacanian like Žižek might put it.[30] Indeed, the imagined rescue by mediocrity oddly expresses the hope that audiences will not react at all. Wagner is saying to Mathilde Wesendonck that he wants them to remain distant from *Tristan,* not only for their own safety and to rescue his public reputation, but also because he can bring those "terrible" passages in the most fevered parts of *Tristan's* third act into being with equanimity only by imagining the neutrality of his listeners.

ENIGMATIC LIAISONS

Wagner gained some remarkable insights into himself and his work during his correspondence with Mathilde Wesendonck. By the time the letters were first published in 1904, their liaison was already the stuff of legend. Indeed, the letters' appearance was a sign that the heirs of the Wesendoncks— Mathilde had died two years previously and Otto six years before that— were acutely conscious that publishing them, in addition to providing valuable information about the composition of *Tristan,* would also confirm some unpalatable truths. The rapidly collapsing barriers between public and private life in the nineteenth and early twentieth centuries, which allowed intimate details of human lives to become an inevitable part of public property, had already taken their toll. And to avoid embarrassment, those at the center of public attention, similar to some celebrities now, increasingly found themselves compelled to half censor or messily reconstruct public perception. Perhaps sensing the inevitable, Mathilde Wesendonck had already gone out of her way in a short memoir published in 1896 to point out that "money matters were never discussed" between herself and Wagner.[31]

It hardly takes a biographer of genius to detect in that statement a diversionary tactic. Wagner was heavily dependent on the patronage of the Wesendoncks at the time of Tristan; and he showed little restraint in upsetting household decorum, not only by expressing his feelings to Mathilde in private, but also by openly flirting with her in front of everyone. The situation eventually came to a head when, on Mathilde's birthday, 23 December 1857, Wagner serenaded her on the steps of the family villa with a chamber orchestration of "Träume" (Dreams), now the fifth song of the Wesendonck Lieder. And straining the good will of everyone to the breaking point as usual, he followed this up with a New Year's gift to her that consisted of the complete first act of Tristan in sketch form, with a highly suggestive poem of dedication wrapped inside it.

Otto was not pleased. Wagner suddenly left for Paris to let things cool down and, sensing a serious threat to his income (not helped by the threat to Otto's fortune posed by economic turmoil in Europe at the time, which, however, like his displeasure with Wagner, soon blew over), he immediately entered into a punishing contractual arrangement with the firm of Breitkopf & Härtel, an agreement that guaranteed him financial support until Tristan was finished and published. As we have seen, the circumstances of the contract had a significant role to play in the way Tristan came into being.

The supposed sexual shenanigans between Wagner and Mathilde Wesendonck have been so grossly exaggerated that it has become all the harder to trace the underlying seriousness of their relationship. Many biographers have implied that on Mathilde's part their relationship was based simply on her craving for fame through association with a brilliant and powerful man. But as Dena Goodman points out in her work on Enlightenment salons, the trouble with this kind of argument is that it all too readily assumes the centrality of men in understanding the actions of women.[32] Wagner biographies, most of them written by men, have obviously played their part, and the images of Wagner and the main characters in his life they contain, even when treated salaciously, are still preserved in the hardened aspic of male-dominated nineteenth-century morality. In their notorious book The Truth about Wagner, first published in 1930, Hurn and Root simply state with the schoolboy enthusiasm of lip-smacking voyeurs that to the end of her life Mathilde Wesendonck "never ceased to titillate at the lot that had been hers when she touched the fringe of greatness."[33] Most biographers, too, have assumed that the compliant, pretty face that blandly gazes into the wings of Johann Conrad Dorner's well-known portrait of her is an accurate reflection of her character.[34] Wagner's Victorian translator William Ashton Ellis fleetingly made her acquaintance in the last twenty years of her life and described her as a "placid, sweet Madonna, the perfect emblem of a pearl, not opal, her eyes still dreaming of Nirvana,—no! emphatically no!" he sputtered on, "*she* could not have once been swayed by carnal passion."[35] One wonders how Ellis—a medical doctor when not working on his time-consuming translations of Wagner's prose works—imagined she had conceived her five children!

Ellis is no less obtuse about her literary works, which include not only the five poems Wagner set to music as the *Wesendonck Lieder* (their modern, though, as we have seen, not their original title), but also several published plays, among them a reworking of the Alceste story, a drama on Frederick the Great, and a volume of folktales and legends. Ellis lists most of them in the "Introductory" [*sic*] to his translation of the Wagner-Wesendonck correspondence, but his apparent generosity in alerting the reader to Mathilde Wesendonck's "mental capacity" is full of problems. He claims that in her works Wagner's "phraseology may be detected here and there"; in fact, it is a surprise to see how unlike Wagner's her writing is, belonging as it does to a "classical" phase of romantic literature dominated by Goethe and Schiller, a characteristic that could be interpreted not just as conservatism plain and simple, but also as a conscious attempt to make her style distinct from Wagner's. He also asserts that her five poems set to music by Wagner "sprang from the depth of her heart" and have survived for that reason, implying, of course, that the rest of her oeuvre did not spring "from the depth of her heart," and has therefore suffered eternal oblivion.

Mathilde Wesendonck's writings in toto are of greater biographical interest than Wagner scholars have claimed, though this is not the same thing as saying that they have great value as works of art. Ellis may not have mentioned her published works at all if Wolfgang Golther, whose edition of the Wagner-Wesendonck correspondence Ellis translated, had not been put under pressure by another woman—no less a person than Cosima Wagner—to bring them to public attention. By the time the letters were about to be published, Cosima clearly sympathized with the past attempts of the recently deceased Mathilde to find a role for herself in the public sphere of the nineteenth century more than she felt any jealousy toward her, thus overriding any qualms she may have had about the quality of the writings. Mathilde Wesendonck's works should be mentioned by Golther in his introduction to the edition, she insisted, because they reflect "her own intellectual life."[36] No more, no less.

As she may have admitted herself, Mathilde Wesendonck was no Madame Geoffrin or Mademoiselle de Lespinasse, two famous and illustrious salonnières of the Enlightenment. Still, in view of her organization of soirées, readings, concerts, and major social events in her Zurich home and in the neighboring "Asyl," she was, like them, a woman determined to shape the social and intellectual life around her according to her own needs.[37] The Enlightenment analogy can also help to explain why Wagner's letters to her were to a large extent far from casual, despite his later attempts to downplay their significance. "To guard against any feeble mistakes," he later told Cosima with unconcealed disdain, "I sent this lady her letters back and had mine burned, for I do not want anything to remain that might suggest it was ever a serious relationship." [38]

In view of what Wagner had told her, Cosima was surprised to learn long after his death that many of the documents were still in Mathilde Wesendonck's estate. "I am astonished that so many letters are there," she wrote to Golther. "They should have been burned a long time ago."[39] What had Wagner been referring to? As good a guess as any (apart from the overly skeptical one that he may just have been inventing a story to placate Cosima) is that he was thinking of the aftermath of the crisis in the Wesendonck household in the first part of 1858 at a particularly sensitive moment during the genesis of *Tristan*, when he was bracing himself for the musical composition of the second act. After his first wife, Minna, had threatened to collect evidence of an adulterous affair, destroying evidence susceptible to serious misunderstanding would have been prudent, to say the least. Indeed, the written communications surviving between Wagner and Mathilde Wesendonck up to the so-called Asyl catastrophe in the late spring and early summer of 1858 are almost all harmless short greetings, invitations to dinner, brief comments, expressions of thanks, and other things of that sort, which have few signs of the intellectual seriousness and sheer length of many of his later letters to her. The single exception is the long letter of 7 April 1858, headed factually (though for more lurid minds provocatively): "Just out of bed." It is in fact a serious attempt to interpret aspects of Goethe's *Faust*. An understandably jealous Minna intercepted it as it was being taken by a servant from Wagner's to Mathilde Wesendonck's quarters on the Wesendonck estate. It is hard to believe that there had not already been others like it, or that it would have survived at all had Minna not decided to keep it as a memento of Richard's supposed unfaithfulness.[40] It was probably also a warning signal to her husband that she was now serious about obtaining real evidence: all the more reason to destroy whatever there was.

This possible scenario is only speculation; but it is notable that Wagner's extant letters to Mathilde after the "affair" had died down continue with some of his most telling and succinct comments about art and philosophy.

Despite its palpable gaps, including its unlikely one-sidedness in all probability caused by Mathilde's attempt to erase her part in it, [41] the correspondence has many of the hallmarks of an exchange of letters between late-eighteenth-century figures—a serious formal engagement, a pact even, with responsibilities on each side, that could be broken after the relationship was over by the return and burning of letters, or their mutilation. One reason why the history of the correspondence is shrouded in mystery, lending it an air of perceived erotic tension that for the most part disguises its essentially formal qualities, is that no one will ever know for certain how many letters the correspondents themselves destroyed. Nor will anyone ever be able to consult the originals that survived to the end of the nineteenth century. The letters were prepared for publication by Golther and Mathilde Wesendonck's heirs and returned to Bayreuth in 1904 after Cosima Wagner had reluctantly agreed to their appearance in print. Beyond sending strong hints to the editors, Cosima did not have final control over the publication (as is often assumed), and only when she got the letters back did she see it as her bounden duty to destroy them out of respect for Wagner's original wishes, suggesting somewhat acidly in an unpublished communication to Mathilde's son Karl von Wesendonck that it was something Mathilde herself should have done long ago: "[I] made the sacrifice, from which your mother shrank."[42]

THE GOLDEN AGE OF PRIVATE LIFE

The trail of destruction that marks the fragmented survival of Wagner's and Mathilde Wesendonck's correspondence is a fitting sequel to the evolution of *Tristan und Isolde* from a tale of unrequited love to an existential account of the annihilation of self. Everyone has heard the cliché that *Tristan und Isolde* is "the ultimate glorification of love."[43] In a sense the work really is the love story to end all love stories: if one understands it well, no other pair of lovers, however star-crossed, can ever be quite the same again. Not even Shakespeare's *Romeo and Juliet*, at first sight perhaps the work *Tristan* most closely resembles, is as bleak. Far from a glorification of love, however, at the core of *Tristan* is the idea that the secret, all-else-excluding passion between two people is just as much an illusion as the public political sphere of human relations that threatens to invade it. They are martyrs in the name of freedom, not only from the public world that has caught them in its vise, but also from the torment of love itself, the dark allure of "night" they both eventually reject as vehemently as they do the bright realm of "day."

The death-devoted rebellion against the public and the private in *Tristan* is undoubtedly one reason for its powerful effect on the nineteenth century, "the golden age of private life,"[44] during which the celebration of a realm of dreams and conflict served as the bulwark of reality and law. But the arc that stretched from the social engineering of the Jacobins in France in the 1790s—a time when the private was considered to have something conspiratorial about it at odds with the national good—to the cult of inwardness and aestheticism in fin de siècle Europe, when the influence of *Tristan* was at its height, also included in its range significant doubts about the equilibrium between the public and private spheres that liberal policy was meant to have achieved. In a sense it is precisely this "equilibrium" that is under attack in *Tristan*. Already in the first act it is the pressure of a public event—Tristan's delivery of "Ireland's daughter, loving and wild" (the sailor's apt description of Isolde at the start of the opera) as Cornwall's future queen—that practically encourages the lovers' fateful recognition of their hidden passion, after which the public and the private retain their tragic dependency on each other almost to the very end. To put it another way: Wagner's staging of the private in metaphysical, quasi-religious form takes on, before its final redemption, a drastic, almost tyrannical character that is not so much at odds with social authority as peculiarly reliant on it.

With its five moons—the five songs of the *Wesendonck Lieder*—*Tristan und Isolde* has therefore not become one of the most alluring planets in the operatic universe simply because it is a love story in extremis. The superficial image only disguises the deep trauma of desire in two individuals in the opera, whose fated relation to each other and the external events that condition it appear to be beyond their control. This existential predicament, which in turn affected the way Wagner misperceived, and subsequently denied, his serious relations with Mathilde Wesendonck, led him to write some of the most searing and emotionally disturbing music ever heard in the theater. Indeed, since *Tristan und Isolde* was first put before its astonished audiences in 1865, nothing quite like it has ever been heard again. The strange tensions between the public and the private encoded in the drama, and even in the way its music unfolds, are doubtless one reason for the hold it still has on our imagination.

12. Postmortem on Isolde

Need I add that hashish, like all solitary joys, renders the individual useless to mankind, and society superfluous to the individual, driving him to unending self-regard, and day by day hastening his approach to the glittering abyss, where he'll admire his face—the face of Narcissus?

CHARLES BAUDELAIRE, *Oeuvres complètes: Les paradis artificiels*

After tea Richard plays for me the Prelude to *Tristan und Isolde* (which the periodical *Signale für die musikalische Welt* once described as "crudely sensual"!). Deeply moved by it, indeed hardly in control of myself.

Cosima Wagner's Diaries, 4 January 1869

In sport and myth, men and women are segregated in terms of the physical demands made on them. Opera, however, is one area where women will always be vocally equal, if not superior. Brigid Brophy wrote in her wonderful study of Mozart's operas that, without denying the beauty of men's voices or their necessary presence in opera, "it is the female voice, and par excellence the soprano, which exerts the most vivid pressure on our imagination."[1] In a prominent review of Catherine Clément's book *Opera, or the Undoing of Women*, Paul Robinson made a similar point, claiming, "Opera is built on one of the great natural equalities, namely, the equality of men's and women's voices. Women can sing as loudly as men, their voices embrace as large a range as those of men and they have the advantage of commanding the heights where they can emit sounds of unparalleled incisiveness. They also enjoy greater vocal facility than men, thus allowing them to convey a sense of tremendous energy."[2] Robinson's complaint about Clément's book is that her indictment of opera is merely an indictment of the libretto. Take, for instance, women's suicide by poison or the knife, or even death without a definable cause: in Clément's hands the operatic heroines who end this way, entrapped in social relations conditioned by men, are just faithful copies of ideas about sex and gender found in contemporary novels, plays, and paintings. It is all very well, Robinson seems to be saying, to talk about swooning divas in the act of self-immolation, as if they were down-market versions of Emma Bovary or Miss Julie. But opera is "above all a musical phenomenon." Warming to what looks like a familiar defense of the enjoyment of music for its own sake, this time with a profeminist wig perched on top of it, Robinson reaches the following conclusion: "The single most important musical fact about opera's female victims is that they sing with an authority equal to that of their male oppressors."[3]

Contrary to the impression given by Robinson, Clément's so-called indictment of opera does include music. Certainly when discussing Isolde, she embarks first on an exotic, extramusical field trip to explore the mythical and anthropological capacities of Wagner's heroine—"Ireland's daughter, loving and wild," as the sailor at the start of the opera aptly calls her. Lovedeath (Liebestod) is not far from Liebelei, "the sad, sweet love of the Viennese shopgirl. Cabbage soup, jam tarts [and] superficial sentiments . . . in the Vienna of decadence."[4] Clément also moves effortlessly from Isolde, the sublimated Viennese shopgirl, to the mythic bad mother who poisons her kind, and the very good mother who feeds, and is kind. She is the "south American opossum," Clément says, "a pretty little animal . . . that stinks" and—though she does not spell out the allusion—one that can feign death.[5] Isolde is a foreigner, too, caught in a social system unable to tolerate her presence. This is how opera reveals its peculiar function: "to seduce like possums, by means of aesthetic pleasure, and to show, by means of music's seduction (making one forget the essential), how women die—without anyone thinking, as long as the marvelous voice is singing, to wonder why."[6]

In Clément's imaginative games with representations of women in opera there are no rules. Roaming around any intellectual terrain that takes her fancy, she seems intent on declaring everything de facto as part of an ongoing dialogue, or what Nietzsche liked to call a perpetual renewal of himself. Which is fine, except that trouble begins "when the sloughing snake"—to stay in the South American jungle for a moment with Ernest Newman's memorable words about Nietzsche—"reviles all other ophidians for not casting their skins at the precise moment when his [or hers] has become an inconvenience to him [or her]."[7] Clément too hastily rejects previous discourse on opera as "deaf," with at least one ironic consequence I shall discuss in a minute. She is right, though, to claim that part of that supposed deafness has been an inadequate critical response to the popularity of women and death as an aesthetic image, and especially women's suicide, which Margaret Higonnet has called a "cultural obsession"[8] of the nineteenth century. Robinson seems unperturbed by the image, at least in opera, holding fast to the idea that vocal equality between the sexes ultimately outweighs their social imbalance. Clément would probably agree about the vocal equality. But for her that is precisely the problem. What is essential about opera for Robinson is music. What is essential for Clément is the brutal oppression of women in myth and history that music, and especially women's capacity for brilliant vocal display, compels us to forget.

Clément is reviving the old argument about music as an agent of dangerous make-believe that ultimately works against us by inveigling us into thinking that our interests are other than they really are. Kierkegaard thought that Mozart's *Don Giovanni*, probably the greatest musical deceiver of all time, embodied the principle. And Nietzsche famously accused Wagner of exploiting it in the name of a spurious religion of redemption. It is not that Wagner's music is true or untrue, Nietzsche claimed; the problem is that it is taken to be true—a point that, as Dahlhaus rather glibly remarks, may be no more than the futile critical ploy of denouncing the theater for being the theater.[9]

Clément senses correctly, however, that there are other things to explore in the ideological landscape of opera, especially among the musical and extramusical strands that librettists and composers have woven into, and displaced in, images of woman and death. In contradistinction to Nietzsche as well, and especially the Nietzsche of *The Birth of Tragedy* (1872), Clément takes as the real goal of her attack the romantic metaphysics of absolute music, even if she is only indirectly explicit about it by simply insisting on its replacement by the category of the social—a demand that, ironically in the context of her narrative, barters one absolute for another. She boldly accuses music, by virtue of its power qua music, of allowing us to forget the reason for Isolde's death. Yet at the same time she turns the social dimension of the image into "the essential." The polarization principally rests on the assumption that the only ideologically significant aspect of the musical score is its ability to hide real social relations. But Clément does not seem to notice that the opposition between the musical and the social oddly dissipates the levels of meaning in the scene by ignoring—paradoxical as it may seem at first sight—the historical residues embedded in Wagner's notion of absolute music. These leftovers from the past inside one of the most deeply affecting moments Wagner ever wrote are surely at the heart of his reputation and its ambiguities. The obvious xenophobia, anti-Semitism and misogyny in his works have linked some of the greatest moments in German culture with the eruption of barbarity. But in a far more problematic and ambiguous way, so too have the seductive high points of his music, with their promise of freedom from social constraint and their utopian celebration of nothingness and death. The overt political gestures in Wagner, in other words, are unobtrusively linked with those moments where his music, appearing at its most pure and "musical," enters into its subtlest contract with the extramusical in order to preserve, as a vision of the absolute, its formidable social power. In the context of Isolde's death scene, it is this contract I want to examine here.

UNRAVELING THE MUSICALLY ABSOLUTE

The prominent musicological discourse on Isolde's death, and the Prelude to the whole opera, is dominated by a formidable phalanx of musical analyses—so many that Jean-Jacques Nattiez had no trouble in devoting a whole article to an analysis of the analyses of the Tristan chord with plenty of material to spare.[10] Nearly all the dissections of the famous musical passages in *Tristan und Isolde* avoid—almost suspiciously so—the extramusical altogether. (I have often wondered whether the inscrutable diagrams and tables in the densest and most obsessive musical analysis of Isolde's death scene included in Benjamin Boretz's article—aptly called "Analytic Fallout"—in the fourth part of his "Meta-variations" are not really metaphorical bomb shelters intended to protect its author from the extramusical meanings that Isolde's death might open up.)[11] At the same time, Wagner created such a stable analogy between the transcendental view of music current in the nineteenth century and the famous night and day symbolism of *Tristan und Isolde* that historians and critics have scarcely noticed it. Wagner really did conceive the work as a monument to the supposed purity of music. It will be the "most full-blooded musical conception," he wrote to Franz Liszt in 1854. And among other similar statements in *Cosima Wagner's Diaries,* Wagner is reported as saying that "he had felt the urge to let go for once in expressing himself completely symphonically, and that led him to *Tristan.*"[12] The countless musical analyses prove time and again that it really did.

Important work done since Adorno's remark that "music's aesthetic autonomy is not its original condition, but a revocable one acquired late and laboriously"[13] has begun to illuminate the gradual evolution of the notion of absolute music at the end of the eighteenth century, and its role in the history of subjectivity in the nineteenth, when it became inseparable from idealistic interpretations of Beethoven's instrumental music.[14] Two basic rules, assiduously dissected by Lydia Goehr, can be summarized as follows: 1) there shall be an essential core of the musical that can be severed from the world of concrete significance and raised to the level of the universal; and 2) the meaning of music shall be moved from its exterior to its structural interior.[15] The high musical ambition of *Tristan und Isolde* and the library of musical analyses that go with it are a near-perfect marriage of these transcendentalist and formalist precepts.

There is, however, a twist. The change from the eighteenth-century notion of music as imitation to the nineteenth-century view of musical autonomy left composers, who were aware of the social role of their music, with a dilemma. Their obligation to the community made them unwilling to loosen the bond between music and the real world completely, though in the name of art for art's sake they were not prepared to tighten it too much either. Thus the problem for some musicians—including Wagner—was how to establish a connection with reality that could underscore the supreme mission of art in society without also sacrificing the purity of music on the altar of a supposedly alien outside world. This is exactly the predicament the young Nietzsche exploits in *The Birth of Tragedy*, in which, memorably, but overdoing things as usual, he asks if anyone, without the extramusical aid of word and image, could listen to the third act of *Tristan und Isolde* as a symphony, "without expiring in a spasmodic unharnessing of all the wings of the soul."[16]

But Wagner did not see the action and poetic text of his opera only as the smelling salts of the sublime, as a way of reviving listeners exposed to the druglike effects of his music. Rather, he regarded them as an encoded image of the sublime itself in which the celebration of German instrumental music he inevitably associated with the sublime played a central role. The essay "Beethoven" (1870)—a belated but nonetheless copious account of the huge philosophical impact of *Tristan* on his theory of theater—was written at the high point of his association with the young Nietzsche. It probably reflects the views of both men on music and its relation to the extramusical (albeit more soberly expressed by the older man), and in particular Wagner's idiosyncratic way of using the philosophy of Schopenhauer to try and resolve the issue. One of the centerpieces of "Beethoven" is a reinvention of Schopenhauer's idea of the allegorical dream that Wagner likens to a purely musical experience, but one still retaining a tenuous link with the conceptual world.[17] The perception of scenic events in his stage works is only the outer surface of an inner musical experience that is analogous to a dream in a state of half-sleep poised delicately between the real and the unconscious world, and often vividly recalled on waking. It is clear from the context that he is referring above all to *Tristan*. (Incidentally, the surreal, dreamlike character of the narrative in Wagner's medieval sources, noted by several commentators independently of the opera, may be one reason he chose to adapt it.) And in a later essay, which appeared in the same year as Nietzsche's *Birth of Tragedy*, Wagner summed up the notion, again with *Tristan* principally in mind, with the ingenious phrase "deeds of music made visible."[18] This was one of the most effective slogans in his campaign to legitimize his concept of symphonic drama, which, on account of its intense concentration on complex music, was in danger of being regarded as fundamentally alien to the theater.

With the idea of the allegorical dream, Wagner provided a door for the extramusical to enter unobtrusively into the bedchamber of absolute music, as it were, and I would like to start opening it with an intriguing literary allusion. As Isolde launches into the final section of her death scene, quickly leading to its famous musical climax, she seems to refer to the ninth stanza of a poem by Nikolaus Lenau called "Beethovens Büste" (The bust of Beethoven):[19]

LENAU	ISOLDE
Sanftes Wogen	Heller schallend,
holdes Rieseln;	mich umwalled,
Sind des Weltmeers	sind es Wellen
kühle Wellen	sanfter Lüfte?
Süß beseelt	Sind es Wogen
zu Liebesstimmen?	wonnige Düfte?
Wie sie steigen,	Wie sie schwellen
sinken, schwellen!	mich umrauschen.

LENAU	ISOLDE
Soft surging	*More brightly ringing,*
sweet rippling;	*floating around me,*
is it the cool waves	*is it the waves*
of the ocean	*of the soft air?*
sweetly inspiring	*Is it the surging, the*
the voices of love?	*sweet fragrances?*
How they climb,	*How they swell*
sink, and swell!	*and roar around me.*

Lenau's poem is a moderately good, typical romantic allegorical effusion celebrating the memory of the dead Beethoven. Its dreamlike language—"soft surging" *(sanftes Wogen)*, "cool waves" *(kühle Wellen)*, "how they climb" *(wie sie steigen)*—is meant to reflect the feelings of the poet on contemplating a bust of Beethoven. Isolde's text has similar phrases—"is it the waves" *(sind es Wellen)*, "is it the surging" *(sind es Wogen)*, "how they swell" *(wie sie schwellen).* The comparison is no more than casual in view of the texts' standard romantic imagery, though in a wider context it is far more significant. Only a year after finishing *Tristan*, Wagner enthusiastically described Beethoven's symphonies as an unprecedented language of "purely musical expression" that can "enthrall the listener" more than any other art, and thereby "reveal an ordering principle of such freedom and daring that it must seem to be more powerful than any kind of known logic."[20] Or, as E. T. A. Hoffmann put it in his review of Beethoven's Fifth Symphony (1810)—a famous pioneer essay in romantic music criticism known to every musician of Wagner's generation—only music can bring about the revelation of that "unknown realm" of the "unsayable," which is "quite separate from the outer sensual world."[21] As Isolde grows oblivious to everything around her, she gradually sinks lifeless into the world of the absolute, which, as the orchestra surges forward with seductive symphonic grandeur, she similarly appears to equate with Hoffmann's and Wagner's supreme musical hero.

THE ASSURANCE OF ECSTASY

E. T. A. Hoffmann was not the only writer in the early part of the nineteenth century to see a relationship between instrumental music and the sublime. Yet it is not at all far-fetched to see him as one of Wagner's principal sources, particularly as he was one of the first to take the category of the sublime as the starting point for an analysis of Beethoven's symphonies. Hoffmann's opera *Undine* (1816) was also a possible model for the visual encoding of the musically absolute at the end of *Tristan und Isolde* in the form of a death that takes place in an otherworldly space. In the original story by Fouqué, who was also asked by Hoffmann to be his librettist, Undine cries her lover to death with tears of love that penetrate his eyes, and then his breast. In the finale of the opera, Undine simply appears in the waters of a fountain, and with a kiss draws her unfaithful lover Huldbrand forever into the kingdom of the immortals. After the fatal kiss, the priest Heilmann remarks that Huldbrand has been "chosen for a pure love-death," and Undine is seen sitting under a fantastically ornate portal made of mussels, pearls, corals, and strange aquatic vegetation. The body of Huldbrand lies in her arms as she "bends softly over him" *(sich sanft über ihn hinbeugt).*[22]

Several similar motifs are embedded in Isolde's death scene, though Wagner both adopts and resists their original meaning, as he usually managed to do with his sources. The scene in Wagner's opera is of course widely known as Isolde's love-death *(Liebestod).* Yet apart from including the

word in the love duet in the second act of Tristan, Wagner actually used it
to describe the Prelude to the opera and not its final scene, which he preferred to call "transfiguration" *(Verklärung)*.[23] The relationship between the
female and male figures is also turned around. Indeed, Nattiez's imaginative
reading of the end of *Tristan* as a kind of domesticated icon of musical
androgyny—"a female-dominated variant in which the female spirit of
music dictates to the poet-composer, telling him what plot he has to construct and what music he has to write"[24]—is actually a more appropriate
metaphor for the end of *Undine.*

A closer look at the genesis of the last scene of *Tristan* and its shape in the
finished work suggests a different reading.[25] It is noteworthy, first of all, that
Isolde hardly features at all in Wagner's initial prose sketches, which are devoted mainly to Tristan's monologue in act 3. (Incidentally, the short prose
sketches with which Wagner usually began an opera, usually writing them
fleetingly in pencil in notebooks and on odd bits of paper, are often important
for sharply characterizing key images later diffused in the finished works.)
Second, when Isolde does appear and kneels down beside the wounded corpse
of Tristan, she says nothing. She just listens. Wagner describes her, and her
death, almost as if she were positioned, mute, inside a stiff Byzantine allegory,
but one in which music is active and tangibly visible, and indeed has to be,
since she eventually throws herself into it and drowns:[26]

> Isolde über Tristan hingebeugt, kommt zu sich u. lauscht mit wachsen-
> dem Entzücken den sich steigenden Liebesmelodien, die wie aus Tris-
> tan's Seele zu ihr aufzusteigen scheinen, anschwellen wie ein
> Blüthenmeer—in das sie sich zum Ertrinken darin stürzt u.—stirbt.
>
> *Isolde, bent over Tristan, recovers herself and listens with growing rap-
> ture to the ascending melodies of love, which appear to rise up as if out
> of Tristan's soul, swelling up like a sea of blossoms, into which, in order
> to drown, she throws herself and—dies.*

As in Fouqué and Hoffmann's *Undine,* including Fouqué's original story,
several famous images come to mind, among them the *Mater dolorosa,* who
wept over the body of the dead Christ, and Narcissus, who died after falling
in love with his own image in the waters of a spring, whereupon a flower
bearing his name grew in his place. (The flower was the last to be gathered
by Persephone before being carried off by Hades.) An important part of the
imagery in *Tristan und Isolde,* too, is the allusion to the Assumption of the
Virgin Mary—a subject that fascinated Wagner all his life and culminated
in his admiration for Titian's famous Madonna, the *Assunta dei Frari,*
which he first saw in Venice in 1861. "We have nothing so perfect in music,"

Cosima recorded him as saying in a conversation about the painting toward the end of his life. "The glowing head of the Virgin Mary," she continued, "recalls to him his idea of the sexual urge: this unique and mighty force now freed of all desire, the Will enraptured and redeemed."[27] Similarly, Isolde is finally freed in death from "love as torment" (die Liebe als Qual),[28] where at least—to adopt a phrase of Julia Kristeva's—she has for her martyrdom a bonus awaiting her: "the assurance of ecstasy."[29]

But the most extraordinary image in Wagner's prose sketch is the graphic description of the music that, before it turns into a sea of sweet-smelling blossoms that will drown Isolde, seems to ascend out of the body of Tristan. Far from being active, as in Nattiez's interpretation, Isolde is transformed into an innocent shell serving only to receive the sounds of Tristan's music. Nattiez's image is in keeping with the view of Leonard B. Meyer, who has gone to great pains in his musical analysis of the scene to show how Isolde's vocal line is an integral and indispensable part of the music.[30] But Meyer misses the possibility that the voice could be heard as passive in relation to the prominent orchestral melody, and the contrast between the two as an acoustical allegory for an extramusical idea that involves the subservience of Isolde to Tristan. Also in keeping with his original concept, Wagner allows Isolde to begin by taking over a melody first sung by Tristan in act 2, as if it were echoing up from his corpse into her own body—a telling reversal of the moment in Wagner's principal medieval source by Gottfried von Strassburg, in which (not unlike Undine's lethal tears of love) Isolde's "secret song" steals "with its rapturous music hidden and unseen through the windows of the eyes into many noble hearts."[31] Wagner's Isolde sings for sixty-eight measures, in twenty-five of which she occasionally touches on the main theme, and in the rest descants in counterpoints. It was Tovey—no sophisticated music analyst certainly, but a sensitive musician quickly able to grasp the aesthetic point of a musical passage—who first asked how many of Isolde's counterpoints anyone, except the singer, could actually remember. "I should not be surprised," Tovey wrote skeptically, "if many of the music-lovers who go to every stage performance of Tristan found themselves unable to quote them."[32]

In terms based on Lacan, Michel Poizat has evolved a sophisticated interpretation of the orchestra's dominance in the last few pages of Tristan, especially the substitution of the orchestra for the voice that completes the trajectory of Isolde's monologue at the end. The substitution, he claims, "is the very image of the function of music in opera, which is . . . to avoid that final step where perfect beauty turns to horror."[33] The point is not dissimilar to Clément's about music as an inveterate deceiver, a purveyor of illusions about unacceptable realities, with the difference that in Poizat's view Wagner actually toys with moments of intolerability, only to use music's power to sidestep them in the end. The orchestra drowns Brangäne's cry of horror at the height of the love duet in the second act, and in the repeat of the same music at the end of Isolde's monologue the cry is replaced by a sumptuous orchestral climax.

But Poizat passes over the moment well before this when the orchestra begins to engulf Isolde in an ever-increasing surge of sound—an acoustical allegory of drowning that confronts violence and the sublime in a way that is provocative even for Wagner. Isolde could have followed the labyrinthine twists and turns of the orchestral melody to the end, as she did with Tristan in their love duet. But from a specific point—and this is confirmed by Wagner's sketches—her vocal line has been carefully rewritten.[34] Her descants on the main melody become, as Tovey noted, barely memorable, and they seem to lose their footing in terms of both audibility and meaningful counterpoint. Moreover, Wagner started recomposing her vocal line at precisely the point ("Heller schallend") where she appears to begin referring to Lenau's poetic celebration of the deceased Beethoven. Indeed, she seems to invoke the memory of the dead hero of music almost as if he were to come alive again in an intoxicating sea of melody, but one that envelops her own voice and eventually kills her.

NEO-MANICHAEAN HERESIES

The long-standing prejudice that ultimately the extramusical cannot meaningfully relate to the music of a work like *Tristan* has also blurred, even sentimentalized, its famous biographical context. The belief in the absoluteness of music even prompted the strange act of vandalism alluded to in the previous chapter that put a question mark over one of its key biographical sources. Cosima destroyed the original letters after they were returned to her by Mathilde's heirs, as I have pointed out—all of them, that is, except for Wagner's beautifully written music examples, which were painstakingly cut out of the letters and placed in an envelope in the Bayreuth archives.[35] Absolute music, it seems, is immune from sordid human affairs.

Wagner, as we have also seen, was infatuated with Mathilde Wesendonck, the wife of a rich Swiss businessman, and for a time lived close to her in a house on the Wesendonck's estate in Zurich. Living "close to her" is probably the wrong way of describing the situation: they clearly lived in separate family circles for most of the time, and in all likelihood they corresponded with each other even more than the number of surviving letters suggests. The famous letter to her about Goethe's *Faust* intercepted by his wife Minna (see chapter 11) also contained a sketch of the *Tristan* Prelude and led to a major crisis that forced him to leave Zurich to compose the rest of *Tristan* in Venice, where, unable to correspond directly with Mathilde any more, he confided passionate thoughts to her in a special diary for himself. Chessick, a psychoanalyst with a professional interest in the relationship, even suggests that the discovery of Wagner's letter by his wife was no accident, because it meant that Wagner's feelings for his "muse" could only thrive properly when he was apart from her and not with her.[36]

As he so often did, Wagner seems to have been living his life as if it were a literary artifact, the source of which here can be traced to his medieval sources. In his famous book *Love in the Western World*, Denis de Rougemont, a Swiss theologian and essayist, saw in the romance of Tristan and Iseult the "one great European myth of adultery"[37] and simple proof of the inescapable conflict in the West between passion and marriage. Constantly stressing the irretrievably narcissistic and segregative character of the conflict that renders the relationship analogous to a drug, de Rougement discovers in the romance a furtive conflict between two religions: an exoteric creed of feudal honor and fealty, and an esoteric creed of unlimited passion. His conclusion is that Tristan and Iseult were in love not with one another, but with love itself. "Each loves the other *from the standpoint of self and not from the other's standpoint*. Their unhappiness thus originates in a false reciprocity, which disguises a twin narcissism."[38] Long before Freud and modern psychology, de Rougement claims, this is what Wagner saw. In their desire for death the lovers feel more fully alive than ever. They live "dangerously and magnificently,"[39] and, as death aggravates desire, their passion secretly wills its own frustrations, irresistibly seeking the bodily death that forever removes it from the qualifications of life, the disappointments of actual possession.

John Updike wrote an elegantly scathing review of de Rougement's thesis almost a decade before the facets of narcissism discussed in the book were taken up in earnest by psychoanalysts. (With its more positive view of romantic love and narcissism, incidentally, the review seems to have been an even stronger stimulus than the book itself for psychoanalysts in the 1970s and early 1980s.) Updike rightly points out that de Rougement's analysis of the Tristan legend is only the center of a virtuoso sequence of ideas that boldly puts the blame for the Western obsession with romantic love on Catharism, a neo-Manichaean heresy that, before being crushed by the Albigensian Crusade, flourished in twelfth-century Provence. In a passage that is more than a match for de Rougement's own stylish text, Updike sums up the sequence as follows:

> Manichaeanism, denying the Christian doctrines of the Divine Creation and the Incarnation, radically opposes the realms of spirit and matter. The material world is evil. Man is a spirit imprisoned in the darkness of the flesh. His only escape is through aestheticism and mystical "knowing." Women are Devil's lures designed to draw souls down into bodies; on the other hand, each man aspires toward a female Form of Light who is his own true spirit, resident in heaven, aloof from the Hell of matter. Moreover, in some permutations of Dualist mythology the Mother of Christ becomes Maria Sophia, sophia aeterna, an Eternal Feminine that preexisted material creation. . . . From such doctrines, de Rougement maintains in his most strenuously and carefully argued chapters, it is a very short step to the erotic rhetoric of the troubadours of Languedoc, and from there to courtly love, epithalamian mysticism, Héloïse and Abelard, Tristan and Iseult, and all the romances, medieval and modern, that torment the West with Gnostic longings.[40]

In this context, Wagner's Isolde becomes the musical prototype of the Unattainable Lady, who diverts attention and adoration from the attainable lady—someone, in other words, who is in legal terms a "wife" and in Christian terms a "neighbor." Yet even though de Rougement tends to see key aspects of the legend through the filter of Wagner's interpretation of it—a point not discussed by Updike—the Isolde in Wagner's opera, given the warmth and presence of the music she has to sing, does not appear at first sight to bear much resemblance to her counterpart in the legend as de Rougement sees her:

> Iseult is ever a stranger, the very essence of what is strange in woman and of all that is eternally fugitive, vanishing, and almost hostile in a fellow-being, that which indeed incites to pursuit, and rouses in the heart of a man who has fallen a prey to the myth an avidity for possession so much more delightful than possession itself. She is the woman-from-whom-one-is-parted: to possess her is to lose her.[41]

Still, a coded language of separation between the sexes in the name of a heightening of pleasure—or twin narcissistic collusion, in psychoanalytical terms—is, I would argue, not only written into Wagner's letters to Mathilde Wesendonck in the 1850s, but also into the music of *Tristan und Isolde*, and into its final scene in particular. Lawrence Kramer has written that "Tristan and Isolde's language about each other, together with the music that conveys it, does little or nothing to articulate the polarity of masculine and feminine—an elision that is drastically at odds with normal nineteenth-century practice."[42] On the contrary, Tristan and Isolde have entirely separate deaths that are inscribed with a multitude of signs that clearly mark them out, dialectically to be sure, as vivid symbols of the masculine and feminine as the nineteenth century understood them. The searing deceptive cadence at measure 17 of the Prelude separates a fraught and complex harmonic progression from a smoother and simpler (i.e., in nineteenth-century terms, more "feminine") one in the cellos. This is why the same cadence reoccurs in an even more agonized, and at the same time pleasurable, form at the moment of Tristan's death, when, only seconds after Isolde's delayed arrival at his sickbed, he separates from her forever.

A deceptive cadence (sometimes called an interrupted cadence) is a cadence that awakens the expectation of a move to the tonic from a chord of the dominant, only to frustrate that expectation by moving to a chord of the sixth degree instead. Bailey insists that it is a mistake to call this moment in *Tristan* a deceptive cadence because he believes that in the advanced harmonic system of the West in the latter part of the nineteenth century, the chord of the sixth degree was no longer perceived as a decorative adjunct when sounded after a dominant chord, but as a substitute tonic of equal weight and validity.[43] This may be right in abstract structural terms; but Wagner also exploited the deceptive cadence as a reference to an earlier musical style, with the rhetorical gesture implicit in its name still intact. Precisely because the cadence has been given such a significant structural role in *Tristan,* its rhetorical force underscores a separation of the music from its expected goal that is therefore made to seem both desired and supremely logical.

The cadence reoccurs at exactly the same pitch level (E/F) in a number of key places in *Tristan,* though one that has received little attention so far is the moment when Isolde begins to regain consciousness in Brangäne's arms just after the bleak oxymoron addressed by King Marke to the dead Tristan "Du treulos treuester Freund!" (You faithlessly most faithful friend).[44] Its importance in the present context is that it leads this time to an evocative pre-echo of the first five notes of Isolde's *Liebestod.* Wagner repeats the idea twice, each time transposed up a semitone, as Brangäne and Marke comment anxiously on Isolde's numb, wordless state, until it reaches the start of the *Liebestod* proper. Aware of the significance of the passage, Wagner was rightly proud that he had made Isolde, to adapt a famous phrase by Novalis, sound homesick for the absolute, and Wagner himself called this series of deceptive cadences "the loveliest moment . . . when the theme enters three times with muted horns and violins, as Isolde's only response to the sympathy of the others."[45]

But like Isolde's response to those around her, the most important thing about her death scene is that, gradually and almost imperceptibly, it seems to separate itself off from the rest of the opera. Indeed, it is part and parcel of the intriguing dialectics of the music of *Tristan* that Wagner managed to convey this feeling of a final retreat from the surrounding external world of the senses, despite the fact that he was repeating, practically note for note, two passages from the love duet in act 2 that, in sharp contrast to the exalted saintliness of Isolde's renunciation of earthly desire in her death scene, is well known as being second to none in its graphic musical representation of the sexual act. Again the intrepid Tovey gropes toward this view in his complaints about the coupling of the *Tristan* Prelude and Isolde's *Liebestod* in the concert hall. "Isolde's dying utterances," he wrote, "emerge into a key not only different from, but totally destructive of the harmonic basis of the prelude."[46]

We shall never know whether Tovey would have been prepared to make the same point about the position of the music at the end of the opera. But here, too, the harmonic logic of the final scene in relation to the rest of the opera is hard to fathom in structural terms if one continues to insist, like Tovey did, that a work must finish in its "proper key" (i.e., the key of its beginning) and be made "as coherent and as exact in its proportions as any movement by Bach."[47] *Tristan* of all works, of course, was hardly ever likely to end "properly," yet the presence of some surface details have led some music analysts to believe that it does. Indeed, it is salutary to study these sophisticated technical readings, if only to see how urgent it has been to contain—perhaps a better term is *to domesticate*—the work's subversive close. Boretz, indulging in what he deprecatingly calls "a bit of derivational tune-detective analysis," claims that "the opening 'Liebestod motto' ($E^{\flat}$ $A^{\flat}$ G) is an obvious permutation of the (A F E) trichord that opens Act I."[48] Even at this simple level Boretz misses the dialectical tension between the two cases. Both have a falling semitone as their second interval. But at the same time the difference between their rising first intervals—respectively a minor sixth and a perfect fourth—also shows that in expressive terms they are worlds apart. Indeed, the chorale-like opening of the *Liebestod* is so sharply contrasted to the yearning, tormented phrase at the start of the opera that one need hardly look further for the clear separation of the two moments.

Both Boretz and Kramer insist, too, that the interval span $G^{\sharp}$–B in the melody of the opening controls the key structure $A^{\flat}$–$C^{\flat}$(B) of the *Liebestod*.[49] But pitches in melodic formations in one key are not necessarily synonymous with the same pitches turned into the centers of different keys. It is true that Wagner structures "the loveliest moment"—the three deceptive cadences leading into the *Liebestod*—with exceptional smoothness and logic by means of straightforward upward transpositions of a semitone. The impression of seamlessness, however, is belied by the simple fact that the music reaches a tonal level, A♭ major, which in terms of the system of key relationships is very distant from the dominant of A minor/major at the start of the transition, and, of course, the beginning of the entire opera as well. The whole point of the key structure of the *Liebestod* is its almost studious avoidance of the polarity A minor/C major that has become associated with the everyday and its tormented human relations during the course of the opera. And if analytical propriety can make out a seemingly good case for the inherent unity of the *Liebestod* with the rest of *Tristan*, it is again the expressive character of the music, as well as its tonal structure, that exposes the spirit of contradiction, the difference in sameness, that the comforting view of organic wholeness usually fails to confront in the looking-glass world at the center of the opera. The sudden reversals from loud to soft, the sudden pullings back and separations from promised high points serving to heighten the intensity of the music, all of which have been heard in a different tempo in the act 2 love duet, take on new meaning in the *Liebestod*, where the earlier torturous striving for togetherness is replaced by a new calm and almost religious illumination now that the lovers are separated. The thwarted dynamic curves of the music no longer crave further disruption and apartness; having found them, they seek resolution instead. Indeed, the most potent musical allegory of the creed that "life is separation even in the midst of union"[50] turns out to be the simplest. The harmonic progression at the start of the Prelude, focused around an unresolved dominant seventh in A minor/major and famous as the central focus of the work's open-ended musical syntax, is unexpectedly given a different function at the very end of the opera and—untransposed—becomes instead an instigator of closure over a quasi-ecclesiastical plagal cadence in B major.

RESURRECTION IN REVERSE

The Christian symbols woven into the *Liebestod*—among them the chorale-like tone of its beginning and ending—reflect similar parallels with religion in Wagner's main medieval source, by Gottfried von Strassburg. (The Bed of Love in the Cave of Lovers serving as the altar and the church where the protagonists are sustained by the sacrament of love are two instances.) Notwithstanding de Rougement's idiosyncratic reading of the

Tristan and Iseult legend, the allusions to religious practice in the medieval poem are in Wagner's *Tristan* without the elaborate philosophical overlay that one might be tempted to call blasphemous were it not for the fact that in many circles in the nineteenth century, aesthetics and the cult of "inwardness" had long since begun to replace theology as the focus of intellectual and subjective experience. The danger here, as always, is to insist on stable analogies between cultural images and experienced reality that, as Elisabeth Bronfen has pointed out, can only defuse the real violence of political domination and the power of representations.[51]

The deceptive cadences and thwarted dynamic curves in the music of *Tristan* that heighten its intensity until it reaches its ultimate climax with the musical casting-off of Isolde, the Unattainable Lady, may or may not owe their existence to an especially turbulent phase of Wagner's life. Yet quite apart from his experiences, the musical image of Isolde's suicide in the *Liebestod*, as she drowns metaphorically in a wash of symphonic sound, is not without an underlying violence that remains disquieting, and also highly provocative in the sense that it appears at the same time as disembodied and drained of this-worldly meaning in its role as a well-nigh perfect allegory of absolute music.

Bronfen has argued persuasively in her discussion of visual representations of drowning women contemporary with *Tristan* that Woman as a cultural construct enacts the fact "that masculinity is constructed as that which lacks death."[52] The erasure of Woman kindles the hope of masculine wholeness and becomes a symptom of that wholeness, precisely because the masculine lacks her relation to death and Otherness. Indeed, not the least important aspect of the *Liebestod* is that it has been written in such a way that it can be played without Isolde as a piece of purely instrumental music.[53] Wagner's musical allegory strives for even greater excess. The exorbitant seductiveness of its music and its enactment in time give it such sensuous immediacy that it seems to be not just a representation of death, but a culturally constructed experience of it with the heightened emotion, the fleeting last-minute vividness of doomed memory, and the final flush of exhausted vitality that one imagines death involves. And for the allegory to work, the Beethoven-inspired symphonism of Wagner's music into which Isolde throws herself, Senta-like, to commit suicide, must itself, after achieving wholeness through Isolde's self-sacrifice, be brought to a close and extinguished.

Immediately after the arrival of Isolde, Tristan dies earlier in the act, accompanied by music that is jarringly incomplete. At the end, the music arising out of his body at last brings to rest the so-called Tristan chord, hitherto unresolved in an identifiable key. Poizat reads both the arrival of Isolde and her death as Tristan's hallucinations and comes to the conclusion that Isolde's death is therefore no more than the death of Tristan and the final dimming of his fantasy of plenitude sought in the Woman.[54] But these final pages can also be seen as Tristan's experience of a second death—an inversion of the Christian doctrine of the resurrection and the life everlasting that presents a hitherto unexplored iconic image in Wagner's theatrical liturgy. (The raised arm of Siegfried's corpse before he is placed on the funeral pyre at the end of the Ring and the opening of Titurel's coffin followed by Amfortas's impassioned dialogue with his dead father in the concluding moments of *Parsifal* are related moments.) Here we have, in fully developed form, the equivalent of a baroque allegory in musical form, which brings with it its own court, the profusion of emblems never absent, as Benjamin reminds us, from genuine allegories.[55] The chorale-like beginning of Isolde's *Liebestod* and the hymn-like gestures in the rest of its music remind us that her monologue is not dissimilar to the kind of baroque *Trauerspiel* described by Benjamin as showing an antinomic relation between Lutheranism and the everyday[56]—a theme pursued, logically enough, in Wagner's next work, *Die Meistersinger*. The difference between *Tristan* and most seventeenth-century allegorical plays is that the ending of *Tristan* shows a melancholic reaction on the part of the sovereign (very much present at the end as he, King Marke, blesses the bodies of the lovers) to the disavowal of religion itself. In sharp contrast to Wagner's medieval sources, the basis of this reaction is not any benign, nontranscendental parallel with religious practice, but a radical reversal of the central categories of that practice—a sensuous redemption in eternal death that actively resists the sense of disenchantment brought about by rigorous, antitranscendentalist Lutheran dogma.

MIRAGES OF ETERNITY

Allowing Isolde's death scene to resonate in its own historical space, so to speak, raises a number of issues about Wagner's notion of absolute music and its consequences. Since Nietzsche and Adorno, the supposed link between his aesthetics and the creation of illusion and hence manipulation of perception has become de rigueur among critics, who lose no time in creating precedents for the cinema, modern advertising techniques, and even fascist political propaganda, many of them based on unquestioned premises. Adorno's line of argument is especially ingenious, positing as it does a process of commodification in Wagner's music, rather like the making of an advertisement, which compels the listener, isolated by society's divisive mode of production, to connive with the powers of discipline by taking refuge in a "mirage of eternity" *(Trugspiel der Ewigkeit)*.[57] The music is stretched, thinned out, and at the same time subjected to a vertical and horizontal process of shrinking to create the impression of endless space, and with it an allegory of the eternal and the mythical.

The argument imputes nefarious intentions to Wagner, the old Klingsor who too often, in his supposed connivance with popular culture, gets the blame for musical conjuring tricks leading to the trivialization of music for propaganda purposes, whether commercial or political. Adorno eschewed any discussion of a fascist aesthetic in his Wagner book, claiming that the music represented merely its roots in the fundamentally bourgeois culture of the nineteenth century. But given the time in which most of his text was written (the late 1930s), the implied connection between Wagner and the propaganda techniques of the Nazi regime is perfectly obvious, as is his ready assumption that there is such a thing as an aesthetic that can be associated specifically with the fascist mind. The work of Siegfried Kracauer was influential; and later writers like Susan Sontag in her essay "Fascinating Fascism" have followed suit.[58] Yet given the pragmatic opportunism and randomness of nearly all functionaries involved with cultural matters in totalitarian regimes, it is exactly this assumption that seems most dubious when the issue is looked at more closely.

Isolde's *Liebestod* is a good test, all the more so because of the studied apartness from the real world it is meant to represent. Indeed, of all the moments in Wagner's works, this is probably the least likely to be associated with anything mundane like politics, though the extramusical allusions built into its musical fabric in the name of the absolute do not by any means exonerate it from reality in terms of its inverted religious codes and psychoanalytical insights, as we have seen. Hitler certainly liked it—in itself a circumstance to set the scholarly policing of it into overdrive—with one witness reporting a specific request that it be played to him. After serving six months for his part in the abortive Munich Putsch on November 9, 1923, Hitler visited the home of Ernst Hanfstaengl, a prosperous early supporter of the National Socialist Party, and, according to Hanfstaengl's memoirs, Hitler immediately asked to hear it:

> He arrived about half past six, in the little blue serge suit of which he was so proud, straining at the buttons with the weight he had put on in Landsberg. . . . I had a big concert grand in the studio and before I could

gather my wits or offer any hospitality, Hitler, who seemed tense and wound up, said, almost pleadingly: "Hanfstaengl, play me the *Liebestod.*" It was one of my party pieces. So I sat and hammered out this tremendous thing from *Tristan und Isolde,* with Lisztian embellishments, and it seemed to work the trick. He relaxed.[59]

A popular picture book on the life of Hitler published in 1936 also includes an unforgettable description by Goebbels of Hitler's reaction to Wagner's music. "His strong inner need for art should have already been clear to anyone," Goebbels wrote, "when, in the midst of the most difficult political negotiations or ennervating tactical battles before coming to power, he sometimes used to sit alone or with a few comrades in arms somewhere in an obscure theater box and hear the heroically elevated measures of a Wagnerian music drama in artistic unison with his political being."[60] Goebbels also added, probably correctly, that there were few people who had heard *Tristan und Isolde* as many times as Hitler had—and not only in the theater.

Despite their respective anecdotal and demagogic status, Goebbels's and Hanfstaengl's remarks suggest that they witnessed in Hitler a strong response to Wagner's music. In an odd way, Hanfstaengl tries to exonerate the music of the *Liebestod* from any suggestion of collusion by turning it, so to speak, into an acoustical therapist, with Hitler, the neurotic patient who was to inflict unprecedented mayhem on the world, responding positively to treatment. Clément's and Poizat's Freudian-Lacanian model comes to mind, a model that posits that not only Wagner's music, but also all music, can recreate the sense of authentic communion with the mother's body, the infantile feeling of wholeness before the intervention of alienating social and cultural codes. This is not necessarily to suggest that the musical image of the divine mother in Isolde's *Liebestod* somehow restored to Hitler, who was at the nadir of his political career, an archaic form of self-regard or "oceanic feeling"[61] that let him relax in a gratifying state of primary narcissism. Rather, according to Goebbels's remark about the artistic unison between Hitler's political being and Wagnerian drama, one could argue that the Führer heard the elevated measures of the *Liebestod* as an equivalent in pure sound of the *völkisch* image of motherhood and homeland, the impression of long-lost oneness and well-being, which he, the long-awaited hero, was setting out to impose on Germany at the time.

In pure sound? Thomas Mann wrote famously in 1940 that he found an element of Nazism not only in Wagner's questionable literature, but also in his "music." The quotation marks are Mann's, as if he wanted to separate Wagner's music from other music, although he admitted in the same breath that even after the outbreak of war he could still be "deeply stirred" whenever a few measures of it impinged on his ear.[62] Hitler also accorded special status to Wagner's music vis-à-vis other musics. Hanfstaengl reports that he never heard Hitler whistle a popular tune in all the years he knew him, though whistling "every note" of the *Meistersinger* overture by heart "in a curious penetrating vibrato, but completely in tune" came naturally. Hitler had little time for Bach and Mozart, and would listen to Schumann and Chopin with interest but no real enthusiasm. In the end, it had to be Wagner.[63]

But did the "music" of Isolde's *Liebestod*, with its thrilling orchestral effects and seductive climaxes, which still cause countless listeners to swoon with pleasure, have a special appeal to a fascist mind like Hitler's over and above the common experience of being emotionally aroused by it? Mann and Adorno have no real answer, though on their behalf one might respond, following Nietzsche, that the discovery of the unconscious was already ideology for Wagner, who from the start of writing *Tristan* relied clear-sightedly on an understanding of music, now familiar from psychoanalysis, as an archaic language capable of simulating a return to a state of primal bonding. In the prose sketches Tristan in his act 3 monologue only has this to say:

> "My mother died as she gave birth to me
> now I'm living, I'm dying of having been born: why?"
> Parzival's refrain—repeated by the shepherd—.
> "The whole world [is] nothing but
> unrelieved longing! How will it ever be stilled?"
> —PARZIVAL'S REFRAIN[64]

In this context, the verb "to still" refers not just to Wagner's Schopenhauerian view of the world, but also resonates in classic Wagnerian fashion with its other meanings—the suckling of an infant, the lulling of it into peaceful sleep, and the death of the infant at birth, that is, being "stillborn." The text also links three conspicuously motherless heroes. Siegfried's words in *Siegfried* on hearing the news of his mother's death at his birth *(So starb meine Mutter an mir?)* are paraphrased by Tristan, who in turn is visited on his sickbed by the wandering Parsifal. All three have been, or will be, guilty of at least one violent act and finally, in the presence of a powerful soprano voice, rectify the badness of life with their own deaths, or with radical self-denial.

Wagner abandoned Parsifal's compassionate response to Tristan to make it the basis of his last opera and left it largely to the music of *Tristan und Isolde* to convey Tristan's anguished sense of self and his return in death to the narcissistic condition the intoxicating sounds of Isolde's

Liebestod re-create on his behalf. By mapping a precise iconic system into the musical fabric of the *Liebestod*, Wagner created, in the name of death, an impression of absoluteness and a total identity with nature—the oceanic sensation described by psychoanalysts and mystics when the (usually) solitary subject feels at one with the world. But what is the rhetorical power of this psychoanalytical premise? And was it adapted by National Socialism for their own purposes in the knowledge that Wagner's music was one of its sources?

The consequences Adorno draws from his arguments about the "commodification" of Wagner's music indeed strongly imply its collusion with the Nazi forces of oppression. His remark about mirages of eternity in Wagner's music as points of refuge for those conniving with the powers of discipline brings to mind a scene like the roll call of the SA and SS and the Commemoration of the Dead at the 1934 Nuremberg Rally in Leni Riefenstahl's film *The Triumph of the Will*. By turning the event into a solemn funeral ceremony for all the dead who had fallen for Germany, Hitler and Goebbels hoped to eradicate memories of the brutal murder, only weeks before, of numerous SA officials and their chief-of-staff Ernst Röhm. Vast rectangular blocks of SA and SS squads flank the tiny figures of Hitler, Himmler, and Lutze, the new head of the SA, as they walk solemnly down the Path of the Führer, wide and brightly lit by the sun, toward the temple of the dead to the sounds of a sub-Wagnerian funeral march by Hanfstaengl. Riefenstahl herself is of course invisible, perched in a specially built lift high up on one of the giant Nazi flagpoles at the back of the huge arena as she films, like a cinematographic Isolde, the ritual of death below. The sheer height of her camera above the ritual gives the image a breath-taking sweep that seems to stretch it out and simultaneously shrink its details to give the sense of endless space. Even Hitler and his two appalling cronies appear as mere specks in the vast quasi-Wagnerian ocean.

Arguing further on these lines, the religious imagery embedded in the *Liebestod* with its meaning polemically altered and the idea of Tristan's second death find vulgar equivalents in the yearly ceremonies organized by the Nazis to commemorate the November Putsch of 1923, which shamelessly borrowed elements, for entirely secular purposes, from the Catholic Feast of Corpus Christi. The uprising ended in disarray with a death toll of sixteen national socialists in front of the Feldherrnhalle in Munich, only a short distance away from the theater, where *Tristan* was first performed, the Bavarian Hoftheater. The commemoration was intended to obliterate all memory of the chaos and indignity of the original event and to turn it instead into a timeless icon of Nazi values and one of the cornerstones of

Nazi mythology. And to achieve this aim, Hitler and Goebbels decided in 1935 to intensify the allegory. The bodies of the sixteen "martyrs" were exhumed and deposited in bronze sarcophagi placed on biers in the Feldherrnhalle, bathed in red light and transfigured by brown drapes and flaming braziers for the occasion. Shortly before midnight, Hitler stood in front of each coffin for a "mute dialogue" with the bones inside, and on the following morning he led a solemn procession toward the Königsplatz, where the names of the sixteen fallen soldiers were read out in a "last roll call." The remains of the martyrs were then placed inside two specially built temples beneath the "eternal flame," where, official Nazi sources claimed, they "passed into the body of the people. Their flesh is dead, but their blood flows, affirming the Führer, to become the baptismal water of the Reich. . . . For us they are not dead."[65]

It is one thing to accuse Wagner of fascist tendencies in the way he constructed his theatrical phantasmagorias, however, and quite another to say that the elevated tone of his music and the almost slavish devotion of the *Liebestod* to the unsayable provided a model that was peculiarly vulnerable to purposive and brutal rationality in the creation of powerful public images by Goebbels's propaganda machine. Even this important caveat assumes that the Nazi image makers were conscious of Wagner's dramas as a specific source, and not only because they are by Wagner, but also on account of their technical ingenuity in assembling suggestive and highly effective acoustic and visual allegories. Alone the sheer eclecticism of the Nazi propagandists, who plundered high and popular culture for whatever happened to be conveniently at hand, makes this virtually impossible to prove. To be sure, there are common dynamics between the amalgam of iconic images in Isolde's *Liebestod* on the one hand and Riefenstahl's death ritual and the allegory of the martyrs of 9 November on the other, including the yearning for everlasting death, the sense of eternal recurrence, the striving for a space beyond history that transcends human frailty, and the "second" heroic death. But given the ubiquitousness of these elements in religious and romantic belief systems before the advent of Hitler, it would be rash to categorize any of them as uniquely totalitarian or fascist.

So why not just give in to the beauty and strength of the *Liebestod*, one of the most affecting moments in all of Wagner's music? This is practically what Michael Poizat does when he claims that this music, standing for all music in opera, avoids "that final step where perfect beauty turns to horror."[66] With Isolde's final scene, however, Wagner does not avoid that final step entirely. One of the paradoxes of the amazing score of *Tristan* and its history is the fact that practically from the moment when Liszt conducted the Prelude at a meeting of professional musicians in Leipzig in early June 1859 (before Wagner had even finished composing the whole opera), the entire work has enjoyed a formidable reputation, particularly among music analysts, in a radically different role as a technical achievement in its own right, a brilliant emblem of "progress" in the cause of absolute music.[67] For many this has continued to be a perfectly justified, even welcome, containment of it inside the Western canon, safely behind glass. Lifting Isolde's concluding monologue out of its case for a moment, I hope to have caught a glimpse of less obvious alliances between the extramusical and absolute music that rather suggest a critical tension between perfect beauty and its opposite. This music is perhaps the most ravishing Wagner ever wrote, though the apartness from the turmoil of human affairs it expresses is, like the yearning of the lovers in the rest of the opera, essentially the projection of an illusion. Frequently heard outside the opera house, it has become a very public fantasy about an endless escape into pure feeling and pleasure—an allegory of the musically absolute itself, inside which remain indelible signs of precisely those harsh realities of human experience it attempts magnificently to exclude.

PART V

Mature Polemics

13. Strange Love, Or, How We Learned to Stop Worrying and Love *Parsifal*

Our great artistic aims also have a political meaning.
Wagner's diary entry to King Ludwig II of Bavaria, 15 September 1865

PRELUDE

Variously described as sublime, vicious, or merely decadent, Richard Wagner's *Parsifal* has always fascinated critics who have seen it either as a "superior magic opera" that "revels in the wondrous"[1] or as a "profoundly inhuman spectacle, glorifying a barren masculine world whose ideals are a combination of militarism and monasticism."[2] More soberly it has been described as a work with an "underlying insistence on assent to a truth outside itself."[3] Yet it is precisely the nature of that truth that has been the subject of unending controversy. Is the work's central theme really the "redemption of an Aryan Jesus from Judaism," as Germany's arch anti-Wagnerite, Hartmut Zelinsky, thinks it is?[4] Can *Parsifal* be interpreted as a Christian work at all, militant or otherwise? Or is it just a benign and rather feeble millenarian fantasy—a kind of Armageddon cocktail with large twists of Schopenhauer and Buddha?

One obvious way to interpret *Parsifal* is to look first at the writings and letters of Wagner and his Bayreuth Circle and to conclude that it is really a sermon on the coming of the "end," the work of a rebel Christian who, resigned and troubled about the progress of modern civilization, became a heretical admirer of Jesus Christ, the supposed redeemer of a decaying Germanic race. To adapt a metaphor once used by the French critic Tzvetan Todorov to describe some authoritarian forms of literary criticism,[5] *Parsifal* turns into a bizarre picnic, with Wagner bringing the images and his interpreters their meaning. And yet the Master always reserved his right to make final decisions about what that meaning was supposed to be. "Although we mercilessly relinquish the Church, Christianity, and even the whole phenomenon of Christianity in history," Wagner wrote to his disciple

Hans von Wolzogen, "our friends must always know that we do it for the sake of that very same Christ . . . whom we want to protect in His pristine purity, so that . . . we can take Him with us into those terrible times that will probably follow the inevitable destruction of all that now exists."[6] Not much later Cosima Wagner reported in her diaries that Wagner told her " 'I know what I know and what is in it *[Parsifal]*; and the new school, Wolzogen and the others, can stick to what it says.' He then hints at, rather than expresses, the content of this work, 'Redemption to the Redeemer' *[Erlösung dem Erlöser]*—and we are silent after he has added, 'it's good that we're alone.' "[7]

Wagner believed that *Parsifal* had a message that could be correctly decoded, at least by initiates. Yet even in private he was reluctant to be specific. A less dramatic explanation is that he simply mistrusted interpretations that were too sharply defined. He sensed his followers' need for a clear understanding of content; but he also needed himself to shroud that content in a veil of secrecy, to surround it with a noise, as it were, that made it less acute. Roland Barthes has said that a photograph whose meaning (though not its effect) is too impressive is quickly deflected, since we consume it aesthetically, not politically.[8] The same could be said of *Parsifal* in the sense that an interpretation of the work that subjects it to a startling array of precise meanings, whether controversial or not, inevitably misfires, because we are affected by its grandeur and the beauty of its music, not because of any doctrinal threads systematically stitched into its allegorical fabric.

I would like to propose, however, that this kind of argument about *Parsifal* is ultimately evasive. The point about the overdetermination of meaning in works of art is of course a commonplace among critics, especially those who still value a dusty connoisseurship that will always promote aesthetics above history. Indeed, those trying to explore the ideological ramifications of a piece such as *Parsifal* inevitably leave themselves open to the accusation of scholarly taxidermy. Nor is this view confined to the adherents of traditional aesthetics. Slavoj Žižek and Mladen Dolar, hardly part of the right-leaning critical establishment, insist:

> It is easy to show how *Parsifal* grew out of timperial *[sic]*, anti-modernist anti-Semitism—to enumerate all the painful and tasteless details of Wagner's ideological engagements in the last years of his life. . . . However, to grasp the true greatness of *Parsifal*, one should absolutely abstract ideas from these particular circumstances; only in this way can one discern how and why *Parsifal* still exerts such a power today. . . . the context *obfuscates* Wagner's true achievement.[9]

Wonderful. But what if the "painful and tasteless" ideas Wagner lavished on *Parsifal* can help to *explain* the power it still exerts? Has the extremely serious charge of anti-Semitism that has been leveled against it really polarized opinion about it to such an extent that the link between its "true greatness" and Wagner's far-from-straightforward ideas about race can no longer be convincingly demonstrated? Is the notion of a racist strain in *Parsifal* so absurd and easy to refute that in reality it has come as a godsend to those seeking an excuse to reaffirm the work's status as an incontrovertible musical masterpiece in the Western tradition?

The very idea seems outrageous until one begins to understand the paradoxes of Wagner's racist views and their inseparability from the experience of supposed cultural decay he wanted to share in *Parsifal*, and not just in a series of seemingly madcap polemics in his late writings. This is indeed a disturbing aspect of the work, and it has taken several crude public spats about the gulf that is meant to separate it from its creator's so-called late regeneration essays to deflect attention from what I believe is the contradictory logic of a more subtle discourse about race at its heart, including its music. I want here to make a brief attempt to bring these bits of him together one more time, hopefully by bringing the dramaturgy of *Parsifal* into sharper focus, and by suggesting that, contrary to what both the left and right flanks in the Western cultural establishment are beginning to think, the closer we look at the way its structure has been entwined with the web of ideas inside it, the less our concerns about it are likely to disappear.

SEX AND THE PITY

Critics of a putative inhumanity in Wagner's *Parsifal* will always find it hard to account for the fascinating beauty of its score and the inconvenient fact that militancy and aggression could not be further removed from its central idea. Wagner himself called the work his "most conciliatory,"[10] as it was based on the notion of compassion *(Mitleid)* borrowed from the philosophy of Schopenhauer and subjected to some characteristically Wagnerian variations. Schopenhauer and Wagner saw compassion as a specific moral response to the violent chaos of the world, a beatific annihilation of the Will, so to speak, achieved through a denial of Eros, and, in Wagner's personal version of the doctrine, a deep sympathy with the suffering of others caused by the torment of sexual desire.

The idea of compassion also influenced Wagner's radical treatment of his main literary source, Wolfram von Eschenbach's early-thirteenth-century romance *Parzival.* Wagner discussed Wolfram and sexual asceticism at length in his letters to Mathilde Wesendonck in the late 1850s (in view of his rapidly cooling feelings toward her after finishing *Tristan,* this was perhaps to be expected), and he came to the conclusion that he would have to compress the enormous 24,810-line poem into just *"three* climactic situations of violent intensity."[11] In effect, he turned the poem into three successive stages of compassion. What begins as a vague feeling in the pure fool (Parsifal) in his response to the Grail ceremony during the first act progresses to a burning insight into Amfortas's suffering at the moment of Kundry's kiss in the second, and ends with two miraculous acts of redemption in the third with the baptism of Kundry and the healing of Amfortas's wound. The epic poem was thus ingeniously transformed into a cathartic theatrical ritual in three cycles, each more drastic than the last.

One of the problems with *Parsifal* is that woven inside its relatively simple outer edifice is not only a skein of memory leading back to a single catastrophic event—Amfortas's serious injury by the spear stolen by his evil rival Klingsor—but also several allegorical threads that are still hard to disentangle. Even the plot is hard to grasp, as Wagner's principal critical enemy, Eduard Hanslick, discovered. After jettisoning its "alleged deep, moral significance,"[12] he simply related the story, only to find it illogical, at least in the way he tried to tell it. King Ludwig II, too, was puzzled. After receiving the first prose draft of *Parsifal* from Wagner in 1865, he immediately wrote back to ask, "Why is our hero converted only by Kundry's kiss? Why does this make his divine mission clear to him?"[13] Wagner's reply—a rare attempt to interpret *Parsifal* with more than just riddles—looks evasive at first, though its cautious elucidation of the story's peculiar logic is clear enough:

> That is a terrible secret, my beloved! You know, of course, the serpent of Paradise and its tempting promise: "Ye shall be as gods, knowing good and evil." Adam and Eve became "knowing." They became "conscious of sin." The human race had to atone for that consciousness by suffering shame and misery until redeemed by Christ, who took upon himself the sin of mankind. My dearest friend, how can I speak of such profound matters except in comparative terms, by means of a parable? Only someone who is clairvoyant can perceive its inner meaning. Adam—Eve: Christ.—How would it be if we were to add to them:— "Amfortas—Kundry: Parzifal?" But with considerable caution![14]

Ludwig, who with his acute sensibility had immediately recognized, amidst the acres of words in Wagner's prose draft, that this was one of its most crucial moments, seems to have accepted this tentative, and in some ways also rather audacious, reading. Only a matter of days after writing it, however, Wagner began sending him one of his most aggressive texts in the form of a diary outlining at some length his plans for the cultural and political renewal of Europe. The text includes disgusting sentences such as "In nature . . . a dying body is immediately found by worms, which completely tear it to pieces and assimilate themselves. In today's European cultural life, the emergence of the Jews means nothing less."[15] Ludwig, who all his life had tolerant views about race and religion, does not seem to have noticed.

The young king could have been making a sensible and shrewd distinction between two texts, the one a grandly ambitious artistic project, the other a reckless political corollary of it, but sixteen years later alarm bells began to ring. In the throes of orchestrating *Parsifal* on 19 September 1881, Wagner wrote to his benefactor that he had decided to accept Hermann Levi as the conductor of the first performances of the work, in spite of complaints from several quarters that "of all pieces, this most Christian of works" was to be conducted by "a Jew."[16] Obviously relieved, Ludwig answered, "It is very good that you do not differentiate between Christians and Jews for your great holy work. Nothing is more repulsive, more unpleasant, than arguments such as these; human beings are basically all brothers, despite their confessional differences."[17]

Wagner shot back an answer to this almost Masonic largesse, an answer that comes as a shock even to hardened Wagner scholars:

> The only explanation I can think of for my exalted Friend's thoughtful judgment on the Jews is that these people never enter the royal sphere. For you they remain a concept, whereas for us they are all too real. My relations with several of these people are friendly, solicitous, and full of compassion; but this is only possible because I regard the Jewish race as the born enemy of pure humanity and everything noble about it. They will be the ruination of us Germans, that is for sure. Perhaps I am the last German who as an artist knows how to survive the Judaism that's already dominating everything.[18]

Note the phrases "full of compassion" *(mitleidvoll)* and "pure humanity" *(reine Menschheit)*, both of which have strong resonances with *Parsifal*. "You and I need fresh water to replenish our bodily fluids. . . . Do you realize that fluoridation's the most monstrously conceived and dangerous Communist plot we have ever had to face?' " Wagner never wrote that: this is Base Commander Ripper (Sterling Hayden) justifying to Group Captain Mandrake (Peter Sellers) his go-it-alone mission to declare nuclear war on the Soviet Union in Stanley Kubrick's film *Dr. Strangelove* (1964). But Wagner's own go-it-alone mission to declare himself an antidote to the decline of the German race is different only in the sense that its black comedy is unwitting. "Whoever attributes the obtuse clumsiness of our public life," he wrote in 1881, "solely to the corruption of our blood brought about by a departure from the natural nourishment of mankind, but above all by the degeneration brought about by the mixing of the hero-blood of the noblest races with that of one-time cannibals now trained to be the skilled business leaders of society, is probably quite right."[19]

WHEN R. MET THE COUNT

Precisely because Wagner's writings are far from being intended as black comedy, it has proved more than awkward to separate *Parsifal* entirely from its creator's thoughts on race, which from the 1848 Revolution onward were indeed obsessed with, but by no means limited to, the Jewish question. Hardly a day in the Wagnerian world goes by without some mention of Wagner's justly notorious anti-Semitic essay *Das Judentum in der Musik* (1850).[20] Far less discussed, apart from some notable exceptions,[21] is the still earlier *Die Wibelungen* (1848–49), in which for the first time, as Ernest Newman rightly says, "a new Wagner comes into view—a boldly speculative philosopher who takes not only music but all literature, history, and life for his province."[22] In this essay, which runs forty pages in his collected writings, Wagner insists that mere "history" can only ever offer us an incomplete picture of the "most intimate, so to speak instinctive, motives of the ceaseless striving and urging of whole races and peoples."[23] The strongest ancient tribes possessed "the purest of blood from which the entire people descended," but which "blurred in the course of time."[24] The "deepest degeneration" *(tiefste Entartung)* of the Frankish royal race would have retained its identity had it not been for its "willing acceptance of Latin depravity" *(willige[r] Annahme der romanischen Verderbtheit)*, and the predecessor of Karl the Great "won and ruled the entire German world" by "getting rid of the deeply degenerate race of the Merovingians."[25] Indeed, the essay floats the idea more than once that the Germanic races always had to be wary of foreign impurity.

The more one tries to penetrate the unlovely exterior of *Die Wibelungen* the more it becomes clear just how integral to Wagner's intellectual strategy are his racial metaphors of cultural decline and its counterforce, "the purest of blood." The four volumes of Count Joseph Arthur de Gobineau's notorious *Essai sur l'inégalité des races humaines* (1853–55) appeared a few years later, soon followed by Bénedict August Morel's now nearly as infamous *Traité des dégénérescences physiques, intellectuelles et morales de l'espèce humaine et de ses causes qui produisent ces variétées maladives* (1857), which first introduced the concept of degeneration into the pessimistic language and quasi-science of early psychiatric studies devoted to heredity and the alleged decline of the human race.[26] But in many respects Wagner was there before either of them, not only making prominent use of words like "blood" *(Blut),* "degeneration" *(Entartung),* and "depravity" *(Verderbtheit)* to describe racial conflict and decay, but also boldly vandalizing the ground rules of political and intellectual history, just as Gobineau was to do, by introducing in their place biological determinism and a free-associative interpretation of myth and ethnology.

Wagner met Gobineau, "racialism's most illustrious representative," as Todorov calls him,[27] for the first time in 1876 in Rome, but he only began to appreciate Gobineau's work on race—then little known except to a smallish circle—when he invited him to Bayreuth in the early 1880s. He came to regard the count as a personal friend and cherished *confrère* in the industry of doom and gloom that was already thriving in the late nineteenth century, and indeed it is no exaggeration to say that Gobineau's later fame in Europe, including the co-option of some of his ideas by the Nazis, was due in some part to Wagner's advocacy, and in particular to the energy of Wagner's disciple Ludwig Schemann, who later translated the *Essai* into German.[28]

Schemann notes that Wagner came across the *Essai* after reading a vigorous critique of it by the etymologist August Friedrich Pott.[29] There are at least two interesting things about this. The first is that Pott's scholarly work on linguistics belongs to the pioneering area of research among German academics in the first half of the nineteenth century that laid the foundations of what we know today as Indo-European comparative philology, and upon which Wagner drew extensively for his work on the libretto of the *Ring.* Second, Pott's detailed attack on Gobineau shows that the study of Indo-European languages had inevitably brought with it the issue of race, about which there was already serious disagreement. Wagner once famously claimed, "Gobineau says the Germans were the last card Nature had to play—*Parsifal* is my last card."[30] But the metaphor, not to be found in the *Essai,* actually originated with Pott, who uses it in a passage laden with irony to sum up Gobineau's absurd notion that around the birth of Christ the Aryan Indo-Germanic races ceased to be *"absolument pure"*[31] because they had opened themselves to racial mixture and hence to eighteen centuries of inevitable decline. After Nature had played its best and final trump card, Pott asks sarcastically, what else was left for it to do?[32]

Pott's book was published in 1856, and obviously Wagner could have come across it at any time after that. There is no evidence to suggest, however, that he was acquainted with it before the early 1880s, when he began to look around in earnest for like-minded spirits to support the ideological superstructure he wanted to build around *Parsifal* in readiness for the public unveiling of the work. All we know is that Pott's "laughable rage against Gobineau," as Wagner's official biographer Carl Glasenapp describes it,[33] made Wagner all the more determined to read the *Essai* for himself. Indeed, when he eventually got hold of a copy with Gobineau's help, he read all four volumes with care, though not without the occasional moan about their length. In particular, the third chapter of the fourth volume, entitled "The Ability of the Native Germanic Races" *(Capacité des races germaniques natives)*, seems to have gone straight to his heart, in all probability because it establishes the supposed superiority of the Germanic races with a discussion of, among other things, some of the old literary sources he had used to write the *Ring* (the poetic Edda, for instance) and racial conflicts such as the one between the Germans and the Merovingians he had already grappled with in *Die Wibelungen*.[34] "In the evening R. reads to the count the pages in his book (volume 4, ch. 3) that he so loves," Cosima wrote in her diaries, "and afterward he plays the Prelude to *Parsifal*."[35]

ALTERED STATES

Wagner thought of his relationship with Gobineau's ideas as "a growing together of two completely independent, but in all essentials deeply related, intellectual worlds."[36] Some friction was bound to occur. A former diplomat who had traveled extensively, Gobineau was far from being a chauvinist or even remotely nationalist. Nor was he an anti-Semite. He regarded the Jews as Caucasians, and therefore a subset of the Germanic race, which meant, not surprisingly, that on the Jewish question Wagner disagreed with him. Wagner also refused to accept his view that the decline of the Aryan race was unstoppable. The "absolute purity" of the Aryan race can indeed be aspired to, Wagner thought, by the intervention of a divine hero, who, although himself the product of racial impurity, is capable of compassion and hence able to resist any further adulteration of blood through an intuitive understanding of human suffering.[37] Indeed, the idea of the superior race no longer in possession of its purity but hoping for salvation is already to be found in embryonic form in the last two sections of *Die Wibelungen*, in which the fallen master race, torn from "its natural racial origin" *(ihrer geschlechtlich-natürlichen Herkunft)*, is left to await its redeemer.[38]

Still, Gobineau was—and these were the two things Wagner particularly liked about him—both a pessimist and a racist with an immense knowledge of racial theory that went back to the heart of the eighteenth century. The overblown scenario of *Die Wibelungen* could not be more different from the smooth elegance of the *Essai*. Yet both writers are at one in their view that race, rather than specific cultural factors, can best explain the trajectory of history; and both give primacy to the undermining of racial origin as the root cause of civilization's impending disaster. Moreover, they are *d'accord* in bringing the whole issue into close proximity with the sacred. Like Gobineau, Wagner believed early on that the original purity of the Aryan race is to be located in the realm of the gods. And he did not hesitate, either, to align the pagan and Christian worlds alongside each other: thus the "abstract highest god of the Germans, Wuotan," is "completely identified . . . with the Christian God,"[39] and the Grail is the original relic of humanity containing the hero blood of the slain sun god Siegfried. In this bizarre scenario, Christ is therefore a reincarnation of Siegfried, and the quest for the Grail replaces "the struggle for the Nibelungs' Hoard."[40]

Not even Gobineau was this reckless. But he, too, was scrupulous in keeping racial theory within the confines of Christian belief, even though the central premise behind it—the essential difference between races—fell well outside Christianity's doctrinal boundaries. Robert Young has analyzed with considerable skill some of Gobineau's adroit maneuvers in circumventing the difficulty of justifying the biblical notion of monogenesis (the descent of different human races from a single source) in a treatise predicated on the decidedly un-Christian idea of polygenesis (the descent of inherently distinct races from different sources). The implication in the *Essai* is that the fall itself caused the everlasting separation of species, much as "Babel produced the division of languages" (Young's own analogy).[41]

As Wagner himself believed in a lost purity of racial division long before he read Gobineau—"everything is according to its kind" (*Alles ist nach seiner Art)*, the Wanderer confides to Alberich in *Siegfried*—it is perhaps not entirely a coincidence that in his reply to King Ludwig II's question about Kundry's kiss cited above he makes his heroine a notional participant in the fall. "But with considerable caution!" Wagner adds, almost as if he were warning that the symbolism of Eve/Kundry's sexual allure is by no means restricted to this biblical imagery, but rather represents a multitude of non-Christian ideas as well, including—so to speak—the splitting of the racial atom. He describes Kundry to Ludwig not only as a figure who experiences "constantly changing reincarnations brought about by a primeval curse," which, "similar to the 'Wandering Jew'," condemns her to life for all time,[42] but also as someone marked by radical difference. She is "as old as time" *(uralt)*, yet "without visible signs of aging." Her hair is black, "loose and wild one minute, beautifully plaited the next." And the color of her skin is subject to startling change, "now pale, then sunburned and dark."[43] One only-too-logical conclusion to be drawn from this vivid description of Kundry's visibly different states of being in Wagner's original prose draft of *Parsifal* for Ludwig II is that it is an ingenious allegory of essential racial difference that, by dint of its creator's own allusion to the fall, manages at the same time to remain rooted in the Christian doctrine of monogenesis.

The deep intellectual relationship that, as Wagner himself thought, existed "in all essentials" between his work and Gobineau's, goes still further. In the final work, Kundry passes through at least three different lives: the exotic animal-like creature in the first act, the young black-haired seductress dressed in "roughly Arabic style"[44] in the second, and the pale repentant sinner in the third. Caught between a masculinized Christian community to the north and a feminized world under Moorish influence to the south, she is a potent symbol not just of racial mixture, but also of a supposed sexual attraction between the races, to which her failed seduction of Parsifal in the opera and her successful seduction of Amfortas in the past both attest.

In his *Essai* Gobineau views the libidinal drive of history almost solely in terms of the attraction of so-called strong masculine races for weaker feminine ones. The idea of gender, of course, is translated here onto an absurdly generalized level and leads to a contradiction at the heart of the theory, which Gobineau happily exploits in the name of a universal view of supposed racial inequality.[45] Because of the sexual attraction of races for one another, tribes fuse with other tribes and form nations of higher culture. Therefore miscegenation, the cross breeding of races, has been inevitable and must account under certain favorable conditions for the existence of successful civilizations. Gobineau even states categorically that the white Germanic races were more inclined to miscegenation and thus stronger and more dominant under certain conditions than the black and yellow races, who have in fact shown greater resistance to racial mixture. The Germanic races have as a consequence become strong and "civilized" precisely because they have mixed their blood with others.

At the same time, in terms of pure racial division, by which Gobineau and Wagner set great store, the mixing of bloods can only lead to an enfeeblement of racial and cultural vitality. This in turn presents a contradiction that greatly appealed to Wagner: the more a civilization gains power through racial mixture, as a result of the sexual attraction of one race for another, the more it becomes vulnerable to decline and decay.[46] The reason for the civilized strength of the Aryan races, the erotic force that has led to the mixing of blood and the dominance of the strong over the weak, is at the same time its fatal weakness and the source of its inevitable degradation. Indeed, with that contradiction in mind, Kundry's baptism and subsequent death at the end of the *Parsifal* can be construed as an allegory of the long-awaited conclusion of this process: the end of racial mixture that caused the whole problem in the first place—the welcome death of hybridity itself.

BEFORE REDEMPTION

What about the music? At the end of *Parsifal*, saturated chromatic spaces are banished, themes appear to be elevated on high, and endlessly consonant harmonic progressions emerge, as if the history of the human races were being embalmed and carried gently to rest by an eternal flame. The music accounts for the perverse sense of inclusiveness in *Parsifal*. Amfortas and his eroticized wound, Kundry with her fraught existence in radically different types of character, and finally Parsifal, who to gain consciousness of the Divine Code must possess no Enlightenment knowledge and renounce carnal desire as if it were the cause of fractured humanity in the first place: through music the whole imbroglio is finally blended together beneath the slogan "Redemption to the Redeemer" *(Erlösung dem Erlöser)*. What does it mean? Probably that the redeemer of mankind is compromised by corrupted blood and is therefore himself in need of redemption by the divine hero, though in the general feel-good wash of sound that ends the work the precise significance of the phrase may not count for much.

Right up to the moment when this high-sounding kitsch begins to take effect in the mother of all Wagnerian closures, the music is far more interesting than it is at the very end. Despite Wagner's differences with Gobineau (and, for that matter, Schopenhauer) about the supposedly inevitable doom of humanity, the best music in *Parsifal* is more in sympathy with the intransigent pessimism of these thinkers than it is with any inscrutable idea of redemption. Humanity is rapidly losing its strength; its best days are gone, and a sense of pervading entropy and the inevitable advent of nothingness prevails. The music seems purposefully to avoid forward movement, or rather to propose it at moments, only to take it back again; and the notes seem to repose constantly in motionlessness, reluctant to do anything else.

Wagner achieves this fluid stasis with an array of ingenious technical devices. Egon Voss has pointed out the numerous pauses that interrupt the movement of the music, especially the general fermatas lasting an entire bar in places where one least expects them (after Amfortas's first entrance and the words *"Ohn' Urlaub!"* for instance).[47] The modernist interest in new musical processes in *Parsifal* has been shared by others (including Adorno and Pierre Boulez), but rarely has anyone seriously asked how they relate to the dramaturgy of the work where the melancholic sense of stasis and decay among the knights of the Grail—a dynamic nihilism, as it were, that gradually takes hold of a community increasingly in danger of collapsing under the weight of its own history—is clearly reflected by the formal and harmonic processes of the music. Repetitive patterns such as the bells in the transformation scenes and circular harmonic sequences create movement while abolishing it at the same time, and indeed the paradox of motionlessness through motion, or motion through motionlessness, pervades the entire score.

Wagner also developed an original relationship between harmony and horizontal line so that both can audibly fold into and out of one another, again creating the possibility of a musical dynamic that paradoxically develops organically by collapsing into itself. Here are a few analytical glimpses at the core of the work. In Amfortas's first mention of "the pure fool," whom he awaits and envisions as his savior, a dissonance, G–B♭–F–D, is introduced at the occurrence of the word "pure," resolving onto a weaker dissonance, G–B♭–E–D (ex. 10b). This tiny harmonic moment with a linear trajectory from "x" to "y" is then used at certain key junctures throughout the work, normally in closed position with the D either changing during the progression, or already changed to D♭ (ex. 10a). Wagner uses the progression as a kind of musical icon, which, precisely because of its basically unchanging pitch identity, imprints significant moments in the action all the more powerfully on the ear of the listener.

These moments include Gurnemanz's highly charged description in act 1 of how Amfortas, drunk with ecstasy in the arms of Kundry, allowed the holy spear to slip away from him (ex. 10c) and the peripeteia of the work after Kundry's kiss, which Parsifal rejects in favor of sudden anguished empathy for Amfortas's predicament. In a single chord, the dissonance is fused with its own resolution (ex. 10d), only to be unfolded at the beginning of the third act with a striking melancholic melody and quasi-invertible counterpoint. Wagner took great care with this in his sketches, starting with a simple two-dimensional solution in the major key (ex. 10e) and eventually arriving at the unforgettable music of the final version in the minor with the

Ex. 10a. *Parsifal*, Recurring dissonance (pitch identity fixed).

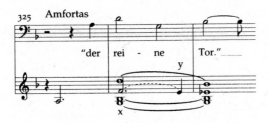

Ex. 10b. *Parsifal*, act 1, mm. 325–26.

Ex. 10c. *Parsifal*, act 1, mm. 528–29.

Ex. 10d. *Parsifal*, act 2, mm. 994–96.

Ex. 10e. *Parsifal,* act 3, mm. 1–2 (Nationalarchiv der Richard-Wagner-Stiftung Bayreuth, A III m 4[(1)] fol. 17r).

Ex. 10f. *Parsifal,* act 3, mm. 1–2 (final version).

Ex. 10g. *Parsifal,* act 3, mm. 623–24.

D♭ of the harmony placed without the preceding D, and the bottom G approached obliquely with an elongated and highly expressive accented G♭ appoggiatura (ex. 10f).

The most controversial moment is in the third act, just after Parsifal's baptism of Kundry, who "seems to weep passionately" like the *Mater dolorosa,* her former eroticism transformed into religious ecstasy. The solemn moment is underscored with an unexpected harmonic shift toward the recurring iconic harmony (ex. 10a), with the linear movement "x" to "y" again intact as it was toward the start of the work. Only this time the bottom G of the chord consists of prescient-sounding strokes on the timpani outlining the rhythm of the "Grail" motif (ex. 10g). Wagner was rightly proud of this striking passage: "the entry of the timpani on G is the finest thing I have ever done," he told Cosima, who described it as "the timpani's sound of annihilation" *(Vernichtungsklang der Pauke)*, or, as Wagner himself described it, "the annihilation of all existence, of all earthly desire."[48]

TERMS OF ENDEARMENT

The music of *Parsifal* has had a powerful effect on composers such as Mahler and Berg, who certainly cannot be accused of sharing in Wagner's barmy racial universe. The distinguished musical lineage is perhaps one reason why many historians have been reluctant to discuss ideas about race in *Parsifal*. A few less cautious scholars, however, have simply distorted history in order to keep the lineage and the undeniable aesthetic power of the work intact. Their tactics have been breathtaking, including the one grasped at by Bryan Magee and Friedrich Spotts, among others, with the claim that the Nazis found *Parsifal* ideologically unacceptable and always tried to ban it, and indeed succeeded in doing so during the Second World War.[49]

An important source of the Nazi's skepticism, as both Magee and Spotts correctly say, was the party ideologue Alfred Rosenberg. Yet neither of them mention the opinion of seasoned biographers of Hitler and the Third Reich that "too much has been made" of Rosenberg's role as chief ideologist of the Nazi party,[50] and that he was "arrogant and cold, one of the least charismatic and least popular of Nazi leaders [who] united other party bigwigs only in their intense dislike of him."[51] Rosenberg's rejection of *Parsifal* as ideologically unsound, in other words, probably counted for less than it seemed to in the Nazi hierarchy, especially if the Führer himself was an admirer of the work.

But even this last point is in dispute. The index to Magee's book has an entry "*Parsifal*: Hitler dislikes,"[52] and Spotts states categorically that in a conversation with Goebbels in the winter of 1941 in Berlin Hitler declared that "After the war, he would see to it either that religion was banished from *Parsifal* or that *Parsifal* was banished from the stage,"[53] which certainly suggests that he harbored significant doubts about it. What Goebbels actually dictated for his diary on 22 November 1941 was this: "Contrary to what has been reported to me, the Führer does not want *Parsifal* to be performed solely in Bayreuth again; he only means that one should modernize the décor and costumes of *Parsifal* somewhat. Either we have to get away from this Christian mystical style, or *Parsifal* in the long run won't be able to retain its place in the modern repertory. The Führer gives me several suggestions, which I will immediately put into effect."[54]

Far from wanting to banish *Parsifal* or its "religion," Hitler had qualms that were clearly directed at the overly reverential treatment of it by theater directors who were in danger of alienating modern audiences by mistaking its sacral content for something specifically Christian. Worried that the public would turn its back on *Parsifal*, Hitler wanted a fresh approach to it, and moreover one in keeping with Wagner's own forthright assertion (cited in the second paragraph of this chapter) that, despite its use of imagery and doctrinal niceties borrowed from the Church, it is a denial of "the whole phenomenon of Christianity in history."

And how did Goebbels think he was going to implement Hitler's suggestions immediately if *Parsifal* were banned? The simple answer is that a ban did not exist. In fact, there had been a performance of *Parsifal* the previous day in Berlin, and another was due to take place that very evening, both of them with a young Elisabeth Schwarzkopf singing the first Esquire and one of the Flower Maidens. Indeed, we need look no further than Alan Jefferson's biography of Schwarzkopf to see that even during the war, groups of three or four performances of *Parsifal* were a yearly, and sometimes twice-yearly, feature in the repertoire of the Deutsche Oper, one of Berlin's principal opera houses. Between 1939 and the end of 1942, when Schwarzkopf began to set her sights on Vienna, there were, according to Jefferson's list of her appearances, no fewer than twenty-three performances of *Parsifal* in this theater alone.[55]

Coupled with the fact that the archives of the *Deutsche Bühnenverein* record no fewer than 714 performances of *Parsifal* within the borders of the German Reich between 1933 and 1939,[56] which hardly sounds like a ban either, the continued presence of *Parsifal* on German-speaking stages after Hitler's ascent to power does not exactly suggest that either he or Goebbels, whose Propaganda Ministry kept a close watch on theater repertoire, were lukewarm about its actual content. Wagner's grandsons Wieland and Wolfgang were also witness to Hitler's ideas about the restructuring of the Bayreuth Festival Theatre after the war, ideas that included *Parsifal*.[57] Indeed, the only reservation Hitler seems to have had, apart from his objections to the dated productions already in existence, is that Bayreuth should never again have a monopoly over the work, suggesting that in his view as many people as possible should get a chance to experience it.

Still, setting the historical record straight on Hitler and *Parsifal* is actually less worrying than disentangling the misunderstandings about race that have clustered around the work, particularly after Zelinsky's frontal attack on it in 1982, the centenary of its first performance. Taking his cue from, among other things, Wagner's description of Kundry's baptism and "annihilation" in Cosima Wagner's diaries ("annihilation" here referring specifically to a quasi-Schopenhauerian negation of self, and not to genocide), Zelinsky suggested that Kundry is "the representative of everything that Wagner associated with Judaism,"[58] including the wish for its destruction. There is no evidence for this whatsoever, and indeed no one, not even Hitler, had ever made quite such an absurd claim. In the last part of his life, Wagner regarded the Jews as incapable of miscegenation ("if ever Jews are mixed with foreign races," he claims in another knockabout, unwittingly blackly comic passage in one of his late writings, "all you get is another Jew").[59] That would mean, according to the historical dynamic of race as he saw it, that they are incapable of both civilization and genuine purity simply because they have never had to reclaim purity from a process of degradation. He did compare Kundry with the "Wandering Jew," as we have seen, but only in the sense that she, too, is the victim of a "primeval curse" that condemns her to wander forever in constantly different guises, never able to die. That does not necessarily turn her into an allegory of Judaism. On the contrary, she seems about as far away from Wagner's idea of the consistent "purity" of the Jews as she can be—the very opposite of the antirace she is supposed to represent, which, quite unlike her ability to wander from one type of human being to another, is according to Wagner all the stronger, and hence all the more dangerous, precisely because of its immutable racial character.

If Zelinsky made the mistake of reducing *Parsifal* to an anti-Semitic philippic of enormous banality, the astonishing invective he provoked made matters still worse. "If Zelinsky is right," Joachim Kaiser thundered, "James Levine—the conductor of the centenary performance of *Parsifal*—should have himself thoroughly denazified. . . . If Wagner planned to put anti-Semitism into *Parsifal*, was he too cowardly to *show* it? Cowardice was not Wagner's way. He could be a bit nutty at times; but he was a damned courageous chap!"[60] Kaiser's macho blather prevented him from pausing to consider the possibility that the very absence of anti-Semitism in *Parsifal* could be significant in ways other than simply providing a welcome relief for the work's uncritical admirers. Carl Dahlhaus also weighed in with the opposite tactic of making Wagner's exclusionary ideas about racial identity so generalized that they cease to have any real meaning. Zelinsky omitted saying, Dahlhaus wrote, that Wagner spoke of "cleansing the redeemer from every

Alexandrian-Judaic-Roman despotic deformation." By this he meant not just the nefarious optimism of the Jews, but also the hidebound church of the Romans and the petrified dogmatism of the Alexandrians. Moreover, in matters of redemption and annihilation, Wagner was prepared to include himself as well as " 'the others': the Jews."[61]

But that does not diminish the role of race in Wagner's way of thinking in the least. As we have seen, it is the Aryan race itself and the inevitable adulteration of its blood with that of others that is for Wagner the central problem in this dimension of his theory; the problem is not the Jews, who are incapable of racial mixture, possess "Rassenkonsistenz" (racial consistency),[62] and hence possess neither history nor humanity. In turn, this should not be taken to mean that they had no role to play in his darkly orchestrated jeremiad on the fate of Germany. *Parsifal* may have been intended as an admonition to the German nation, an imploring cry for self-examination of identity and belief, together with an awakening of "divine compassion streaming throughout the whole of the human race."[63] But it was premised on the conviction that the failure of the "noble" races to submit themselves to this arduous process would result in their collapse and a consequent invasion by the Jewish antirace, which was supposed to be eagerly waiting in the wings for the negative outcome of the Germans' painful confrontation with their racial past.

NOT ABOUT REDEMPTION

As Hannah Arendt said long ago, opinions about race in the middle and later nineteenth century were still judged by the yardstick of political reason.[64] As early as 1853 Tocqueville wrote to Gobineau about the latter's doctrines that "they are probably wrong and certainly pernicious."[65] We have also heard that not much later a scholar like Pott roundly condemned Gobineau with an entire book, and that no less a person than King Ludwig II of Bavaria eventually plucked up enough courage to congratulate Wagner on his apparent retreat from his rabid anti-Semitism. But Gobineau's ideas about a racial law of decay fired Wagner's enthusiasm to such an extent that they cannot be entirely airbrushed out of the picture we would like to have of *Parsifal* now, particularly as he had already come to his own conclusions about racial conflict since the dawn of humanity well before he had even heard of Gobineau's *Essai*.

I am also suggesting that *Parsifal* is a rather broader fantasy about race than is generally realized, couched as it is, like Gobineau's *Essai*, in terms of a powerful myth about humankind and its supposed demise that is likely to attract like-minded listeners from moderates to zealots for some time to come. It has to be stressed that there is no evidence at all that Wagner considered genocide to be the logical conclusion of his ideas. We can say of him, as Todorov says of Gobineau, "the victim of his own literary talent," that he "ought not to have spawned any political activists proposing to rid the world of inferior races."[66] But that may just be wishful thinking; a more exact insight into the relationship between *Parsifal* and race is perhaps unlikely to diminish audiences' love for its sublime music. On one level far from trivial for Wagner, however, its final unity and intensity of utterance is a conciliatory resolution of often-misunderstood ideas about racial identity and decay that are equally unlikely to persuade us to stop worrying entirely.

14. Mendelssohn and the Strange Case of the (Lost) Symphony in C

Mendelssohn Is on the Roof, the last novel of the Czech writer Jiří Weil, begins with the following story.

After the German invasion of Czechoslovakia, the Academy of Music in Prague was about to be transformed by the National Socialists into an institute devoted entirely to German art. The building of the academy had a balcony on which there were many statues, each one representing a great composer of the past. Among the statues was one of Felix Mendelssohn. Because of Mendelssohn's Jewish descent, his statue wasn't allowed to stand on the roof of a National Socialist institute, and an aspiring SS candidate named Julius Schlesinger was ordered by his superiors to remove it. Schlesinger was a nervous person. He wasn't a Jew, but Schlesinger sounded like a Jewish name, creating doubt everywhere, which is why he always carried his Aryan papers with him—papers going back to his great-great-grandfather and great-great-grandmother.

Nobody could make Schlesinger go onto the roof himself, because he was afraid of heights. So he ordered two Czech workers, Antonin Becvar and Josef Stankovsky, to climb onto the balustrade and remove Mendelssohn's statue. "Walk around the balustrade and look at the plaques until you find the name Men-dels-sohn," Schlesinger snapped, distending the composer's name syllable by syllable, so the stupid Czechs could understand

"But there aren't any plaques on the pedestals, Boss," replied Becvar. "How are we supposed to tell which one is Mendelssohn?"

Schlesinger was beside himself. His future career in the SS suddenly seemed threatened by his failing to carry out the order to remove the statue. But neither could he get onto the roof himself, nor did he know enough about the history of music to be able to recognize Mendelssohn's statue. What could be done?

Suddenly he had an idea. He remembered taking a course at school called "World View," with lectures on "racial science." There were slides of lots of noses, he recalled, with measurements next to them. Every nose had been carefully measured. It was a very deep and complicated science, but its findings were simple. The biggest noses belonged to the Jews.

"Go around the statues again and look carefully at their noses," Schlesinger called up to the workers. "Whichever one has the biggest nose, that's the Jew."

Becvar and Stankovsky walked around the statues. "Look," yelled Becvar. "That one over there, none of the others has a nose like that." They put a rope around the neck of the statue and pulled. The statue began to wobble.

Schlesinger looked up to see what they were doing. Suddenly he started sweating with terror. He didn't know what Mendelssohn's statue looked like, but he certainly recognized this one. My God, it was Wagner, the greatest German composer and one who had helped build the Third Reich. "Stop, I'm telling you, stop!" he yelled.

Confused, the workers dropped the rope. The noose swayed around the neck of Richard Wagner. Slowly, Becvar and Stankovsky removed it. Schlesinger walked hesitantly back to Prague's town hall to report to his superior that the order hadn't been carried out. Relieved, the workers went to lunch, and Felix Mendelssohn's statue stayed on the roof of the Prague Academy of Music. And—a bit less securely than before—so did Richard Wagner's.[1]

Jirí Weil's story is a fiction that reflects the reality of National Socialist policy toward Mendelssohn in at least one respect: the high-wire dance in cultural matters between racist policy on the one hand and the clumsy implementation of that policy on the other. Marion Kant has pointed out the mind-boggling political machinery that was set in motion to formulate an official policy on swing dancing that tried in vain to reconcile its immense popularity in Germany in the 1930s and 1940s with its supposedly degenerate origin in so-called "nigger jazz."[2] Mendelssohn, on account of the quality and attractiveness of his music, could be a problem too. All Mendelssohn's works were banned from performance by the National Socialist Reichsmusikprüfstelle, the official musical testing office of the Reich that each year gave each piece of music a kind of racial certificate of political roadworthiness that would allow it to be performed. But on 11 February 1937, from within the ranks of the "avant-garde" racist journal of the SS, *Das schwarze Corps,* an assistant editor felt obliged to suggest privately to *Reichsdramaturg* Dr. Rainer Schlößer, a former assistant of Goebbels now in charge of all theater performances in Germany, that it was time to stop the feeble attempts to replace Mendelssohn's music for *A Midsummer Night's Dream:* "In my opinion everything that has so far been offered as a replacement is not nearly as good as Mendelssohn. Do you think it is psychologically wrong to admit that openly in public? I find that in such a striking case, where one really cannot speak of subversion, it is more effective propaganda if one points out that there are much better examples than Mendelssohn proving the subversive Jewish influence on German music."[3]

But Weil's story about the statues on the roof of the Prague Academy of Music is not just about the tension between aesthetics and politics. It is an allegorical tale about the figures of Mendelssohn and Wagner marked by intended rejection, but also by dependence and doubling. In short, despite sometimes vicious hostility toward Mendelssohn, Wagner needed him so that his own life as an artist could reach perfection. He also seemed to believe that Mendelssohn needed *him*, Richard Wagner, in order to strive after the grand totality of German art.[4] Unlikely as it sounds, this was not just arrogance, but it was also rooted in Wagner's belief that, as a totality, German art had something imperfect and uncertain about it. In other words, Wagner seems to have needed to inscribe, dialectically and with racist formulas, an image of Mendelssohn in his works and in his own artistic ego in order to ensure their social and historical success. This process of dialectical inscription is what I am briefly concerned with here.

ANOTHER TALE BEGINNING IN PRAGUE

My own story about Wagner and Mendelssohn also begins in Prague. In November 1832, Dionys Weber conducted a rehearsal of Wagner's Symphony in C Major with a student orchestra and with the composer in attendance at the Prague Conservatoire. A second performance of the symphony, this time in public on 15 December 1832, was conducted by Wagner's first composition teacher, Christian Gottlieb Müller, at the Leipzig music society Euterpe a few days after Wagner's return. According to Wagner himself, this event was in some ways just a rehearsal for the performance of the symphony on 10 January 1833 in the subscription concerts of Leipzig's famous Gewandhaus—by any standard a prestigious event for a young composer just approaching his twentieth birthday.[5]

Fifty years later, almost at the end of his life, on Christmas Eve 1882, Wagner directed another performance of the symphony at the Teatro La Fenice. Shortly afterward, he wrote what he called a "Report on the Revival of an Early Work," which he published in the form of an open letter to the publisher and editor of a weekly music magazine called the *Musikalisches Wochenblatt*. He began his account as follows:

> In Leipzig in Christian premodern times . . . the so-called Gewandhaus concerts were accessible even to progressive beginners like myself. . . . People were good to me in Leipzig then: a little admiration and goodwill stood me in good stead for the future. But that future greatly changed. I chose to be a composer of operas. And coziness in the Gewandhaus came to an end when Mendelssohn took up the reins a year or two later. I was astounded by the ability of this master, who was still very young at the time. . . . Yielding to a curious inner need, I handed him . . . the manuscript of my symphony with the request not even to look at it, but just to keep it by him. Of course I hoped he would peep into it anyway and, some day, say a word to me about it. But this never happened. In the course of time our paths often crossed; we met, had meals, and even made music together; he attended one of the first performances of *Der fliegende Holländer* I conducted in Berlin and said that, as the opera hadn't quite proved to be a total flop there, I could be satisfied with its success. On the performance of *Tannhäuser* in Dresden, too, he said that a canonic entry in the Adagio of the second finale had greatly pleased him. But he never said a word about my symphony and its manuscript, which was sufficient cause for me never to ask about its fate.[6]

Mendelssohn is presented by Wagner as a man who lavishes faint praise on foreground technical details and whose readiness to make do with only moderate success hardly qualified him as an enthusiast for the heroic vitality of Wagner's art and its meaning for the future. But later in the "Report" Wagner presents *himself* as a youthful Biedermeier artist who, with hardly a trace of the future intellectual composer of music drama, imitated his favorite composers Mozart and Beethoven with boundless confidence, and who reveled in the contrapuntal working-out of themes until every possibility had been exhausted.

At first sight, this looks like an honest confession by an aging composer about the artistic sins of his youth, but the confession is deceptive. On the one hand, the brilliant new director of the Gewandhaus concerts, Felix Mendelssohn, could have saved Wagner from his Biedermeier coziness and the humble origins of his symphonic work in Prague had he paid some attention to the C-major Symphony instead of losing it. (The original manuscript of the symphony, by the way, has never been recovered.) On the other hand, Wagner's description of himself as a young composer is nothing less than an accurate replica of a description of Mendelssohn: the astonishingly able composer who has mastered form and every technical device in music, but whose fascination with music as artifice prevents him—at least for the moment—from achieving *real* mastery, that is, the intuitive ability to express proud, genuine feelings in a life-affirming musical language that is truly heroic and new.

DREAMS ABOUT MENDELSSOHN

Wagner had already published his anti-Semitic views about Mendelssohn in his essay "Judaism in Music" in 1850, as well as in a lengthy, even more virulent appendix attached to the republication of the essay in 1869.[7] Many scholars have asked why Wagner saw fit to publish his views in the late 1860s, when the mood in Germany, through Bismarck's reforms, was decidedly pro-Jewish. A little-known letter to his brother-in-law Oswald Marbach, who was a lecturer at Leipzig University, suggests that Wagner intended the republication of his essay as a memorial to his friend Franz Brendel, an influential critic and historian who died on 25 November 1868.[8] According to Wagner, Brendel put himself on the line by supporting the publication of the original article against all opposition. And he did so with such courage and heroism that his very existence as a citizen was threatened:

> Leipzig, where Brendel was a professor at the Music Conservatory, had received an actual Jewish baptism of music because of the influence of the many years of rightly and deservedly honored work Mendelssohn had put into the musical life of the city. As a reviewer once complained, blond musicians had become an ever-greater rarity there. The place was once distinguished in every walk of German life for its university and important book trade. But in music it was learning to forget the most natural sympathies of local patriotism so willingly evinced by every other German city. It became, exclusively, the metropolis of Jewish music.[9]

Even at his most libelous Wagner is willing to praise Mendelssohn's "many years of work in Leipzig," which, he says, are still "rightly and deservedly honored." Alongside the maliciously exaggerated rhetoric, then, it is possible to see a moment of identification with the goal of Wagner's philippic.

The later history of the C-major Symphony is instructive here. In March 1876 Wagner commissioned the Berlin writer Wilhelm Tappert to start looking for the lost manuscript. Tappert eventually found a set of parts in a trunk in Dresden; they had been copied in 1832, either in Leipzig or Prague. Anton Seidel, who was then Wagner's assistant, immediately set to work reconstructing the full score. Wagner himself could not remember a single note of it, but it is interesting that as the symphony gradually reemerged, he began to remark more and more on his relationship to Mendelssohn and the direction taken by nineteenth-century music via the oratorio, chamber music, and, above all, the symphony. Apart from Wagner's own plans to write symphonies, the reason for his intense interest in the Mendelssohn tradition as he saw it was the success of Brahms's First Symphony in 1876. This had suddenly made Wagner's famous opinion of Beethoven's Ninth as the "last symphony" look precarious, to say the least. In Wagner's view of things, Brahms was, like Mendelssohn, a representative of music as *künstliche Kunst*[10]—literally "artifice art"—that is, an art in which artifice, as opposed to inspiration, is predominant. Or, to put it another way, an art guided not by transcendence or the sublime, but simply by the masterly control of musical materials that "imitate" nature but hardly delve into its innermost being. For this reason, for Wagner the name Brahms was practically synonymous with the name Mendelssohn. Even though Brahms was not Jewish, Wagner insisted on believing that Brahms had thought out a way of composing that was modeled on that of Mendelssohn, and that he received powerful support from Jewish and half-Jewish artists and critics such as Ferdinand Hiller, Joseph Joachim, and Eduard Hanslick. Wagner, who equated Jews and the French with the lower primates at best, put them all into the category of musical apes. Indeed, he liked to suggest that to mistake an ape for a human was akin to mistaking a Jew for a German. A Jewish artist, to paraphrase Wagner's ghastly punning metaphor, who can only "ape" nature—that is, imitate or mimic it realistically—is the antithesis of the German artist, who can discern the ideal meaning behind natural phenomena and imbue it with profound feeling.[11]

But was Wagner afraid, or did he simply know that he belonged in the zoo himself? In June 1875 he presented Brahms with a printed score of *Das Rheingold* with the following words inscribed in an accompanying letter: "It is probably not uninteresting to observe how, in relation to the other scores of the *Ring of the Nibelung*, I knew how to form all kinds of musical thematic material out of the theatrical images set up in this first work of the cycle. In this sense, it is precisely *Das Rheingold* that will perhaps receive your friendly attention."[12] Wagner implied, of course, that his skill of symphonic development in the whole of the *Ring* was comparable to Brahms's own renowned talent for it, despite the theatrical origin of the *Ring*'s themes. And in an unpublished letter to Wilhem Tappert in 1878 about his own symphony, which, as he always implied, Mendelssohn had lost on purpose, he wrote the following:

Just getting to know my symphony again would be tremendously interesting to me—but perhaps I'll be disappointed. Still, I have to confess my weakness that I expected to learn something, and that I was all the more curious when I recently looked through Brahms's [First] Symphony. I was really quite astonished at how a trained composer can get along without any kind of inspiration. I've never been able to do that, and assumed that I'd be able to study my own symphony, to see whether I ever could. . . . Now Seidel has to put the whole thing in score. . . . That is going to take some time, until I nevertheless arrive at some insight about myself, which will probably make me realize that I'm more related to Brahms than I thought I was.[13]

Wagner could just as well have written "more related to Mendelssohn than I thought I was." At any rate, only a few months later, Cosima Wagner reported the following in her famous diaries: "R[ichard] dreamt that Mendelssohn said 'you' to him" *(R[ichard] träumte von Mendelssohn, daß er ihm du sagte).*[14] In other words, he dreamt that Mendelssohn addressed him with the intimate *du* form and not with the formal *Sie*. Indeed, Cosima's diaries are full of entries that prove time and again that Wagner's view of Mendelssohn involved not just a rejection of him but also an identification with him. Wagner himself takes on the negative character traits he detected in Mendelssohn while also turning them against the object of his criticism. At one point he talks to Cosima about strangely malicious traits in Mendelssohn's character: how, for example, during an academy examination he had amused both himself and the other examiners by caricaturing the students who were playing for them, one of whom was deformed.[15] But Wagner didn't hesitate to turn a similarly wounding insult against Mendelssohn's own body. "The same thing happened to Mendelssohn's personality," he said, "as to certain apes who, so gifted when young, become stupid as their strength increases. I saw him after his marriage, and he looked so fat, so unpleasant—an unsavory man!"[16] Not surprisingly, Wagner blows hot and cold about Mendelssohn's music. At one moment Cosima reports how Richard delights in the *Hebrides* Overture and calls it a "beautiful work."[17] At another, however, Wagner compares a Mendelssohn Song without Words to a Schubert song. The Schubert song, he claimed, demonstrates what melody and feelings really are, in contrast to Mendelssohn's song and its "Semitic excitability."[18]

AN ANTI-SEMITIC SONG WITHOUT WORDS

Wagner gave Mendelssohn the score of his C-major Symphony in 1836 with a letter that described it as "a present."[19] That was probably just a polite way of saying that Wagner expected Mendelssohn to conduct it in his

Gewandhaus concerts. But later Wagner saw this "present" and the subsequent loss of the score, at least in part, as the start of an imaginary dialogue about the validity of what he considered to be two entirely opposed methods of composition. According to Cosima's diaries, Wagner spoke of the "malice of Mendelssohn's silence" about the symphony.[20] And even before the work was rediscovered by Tappert, Wagner complains to Cosima that he cannot show it to her; Mendelssohn probably destroyed it, he said, possibly because it revealed certain things he found unpleasant.[21]

Wagner implied with that remark that there are already places in the C-major Symphony that for him were a kind of aesthetic premonition of his later music. It would be too banal to assume, however, that he was simply concerned with proving his superiority over Mendelssohn and tracing it back to as early as 1836. Rather, for Wagner the story of the symphony was a dialectical doubling of two positions in the aesthetics of composition, which he was at pains to inscribe ideologically in his life and postrevolutionary music dramas. It was not entirely a coincidence, perhaps, that when he became interested again in his symphony he decided to use the Dresden Amen as one of the central motifs of his last music drama, *Parsifal*—a motif that is tolerated, so to speak, in prominent places in the first movement of Mendelssohn's "Reformation" Symphony as a sensuous Catholic symbol alongside an austere Lutheran chant.

Everything is mythic and unreal in the blasphemous thrillerama of *Parsifal*. Yet in its ritual moments it can also be seen to be—like Mendelssohn's "Reformation" Symphony—as solid and substantial as a Victorian drawing room. Not surprisingly, Wagner himself damned the Biedermeier, thisworldly, materialistic aspect of the "Reformation" Symphony in obviously anti-Semitic terms when he heard it in February 1876, remarking that the second movement reminded him of the satiric couplet *"wenn das Geld im Kasten klingt,/ die Seele in den Himmel springt"* (when the money in the cashbox rings, / the soul at once to heaven wings).[22] Wagner therefore clearly went out of his way to listen critically to the "Reformation" Symphony in the period immediately before beginning work on the music of *Parsifal*. And in contemplating the appropriation of Mendelssohnian ideas he was intrigued by the possibility of both reversing their meaning *and* retaining a residue of their original aura as he saw it, precisely in order to make the reversal in meaning all the more effective. Marc Weiner has rightly said that Wagner relied in instances like these on romantic paradigms of self-reflection and irony in the writings of Novalis, Friedrich Schlegel, and E. T. A. Hoffmann to define, with several characteristic Wagnerian twists, the difference between the superficial material of the sign and the meaning that transcends this base materialism. According to Wagner, the Jewish artist is limited to the first, and only the truly German artist is able to discern the second.[23]

It is certainly clear enough from Wagner's writings that one of his aims was to reduce to racial categories the idea that a work of art can metaphorically dramatize the tension between the material of representation and another realm it strives for, but is incapable of actually reaching. The notion that in the name of transcendence a work of art can reflect on the limitations of its own materiality is bundled together with an ideological program in which the ability or inability to create "higher" art is turned into a question of race. In Wagner's opinion, the sovereign German artist is capable of devotion to the ideal, while non-Germans, because of their innate limitations, have to make do with realism, with the material of the sign, and with merely surface meaning. As all Jewish artists in Wagner's program count as *"nicht-deutsch-fühlend"* (not German in feeling), Mendelssohn obviously plays a significant role. According to the original version of "Judaism in Music":

> Mendelssohn has shown us that a Jew can possess the richest store of individual talents and may be in possession of the finest and most varied culture . . . yet is incapable, without these advantages, of bringing about, even for a single moment, the profound effect that moves heart and soul that we expect from art, because we know art is capable of it, and because we have felt it countless times, the moment a hero of our art simply opens his mouth and speaks to us.[24]

Accordingly, the talented Jew can only practice music as *künstliche Kunst*, that is, as technique, as counterpoint, and in terms of the working-out of themes and orchestration. "The incapability of the musical art form itself," Wagner wrote elsewhere in the same essay, "is reflected for us by the artistic influence of Mendelssohn—that musician of especially immense talent."[25] For Wagner there were always two kinds of music: pleasurable music, the product of fabulous talent bound to the materiality of technique and the sign, and inspirational music, identical with the outpouring of profound feelings from the soul of the (Germanic) hero of art reaching beyond the surface of appearances.

Wagner had to appropriate the Mendelssohn tradition as he saw it, however, in order to present all the more powerfully the tension between music as mimesis of a material, technical world on the one hand and the idealistic ambitions of the music drama on the other. Here I merely want to make a point about the confrontation between Mime and Siegfried in the third scene of the second act of *Siegfried* that is not made in the penetrating analysis of this scene by Weiner.[26] In my view, this scene in particular can be interpreted as a replica of the myth created by Wagner about his relationship to Mendelssohn. Mime's creative talent and miraculous technical ability (Siegfried calls him a "Master"[27] in the early drafts of the *Ring*) is, like Mendelssohn's, supposedly vitiated by his racial origin. Mime intends to poison the hero so that he can win the ring and the Nibelung hoard for himself. He approaches Siegfried to kill him, but he hides his real feelings behind a facade of friendliness and fun-loving affection. The Forest Bird has already warned Siegfried of Mime's true intentions, with the result that Siegfried and the audience hear the real content of Mime's thoughts. The text the audience actually hears from Mime therefore does not correspond with the meaning he is trying to convey. The music does it for him. It mirrors the text he wants to sing by becoming smooth and without problems. According to Wagner's directions, the music has to sound hypocritical: "sweetly," "tenderly," "as if praising Siegfried," "as though he were promising him pleasant things," "as though he were ready to give him his life," "with evident pains," "with an expression of heartfelt concern," and so on. The music accompanying Mime's vocal line does all of this. Using the musical codes of lullabies and familial love—lilting, unctuous, and sycophantic, as Wagner perceived the smooth, sophisticated, and fundamentally dishonest surface of Mendelssohn's music to be—Wagner creates music for Mime that acts as an approximation of a verbal text that is never heard. At his most insincere, Mime sings, quite literally, a Song without Words.

THE LIMITS OF PARADISE

Wagner's thoughts about Mendelssohn, which came to a head at the end of his life during his preoccupation with the C-major Symphony mean perhaps that the many-layered symphonic character and contrapuntal ambition of his music dramas, much praised by Richard Strauss, among others, can be seen in a different light. The musical techniques that are part of Wagner's conception of symphonic drama are usually viewed as constituent parts of his musical structures. But perhaps it would be more interesting to hear them—as Nietzsche already did—as rhetorical components secretly harboring alien elements such as contrapuntal and orchestral ingenuity for its own sake and a virtuosity in the handling of themes that Wagner associated with the Mendelssohn "tradition." And all of them were composed in the name of an all-embracing ideology reinforcing the message of a utopian paradise of German art, while at the same time defining its limits. In very simple foreground moments, how can one forget the canonic E♭ entries of the lumbering giants as they confront Wotan in *Das Rheingold,* or the odd fugue on Siegfried's horn call as Siegfried journeys up the Rhine in *Götterdämmerung?* Both sound as if they had been served up as instant composition lessons in counterpoint rather than organic constituents of a musical or dramatic structure. In fact, they present, using strict musical technique as metaphor, the social world of reason and legality from which the two heroes of the *Ring* are either trying to escape, or unwittingly enter into. The giants announce to Wotan that he is bound to social contracts, like Odysseus to his ship's mast. And Siegfried enjoys the fugue, as if improvised out of his horn call, when he leaves the sunlit brilliance of Brünnhilde's rock to join the darkness of real human relations in the Gibichungs' Hall. The fugue occurs at just the moment, in other words, when Wagner's anti-Enlightenment myth of heroic vitalism leaves its world of dazzling light and begins to veer tragically toward its end.

There has been no fundamental study of how Mendelssohn's music influenced Wagner. Nor has there been any significant appraisal of the effect Wagner's sharp criticisms of Mendelssohn—here I mean Wagner's criticisms after the full implications of the loss of his symphony score due to Mendelssohn's supposed neglect began to take shape—have had on the reception of Mendelssohn's music. It is obvious that Wagner's prejudices against Mendelssohn's music that are still with us (now usually, but not always, without any kind of anti-Semitic ballast) need to be looked at carefully. And certainly it would be naïve to dismiss Wagner's criticisms out of hand as just another one of those undesirable bits of his personality, or indeed as entirely wrong. What I am interested in is trying to understand the self-reflective moments in the scores of Wagner's music dramas a bit better. In these moments, his interpretation of Mendelssohn's aesthetics—not only as parody, but also as part of his symphonic ambition—is woven into the musical texture of the dramas, and hence also into the refined ideological complexity of those dramas in order to ensure their success, but also possible failure, in the utopian age of the drama of the future. Mendelssohn's statue, we remember, stayed on the roof of the Prague Academy of Music. And Wagner's did as well, though a bit more wobbly than before, after the noose had been removed from his neck.

15. Unfinished Symphonies

Old age: gradually receding from appearance.
JOHANN WOLFGANG VON GOETHE, *Maximen und Reflexionen*

Cosima Wagner once recorded the following statement by her husband: "I shall have to write something one day about the manner in which the life of the intellect goes its own way and has nothing to do with actual experiences—indeed, it is rather the things one does not find in life that provide the images."[1] Wagner was objecting to Ludwig Nohl's recent and pathbreaking biography of Beethoven, and in particular to his dovetailing of *Fidelio* (1814) with an episode in Beethoven's love life.[2] By implication he was also referring disparagingly to those who saw his famous amours as the moving force behind works like *Lohengrin* and *Tristan und Isolde*.

The statement seems provocative, given that it was uttered by the man who inspired more literature of the life-in-the-works variety than just about any other composer. Indeed, Cosima's diaries are filled with Wagner's scornful remarks about just the kind of publication that would, twenty years after his death and at the height of his influence, become the mainstay of the literature about him. To this day, the apparent plenitude of his works and writings prevents commentators from asking what his life did *not* bring him, what he did *not* do, or indeed what he sensed was lacking in his own life that provided images for his voracious intellect.

His final work, *Parsifal*, is itself about a lack, a void at the center of a community—a kind of death among the living—that is symbolized by the character of Titurel, a tragic, Frankenstein-like wreckage of humanity who is the father of Amfortas, the leader of the knights of the Grail. That lack has to be made good by the hero, Parsifal, whose active avoidance of Eros grants him the spiritual strength he needs to escape delusion and restore wholeness to the community of the Grail. *Parsifal* is not just a work written in the last years of Wagner's life; it is also, on a personal and a communal level, about old age itself, the repressed knowledge of the gradual

189

receding of vitality, and the pain of not having experienced something essential in the past.

Hannah Arendt noted in *The Human Condition* (1958) that death can seem to appear among the living in old age. She points to the old-age self-portraits of Rembrandt and Leonardo da Vinci, in which the intensity of the eyes seems to dominate the receding flesh, and she cites Johann Wolfgang von Goethe: "Old age: gradually receding from appearance."[3] We can see something of this in one of the last photographs of Wagner, which could not be published in the epoch of his greatest fame because it showed all too clearly the signs of premature aging (see frontispiece). Large, confident eyes command the slightly sunken cheekbones and a forehead that somehow looks parched: his face is a lunar landscape still inhabited by sharp intelligence. Nine months after the photograph was taken Wagner was dead; he was only sixty-nine.

During the last few months before his death, Wagner composed nothing of any consequence, mainly because his time and energy were above all given to the first performance of *Parsifal*, which was staged in Bayreuth in the summer of 1882. It was a huge artistic achievement and a fitting end to an astonishing body of work, which, though marred by a dubious political legacy, he had spent a lifetime creating. In the process, he changed opera, tragedy, music, drama—the nature of culture and theater tout court. Yet for a good deal of the time he was composing *Parsifal* (between 1877 and 1881) and then putting it into production, his mind was frequently on something else, on something he had wanted to do all his life and for various reasons had never managed to complete. It is no wonder that this great lacuna preoccupied him in his last years as much as it did, and probably only his death prevented it from leading to any significant creative results. There is nothing complicated about it: he simply wanted to write symphonies.

THE SYMPHONIST IN SPITE OF HIMSELF

It does not follow from Wagner's meager contribution to the symphony that he would have been incapable of writing good instrumental music if he had chosen to do so. Indeed, the evidence of Cosima's diaries and his late sketch fragments, which I shall discuss later in this chapter, suggest that despite blowing hot and cold about the idea, he was more confident about writing instrumental music after *Parsifal* than is usually realized, and he was certain that it would not be incidental to his life's work.

Was this confidence misplaced? Nietzsche was firmly convinced that

Wagner had always been incapable of writing music that could stand on its own without indulging in a patchwork of motifs, gestures, and the like that needed a "literature" to persuade the world to take it seriously. According to Nietzsche, Wagner's abandonment of, and arguments against, the writing of instrumental music throughout his life amounted to a single, unstated law: "Everything Wagner can *not* do is reprehensible."[4] Thomas Mann's suggestion that there were "dilettante" traits in Wagner's creative make-up (mentioned in chapter 8 of this volume), an idea that was later elaborated by Theodor W. Adorno, belongs to the same line of reasoning. This is also true of an important book on Wagner's instrumental music by the German musicologist Egon Voss, who insists that Wagner compensated for his weaknesses in facing up to the demands of purely instrumental composition—even his literary or dramatic conception of it—by seeking refuge for his symphonic ambitions in the music drama.[5]

Nietzsche's argument and its sundry variations are belied by Wagner's most famous instrumental work, the *Siegfried Idyll*, which can beguile listeners who have no knowledge at all of its composer's ideas about music drama. Even an early work like the Symphony in C Major makes up for its heavy reliance on Beethoven with its technical assurance; it may not be original, but it is certainly not the work of a dilettante. The main problem with Nietzsche's view is that in deliberately spurning Wagner's philosophical ideas, he seriously underestimated their role as active agents in guiding the creative decisions made by Wagner, some of which, after all, turned out to be momentous.

Wagner's quasi-Hegelian interpretation of world history and his place in it—a view that Stravinsky once cheekily, but with deadly accuracy, referred to as "Bayreuth or bust"[6]—began in 1834, when he became involved with the Junges Deutschland (Young Germany) movement, a loose conglomerate of liberal, nationalist, and left-Hegelian writers like Heinrich Laube and Theodor Mundt, whose writings on art left an indelible mark on Wagner's thinking. The year 1834 saw the publication of Wagner's first essay, "Die deutsche Oper" (German opera), in which he lavished praise on the Italian bel canto and expressed a distrust of instrumental music that was typical of many nineteenth-century philosophers. In the same year he conducted his first opera *(Don Giovanni)* and began a lifelong devotion to the art of one of the most famous singers of the era, Wilhelmine Schröder-Devrient. The soprano was the heroine of Junges Deutschland, for whom she symbolized, in their words, a new age concerned with "strong emotions" as opposed to the "affairs of state," represented by her more classically oriented and well-connected rival, Henriette Sontag.[7] In other words, new subjective forms of vivid musical drama were "in"; the empty civic genre of opera and obscure purely musical forms like the symphony were "out."

It is hardly a coincidence that in 1834, the year of Wagner's philosophical awakening, he left his Symphony in E Major unfinished. He started sketching the first movement on August 4 and finished it just over three weeks later. While working on the slow movement, he suddenly announced in a letter to a friend that there was "no way" *(auf keinen Fall)* he could finish it.[8] It is still not clear exactly what he meant by that. Toward the end of his life he intimated that giving up symphonies in his youth "had indeed a serious reason" *(hatte wohl seinen ernstlichen Grund)*,[9] but again, he provided no concrete explanation.

The phrases "no way" and "serious reason," however, suggest that some kind of philosophical grand design was in play. The same is suggested by the way Wagner described the fate of another of his unfinished symphonies, the projected Faust symphony of 1839–40. In chapter 2 we saw him speak in 1852 about his "escape" from "the fog of instrumental music" in this work into the "clear-cut" dramatic definition of *Der fliegende Holländer,* and here, too, one suspects another perceived aesthetic and philosophical confrontation with history. In terms of national rivalry alone, it makes sense that a young German in Paris in the late 1830s should write a purely instrumental Faust symphony that included allusions to Beethoven and Weber as a counteroffensive to the powerful French example of Hector Berlioz's symphony *Romeo et Juliette.*[10] In 1839, at its first performance, Berlioz's symphony had a great impact on Parisian musical life. But Wagner went a step further with his own project: he not only disqualified the projected symphony from membership in a historically prestigious, though now redundant, genre by completing only the first movement, eventually calling it merely *Eine Faust-Ouvertüre* (A Faust overture), but he also replaced it with something that immediately put it on a higher level of historical truth as he saw it: *Der fliegende Holländer,* his first foray into "drama."

The *Siegfried Idyll* repeats a similar, though more complicated, pattern. Wagner conceived it as a one-movement symphony that would use, as did the Faust overture, an ingeniously modified sonata form. When he allowed the piece to be published in 1878, Wagner omitted the word "Symphony" emblazoned at the head of the manuscript of the *Siegfried Idyll* and replaced it with a harmless (and possibly mischievously misleading) title with obvious autobiographical allusions.[11] It was a perfectly logical step for a composer still engaged with his lifelong project of "drama," and who, logically enough, had announced in 1850 that, with Beethoven's Ninth Symphony, "the last symphony has already been written" *(die letzte Symphonie [ist] bereits geschrieben).*[12] Or, to put it another way, after a period of almost thirty years during which his idea of the "end" of the symphony had proved to be highly influential in progressive musical circles, Wagner did not want to be caught refuting one of the cornerstones of his artistic and philosophical credo.

THE NEW SYMPHONY AFTER BEETHOVEN

The tension between Wagner's private creative need to write symphonies and his official public position on the symphony increased markedly toward the end of his life. This is perhaps why the true extent and intensity of his preoccupation with instrumental music, and particularly the symphony, has still to be fully recognized.[13] In the period from the early 1870s to his death in February 1883, frequent mention is made in Cosima's diaries of his plans to write instrumental music. Twice, on 4 July and 8 September 1878, Cosima writes that Wagner speaks of writing a quartet; once, on 9 February 1881, he holds forth more generally about "instrumental compositions." As a rule, however, he called the works he was planning "symphonies." The earliest diary entry that mentions such a plan is dated 8 October 1877: "In the evening R. plays me a wonderful theme for a symphony and says that he has so many themes of this kind, they are always occurring to him, but he cannot use such healthy things for *Parsifal*."

Cosima's diary does not make it clear whether Wagner notated this theme or not, and, unfortunately, many of her other entries are similarly silent on the subject. Clearly Wagner was not in the habit of regularly writing down everything that occurred to him. On 28 March 1878, Cosima writes, "Then he sang me a theme: 'the Andante of your symphony,' I say. . . . He gets back to his work; my telling him to write down the theme has distracted him, he says, and now he also has the finale. He plays it." Wagner then asks Cosima, "What key shall I write my symphony in?" Probably without waiting for an answer, he continues, "When *Parsifal* has been composed, I shall write nine symphonies, the ninth with choruses: Schmerz, schöner Höllenfunken—Püffe gabst du uns und Stöße, einen Feind beschmiert mit Kot." Apart from the obscene punning on Friedrich von Schiller's famous lines in Beethoven's 1824 Symphony No. 9 in D Minor ("Choral")—I leave readers to translate it for themselves—the only thing that is really clear from the entry is that Cosima had to ask Wagner specifically to write down his musical ideas. Whether he actually did so is another matter, though naturally he often notated ideas without being asked. On 11 January 1879, Cosima notes that Wagner had written down "another theme for a symphony," and on 11 June 1882 we read that he wrote down a symphonic theme "on coming in from the garden."

The correlation of the diary entries about symphonies and symphonic themes with surviving sketches in Wagner's hand is unfortunately far from straightforward. The sketches are only occasionally provided with dates, and even these few pieces of concrete information do not correspond with diary entries. There is, in fact, only one sketch with a heading indicating that it was intended specifically for a symphonic movement (ex. 11). It is not impossible that this sketch has something to do with the Andante mentioned by Cosima on 28 March 1878.

One precise connection between the diaries and the sketches can be made. On 11 February 1883, two days before Wagner's death, Cosima writes, "Around noon he came into my room. 'I have a letter from Cyriax.' 'Is there anything in it?' 'You'll soon see.' As soon as I've dried my hands I take a look: it's a scherzo theme, written down on an envelope from Cyriax—he then plays it on his piano." The "scherzo theme" was neatly written out again in a separate sketch (ex. 12). But a rough preliminary version of it was notated beneath an embossed stamp of the law firm Cyriax on the back of an envelope postmarked in London on 14 March 1879 that is now preserved in the Bayreuth Nationalarchiv.[14] Other entries in the diaries around this time make it clear that just before his death Wagner was busy putting his sketch fragments in order, and it is likely that he came across the Cyriax envelope while doing so. The sketch itself possibly has some connection with this diary entry, dated 25 March 1879: "He is working [on the third act of *Parsifal*], but nothing comes to him, he says, except a few odds and ends, among them a scherzo for a symphony."

Besides inventing fragments of music intended for the symphonies he was planning, in his last years Wagner was also keen to explore ideas relevant to their content and form. On 8 February 1878, Cosima notes that "R sketches out a canon for a domestic symphony." Some weeks later, on 22 February, we read, "R speaks of a symphony that he wants to dedicate to Fidi [his son Siegfried], a theme for it has occurred to him again today; it will be spirited and friendly, just like the boy." These ideas for a domestic symphony correspond, too, with an entry on 19 March, which notes that Wagner wanted to write "many more things like the *Siegfried Idyll*." Yet another example is an entry for 20 March 1881, which recounts how he was considering the title "From My Diary" for his prospective symphonies. "How much he would like to write symphonies," Cosima enthuses, "how much he enjoys working with orchestras, how little with theater singers"; she then adds that Wagner—whose sharp critical judgment had already

Ex. 11. Richard Wagner, sketch, 1878? (Nationalarchiv der Richard-Wagner-Stiftung Bayreuth, A II a 6, fol. 24v).

Ex. 12. Richard Wagner, sketch, 1879? (Nationalarchiv der Richard-Wagner-Stiftung Bayreuth A II a 6, fol. 28r).

brought him back from the brink of execrable taste many times in his life—found the title "too pretentious."

A few weeks later, on 17 April 1881, Wagner is recorded as saying, "I shall set the Christian religious holidays to music—these will be my symphonies." Obviously he was not being completely serious, and he gave up the idea three days later: "He observed in the morning," Cosima wrote, "that in the end the Christian festivals idea will not work, as he has too many high-spirited themes, and that is not Christian." Indeed, some of Wagner's ideas were so short-lived, and his lurches between seriousness and

high comedy so frequent, that it is hard not to conclude that he was unde-
cided about putting his plans for symphonies into practice.

It is hardly a surprise that the earliest surviving statement about the
form of the symphonies Wagner was planning, recorded by Cosima on 22
September 1878, is laced with a blend of ribaldry and earnestness. This time
the butt of his humor is Kundry, one of the main characters in *Parsifal* and
a veritable compendium of female hysteria, as the late nineteenth century
understood it. Kundry, bizarrely, seems to have inspired musical ideas that
could not have been further removed from the neurasthenic art nouveau
world she is supposed to inhabit.

> He complains with indescribable humor that now he has to compose
> Kundry nothing comes into his head but cheerful themes for sym-
> phonies. . . . He says he will call his symphonies "symphonic dia-
> logues," as composing four movements in the old style is not for him;
> rather, one must have theme and countertheme, allow them to converse
> with one another. He says there is nothing like that in the whole of
> Brahms's [first] symphony.

Wagner offered a pendant to these remarks on 19 November: "I want to be
writing symphonies where I can write whatever comes into my head—I am
not lacking in ideas. . . . I shall probably return to the old symphonic form, in
one section, with an andante in the middle. After Beethoven, four-movement
symphonies cannot be written any more, they just look like imitations—if
one were to write a large-scale scherzo like one of his for example."

The idea of the one-movement symphony was retained, however, even
though Wagner's opinion about its form and character tended to change. On
17 December 1882, he told Liszt, "If we write symphonies, Franz, then let
us stop contrasting one theme with another, a method Beethoven has exhausted. We should just spin a melodic line until it can be spun no further—
only nothing of drama." A later entry in Cosima's diaries, dated 30 January
1883, is in a similar vein: "At the end of the evening he tells me that he can
still imagine one-movement symphonic works of a kind like, for example,
the *Kaisermarsch*, written in the aftermath of the Franco-Prussian War in
1871, in which themes are not contrasted, but each merges out of the other.
But he says he will make no more music—it excites him too much."

MELODIES AND THEMES

Frequent mention is made in Cosima's diaries of themes, either played by
Wagner on the piano or notated, that appear to be independent of his plans

to write symphonies. A few times, particularly in the last months of his life, the word "melody" is used instead of "theme." It is not impossible that he intended to use some of these melodies and themes for the symphonies that he wanted to compose. The reasons for the existence of these fragments, and the functions they were meant to fulfill, however, remain open questions.

Most of Wagner's notated themes and melodies are contained in the same group of sketches in the Nationalarchiv in Bayreuth as those that are more clearly relevant to Wagner's ideas about his symphonies-to-be. Indeed, if it could be conclusively proved that Wagner was solely responsible for collecting the sketches together, this might suggest that that they have something to do with one another. Unfortunately, it is not known for certain who assembled the sketches; nor is it clear why they were put together in the way they were. It is also impossible to be absolutely certain that most of the themes and melodies mentioned by Cosima are identical to those in this particular collection.

It is possible nonetheless that Wagner had something to do with the grouping of the fragments, as there is clear evidence that he was keen to collect scraps like this himself. On 17 October 1878, Cosima writes, "With our morning conversation at an end . . . we go our own separate ways when he says: 'Now I am going to collect runaways *[fuyards]*.' . . . He means all the musical ideas he has hastily written down." And on 9 February 1883, four days before Wagner's death, Cosima speaks of him "arranging his papers" *(Ordnen seiner Blätter)*, although the precise meaning of this is not clear.

Significantly, perhaps, both statements are adjacent to others about symphonies. After citing Wagner on the *fuyards*, Cosima mentions that he had told her the day before that most of all "he would like to write some symphonies—cheerful, friendly works in which he wouldn't get carried away too much. He absolutely feels the need to give vent to this side of himself." Immediately preceding *"Ordnen seiner Blätter,"* she records that "he will still do his article about masculine and feminine, then write symphonies." In the same diary entry, however, Cosima speaks of Wagner sorting out his bits and pieces of music *(Ton-Schnitzel)*, then quotes him as claiming that "he will never make any use of them."

But some of these sketches seem to have been particularly important for Wagner, since, like the "scherzo" theme on the Cyriax envelope, they were all sketched at least twice. Ex. 13a and 13b show the earliest of these fragments, the second of which is dated 1876, proving that it was written shortly after the premiere of the *Ring* cycle in Bayreuth, while Wagner was staying

Ex. 13a. Richard Wagner, sketch, 1876? (Nationalarchiv der Richard-Wagner-Stiftung Bayreuth, A II a 6, fol. 29r).

Ex. 13b. Richard Wagner, sketch, 1876 (Nationalarchiv der Richard-Wagner-Stiftung Bayreuth, A II a 6, fol. 30r).

Ex. 14a. Richard Wagner, sketch, 1876? (Nationalarchiv der Richard-Wagner-Stiftung Bayreuth, A II a 6, fol. 9r).

Ex. 14b. Richard Wagner, sketch, 1876? (Nationalarchiv der Richard-Wagner-Stiftung Bayreuth, A II a 6, fol. 30r).

Ex. 15a. Richard Wagner, sketch, 1882? (Nationalarchiv der Richard-Wagner-Stiftung Bayreuth, A II a 6, fol. 3r).

Ex. 15b. Richard Wagner, sketch, 1882 (Nationalarchiv der Richard-Wagner-Stiftung Bayreuth, A II a 6, fol. 15r).

in Naples. The sketch transcribed in ex. 14b is on the same sheet (a rough preliminary notation in another sketch is ex. 14a); it was clearly written down in Naples as well, probably at the same time.

The provenance of these sketches is not so clear, however, in sharp contrast to the direct connection that can be demonstrated between entries in Cosima's diaries and the various versions of the theme shown in ex. 15a–d. Cosima provided the fourth notation of this theme in the manuscript with the words "Melodie der Porazzi!" referring to the Piazza dei Porazzi in Palermo, on which Wagner lived between 2 February and 19 March 1882. The four sketches provide a classic example in miniature of the care with which Wagner evolved small units of highly suggestive melodic sequences. The pallid octave leap in measures 2–3 of the initial sketch (assuming that the lower E♭ in measure 2 is integral to the melodic line) is changed to a colorful flattened seventh in measures 1–2 of ex. 15b, and measure 4 of 15b evolves into a heightened, as well as a more logical, harmonic progression in ex. 15c and 15d.

4 März Anders

[sic]

Ex. 15c. Richard Wagner, sketch, 1882 (Nationalarchiv der Richard-Wagner-Stiftung Bayreuth, A II a 6, fol. 25r).

Ex. 15d. Richard Wagner, sketch, 1882 (Richard-Wagner-Gedenkstätte Bayreuth Hs 120/NNr).

Wagner's dating of the second and third sketches in ex. 15b and ex. 15c corresponds closely with entries in Cosima's diaries. On 2 March 1882, she reports that Wagner "writes down a melody, then shows it to me, saying that he has at last found the line he was looking for." Indeed, this also suggests that the theme had been worked on before ex. 15b was written down. Then, on 5 March 1882, Cosima notes that "after supper R plays the new melody, which he has altered a little." Cosima particularly liked this theme (or melody), and Wagner often played it to her. On 2 May 1882, she writes, "and while I am in my bath, I hear him play the Porazzi melody!" In each diary entry she includes the title "Porazzi," which proves beyond a doubt that this is the legendary "Porazzi theme," and not the theme in A♭ major (ex. 16), which for many years was mistaken for it, even by the best of Wagner's biographers.[15]

The theme in A♭ major is also connected with Cosima's diaries, albeit less firmly. On 9 February 1883, Cosima reports that Wagner played her "a melody that sounds very beautiful," further noting his surprise at finding it among his "bits and pieces of music." Suddenly he remembered that he had intended it as a "dedication page" *(Widmungs-Blatt)* for the manuscript

Ex. 16. Richard Wagner, former Porazzi theme, 1858? and 1881? (Richard-Wagner-Gedenkstätte Bayreuth Hs 120/JJ photocopy).

score of *Parsifal*. All the evidence suggests that Wagner sketched the first eight measures while he was writing the music of *Tristan*, and the rest, in lilac ink, at some point during the composition of *Parsifal*.[16] Moreover, his daughter with Cosima, Eva Chamberlain, wrote on the fair copy of the sketch, which she presented to Arturo Toscanini in 1931, that it was a "dedication page for Mama placed in the score of *Parsifal*." The evocative fragment has since achieved a modicum of fame, especially since the appearance of Luchino Visconti's film *Ludwig* (1972), in which Franco Mannino's different orchestrations of the theme reinforce its ubiquitous presence on the soundtrack. We shall never know whether Wagner would have orchestrated it himself. As we saw earlier, after discussing the "beautiful melody" with Cosima, he confirmed in practically the same breath that he wanted to "write symphonies." That does not necessarily imply, however, that his projected symphonies would have included any of this strikingly melancholic music.

CONCERNING LISZT AND NIETZSCHE

Wagner's late thoughts about his plans to write symphonies throw some new light on his relations with Liszt. The two men had less in common than is usually thought, which is probably why they got on tolerably well. Yet Cosima's diaries reveal that the famous friendship received some severe body blows. Wagner was moving closer to Liszt's skepticism about the "drama"—the word that Wagner liked to use to refer to his entire aesthetic-philosophical system—and Liszt's lifelong belief in the historical validity of instrumental music after Beethoven. At the same time, he continued to be a sharp critic of Liszt's music, although for the most part he kept silent about its aesthetic weaknesses while praising (and learning from) its technical cunning. But the more he felt the need to write instrumental music himself, the more he began to speak the unspeakable—all of it dutifully recorded by Liszt's daughter. It is almost as if he wanted to change identities with his father-in-law. On 26 February 1882, Cosima reports that Wagner had dreamt about a "Gretchen theme." It is not clear whether Wagner meant his own (which, as we saw in chapter 2, he discarded from the Faust symphony he was planning in 1839) or was referring to the second movement of Liszt's *Eine Faust-Symphonie in drei Charakterbildern* (Faust symphony in three character portraits, 1854). Either way it hardly matters, since the subliminal exchange is clear enough: "From the street outside I looked up at your father's room; there was a piano in the window; nimble as I was, I climbed up and played the Gretchen theme to your father as he returned; he looked up from the street in astonishment; so that he would not know who it was, I tried to go back through the window, but I stumbled, and then woke up."

The more Wagner voiced his criticisms of Liszt's music, the less underhanded and guilty he felt. Only a few days after his dream about the "Gretchen theme," on 2 March 1882, he described the "Porazzi" theme specifically as an "antidote" to Liszt's second "Mephisto Waltz" (1881). Toward the end of the year he was even more explicit, referring to Liszt's latest compositions as "budding insanity."[17] It is also clear throughout his late years, on the other hand, that Wagner looked to Liszt for the bridge between those teasing fragments in the Bayreuth archives and the symphonic structures he might have made out of them. The statement to Cosima that he wanted to write "many more things" like the *Siegfried Idyll* was as good as saying that he intended to elaborate further Liszt's solution to the merging of ornate sonata forms and extramusical programs: the work is, in effect, a miniature symphonic poem that does precisely this.[18] He admired, too, Liszt's ambition to abolish form in favor of idea in his late works, letting freedom triumph over authority. Wagner was prepared to accept this in instrumental music, even though it meant relinquishing the two essential pillars of his aesthetic-philosophical system: Beethoven and music drama.

Wagner's relationship with Nietzsche also begins to appear in a different light when Cosima's diaries are closely read. In private, Wagner expressed views about himself and his life's work that would not have been out of place in Nietzsche's later polemic against him in *The Case of Wagner* (1888). Several remarks show that Wagner was just as disconcerted by the reality of Bayreuth—including the beer-swilling philistines haunting the restaurants during the intervals—as Nietzsche was. Furthermore, he seems to have been prepared on occasion to jettison the ideology of the "drama" and the idea of redemption for the sake of writing music that was going to be "healthy," "cheerful," "simple," and "high-spirited." This is precisely what Nietzsche later accused him of never wanting to do. Indeed, the impression is inescapable that Nietzsche's shrewd observations on Wagner's music are simply negative versions of Wagner's own, private thoughts. Nietzsche has been accused many times of telling tales out of school, particularly about Wagner's reputedly Jewish father, but few realize that these insights also extend to Wagner's view of himself as a musician. We can almost hear Wagner saying, "Music should be Mediterraneanized" *(Il faut méditerraniser la musique)*, the famous phrase Nietzsche coined in French when he compared the Mediterranean simplicity and warmth in the music of Georges Bizet's *Carmen* (1875) with the dampness of the north and the "steam" of the Wagnerian ideal.[19] Wagner told Cosima on 4 February 1879 that "people will be amazed when I publish my symphonies to see how simple they are," and he spoke repeatedly of giving vent musically to a side of him the public had never heard.

This remarkable self-knowledge may well have been the weapon Nietzsche later used publicly against Wagner. Certainly the surviving fragments for Wagner's unwritten symphonies throw some light on at least one enigmatic passage in *The Case of Wagner*, suggesting that Nietzsche had an intimate knowledge of Wagner's secret musical thoughts and the assiduousness with which he collected them for future use. Also interesting here is that Nietzsche interprets the happiness and simplicity Wagner thought he was investing in these fragments as another form of melancholy—the cheerful pessimism, perhaps, that both men had discovered in the philosophy of Arthur Schopenhauer. This philosopher's advocacy of compassion, which Wagner adopted wholeheartedly, is dismissed by Nietzsche as merely a virtue of the Décadents: Wagner, in Nietzsche's view, was one of their most prominent representatives. Like Wagner, however, Nietzsche regarded these fragments as "other": they were a gathering of precious stones, so to speak, secreted away by a master of seductive large-scale effects who is afraid of revealing a side of himself that could shatter the illusions he sets out to create:

Apart from Wagner the hypnotist and alfresco painter, there is another Wagner, who laid aside small jewels: our greatest melancholic in music, full of glances, gentleness, and words of comfort that no one has anticipated before him, a master in tones of a heavy and sleepy happiness. . . . A lexicon of Wagner's most intimate sayings, simply short things from five to sixteen measures, all of it music *nobody knows* . . . Wagner had the virtue of the Décadents: compassion.[20]

IN SEARCH OF THE SYMPHONY

Wagner was never clear about what he meant by the "symphony" or the "symphonic." At one moment he means the decline of classical forms; at another he is referring to Beethoven's perfection of the sonata form, in which he saw the seeds of the so-called unending melody. Then we read about something called "symphonic melody" *(symphonische Melodie)*,[21] a snazzy term that is supposed to define "the true purpose of music, which the poet has completely internalized in a poem that corresponds to it and can explore its finest and most intimate nuances."[22] Finding exact analytical equivalents to all this is a hopeless exercise. Wagner's philosophizing can sometimes tell us precious little about his art, although it does shed light on some influential analyses of it by those who have studied the Master's writings more eagerly than they have listened to his music.

Two crass examples, the specters of which still haunt modern analytical studies, are Alfred Lorenz's insistence that *Tristan und Isolde* has the identity of "an infinitely large symphonic movement" *(eines unermeßlich großen Symphoniesatzes)*, with a main section, a middle section, and a recapitulation, and his disciple Hans Albert Grunsky's view that part of the third act of the opera is a regular four-movement symphony with an Allegro, Adagio, Scherzo, and Finale.[23] This is obvious nonsense; nonetheless, the idea that *Tristan* is a symphony in disguise became an article of faith among Wagner's disciples and was hard to refute for a long time. Wagner was indulging in a grandiose metaphor when he told Cosima that with *Tristan* he "just felt the need to go to the brink musically," as if he had been "writing a symphony," and, a few months later, that "he had felt the urge to let go for once in expressing himself completely symphonically, and that led him to *Tristan*."[24] Overly literal interpretations by the Bayreuth faithful not only gave these words mythical significance, but they also had the paradoxical effect in less subtle minds of belittling Wagner's true role in the history of the symphony by confusing influential musical techniques and ambitions with historically vacuous generic labels. Wagner's suggestive remarks about *Tristan* in the final years of his life were not a serious attempt to recast the work; rather, they were a reflection of his preoccupation with the planning and writing of symphonies at the time. *Tristan* is not a symphony by any stretch of the imagination, but for an older Wagner, full of memories about his intense life-long need to imagine a symphony that was genuinely new and philosophically resilient, it was the nearest he had ever come to writing one.

What do Wagner's late thoughts about his plans for symphonies tell us? Do they suggest that he ultimately gave up trying to find purely musical solutions to the problem of writing symphonies after Beethoven? Are they just the remnants of a symphonic ambition that had already been absorbed into his music dramas, where processes typical of the symphony could be exploited in a medium more congenial to his musical limitations? Does the elusive evidence suggest that ultimately Wagner wanted to reaffirm or to ignore his idea about the "end" of the symphony? Or was the idea simply a piece of Hegelian hocus-pocus, philosophical sleight of hand meant to disguise the fact that Wagner thought he would never be able to create a viable work that would assure the future of the genre? Wagner's late plans for symphonies may not help to explain why *Tristan*, with the apparent authority of its composer, has been mistaken for a symphony; but they could offer at least one answer to the above questions.

I have always wondered why Wagner's famous 1879 essay *On the Application of Music to the Drama* was given that particular title.[25] The essay is full of thinly disguised sallies against the famous leitmotif guides invented by his colleague Hans von Wolzogen, as well as more forthright criticisms of the Brahms school, which Wagner accuses of serving up symphonies that are little more than chamber music writ large. The essay is really a discourse about the writing of symphonies, as distinct from music dramas. Indeed, on 11 September 1879, Cosima notes that Wagner called it an essay about the "character of symphonic music." Just as he suppressed the word "Symphony" in the manuscript of the *Siegfried Idyll*, it seems that he felt obliged to give the essay a different designation in public. The composer who for many years had been confidently announcing the demise of the symphony was now tangled in a philosophical dilemma: were he to write symphonies and justify their place in history, he would be forced to rescind his argument that the music drama had finally superceded the symphony as a historically valid form of art. It was not Wagner's lack of ability in writing instrumental music, but his own polemic about the symphony and its future, that in the end may have been responsible for his inability to compose one. The will to write symphonies remained with Wagner to his death, but no matter how much the aging composer brought his still lively intelligence to bear on the problem, he remained struck compositionally silent by a lifelong allegiance to a different point of view.

PART VI

Operatic Futures

16.   Configurations of the New

> The future was given something of a chance, but not much
> of one.
>
> CARL DAHLHAUS

SECULARIZING PROGRESS

On 16 September 1989 a national British newspaper, *The Independent*, carried a full-page advertisement placed by Technics for their latest "Hi-Fi Midi System for Music Lovers," the CDX3.[1] At the top of the page, Wagner's furrowed brow and glaring eyes, slightly askance, stared out as if insisting on, though not quite peremptorily demanding, a close reading of the text beneath. The text began as follows (comments in brackets are mine):

> To hear what he [Wagner] intended a hi-fi system has to be perfectly composed.
>
> The insane glint in Wagner's eyes may have something to do with the events that unfolded before them. Between spells in debtors' prison [untrue], he founded a revolutionary movement [untrue], married Liszt's daughter [true] and had an affair with King Ludwig II [undocumented].
>
> He was also a composer whose originality completely changed the way music was written and performed.

According to the Italian philosopher Gianni Vattimo, reading the newspaper is "the morning prayer of the truly modern man."[2] What Vattimo means is that, with the ability to construct a global image of human affairs and transmit it quickly via the media, modern man has been able to experience day by day, almost in a spirit akin to a religious duty, the sense of living in history as a moment conditioned and sustained by a unitary process of events. At first sight the Technics CDX3 advertisement looks as if it had been tailor-made for a key article of faith in this credo of modernity, the belief that history proceeds logically and rationally through a process of constant critical renewal, and toward a utopian goal of universal

210 / Operatic Futures

perfection: "events that unfolded," "revolutionary movement," "completely changed," "perfectly composed." Even the association of madness with genius—"the insane glint in Wagner's eyes"—is a notion that, although it goes back to the Greeks, has also become a topos of the modern: as Nietzsche put it in his preface to *The Case of Wagner* (1988), decadence and sickness are equated with the "labyrinth of the modern soul." For Technics apparently, as for Nietzsche, "Wagner sums up modernity."[3]

The advertisement, however, has another dimension. Technics is not simply exploiting Wagner to re-create a hoary emblem of modernity, with its grandiose notions of historical change and unshakable faith in the value of the new. The hit-and-miss "events" of Wagner's life that Technics presents actually celebrate a blithe disregard for history. (No one would seriously claim that Wagner's mountainous debts and adulterous liaisons were well within the moral boundaries set by mid-nineteenth-century society. Nonetheless, it is virtually certain that he did not go to prison, and his relations with Ludwig II, despite the literary effusions of their letters, were in reality cool and anything but sexual.) The rest of the Technics text—too long to be cited in full here—evokes personal, softened images of history that are brought into such close proximity as to be drained of meaning. The equation of genius and insanity dwindles into instant talent and momentary derangement ("you can present a choice of up to 24 bewildering channels"). The classical ideal turns out to be the ultraclean sound ("every part of the orchestra gets perfectly reproduced"), and the hankering of modernity after a utopian future and its secret affinity with the classical turns out to be little more than keeping up with the neighbors ("a host of features which are years ahead . . . The CDX3 will be a classic"). Everything, including Wagner, tends toward the one-dimensional, a flattening out of the sense of history at the level of the "now" and the simultaneous. Even progress itself is presented as little more than a routine decked out with a string of obligatory clichés ("boasts the latest 18-bit technology . . . designed on true hi-fi principles").

On one level the Technics advertisement is an example of how, to use Arnold Gehlen's famous phrase, "progress" has become "secularized."[4] Gehlen's notion of secularization presupposes a condition in which it is recognized that the premises of the Enlightenment, in particular its idealization of progress, are dead and that only their consequences live on. Doubts about progress are hardly new, even in the relatively secluded area of music history. Franz Brendel was already proclaiming in 1850 that "our age is the end of music as we know it,"[5] and not much later A. B. Marx echoed these sentiments when he asked whether music had "reached the boundary of progress—the end? Or will creative genius reveal itself in a new form?"[6] The difference is that Brendel and Marx were writing after the 1848–49 Revolution, were still within sight of the Young Hegelian banner, and were therefore willing to exhort the history of ideas and its continuation to remain steadfast, in this case with the old trick of conjuring up threatening images of its imminent demise. Gehlen, however, believes that this history has already led to its own negation. Since progress has been reduced to the perpetual act of providing further progress in a guise that is always new, it has been deprived of a final destination and removed from the pedestal of the ideal. Progress has been secularized, and thereby its very notion has been dissolved. Because metaphysics is exhausted, we have arrived, thinks Gehlen, at the condition of "post-history."[7] It is only a small step from this to the notion of the "postmodern." Without the Spengler-like doom hovering around Gehlen's writings, this notion is in brief a philosophical and—to judge by the more entertaining level of the Technics advertisement—an ostensibly cheerful coming-to-terms with the sense that history is at an end. That does not mean all and every history, but an experience of the past dominated by the Enlightenment model.

Wagner, whose output from the 1840s on stands in the shadow of the Young Hegelians and the beginnings of aesthetic modernity, has played a role in the history of the modern and the postmodern that has still to be properly assessed. Like most things about Wagner, this role is full of paradoxes and subtle shifts and countershifts. I want to touch on just two aspects of it: first, his "strong" belief in the Young Hegelian version of the power of history, which was the driving force behind his Zurich writings and the initial conception of the *Ring;* and, second, the idea that, especially after his discovery of Schopenhauer, this belief went hand in hand with a "weak"[8] modification of the notion of the new as a perpetual critical overcoming of tradition, which brought him closer to the subversive strategies of postmodern thought than he is usually thought to be.

NOT DEFINING THE POSTMODERN

This is not the place to vainly try once more to define the controversial term "postmodern", nor to trace the idea's origins or enter into yet another worldly debate about its relevance to music.[9] To offer a watertight definition or to indulge in any monumental evaluation of the notion in any case runs the risk of turning it inside out, precisely because it is supposed to denote a condition in which Enlightenment rationality and the "organic" view of unified historical progress no longer make sense. If this has been an abiding contradiction in a rapidly proliferating debate, nearly everyone at least agrees by now that the shift in sensibility we loosely describe as post-modern began with Nietzsche, the first philosopher seriously to question the increasingly frantic search for stable foundational thought in the late nineteenth century, and the only top-ranking thinker of his day to seek escape routes from the dilemma of modernity that did not simply lead back to the process of critical overcoming.[10]

Nietzsche's first polemic against the "power of history" was the second of his *Untimely Meditations,* "On the Uses and Disadvantages of History for Life" (1874), written when he was still relatively close to Wagner. One of its themes is that a surfeit of historical consciousness (nourished mainly by Hegel) had stunted the ability of the nineteenth century to create history that was truly new. Hegel ought to have said, Nietzsche wrote sardonically, that all things coming after him were actually to be thought of only as "a musical coda to the world-historical rondo or, even more properly, as superfluous." But Hegel did not say this, with the result that generations after him, soured by his example, claimed to admire the "power of history" when they were really admiring "success" and idolizing "the factual."[11] Modernity, drained of its vitality, has therefore dwindled into a meaningless relativism. Nietzsche's solution, however, is not to subject the issue to a rationalist critique that would promote reason once more as a driving force of modernity. The antidote to the historical, he suggests, is the "unhistorical" and the "supra-historical," "the art of being able to forget and to enclose ourselves within a bounded horizon" and "the powers" that can lead us toward the "eternal and stable, towards art and religion."[12] It is obvious from the context of the essay (including some heavy borrowing from Wagner's Zurich writings) that by "art" Nietzsche means above all Wagnerian art, a message that ensured, at least at first, a positive response from Bayreuth.[13]

Dispensing with an affirmative belief in the reformative power of art, Nietzsche, after his break with Wagner, went on to even more radical diagnoses of, and ways of escape from, modernity. However, one of the little-noticed aspects of the reception of "On the Uses and Disadvantages of History" is that Wagner seems to have accepted its basic argument. To Cosima he was critical of the repetitiveness of the essay and bemoaned the fact that Nietzsche did not quote actual examples from history (ironically, he sounded rather like one of the academic professors against whom its polemics were directed).[14] But to Nietzsche himself, Wagner wrote a genuinely enthusiastic letter:

Eight days ago we received your latest publication from the bookseller, to which we devoted three evenings of thoughtful reading. . . . As I have to be brief, there is only one thing I would like to say to you, and that is that I feel very proud no longer to have to say anything, and to be able to leave all the rest to you. All the "rest"? That is certainly something we should be worried about! But it's always comforting to know that the matter is being dealt with in the right way.[15]

Wagner's concern about "all the rest" *(Alles Weitere)*, by which he meant both the near and the distant future and its dwindling prospects, is strikingly different from his position in the Zurich writings. There the task of the "artist of the future" had been to restore the vanished harmony of art and community (supposedly) known to the Greeks by moving "modern" consciousness away from its center of interest in money and success and restoring to it a long-lost sense of unity and well-being. By 1874 the pathos of the future and the simultaneous celebration of fundamental origins were being abandoned. In contrast to the Hellenistic optimism of the Zurich writings, the grave doubt about the utopian content of art can be attributed conveniently to Wagner's famous so-called pessimistic mode à la Schopenhauer. It is more illuminating, however, to see it specifically as part of a redefinition of, and significant shift in, his perception of modernity and the value of the new, to which the issue of modernity was inevitably linked.

Four years after receiving Nietzsche's essay, Wagner wrote for the *Bayreuther Blätter* a short and little-known article entitled "Modern" (1878). Apart from its loathsome anti-Semitic bias, the piece is not insignificant in the present context because in it Wagner offers a definition of modernity that not only describes the contemporary world as narrowed and enfeebled by positivism (as his Zurich writings and Nietzsche's essay nearly always tend to do), but also clearly defines a dynamic concept of modernity that has its origin in Hegelian philosophy. Habermas has trenchantly described the Hegelian notion of the "modern" as one that "can and will no longer borrow the criteria by which it takes its orientation from the models supplied by another epoch; *it has to create its normativity out of itself*" (Habermas's emphasis).[16] Wagner's definition, though decidedly more skeptical, is not much different:

To begin with there is "the modern world." Where this does not simply mean the world of today, the time in which we live—the "now-time" *[Jetztzeit]*, as it is so euphoniously styled in modern German—it means, in the heads of our latest purveyors of culture, a world such as never existed before: a "modern" world, unknown to the world in any previous epoch: an entirely new world, in fact, that has nothing at all to do with the worlds preceding it, and therefore develops as it wants according to values that are completely its own.[17]

Wagner's understandable distaste for the ugly compound *Jetztzeit* and his deprecating reference to the "latest purveyors of culture" *(die neuesten Kulturbringer)* clearly show that he is rejecting the "modern" both in the descriptive sense of "modern times," with its connotations of materialism and alienation, and in the philosophical sense of a critical overcoming that feels compelled to set a new agenda vis-à-vis the orthodoxy of a past epoch that is rapidly growing old. Moreover, he is also aware, even if he expresses the complexity of the problem with a negative gesture (as he nearly always did in his late writings), that the issue of modernity has little to do with the age-old opposition between ancient and modern. "To explain what 'modern' really means is not as easy as the Moderns imagine," he writes. "We deem it useless here to trace the history of the concept 'modern,' a term originally allotted to the visual arts in Italy to distinguish them from the antique."[18] Such histories have since been attempted, notably by Gumbrecht and Jauß;[19] they not only trace the idea of being "modern" back even further, but also confirm one of Wagner's main points, namely that the notion of the "modern" as a new world, which does not refresh, but negates, all previous worlds, was a relatively recent development beginning in the realm of the fine arts not much earlier than the middle of the nineteenth century.

The use of "modern" and "modernity" as nouns to mark an aesthetic rupture with the past is usually traced to Baudelaire's famous essay on Constantin Guys, "Le peintre de la vie moderne" (1859), where they are part of an elusive and paradoxical notion of *modernité* that would take too long to unravel here. Wagner neither mentions Baudelaire nor embraces the ambiguities of the latter's definition of modernity. He does suggest, however, that the term "modern" in the sense of something radically new in the history of art, something that consciously did not relate to, or develop out of, the achievements of a past epoch, began to develop as an "abnormal growth" *(Mißwachs)* on the field of German literature as early as the 1830s and 1840s with the rise of the Young German Movement. "I myself," he writes sardonically, "beheld the early flowering of the plant."[20] What he does not say is that starting in 1835, with his friend (and later enemy) Heinrich Laube, he was not just a witness to the growth of the plant, but he was very much a part of it. Moreover, he also omits to mention that his rebellion against "orthodoxy" on an aesthetic level at the side of the Young Germans later combined with a concept of the "modern" influenced by the Young Hegelians in the most important of his Zurich writings, *Opera and Drama*—a treatise, incidentally, that Baudelaire claimed to have read in English translation.[21] It is almost as if Wagner violently rejected the "modern" because he felt entrapped by his own role in helping to create it. Certainly the more one reads beneath the murky polemics of his late writings, not to mention the statements frequently recorded in Cosima's diaries about the symphonies he wanted to write after *Parsifal* (discussed in the previous chapter), the more one senses the true scale of his intellectual tussle with his own past philosophizing. It was, after all, a much younger Wagner, enraptured in his late thirties by Young Hegelian ideas, who had been one of the most vociferous advocates of the radically new, not only in establishing the influential (but already, by the late 1870s, eccentric-looking) idea that with the Ninth Symphony Beethoven had written the "last" symphony, but also in proclaiming very publicly that opera was dead, and with it the old world it represented.

GOODIES AND BADDIES

I agree with Richard Rorty that one of Habermas's basic propositions is that the notion of modernity the Young Hegelians took from Hegel and adapted remains fundamental in determining our own sense of the modern.[22] Those who espouse the postmodern cause, Habermas insists, are really just another group of moderns entangled with Hegel's original concept.[23] In other words the "posties" are still "contemporaries" of the Young Hegelians, who distanced themselves from Hegel and philosophy in general with the strategy, first perfected by Hegel, of simply showing how and why their predecessors were out of date. It was, and still is, Habermas seems to be saying, a high-stakes game of philosophical roulette and, as far as the Young Hegelians were concerned, one directed against Hegel, the master croupier himself. Expressing Habermas's notion in a more laconic way, Rorty calls it a game with two rules. Rule number one: you make a convincing case that you are more modern than your predecessors because you are more acutely aware of the pattern of the past and the needs of the present, and therefore you have to set your own agenda. Rule number two: you ferret out a basic definition of everything that has so far been called philosophy, point to its central flaw, and reject it. Then you simply announce the end of philosophy.

Wagner states in his autobiography that in 1849 he was drawn to Ludwig Feuerbach, a leading Young Hegelian, mainly because he had heard him described as the sole adequate philosopher of the modern age. The most attractive aspect of Feuerbach's ideas, Wagner writes, was his "conclusion, which had led him to abandon his original master, Hegel: namely, that the best philosophy is to have no philosophy at all."[24] This does not mean that Wagner (or Feuerbach) rejected Hegel's world-historical view of the "modern." On the contrary, Wagner adopted it, but he moved it from the abstract into the physical realm—the "purely human," as he liked to call it—as if Hegel's "absolute" way of thinking had merely separated the two. Sticking to the rules of the game, Wagner replaced Hegel's abstract categories with ones that were specifically critical and technical, while at the same time remaining on Hegel's "higher" level of discourse. His naming of names and analytical blueprints—in particular, the passages on *Stabreim* and the "poetic-musical period," ostensibly new ways of constructing text and music for the "Artwork of the Future"[25]—gave the impression that he was a practical artist with his feet on the ground. And his devastating critique of other composers and his didactic emphasis on method were also the counters, so to speak, in the game of critical overcoming that was still being played, in true Hegelian fashion, in the name of the World Spirit.

As was usual in Wagner's intellectual scenarios, there is no danger in his Zurich writings of confusing the goodies with the baddies. Virtue triumphs over evil in the end even if it has to make its own historical "mistakes." Application of rule number one: the crisis of "absolute" music, the increasing isolation and inadequacy of classical forms to express the needs of the modern age, came to a head with Beethoven's Ninth Symphony. The crisis has made me, Wagner, aware of the direction that postrevolutionary art must take. Application of rule number two: the genre of the symphony is the embodiment of the age of "absolute" thought. Beethoven's "error" was that he tried to find a means of expression that reached beyond bourgeois and naïve Christian consciousness within the framework of a purely instrumental genre that had fulfilled its historical task. Thus Beethoven's imitators, and even Beethoven himself, did not realize what I, Wagner, now feel called upon to announce: the fact that after Beethoven's Ninth Symphony, "the last symphony has already been written."[26]

Still at the beck and call of the World Spirit, Wagner was then obliged to place his hero in full-bodied dialectical relationship with his villains. In other words, before he could properly announce the "end" of the symphony and its overcoming in the symphonic Drama of the Future, he had to abide by the rules and provide Beethoven's magnificent but misguided effort to escape the confines of "absolute" music with an antithesis in the form of Rossini's and Meyerbeer's malevolent deeds in the realm of opera—not, however, before making a grandiose comparison with the ancients.

According to rule number one, Greek antiquity represents the long-lost ideal of a close relationship between art and state that has been rent asunder by the power interests of industry, state, and church. The deep divisions in our Alexandrine culture have made me, Wagner, aware of the need for an antidote that can restore this lost sense of unity. My new agenda is this: not one art alone, but only all the arts in a truly humanistic relation to one another, can help mankind reject history and lead it back to the heart of nature. The goal of humanity is thus that pristine, unalienated state it once knew at some distant point in its past.[27] The future of man is therefore a return to his fundamental origin.

It was then a relatively simple matter to dismiss opera according to rule number two. Opera is a genre in which different arts only appear to be unified. In reality they vie with one another for domination—absolute music usually playing the dominating role—and as such are a true reflection of the ruling egotistical and capitalistic thinking of the age. Rossini sacrificed drama for the sake of melody. Meyerbeer demoted his librettist, Scribe, to the role of a "poetic private secretary."[28] A Meyerbeer opera is nothing but an "effect without cause"[29] that merely allows a suitably costumed tenor, say, to sing as beautifully as possible while "behaving a little bit like a communist so that at the same time people will at least have something titillating to think about."[30] Thus opera has a central flaw: "the means of expression (the music) has been made the purpose, and the purpose (the drama) has been made the means."[31] Music is capable of expressing sublime truths if it can interact with the other arts, but opera composers, who insist on keeping music locked in the closet of absolute beauty, prevent it from doing this. Opera is impotent because it promotes an egotistical imbalance of, and a contractual relationship between, the arts. This ensures that the arts remain isolated from one another, incapable of fertilizing music to create a dramatic form that would place music among the gods. Opera can thus be neither truly dramatic nor socially critical, let alone an adequate vehicle for the utopian drama of the future that could show humanity its full potential and the way back to its primal, unalienated state. I, Wagner, therefore announce the end of opera.

PARRICIDAL IMAGES

One of the first things Wagner did after finishing his Zurich writings was draft the libretto of *Siegfried*. He seriously thought of setting it to music there and then, before he made the decision to expand the *Ring* further still by prefacing *Siegfried* with *Die Walküre* and *Das Rheingold*. Various sketches for nature motifs, such as "Fafner" and the "Woodbird," written down in 1851, as well as various remarks in Wagner's correspondence, have survived to prove the point.[32] *Der junge Siegfried* (as it was then called) was the first work he had in mind to try out his system of leitmotifs, a system he promised in *Opera and Drama* would guarantee the evolution of perpetually new forms bound together by symphonic "unity" and hence provide a powerful analogy to his ideal of an undivided community capable of constant renewal. He also conceived the dynamic of the work's overall form as an ingenious metaphor for his utopian vision of the future.

Siegfried is rightly regarded by many Wagner critics as his most modern and advanced score. Indeed, the "strange pathos of purity" that Peter Bürger detected in the modernist project of the 1950s and 1960s[33] is already part of this work written a hundred years earlier. No choruses; starkly ritualistic forms (the riddles scene in act 1, for instance); brittle, facetlike orchestration that can disintegrate and recombine like the fragments of Siegfried's sword;[34] the simple fact that Wagner has pruned the action down to very few characters: these are all features of *Siegfried* that can make it seem almost forbiddingly rigorous, a "wonderfully austere primeval image of youth,"[35] as Nietzsche aptly called it.

But after Wagner completed two acts, the composition of *Siegfried* ground to a halt for twelve years, during which time *Tristan und Isolde* and *Die Meistersinger von Nürnberg* came into being instead. Exactly why Wagner stopped Siegfried in his tracks on his way to the "new age" is still not entirely clear. His transformation of Schopenhauer's misanthropic quietism into a far from inactive triumph of the will clearly made a difference. Yet, as Rainer Franke has pointed out, it hardly amounted to a rejection of Feuerbach.[36] On the contrary, Wagner's highly idiosyncratic espousal of Schopenhauer's nihilism had the odd effect of actually reinforcing his belief in the necessity of social change and radical renewal, while at the same time shrinking his faith in the future, and metaphysics and humanism in general. The paradox is one reason for the apparently contradictory symbols and ideas that vie for attention in his late works and writings, which as a result frequently resemble the opaque profusion of a baroque allegory.

The severe image of critical overcoming in the last act of *Siegfried* (the bondage to the past, represented by the Wanderer's spear, that is smashed by the sword of the hero of the future) may have persuaded Wagner that he had overstated the case against history. Whatever his reasons for abandoning the work in 1857 to write *Tristan*, there can be no doubt that it was at this time that he began seriously to question the high premium he had placed in his Zurich writings on a notion of the "new" that, with its insistence on a complete break with the past, would open the way to an independence from traditional formal categories, and hence to "the great, all-embracing artwork of the future" capable of permanent, "endless" renewal.[37] Wagner himself seems to have deliberately taken the notion to an extreme in *Tristan*, almost in order to undermine it. Only a year after finishing the music, he wrote to Mathilde Wesendonck, "in a certain, very deep sense that only the World Spirit *[Weltgeist]* can understand, all I can do now is to repeat myself with new works; I am unable to reveal any more essential truths."[38] It is not out of the question that with this intoning of a quasi-Hegelian *Weltgeist* Wagner was trying to touch on a serious philosophical issue about the ever-tightening circle of endless overcoming in store for artists who, in the Young Hegelian sense, still placed their faith in the radical notion of permanent innovation at all costs. Nor is this extraordinary statement an isolated example. Eighteen years later, on 26 March 1879, Cosima Wagner wrote in her diary, "In fact, he says he has produced nothing new since *Tristan*, whereupon I observe that even from a technical point of view, *Die Meistersinger*, *Siegfried*, and *Götterdämmerung* contain new ideas." At first sight Cosima's protest seems reasonable, but it misses Wagner's implicit philosophical point about the specific value he had attached to the new in *Tristan*, not to mention the searching scrutiny to which he had exposed it in that work.

In the third act of *Tristan*, as in *Siegfried*, the hero is poised provocatively between the old and the new. The difference is that whereas Siegfried is himself a kind of tabula rasa, a new beginning, Tristan is compelled to confront his own history before he can arrive at a point that he senses is a new departure. In a way similar to each act of *Siegfried* (see chapter 6), the so-called "delirium scene" in the third act of *Tristan* rises in ever-widening arcs from the leaden F minor of the old song, *die alte Weise*,[39] to the shepherd's new, jubilant melody in C major announcing the arrival of Isolde. Joseph Kerman has rightly pointed out that the scene is a double cycle, each part following the following plan: "recollection—curse—relapse—anticipation."[40] One thing missing from the scheme, however, is Tristan's impulsive will to forget—*ew'ges Urvergessen* (eternal oblivion), he sings longingly at one point—or rather (and this shows the philosophical complexity of Wagner's idea) the paradox that as Tristan tries to forget the old, he is at the same time compelled to remember it, to delve into his fundamental origins as well as his recent and traumatic history. In other words, the more Tristan tries to obliterate the past, the more it entwines him, until, forced into reinventing it, he turns it against himself. His despairing self-accusation at the climax of the scene—that it was he who brewed the love potion—is, to put it prosaically, quite simply a rewriting of history in the name of a recovery from it, a desperate attempt at recovery that appears to be only momentary, and ends in death.

It is hard to imagine that Nietzsche, who accurately described *Tristan* as an *opus metaphysicum*, did not have the delirium scene in mind when he wrote, in "On the Uses and Disadvantages of History":

> For since we are the outcome of earlier generations, we are also the outcome of their aberrations, passions and errors, and indeed of their crimes; it is not possible wholly to free oneself of this chain. If we condemn these aberrations and regard ourselves as free of them, this does not alter the fact that we originate in them. The best we can do is to confront our inherited and hereditary nature with our knowledge of it, and through a new, stern discipline combat our inborn heritage and implant in ourselves a new habit, a new instinct, a second nature, so that our first nature withers away. It is an attempt to give oneself, as it were *a posteriori*, a past in which one would like to originate:—always a dangerous attempt because it is so hard to know the limit to denial of the past and because second natures are usually weaker than first.[41]

A number of problems touched on in this remarkable passage also preoccupied Wagner, including one that may not be immediately obvious: the search for boundaries in rejecting the past. Kerman is right when he says of *Tristan* that the shepherd's "new" melody in C is of "miserable quality."[42] In a sense its musical weakness is deliberate: Wagner allows Tristan to overcome the quasi-natural inflections of *die alte Weise* by forcing him to invent a past in which he would like to originate (as opposed to the one in which he actually did originate) and by superimposing over his "first nature," represented by the old melody, the tortured, chromatic sounds that for Adorno were on the threshold of the Second Viennese School and the New Music.[43] According to Adorno, this is where, in the phrases following Tristan's words *"der furchtbare Trank"* (the potion so dread), Wagner's music at last unmasks its own illusions and becomes truly modern in the sense that it directly confronts the historical necessity of resisting and overcoming the crisis of humanism. But the outcome of Tristan's ruthless blindness about the past (a blindness already suggested metaphorically by the plot of *Siegfried*) is not the near atonality after *"der furchtbare Trank,"* but the thinly triumphant melody in C presaging the arrival of Isolde. At this point in the drama, Tristan's wish to extricate himself from the errors of the past has led, in Nietzsche's words, to the "dangerous attempt" of combating his real heritage and planting in himself "a new instinct, a second nature," which turns out to be more frail than the one it replaces.

Paul de Man has already pointed out the parricidal imagery in Nietzsche's text, as the weaker son condemns and kills the stronger father.[44] The same imagery is at the core of act 3 of *Siegfried*. The sharp blade of the fated hero's sword brutally cuts through the Wanderer's spear and clears the hero's path to Brünnhilde and a triumphant concluding duet. The third act of *Tristan* is almost certainly intended as a more complex version of the same process, presented this time as a slow and painful convalescence that can only lead to the new in a "weak" sense as something enfeebled and transient.[45] This is not to deny that the introduction of the female voice at the end of the work creates a powerful sense of closure. Isolde's so-called *Liebestod* is often regarded as a sexual image of orgasmic ecstasy that overcomes, in a "strong" sense, the metaphysical crisis at the center of the work. But it is actually a different kind of resolution, one that moves away from an emphatic triumph over the "errors" of the past toward a resignation to, and at the same time a recovery from, them. The sense is not so much one of permanent renewal after the critical over-coming of the "end," the main purpose of Wagner's philosophical agenda in *Opera and Drama*, but one of an acceptance of crisis and of an attempt to heal the wounds it has opened.

I have deliberately nudged this reading close to the notion of "weak" over-coming that Vattimo places at the center of the debate about the end of modernity.[46] I am not suggesting, however, that *Tristan* is therefore a post-modern work pure and simple, or that Wagner in his mid-forties simply began to turn into a postmodernist *avant la lettre*. Even the rejection of "post-modern" as an epochal term would leave us with the difficulty that *Tristan*, like the famous hybrid chord at its start, faces in several directions at once. If, as Adorno insists, the black, jagged music of *"der furchtbare Trank"* unveils the demise of humanism in a truly modernist spirit, Isolde's *Liebestod* can equally be said to react against the Western tradition of metaphysics alto-gether, with a call, in Vattimo's provocative words, "for humanity to heal it-self of humanism."[47] The compromise also had consequences, including the decision in 1860 to revise, but not entirely to retract, the original, austerely

triumphant ending of the overture to *Der fliegende Holländer* and the parallel conclusion of the opera by introducing the gently soothing "feminine"
theme from Senta's Ballad over a shimmering plagal cadence in the last few
bars instead of the abrupt conclusion of the original version from the early
1840s. Another outcome of *Tristan,* and its third act in particular, was Wagner's last work, *Parsifal.* The open, unhealable wound of Amfortas—a wound
resulting from a past transgression—is miraculously closed by the pure fool
Parsifal, who gains access to divine knowledge precisely because he learns to
understand, and to accept, Amfortas's condition.[48] At issue is not the "right"
classification of *Tristan* or *Parsifal* (or even *Holländer*) as modern or post-
modern, but Wagner's growing critical attitude to the new in terms of its ambition to overcome and "correct" the crisis of European humanism. Doubts
about the survival of the new as a utopian ideal are readily attributable to
Nietzsche, whose willingness to scrutinize modernity and the conditions of its
possibility have made him such a familiar (though far from always reliable)
witness in the debate about the postmodern.[49] But rarely, if at all, has an even
remotely comparable consciousness been accredited to Wagner.

FAILING TO BREAK WITH THE PAST

The more one looks at Wagner's reaction to his own obsession with the new,
the more one senses the need for a less sanctimonious view of the "modern," including its self-destructive instinct, in order to understand some of
the paradoxes of his influence and reception, not to mention some surprising lapses on the part of otherwise powerful critics to certain problematic aspects of his works. Adorno once summed up his mixed feelings about Wagner by referring to the impossibility of separating "progress and reaction"
in his music "like sheep and goats."[50] In reality it was a serious failure of
critical nerve, apparent in Adorno's disappointing response to the ending of
the *Ring* discussed in chapter 8. The sense of triumph in the orchestral fire-
works display that concludes the work is obviously one of crisis magnificently overcome. Yet Wagner also made the bold decision to turn the very
last bars into a "weak" ending that, in a similar way to Isolde's *Liebestod,*
conveys the rather different, if enigmatic, sense of healing and repose, of
convalescence after a long illness accompanied at the same time by strong
hints of melancholy and resignation. Accusing Wagner of not providing
something "qualitatively different" just at the moment when, with the fall
of Valhalla, it would have been most needed,[51] Adorno could not take on
board the possibility that Wagner had had good reason to adjust the

unequivocal celebration of the advent of a new order contained in the ending written in the early 1850s under the influence of the Young Hegelians. It was also anathema to Adorno and his systematic way of thinking that Wagner had arrived at the highly original solution of allowing both part of the earlier concept and its modification, with its faintly postmodern air of kitsch and loosely piled musical imagery, to stand side by side in the final work like distracted icons.

Not only the remainder of the *Ring*, which for Wagner became a work significantly different in tone after the experience of writing *Tristan*, but also in a more obvious sense the fake Lutheran chorales and amusing parodies of baroque musical figures in *Die Meistersinger*, are Wagner's nearly nihilistic and at the same time ironic reaction to the heroic revolutionary phase of the 1850s. When Sachs muses in the second act that Walther's first (unsuccessful) song "sounded so old, and yet so new" *(Es klang so alt, und war doch so neu)* and asserts in the third act that Walther's new (successful) song "retains strength to live" *(Kraft behalte zum Leben),* he is deliberately reversing the categories of *Tristan*. The belief in the jettisoning of history and the feeling of transience and sickness turn into a judicious reabsorption of the old, a seemingly resolute faith in tradition and health. One set of values, however, is not merely exchanged for another. The import of *Tristan* is still palpable, but placed in the background in such a way that its substitution comes to serve as an ironic contrast, with the result that the new values appear, as it were, in quotation marks. While appearing to celebrate a traditional concept of the new in *Die Meistersinger* (the new, that is, as a variation of the old within the confined limits of genre), Wagner is actually setting its opposite into sharp relief, thereby placing his utopian faith in the new as radical renewal and negation of the past in an even more complex and melancholy light than he had done in *Tristan*.

Nonetheless, the reduction of history to a decorative status in *Die Meistersinger,* and even more so in the music of *Parsifal,* has obscured a real connection between the new music of the post-1945 era and Wagner's radical views of musical material almost a hundred years earlier. This is particularly true of Wagner's novel approach to musical form and his technique of refiltering traditional musical gestures—the allusions to the French *opéra comique* in the opening scene of *Das Rheingold,* for instance—so that they are heard critically, if problematically, in their new context.[52] Indeed, the parallels are striking: the critical negation of traditional language, the correction of historical "mistakes," the limitless transformation of musical material to create endlessly new forms[53]—these three pillars of modernist musical wisdom alone are already part of Wagner's credo in the early

1850s. Even Schoenberg, who was not slow to admit the influence of Wagner on his early tonal music, preferred to chide *Tristan* for its "inferior method of construction"[54] rather than acknowledge the quality of permanent newness in the music, its open-ended syntactical logic, and its endless musical proliferation. *Herzgewächse*, for instance, a nontonal work written in 1911, is clearly indebted to the radically modern aspect of *Tristan:* not only does the vegetal imagery of Maeterlinck's poem *Feuillages du coeur* resemble Mathilde Wesendonck's *Im Treibhaus*, which Wagner described as a "study" for *Tristan* after he had he set it to music; but each strand of musical material also grows forward without insisting on closure and remains, so to speak, ecstatically deaf to the past.

That newness is an aesthetic factor intimately bound up with the earliest of Schoenberg's atonal works has been pointed out by Dahlhaus, who claimed that even "half a century later it can be felt in almost undiminished form."[55] But the transient sense of incipient beginning, of "for the first time," is inextricably linked as an immediate aesthetic quality to the *Ring* and *Tristan* as well, both of which were conceived more than fifty years earlier. Although the compound meter and drone bass in the famous opening of *Das Rheingold* are familiar from the tradition of the pastorale, they are distended and applied in a way that creates the illusion that the music is fundamentally new, with no tradition at all behind it. Wagner privileged in the first bars of *Tristan* a harmonic progression that had been used previously only as a passing expressive detail in works by (among others) Mozart and Spohr.[56] By catapulting it into a prominent position at the start of the work and by dwelling on it at greater length, Wagner gave what was in the hands of others merely a transitory chromatic sequence a paradoxical aura of "newness" and permanence that has been cited—and pilloried—as an emblem of the first stirrings of musical modernity ever since.

The first bars of the *Ring* and *Tristan* are ingenious acoustical metaphors of a new beginning. By deliberately turning the tables on the past, Wagner obeyed the rules of the Young Hegelian game of critical overcoming in his music just as much as he did in his Zurich writings. In the name of a radical modernity, the music is its own agent, so to speak, which perhaps explains why Baudelaire and Nietzsche could be initially bowled over merely by hearing it in the concert hall. In the long run, however, the agenda behind the music has in a sense been arguably more influential, if only because composers of opera after Wagner who wanted to keep the spirit of modernity alive were compelled by the same logic of critical overcoming to reject Wagner in turn as a relic of the past. Kurt Weill, for instance, effectively turned Wagner's thesis about a supposedly socially determined "flaw" in opera that must be "corrected" in a truly "new" approach to the genre against Wagner himself when he declared to a Viennese newspaper in 1929 that the type of music in *The Threepenny Opera* "signifies the complete destruction of the concept of music drama."[57] Brecht, of course, did much the same with his concept of epic opera, which among other things systematically reverses the categories of Wagner's "out-of-date" *Gesamtkunstwerk*. The aggressively apodictic tone and the mechanics of the overly paradoxical arguments in favor of a renewal of opera as a moral institution are uncannily familiar.

There is no need to stay in the anti-Wagnerian camp. Ernest Chausson lamented with well-rehearsed self-mockery that his opera *Le roi Arthus* was "Wagnerian in subject and Wagnerian in music."[58] He carefully omitted saying that he went out of his way not so much to imitate the plot of *Tristan* as to turn it inside out. The adulterous lovers Lancelot and Guinevere, instead of celebrating their relationship, feel guilt and remorse, and exaltation of duty, beauty, and moral grandeur in the opera are substituted for eroticism and death. Moreover, most of the music sounds decidedly unlike Wagner's.

Richard Strauss was also a virtuoso inventor of anti-Wagnerian agendas when he wanted to be, while at the same time presenting his operas suavely with impeccable Wagnerian credentials. He called *Salome* a "drama" or "musical drama" (the printed scores are inconsistent on this point), yet the work is a ready-made play by one author set to music by another—an idea completely at odds with *Opera and Drama*, which stipulates unequivocally that only the composer of the Drama of the Future can also write its libretto. Furthermore, the leitmotifs and harmonic vocabulary of *Salome* resemble Wagner's only superficially.[59] Finally, its fatal conclusion is so obviously alien to Wagner's affirmative religion of redemption that the peremptory killing of the female protagonist to the sound of clattering brass must have surely been consciously intended as a negative image of the famous closing soliloquies of Isolde and Brünnhilde in *Tristan* and the *Ring*.

Strauss has been heavily criticized for betraying the modernist cause after *Salome* and *Elektra* with his retreat into the cozier world of *Der Rosenkavalier*. And it is not a coincidence that the plot of the latter opera should resemble *Die Meistersinger*, with the young and old vying for the same young lover, while the philistine (Beckmesser/Baron Ochs) sets it all into comic relief. In any case, retrenchment from the radically new, which boasts (or more discreetly disguises) a sharp break with the past, is a familiar recurring motif in twentieth-century music. In the 1920s and 1930s Schoenberg corseted his music in old forms. Stravinsky carried on a love affair with neoclassicism, and Weill headed for Broadway. For Adorno (who did not spare Schoenberg in this respect), this was tantamount to flinching in the face of the World Spirit and permanently averting one's eyes from the forces of reaction. The logic of critical overcoming and radical innovation, however, which is based on the premise that the pursuit of the new can only achieve its aim through rupture and discontinuity, is a burden the moment it embraces the possibility of failing to break with the past. The historical pattern, which Adorno bemoaned as the decline of the new, was rooted in this dilemma long before it became a major aesthetic and philosophical issue in the so-called age of the postmodern. It was also a pattern anticipated by Wagner, who broke off work on the *Ring* to create in *Tristan* another powerfully immediate image of the radically new, but this time one already haunted by the specter of its own demise.

17.   Wagner and Beyond

MYTHS AND REALITIES

Wagner was not the only one to change the course of opera's history in the nineteenth century and into the twentieth. And, indeed, only his most fanatic admirers have ever thought otherwise. It is hard, nevertheless not to think of him as someone who left an indelible stamp on twentieth-century opera. Every figure of importance is said to have reacted to him, and rarely indifferently. The possibility exists that this is just another part of the Wagnerian myth that has, in spite of formidable opposition, circled like a vulture over Western music since the end of high romanticism. The great conductor Hans von Bülow insisted with his usual caustic wit that Richard Strauss should be called Richard III in the dynasty of German music, since a Richard II after Wagner was inconceivable.[1] Auden ventured to suggest that Wagner had no real successors at all, calling him "a giant without issue."[2] Not everyone needed to take an interest in him after all, while some of those who did paid him the briefest of respects and quickly went their own way. Igor Stravinsky tells a nice story of how in 1912 Diaghilev persuaded him that on short notice they should go together to Bayreuth to see *Parsifal*, even though it meant interrupting work on *Le sacre du printemps*.[3] With dismay Stravinsky noted the mausoleum-like interior of the festival theater, deplored the cultlike performance, lambasted the Wagner faithful for putting up with it, and then simply fled. He did admire "the web-like blending of the orchestra from under the stage," which meant that *Parsifal* might have been a headache, but at least it was "a headache with aspirin."[4]

But the driest of statistics can still hint at the scale of Wagner's presence in the twentieth century, including some of its contradictions. The well-known distaste for him among the modernists of the Weimar Republic shrinks not a little in significance when set against the cold facts of operatic life at the time. Performances of Wagner's operas in German-speaking theaters in 1926–27 amounted to 13.9 percent of the total operas performed, easily beating Verdi in second place (11.3 percent), Puccini in third (7.8 percent), and Mozart in fourth (6.6 percent). In contrast, the number of performances of *all* new operas amounted to a mere 4.5 percent.[5] In the 1920s and 1930s Wagner was excoriated by progressive thinkers and linked musically by scurrilously minded theater composers to perilous subjects. When Paul Hindemith cited King Marke's music from *Tristan und Isolde* in the castration scene in his one-act opera *Das Nush-Nuschi* (1921), his morally hidebound audience (predictably) prompted a scandal. And among other memorable Wagner-deflating moments is the line "cash makes you randy" in Brecht's and Hanns Eisler's *Die Rundköpfe und die Spitzköpfe* (composed in 1934–36), a line sung by a bawdy procuress to the opening of *Tristan* with obvious relish. Avant-garde antics like these, however, only served to enhance the popularity of Wagner's works, which continued to dominate the operatic stage with ease.

Except for the unwary, the precise nature of Wagner's influence will probably always be elusive. Part of the problem is Wagner himself, or rather the way circumstances led him to present his work to the world. The simple fact is that the daring project about opera and drama he launched in literary form in Swiss exile soon after the Dresden Uprising of 1849 unleashed a war of words on an international level that, as the reaction of the influential Belgian critic François-Joseph Fétis shows, set the tone of the debate about his fight for the soul of opera before a note of the major works on which his reputation now rests had been composed, let alone heard. (Fétis attempted to disavow Wagner's writings on the future of opera and drama in a seven-installment philippic in the Paris periodical press in 1852, followed by another three polemical articles a year later, despite the fact that he still knew practically nothing of Wagner's music except the overture to *Tannhäuser*.)[6] Indeed, by the end of the 1850s the battle and its terms of engagement—"Total Work of Art" *(Gesamtkunstwerk)*, "Music of the Future" *(Zukunftsmusik)*, and "Unending Melody" *(unendliche Melodie)* are just a few of the slogans Wagner bandied about—were already notorious among cognoscenti and to some extent the public at large, even though there had been virtually no exposure to the music to which they actually related. In its edition of 20 November 1858, the satirical London weekly *Punch*—to cite just one example—referred disparagingly to Wagner and "other crotchet-mongers of the *Music of the Future.*" How that squared with the pieces by Wagner best known in London at the time, the

Tannhäuser Overture and the Bridal Chorus from *Lohengrin*, both of which were extremely popular precisely because they looked back to Mendelssohn rather than to a brave new operatic world in the future, is anyone's guess.

If the controversy about Wagner began to rage in Europe while *Der Ring des Nibelungen* (composed in 1848–74) and *Tristan und Isolde* (composed in 1856–59) were still incomplete and unperformed, it is hardly surprising that similar splits between theory and practice in the debate about his influence exist to this day. Certainly it was unhelpful that theory and practice initially appeared largely in reverse order. When Wagner's ideas about opera were discussed with such harsh polemics in the early 1850s, the chances were strong even then that certain slogans would stick no matter what the reality of the works to which they were related turned out to be. These same slogans, plus a few ingrained habits arising from them such as the Great Leitmotif Hunt or the chase for the proverbial *Gesamtkunstwerk*, in which all the arts are supposed to find themselves miraculously on an equal footing, inevitably spilled over with disconcerting regularity into accounts of operas by other composers where they were used—and often still are—like Rorschach tests to diagnose "Wagnerian" tendencies.

In fact, not a single stage work by Wagner uses so-called leitmotifs in the same way as the next. The point is obvious that composers after him often used recurring motifs in a manner derived from other, usually non-German, sources, or from the relatively primitive use of motifs in Wagner's early operas while also alluding—confusingly, for some historians—to his later music dramas in terms of harmony and melody.[7] It seems pointless, therefore, to take the existence of motifs as a hard-and-fast rule for detecting his influence without first defining more closely the different ways he used such a technique himself. Nor is all the talk about a supposed synthesis of the arts in most cases much more than shallow high-mindedness. The claim that Wagner wanted to put his music on the same level as the other arts is to confuse an argument about particularism (he took the fairly standard Hegelian Left line that the separation of the arts reflected the deleterious fragmentation of modern industrial society and the resulting alienation of the individual) with a bland notion of equality. Admittedly, a misunderstanding of the issue in his so-called Zurich writings (1849–51) has arisen in part because of Wagner's love affair at the time with Hegelian Left dialectics, which to the uninitiated can appear mainly inscrutable. He basically constructs a quasi-Hegelian argument for music, which involves both its subservience to the other arts and, precisely because of that subservience, its ultimate redemptive power. Thus we read in the essay "The

Artwork of the Future" of "the power [of music] to deny itself in order to hold out its redeeming hand to its sister arts" and, in "Judaism in Music" (which, despite its revolting racism is in Wagner's terms actually a seminal essay about music), that "music can articulate the most sublime of truths through renewed interaction with the other arts."[8] In other words, well before he read Schopenhauer, who famously placed music at the center of his philosophical ideas, Wagner always made it clear that music is the crown jewel of the arts. He refers not to the classical music of old, to be sure, but to a different kind of music that needed the other arts more than it had ever needed them before. It must interact with them, derive its power from them, let them act as catalysts in allowing it to grow up, to come of age.

Despite all the impressive talk of *Wagnérisme*—fundamentally a literary concept—or "the birth of film out of the spirit of [Wagner's] music,"[9] there is no getting away from music as the *fons et origo* of the entire Wagnerian project. Given the huge cultural responsibility Wagner wanted music to bear, this by no means excludes politics, and it is true even when the emphasis is placed on words, despite serious misapprehensions about this issue in particular. There is some truth to the idea that the strange alliterative language Wagner first used in the opening work in the *Ring* cycle, *Das Rheingold,* which has the effect of everyday speech rather than verse, and the first successful setting of a libretto in actual prose, the tavern scene in Modest Musorgsky's *Boris Godunov* (written 1868–69, revised 1871–72), both anticipate a later fashion for the operatic "bleeding slice of life," as Tonio expresses it in the prologue of Ruggero Leoncavallo's *Pagliacci* (1892). And indeed, realistic operas with prose libretti like Charpentier's *Louise* (1900) became immensely popular in Europe around the turn of the century. But *Das Rheingold* is far from being "the musical equivalent of prose drama," a condition accounting for the "inspirational limitedness" of its music,[10] or an instance where "word and tone, each contributing to its share of the synthesis, are blended inseparably into a single unit."[11] If a work so obviously dominated by rich musical invention can be misjudged this badly, it is hardly a surprise that the fabled *Gesamtkunstwerk*, still rising to the surface of the Wagner literature and its vast oceans, has yielded scant insight into the composer's historical role.

WAGNER'S TEN COMMANDMENTS

If we abandon the Great Leitmotif Hunt and the chase for the *Gesamtkunstwerk*, what do we have left? Carl Dahlhaus has already said in an important essay on Wagner's influence that no historian in their right mind would ever claim that the composer's theory contains the only valid criteria by which to judge his successors.[12] Nor, it should be added, are the claims set out in Wagner's prose works the only means of measuring his own achievements, except perhaps by the most dogmatic of his admirers (and enemies). Nevertheless, it makes sense to look at the bold and intimidating attack he launched against "opera" and his insistence on the rise of what he liked to call "drama" over its ashes, if only to understand the enormous impact his work made on other composers, and why even the strongest of them seem to have reacted with surprising reticence, much as an attentive schoolchild might to a stern and charismatic teacher, in the presence of whom even the mere thought of a spirited riposte can feel less than wise. The scholar Edward Locksspeiser once remarked that the almost brutal finality of Wagner's idea of drama was in itself an aggressive obstacle for anyone brave enough to want to contribute meaningfully to the operatic stage after his death. And Locksspeiser rightly compared the historical stop sign that his work seemed to present with Claude Debussy's reluctance to complete certain of his most cherished projects for the stage—a reluctance he expressed in a letter to Pierre Louÿs in 1895, and which remained with him for the rest of his life.[13]

The dreamlike incompleteness of Debussy's work does indeed make a striking comparison with Wagner's goal-directed obsessiveness. Moreover, it is easy now to underestimate Wagner's powerful presence on the musical scene in Europe during the final decade of his life, let alone that of his second wife, Cosima, who after his death dominated his heirs and other keepers of the Bayreuthian flame, sometimes with brutal language reminiscent of a military campaign. In a letter to Richard Strauss dated 7 January 1890, for example, she speaks of "purging" the Rhineland and the area around the River Main and "occupying" it with her favourite Bayreuth luminaries, who, thanks to her formidable influence, held (or were about to hold) important theater posts in that part of Germany.[14] Indeed, apart from Engelbert Humperdinck's *Hänsel und Gretel* (1893)—an exception that proves the rule—the impressive number of operas listed near the start of Dahlhaus's essay that were written with obvious allegiances to Wagner—Ernest Reyer's *Sigurd* (1884), Edouard Lalo's *Le Roi d'Ys* (1888), Richard Strauss's *Guntram* (1894), Hans Pfitzner's *Der arme Heinrich* (1895), Vincent d'Indy's *L'étranger* (1903), and August Bungert's *Homerische Welt* (1896–1903), a list to which many more could be added, including Felix Weingartner's *Genesius* (1892)—owe their place in the admittedly capacious graveyard of past operatic disasters not only to inferior talent, but also to a puritanical party line emanating from Bayreuth that simply inhibited the progressively minded operatic composers of the day. Certainly it may not be a coincidence that strong works with clear links to Wagner, such as Debussy's *Pelléas et Mélisande* (1902) and Strauss's *Salome* (1905), only really began to emerge in the first decade of the twentieth century, when the influence of the Bayreuthians was already in sharp decline and the copyright restrictions imposed on Wagner's works for thirty years after his death were nearing their end.

Still, Wagner was always more than happy to explain his mission to anyone willing to listen. And against expectations he usually did so with exceptional clarity and succinctness. On 17 January 1873 in Berlin he read the libretto of *Götterdämmerung,* the fourth part of his *Ring* cycle, to an invited audience and prefaced the reading with an exposition of his entire program for the future of "drama."[15] It reads today like a manifesto—one of the clearest and shortest he ever wrote—and like all good manifestos it is pithy and shrewdly polemical. It needs to be emphasized, perhaps, that Wagner, who on this occasion was in distinguished company, including that of Prince George of Prussia and the crown prince of Württemberg, almost certainly did not intend to unfurl his project to his exalted listeners like holy commandments thundering down from Mount Sinai. But one wonders, nevertheless, whether the ten points he made in his talk came across like that to some. A composer who believes in true drama, he said in so many words, shall:

1. write no more operas;

2. attend to the dramatic dialogue, the focus of the music;

3. not covet the lyrical in opera;

4. regard German music as victorious over all its rivals;

5. marry music and drama in a way that appeals not to abstract reflection, but to feeling;

6. allow music to reveal the most intimate motifs of the drama in all their ramifications;

7. regard the modern orchestra as the greatest achievement of the modern age;

8. allow the modern orchestra to combine the archetypal *moments* provided by music in ancient tragedy with the action of the *entire* drama (Wagner's emphasis);

9. extend the dramatic dialogue over the entire drama like a spoken play, but articulate it solely in music;

10. create a new kind of drama that appeals not to opera-lovers, but to truly educated persons concerned with the cultivation of a genuine German culture *(eine originale Kultur des deutschen Geistes)*.

THE SUPPOSED DEMISE OF OPERA

It is true, as scholars always insist, that Wagner was not the sole destroyer of the so-called number opera inherited from the seventeenth and eighteenth centuries. Greater continuity and flexibility in adapting dramatic moments into wider musical expanses without the stop-and-go character of older opera divided into recitatives, arias, choruses, and ensembles is also noticeable in the most interesting French and Italian works for the musical stage in the nineteenth century. That Wagner himself learned a thing or two from these non-German sources, in particular the operas of Scribe and Meyerbeer, is indeed one of the great unstated facts in his public pronouncements about his own project, though in private he tended to be more frank about it. It is difficult to deny, however, that the widening of tonality and thematic continuity in his mature works, and their vast tracts of music with swift changes in stylistic level and syntax, together constitute a bold adventure in harmony and large-scale structure that left an indelible mark on opera and the history of music in general.

The (now underestimated) literary impact of Wagner's manifestos against opera contributed to its supposed demise not only with polemical brevity but also with eye-crossing tedium in longer theoretical treatises that nevertheless seem to have impressed influential figures in the later part of the nineteenth century like Friedrich Nietzsche and Richard Strauss.[16] Still, his music dramas were undoubtedly the main reason for the declining status of "opera" in the nineteenth century—opera, that is, as a series of items performed exquisitely by renowned singers for the sake of sheer enjoyment and in which meaningful drama (at least according to Wagner) had only peripheral status. Adorno was not being entirely perverse when he pointed out that the revival of the number convention in Stravinsky's *The Rake's Progress* (1951)—an opera that at first sight seems about as far from Wagnerian drama as can be imagined—was only possible as ironic stylization because the damning verdict that Wagner as theorist and as artist had long since delivered on the obligatory division between arias, recitatives, and other set pieces Stravinsky sought lovingly to resuscitate still retained its validity.[17]

It is even likely that Wagner's own works would have stood little chance of survival had they not paid more than just a few respects to the opera industry they were supposed to be undermining. Beloved moments like Siegmund's Spring Song in *Die Walküre* and the famous Quintet in *Die Meistersinger* have served the popularity of his music well. Nor is it exactly a secret that the Wagner repertoire has had more than its fair share of formidable singer cults, even if they have become increasingly eccentric and isolated over the years. (The rarity of first-rate Wagner singers in the twenty-first century has practically turned them into the equivalent of the northern right whales of the western Atlantic, whose pending extinction is always woefully—and not unjustly—predicted by small groups of dedicated activists.)

The war against opera and its supposed vices was therefore never completely unsympathetic to composers who continued to believe in the object at which Wagner's intellectual aggression was directed. Giacomo Puccini, for one, was always willing to learn from *Tristan und Isolde* (1865) and *Parsifal* (1882) in particular. And exactly for this reason German critics felt compelled at once to appropriate Puccini's first substantial European triumph, *Manon Lescaut* (1893), as part of the Wagnerian legacy. A typical example of such a critic is Alfred Kühn, who wrote enthusiastically of Puccini that "no one has ever understood so well how to make such beautiful *music* out of Wagner's *musical initiatives*."[18] Given Wagner's and Puccini's almost antithetical use of music for dramatic purposes (as we shall see), the author's emphases could hardly be more misleading.

The real cause of the preemptive critical strike was that alongside Pietro Mascagni's hugely successful *Cavalleria rusticana* (1890), Puccini's opera actually posed a threat, showing modern international audiences that an entirely different kind of operatic dramaturgy was still possible. Vivid characters, believable situations, scenery without heavy mythological detail, and shameless coveting of the lyrical, fast-moving dialogue and the very roots of drama itself were brought back to real life, as it were, well beyond the reach of the internalized subjectivity of Wagner's phantasmagorias. Indeed, no one was clearer about this than Puccini himself. In an interview with a German journalist defending the right of the Wagner family to continue to restrict performances of *Parsifal* to Bayreuth (its copyright was about to run out in 1913), he said, "I am not a Wagnerian; my musical education was in the Italian school. Even though, like every other modern musician, I have been influenced by Wagner in the way I use the orchestra for illustration and in the thematic characterization of persons and situations, as a composer I have always remained, and still remain, Italian. My music is rooted in the peculiarity of my native country."[19]

Puccini was being ingenuous, perhaps, in insisting on a counterweight

to Wagner's fourth and tenth commandments, which demanded the cultivation of a genuine German culture by educated persons. An Italian school
of opera seemed to be still alive and kicking. Moreover, for some high-
minded intellectual elites, it was proving to be disconcertingly popular,
showing little sign of fatigue. But in view of the increasingly cosmopolitan
strategies of opera composers around the turn of the century (to which the
overtly nationalist stance of Wagner and Puccini had ironically contributed), Puccini's point about his supposed Italian roots is surely less significant than his fundamental difference of opinion with Wagner about the
nature of opera—a difference that on a broader level was to have palpable
consequences for the whole future of the genre.

WAGNER'S NEW DRAMA AND ITS CHALLENGERS

Like Puccini and many other composers of opera around the turn of the
century (Claude Debussy and Richard Strauss immediately spring to
mind), Wagner had all his life been interested in the spoken theater. The
fundamental question he kept asking himself was: What precisely is the
difference between a drama that relies on words and one whose raison
d'être is music? His response is embedded in his eighth commandment
(with rallying support from the second, fifth, and sixth), which advocates
a link through music between the individual moments of a drama and its
entire action. What he meant was that in musical drama it was possible to
create a logical chain of structured presence infinitely greater in depth and
power than it ever could be in a spoken play precisely because it was always
musically bonded with other moments, both future and past, inside the
same dramatic structure.

Admittedly the idea was not without its rhetorical baggage, including a
specious comparison with music in ancient Greek tragedy and Wagner's
much-trumpeted intention to revive the spirit of Aeschylean drama in a
modern guise using newly invented myths of his own based on sources from
the Middle Ages. A more accurate and insightful account of what he actually
achieved, however, comes not from Wagner, but from one of his most
imaginative interpreters. In 1895, at one of the most significant moments in
the history of Wagnerism, three hundred copies of Adolphe Appia's *La mise
en scène du drame wagnérien* were published in Paris and rapidly devoured
by small groups of symbolist poets, antirealists, producers, composers—
anyone interested in the artistic avant-garde of the day. And in this ground-
breaking document they found a definition of Wagnerian drama that comes

extremely close to its oneiric world and internally prescribed sense of time that in literature and music were already turning out to be the most durable aspects of Wagner's legacy:

> What characterizes Wagnerian drama and constitutes its high value is the power it possesses, by music, to *express* the interior drama, whereas spoken drama can merely *signify* it. As music is *Time*, it gives to the interior drama a duration that must correspond to the length of the performance itself. . . . Therefore, given the special nature of music, the interior drama cannot possibly find a satisfactory model for its development in the time-frame provided for spoken drama by life itself.[20]

The musical realists of the 1890s, taking their cue from George Bizet's *Carmen* (1875), had already thrown down the gauntlet to music's supposed exclusive right to create "interior drama" by inventing a new kind of opera in which music, and not just the spoken word, had the right to an exterior temporality—or at least an illusion of it—driven by "life itself." The idea of fast and furious events conditioning internal emotional states within a dramaturgy taking leanness and concision to a radical extreme was the prerogative of Giuseppe Verdi. But with the huge success of Wagner's example to contend with, Verdi's successors were all the more determined to put "life" to the fore with realistic action with which any audience could immediately identify, as opposed to the internal states of mind in Wagnerian drama that claimed to exist outside real time.

These starkly opposed views of operatic dramaturgy were highly influential in the twentieth century, and some of the most interesting operas of the era took a radical stance on either side. Arnold Schoenberg's one-act opera *Erwartung*, composed in 1909, is frequently cited as a daring experiment in atonality with a lineage that can clearly be traced back to some of the bolder moments in Wagner's harmony, which stretch tonality to its limits. But what is really Wagnerian about it is its almost self-consciously interior sound-world that continuously threatens to engulf its neurasthenic protagonist (a woman searching frantically for her dead lover), and its references to the language of dreams inside a dramatic space "on the border of a forest"—the opening stage direction—which is essentially without concrete social identity. True, accepting Wagner's premise unconditionally, as Hans Pfitzner did in *Palestrina* (1917), could also bring with it a sense of high-minded didacticism and belatedness. *Palestrina* looks at first sight as though it should be a historical drama about a sixteenth-century Italian composer. In fact, using Wagner's *Die Meistersinger von Nürnberg* (1868) as a model, it is an allegory with considerable ahistorical pretensions about the superiority of German music, an allegory that Pfitzner himself described as "autumnal"—a melancholic farewell to the Wagnerian ideal.

Jettisoning Wagnerian interiority altogether on the other hand, or half-parodying it, as in Jim's defiant aria to the coming of day in Bertolt Brecht's and Kurt Weill's *Aufstieg und Fall der Stadt Mahagonny* (1930), only served to expose the hollow ambitions of full-scale works that had nothing really significant to put in its place in the long term. The outstanding exceptions are nearly all the mature operas of Leoš Janáček. Indeed, there could hardly be anything less like Wagner's lengthy psychological explorations of character entwined in labyrinthine musical structures. Janáček's best works for the stage are justly admired for their concision, raw emotion, sinewy harmony, bare textures, direct expression, and a dramatic immediacy that goes directly to the heart of the listener. Even some of his subjects are simply inconceivable in the context of Wagner's concept of temporality, in which real historical time can never exist, even in its most grotesque forms. Consider the journey of the philistine Prague landlord Brouček to the moon and the fifteenth century in *The Excursions of Mr. Brouček* (1920), for instance, or, in *The Makropulos Affair* (1926), the heroine Emilia Marty, who can live for three hundred years.

Apart from Janáček, most valiant efforts to recapture or to reject Wagner's idea of drama pale before the achievement of Alban Berg's *Wozzeck* (1925), one of the undisputed masterpieces of modern opera. Berg had to twist the knife twice: in addition to turning Wagner's concept of temporality psychologically on its head, he also set it on a dangerous collision course with its challengers. In his 1929 lecture on *Wozzeck,* Berg himself formally eschewed "the Wagnerian recipe of 'through-composing,' "[21] and he famously relied on traditional forms like the passacaglia and the sonata to ensure musical cohesion. Indeed, to describe *Wozzeck* as a post-Wagnerian opera without careful qualification can be seriously misleading. On one level it is a realistic melodrama on a par with Puccini's *Tosca* (1900), in which its protagonist also suffers appalling abuse. (Not insignificantly, both operas take their time frame of "life itself" from spoken plays.) But, on another level, its fifteen scenes are highly subjective musical journeys into deracinated states of mind closer to the central idea behind Wagnerian drama—from which, as we have seen, Puccini explicitly distanced himself. The complex orchestral environment each time envelops the characters, not to explore rich Wagnerian lives to be sure, but to examine human existences that have been devastated and emptied out by modern social conditions. Berg's compassionate spirit, which owes not a little to a profoundly ironic adaptation of Wagner's idea of interior drama on an ambitious musical scale, is never more in evidence than in this astonishing work.

Thus, for composers working in a post-Wagnerian environment, negotiating between Wagner's example and a radical rejection of it was often more important than adhering rigorously to the one or the other. Not that this was a recipe for avoiding disaster. Franz Schreker's *Der ferne Klang* (1912) and Ernst Krenek's *Jonny spielt auf* (1927) veer awkwardly between idealized musical spaces and realistic scenes of petty bourgeois life (e.g., the bizarre scene in Krenek's opera in which the hero, Max, shares his sorrows with a singing glacier outside his hotel in the Alps). It is doubtless this uncertainty of dramatic aim that has helped to consign these works, and others of the same ilk, to the limbo of Fascinating Operas of the Past (FOPS), operas that are occasionally revived but stubbornly grounded on the remoter borders of the repertoire.

Admiring historical studies of FOPS from the 1920s and 1930s will probably never be in short supply. What is sorely missing, however, is a sober critical investigation into the reasons for their initial success and their long-term failure, an investigation that takes a hard look at their Wagnerian and anti-Wagnerian pedigree. *Jonny spielt auf*—probably the most famous example—was taken up by more than thirty stages in German-speaking countries during its first season, and by about twenty foreign theaters during the next two years, making it one of the greatest operatic hits of all time. But history has been less than kind to it, and it is simply no good blaming its subsequent lackluster fame solely on the influence of Goebbels's Nazi propaganda machine. (The Nazis notoriously excoriated the work, among other reasons because the character Jonny is a "Negro" jazz-band musician who first enters carrying a golden saxophone, a sexually uninhibited image that could hardly be further removed visually and musically from the interior spaces of Wagner's music dramas.) Indeed, the resolute refusal of Wagnerian drama to move outside the subjective musical worlds of its characters, thus measuring itself idealistically against the "impurities" of real life, was shamelessly exploited by Hitler, whom—as we saw in chapter 12— Goebbels described as listening to Wagner as if "the drama were in artistic unison with his political being."[22] It was only logical, therefore, that the image of Jonny should be emblazoned over the brochure for the Nazis' notorious 1938 Düsseldorf exhibition "Entartete Musik" (Degenerate music) as a telling symbol of everything opposed to the racist musical ideals of the Third Reich.

But public demand for performances of Krenek's opera had already begun to wane before the Nazis assumed power in 1933. Unsettling though the political upheavals surrounding the so-called *Zeitopern* (operas of the times) of the 1920s and early '30s were, their deliberately ephemeral topicality is not quite enough to explain their weaknesses. Alone the label *Zeitoper* marks the opposition of these works, including Hindemith's *Neues vom Tage* (1929) and Caspar Neher's and Weill's *Die Bürgschaft* (1932), to the Wagnerian ideal of an operatic dramaturgy beyond history. Indeed a more fruitful line of critical enquiry could well lie in a closer scrutiny of the role of music in relation to the perception of dramatic time, which composers were often confused about or simply miscalculated—an understandable failing, perhaps, in view of the social pressure that was increasingly being brought to bear on opera, especially after the First World War. If reflection on Wagner's influence can teach us anything, it is that he raised the stakes of opera to such a pitch that it proved extremely difficult for those after him to choose the right form of musical dramaturgy, and to reconcile that choice with the heavy demands placed on works of art in the modern era. In the case of opera, that included a growing sense of unease about its validity that, from the middle of the nineteenth century onward, Wagner himself had already forcefully expressed.

Abbreviations

CD   *Cosima Wagner's Diaries*, ed. Martin Gregor-Dellin and Dietrich Mack, trans. and with an Introduction by Geoffrey Skelton, vol. 1: 1869–1877 (London: Collins, 1978); vol. 2: 1878–83 (London: Collins, 1980). German edition: *Cosima Wagner: Die Tagebücher*, 2 vols. (Munich and Zurich: R. Piper & Co. Verlag, 1976–77). I have used the published English translation, modified where noted. All citations include the date of the relevant entry, and hence are easily located in either edition.

ML   Richard Wagner, *My Life*, ed. Mary Whittall, trans. Andrew Gray (Cambridge: Cambridge University Press, 1983). All citations are to this edition, which is based on the complete, fully annotated 1976 German edition by Martin Gregor-Dellin.

PW   *Richard Wagner's Prose Works*, trans. William Ashton Ellis, 8 vols. (London: Kegan Paul, Trench, Trübner & Co., 1892–99; Lincoln and London: University of Nebraska Press, 1995). This notorious, though by no means always misleading, translation is based on Wagner's original ten-volume edition (see SSD) and has been modified throughout.

SB   *Richard Wagner: Sämtliche Briefe*, ed. Gertrud Strobel and Werner Wolf (vols. 1–5), Hans-Joachim Bauer and Johannes Forner (vols. 6–8), Klaus Burmeister and Johannes Forner (vol. 9), Andreas Mielke (vol. 10), Martin Dürrer (vols. 11–13, 16), and Andreas Mielke (vols. 14–15) (Leipzig: Deutscher Verlag für Musik 1967–2000 [vols. 1–9]); Wiesbaden, Leipzig, and Paris: Breitkopf & Härtel, 2000– [vols. 10–]). To avoid cumbersome references to endless other volumes, the letters are referred to by date and can therefore be easily located, if necessary, in German and English editions not cited, though not all of the letters have been published or translated before. Translations are mostly from the original German text. I have profited greatly from the excellent translation of some of the letters in *Selected Letters of Richard Wagner*, ed. and trans. Stewart Spencer and Barry Millington (London and Melbourne: J. M. Dent & Sons Ltd., 1987).

SSD   *Richard Wagner: Sämtliche Schriften und Dichtungen*, Volks-Ausgabe, 16 vols. (Leipzig: Breitkopf & Härtel and C. F. W. Siegel [R. Linnemann], 1911 [vols. 1–12], 1914 [vols. 13–16]). First published under the editorship of Wagner as *Richard Wagner: Gesammelte Schriften und Dichtungen*, 10 vols. (Leipzig: E. W. Fritzsch, 1871–83), later expanded to 12 vols. in 1911, when it was edited by Richard Sternfeld. The pagination of SSD and the different editions of the *Gesammelte Schriften* do not always correspond, which is why I have always cited the former. If there is a discrepancy, a basic concordance is provided in SSD 16: 261–326.

SW   Richard Wagner, *Sämtliche Werke*, 31 vols. [projected] (Mainz: B. Schott's Söhne/Schott Musik International, 1970–). Titles, editors, and dates of publication are cited when relevant volumes are first referenced within chapters.

WWV   John Deathridge, Martin Geck, and Egon Voss, *Wagner-Werk-Verzeichnis (WWV): Verzeichnis der musikalischen Werke Richard Wagners und ihrer Quellen* (Mainz, London, New York, and Tokyo: B. Schott's Söhne, 1986, 1987).

Notes

1. WAGNER LIVES

1. For a summary of Wagner in film, see Ulrich Müller, "Wagner in Literature and Film," in *Wagner Handbook,* ed. Ulrich Müller and Peter Wapnewski; trans. ed. John Deathridge (Cambridge, Mass., and London: Harvard University Press, 1992), 373–93.

2. The *Gesammelte Schriften,* originally in ten volumes, expanded posthumously into sixteen (see SSD).

3. First published privately in four volumes in 1870, 1872, 1874, and 1880, and later published publicly, with minor cuts, in 1911. All references are to the modern English translation (ML).

4. The most interesting are the so-called "Red Pocket-Book" *(Die rote Brieftasche),* reproduced in SB 1: 81–92; the "Brown Book," in *Das braune Buch,* ed. Joachim Bergfeld (Zurich: Atlantis Verlag, 1975), trans. George Bird (London: Gollancz, 1980); and the diary written for the eyes of King Ludwig II in 1865, included in *König Ludwig II und Richard Wagner. Briefwechsel,* ed. Otto Strobel, 5 vols. (Karlsruhe: G. Braun, 1936–39), 4: 5–34 (hereafter *Ludwig-Wagner*).

5. See Martin Geck, *Die Bildnisse Richard Wagners* (Munich: Prestel-Verlag, 1970).

6. See SB and *Wagner-Brief-Verzeichnis* (WBV), ed. Werner Breig, Martin Dürrer, and Andreas Melke (Wiesbaden, Leipzig, and Paris: Breitkopf & Härtel, 1998).

7. See Stewart Spencer, *Wagner Remembered* (London: Faber and Faber, 2000).

8. John Deathridge, "A Brief History of Wagner Research," in *Wagner Handbook,* 202–23. The only major biography to be published since is Joachim Köhler's *Der letzte der Titanen: Richard Wagners Leben und Werk* (Berlin: Claassen Verlag, 2001); trans. Stewart Spencer as *Richard Wagner: The Last of the Titans* (New Haven and London: Yale University Press, 2004). Despite some welcome critical moments, its wearying length and naïve fusion of art and life ("Like the

composer, the young hero [Siegfried] grows up in straitened circumstances," 363) ultimately turn it into yet another low-grade *biographie romanesque*, of which, as I suggest in my earlier essay, there are already more than enough. Despite all attempts at critical distance, its journalistic hyperbole is a crude mirror image of Wagner's own methods and does scant justice to his importance as a formidable bellwether of German ideology.

9. The definitive account is Samuel Schoenbaum, *Shakespeare's Lives* (Oxford: Clarendon Press, 1970). An abridged and updated edition was published in 1991. A notable and actually well-grounded attempt is Stephen Greenblatt, *Will in the World: How Shakespeare became Shakespeare* (New York and London: Pimlico, 2004), which derives many suppositional details from reading the dramatic texts against the record of politics and daily life in London during the years Shakespeare was active there.

10. Unfortunately, none of the key texts concerning this important issue have been translated. See Winfried Schüler, *Der Bayreuther Kreis von seiner Entstehung bis zum Ausgang der wilhelminischen Ära*, Neue münsterische Beiträge zur Geschichtsforschung 12 (Münster: Aschendorff, 1971); Michael Karbaum, *Studien zur Geschichte der Bayreuther Festspiele* (Regensburg: Gustav Bosse Verlag, 1976); Hartmut Zelinsky, *Richard Wagner: Ein deutsches Thema—Eine Dokumentation zur Wirkungsgeschichte Richard Wagners, 1876–1976* (Frankfurt am Main: Zweitausendeins, 1976).

11. Lytton Strachey, *Eminent Victorians* (London: Chatto & Windus, 1974; first published 1918), 7.

12. Carl Friedrich Glasenapp, *Richard Wagner's Leben und Wirken*, 2 vols. (Cassel and Leipzig: Carl Maurer's Verlags-Buchhandlung, 1876–77); *Das Leben Richard Wagners in sechs Büchern dargestellt*, 6 vols., 3rd–5th ed. (Leipzig: Breitkopf & Härtel, 1908–23).

13. ML 741.

14. CD, 21 March 1873.

15. Theodor W. Adorno, "Wagner, Nietzsche, Hitler," in *Gesammelte Schriften*, vol. 19, ed. Rolf Tiedemann and Klaus Schultz (Frankfurt am Main: Suhrkamp, 1984), 405.

16. CD, 9 February 1883.

17. From a letter of 25 January 1880 in *Ludwig-Wagner*, 3: 169.

18. From the Neuchâtel preface to Rousseau's *Confessions*, cited in Laura Marcus, *Auto/biographical Discourses: Theory, Criticism, Practice* (Manchester: Manchester University Press, 1994), 23.

19. See, e.g., Trev Lynn Broughton, *Men of Letters, Writings Lives: Masculinity and Literary Auto/Biography in the Late Victorian Period* (London and New York: Routledge, 1999), in particular chapter 3 on the famous Froude-Carlyle debate and "married life as a literary problem" (83–112).

20. Cited in Marcus, *Auto/biographical discourses*, 46.

21. ML 108, trans. modified.

22. From a letter of 12 November 1864, in *Ludwig-Wagner*, 1: 36–37.

23. First published in its entirety in *Das braune Buch*, 111–47.

24. Otto Strobel, foreword to *Ludwig-Wagner*, 1: ix (original emphasis).

25. Georges Gusdorf, "Conditions and Limits of Autobiography," in *Autobiography: Essays Theoretical and Critical*, ed. James Olney (Princeton: Princeton University Press, 1980), 38. See also the discussion of Gusdorf's seminal essay in Marcus, *Auto/biographical discourses*, 154–62.

26. Gusdorf, "Conditions and Limits of Autobiography," 43.

27. John Deathridge and Carl Dahlhaus, *The New Grove Wagner* (London: Macmillan, 1984), 7. See also, e.g., Klaus Kropfinger, *Wagner and Beethoven: Richard Wagner's Reception of Beethoven*, trans. Peter Palmer (Cambridge: Cambridge University Press, 1991), 32–33. After coming up empty-handed, Kropfinger, whose innate conservatism in any case makes it difficult for him to challenge Wagner's authority, asks a bit desperately, "was there . . . ever any need for such a falsification? Does Wagner's extraordinary—and well-documented—early commitment to Beethoven's Ninth not speak for itself?" Well, yes and no: from a psychoanalytical perspective alone, not to mention for its ideological ramifications, Wagner clearly needed to invent an autobiographical myth in which a powerful female (mother) figure is fused with a dominant (paternal) male authority. That would have been much harder to do with the Ninth Symphony, given the absence in it of famous solo arias, and hence the lack of an iconic woman singer with whom it could be unmistakably identified.

28. See the brilliant rereading of it in Tamara S. Evans, "Am Mythenstein: Richard Wagner and Swiss Society," in *Re-Reading Wagner*, ed. Reinhold Grimm and Jost Hermand (Madison: University of Wisconsin Press, 1993), 3–22.

29. See Egon Voss, "Die Wesendoncks und Richard Wagner," in *Minne, Muse und Mäzen: Otto und Mathilde Wesendonck und ihr Zürcher Künstlerzirkel*, ed. Axel Langer and Chris Walton (Zurich: Museum Rietberg, 2002), 117.

30. ML 424, trans. modified.

31. ML 483.

32. Cited in Evans, "Am Mythenstein," 17.

33. Max Fehr, *Richard Wagners Schweizer Zeit*, 2 vols. (Aarau: H. R. Sauerlander, 1934–54), 2: 21.

34. Richard Wagner, *Eine Mitteilung an meine Freunde*, in SSD 4: 239, 244; cf. PW 1: 278–79, 283 (original emphasis).

35. SSD 4: 240; PW 1: 280.

36. Laura Marcus, "The Newness of the 'New Biography'," in *Mapping Lives: The Uses of Biography*, ed. Peter France and William St. Clair (Oxford: Oxford University Press, 2002), 194.

37. Wagner was an admirer of Thomas Carlyle's biography of Frederick the Great, but as one example among many writers of biography, he chastised the author of this one for the "completely unphilosophical cultivation of his mind" (CD, 21 March 1873; trans. modified).

38. At the end of the score of *Die Meistersinger*, for instance, is the entry: "Thursday, 24 October 1867/Evening 8 o' clock." See WWV 478.

39. SSD 1: vi; PW 1: xviii (original emphasis).

40. SSD 1: iv; PW 1: xv–xvi (original emphasis).

41. SSD 1: 19; PW 1: 19.

42. Compare the original text of the passage in the *Autobiographical Sketch* (SB 1: 100) with the "official" 1871 version (SSD 1: 9; PW 1: 8).

43. SSD 1: 160; PW 7: 95.

44. Compare the text in SSD with the French original, titled *De la musique allemande,* in *Revue et Gazette musicale,* Paris, 12 and 26 July 1840. The French original can also be found in *Oeuvres en prose de Richard Wagner,* trans. J.–G. Prod'homme (Paris: Libraire Delagrave, 1928), 1: 152–80, esp. 179. Prod'homme has placed the passages cut in the German version in square brackets. I am grateful to Jean-Jacques Nattiez for drawing my attention to this edition and for providing me with a copy of it. Ellis dutifully provides one of the cut sentences in a footnote to his English translation of the essay, but oddly leaves it in French. See PW 7: 101.

45. For evidence that Wagner was still working on the essay during 1849, see WWV 329–30. In a letter of 16 September 1849 to Theodor Uhlig, he states explicitly that he is expanding and reediting the piece "in a whole variety of new ways" *(mannigfach neu).* See SB 3: 122.

46. SSD 10: iii; PW 6: vii.

47. Richard Wagner, *Mein Leben,* ed. Martin Gregor-Dellin (Munich: List Verlag, 1976), 786. The phrase is not in the English edition (ML), which excludes the "Annals."

48. ML 758.

49. See, for example, Ernest Newman's entirely convincing exposure of Wagner's and Cosima's ruthless behavior toward Malvina Schnorr von Carolsfeld (the first Isolde), who threatened to expose their illicit relationship to King Ludwig II. The official Bayreuth legend had it that Wagner was human kindness itself in his treatment of the singer. Ernest Newman, *The Life of Richard Wagner,* 4 vols. (Cambridge: Cambridge University Press, 1976), 4: 3–37.

50. Friedrich Nietzsche, *The Will to Power,* trans. Walter Kaufmann and R. J. Hollingdale, ed. with commentary by Walter Kaufmann (London: Weidenfeld and Nicolson, 1968), 272 (original emphasis).

51. Roger Hollinrake, "The Title-Page of Wagner's 'Mein Leben'," *Music and Letters* 54, no. 1 (October 1970): 416.

52. Letter of 15 August 1888 from Köselitz to Nietzsche, in *Nietzsche Briefwechsel,* ed. Giorgio Colli and Mazzino Montinari, III/6: Briefe an Friedrich Nietzsche: Januar 1887–Januar 1889 (Berlin and New York: Walter de Gruyter, 1984), 270.

53. Friedrich Nietzsche, *The Birth of Tragedy and the Case of Wagner,* trans. with commentary by Walter Kaufmann (New York: Vintage Books, 1967), 182.

54. Letter of November 1872 to Rohde, *Nietzsche Briefwechsel,* II/3: Friedrich Nietzsche Briefe: Mai 1872–Dezember 1874 (Berlin and New York: Walter de Gruyter, 1978), 86.

55. Nietzsche, *The Birth of Tragedy and the Case of Wagner,* 166.

56. Cited in Broughton, *Men of Letters, Writings Lives,* 141.

57. Isolde Vetter, "Wagner in the History of Psychology," in *Wagner Handbook,* 118–55.

58. Letter of 5 December 1866 in Cosima Wagner and Ludwig II of Bavaria, *Briefe,* ed. Martha Schad, with assistance from Horst Heinrich Schad (Bergisch Gladbach: Gustav Lübbe Verlag, 1996), 301.

59. Cited in Newman, *The Life of Richard Wagner,* 1: 80.

60. ML 751–52.

61. Gusdorf, "Conditions and Limits of Autobiography," 39.

62. Cited in Vetter, "Wagner in the History of Psychology," 125 (original emphasis).

63. SSD 2: 2; PW 7: 226.

2. "PALE" SENTA

1. Translated from the German text in Heinrich Heine, *Historisch-kritische Gesamtausgabe der Werke,* ed. Manfred Windfuhr, vol. 5 (Hamburg: Hoffmann und Campe, 1994), 147–95.

2. Transcribed in SW 24, *Dokumente und Texte zu "Der fliegende Holländer,"* ed. Egon Voss (Mainz: Schott Musik International, 2004), 171–72. English trans. by Peter Bloom in *Richard Wagner: "Der fliegende Holländer,"* ed. Thomas Grey, Cambridge Opera Handbook (Cambridge: Cambridge University Press, 2000), 169–73.

3. "*[D]'un petit opéra en un acte.*" See SW 24: 22.

4. SW 24: 175.

5. SW 24: 176.

6. SW 24: 178–80. The first half of the scenario is missing. English trans. by Stewart Spencer in *Richard Wagner: "Der fliegende Holländer,"* 173–78.

7. SW 24: 183.

8. SW 24: 183–88.

9. "*Ach, liebes Mädel, blas' noch mehr,*" as in the original layer of the first draft of the libretto. See SW 24: 187.

10. This extends to the orchestration that was greatly refined over the many years that Wagner tinkered with the opera. Compare the original version of 1841 with the versions 1842–80 in SW 4/I–II, *Der fliegende Holländer (Urfassung 1841),* ed. Isolde Vetter (Mainz: B. Schott's Söhne, 1983), and SW 4/III–IV, *Der fliegende Holländer (Fassung 1842–1880),* ed. Egon Voss (Mainz: Schott Musik International, 2000–2001).

11. Paul Barber, *Vampires, Burial, and Death: Folklore and Reality* (New Haven and London: Yale University Press, 1988), 67. This book is by far the best on vampires I have read.

12. The crucial adjective, present in the brochure *Bemerkungen zu Aufführung der Oper "der fliegende Holländer"* (Remarks on the performance of 'Der fliegende Holländer'), first published in Zurich in 1852–53, is oddly omitted in the first edition of Wagner's writings, edited by himself in ten volumes

in 1871–83, only to emerge intact in the expanded, posthumously edited sixteen-volume Volks-Ausgabe edition published in 1911 and 1914. It could just be accident-prone editorial procedure. Nowhere is any reason given, however, for this hide-and-seek game with a far from trivial moment in the original text, the relevant part of which can be found in SSD 5: 168; PW 3: 216, and SW 24: 112.

13. A new allegro finale for Aubrey's aria (no. 15), written for his brother Albert, who sang the role in Würzburg in 1833. See WWV 120–21.

14. On Schröder-Devrient as Fidelio and Romeo, see Jean-Jacques Nattiez, *Wagner Androgyne: A Study in Interpretation*, trans. Stewart Spencer (Princeton: Princeton University Press, 1993), 183–84. In his "official" biography, Wagner, in contradistinction to other sources, emphasizes only the impression she made on him in the former role, preferring to ignore the Italian work. See ML 37.

15. ML 241.

16. See the facsimile in SW 18/II, *Orchesterwerke*, ed. Egon Voss (Mainz: Schott Musik International, 1997), xxxv. The facsimile of the two sketches was first published in my article, the relevant part of which I have expanded here, "Richard Wagners Kompositionen zu Goethes *Faust*," in *Jahrbuch der Bayerischen Staatsoper 1982* (Munich: Bayerische Staatsoper, 1982), 90–99.

17. Letter to Theodor Uhlig of 27 November 1852. See SW 18/II: xl and SB 5: 122.

18. SW 17, *Klavierlieder*, ed. Egon Voss (Mainz: B. Schott's Söhne, 1976), 22.

19. Cf. Julia Kristeva, "Stabat Mater," *Poetics Today* 6, nos. 1–2 (1985): 144. I have deliberately given Kristeva's words a negative twist appropriate to the nihilistic logic of the opera.

20. SW 30, *Dokumente zur Entstehung und ersten Aufführung des Bühnenweihfestspiels "Parsifal,"* ed. Martin Geck and Egon Voss (Mainz: B. Schott's Söhne, 1970), 70.

21. SW 24: 19. The words in this essay devoted to the subject of the "Scottish" version and the autobiographical reasons for its subsequent transformation are taken largely from John Deathridge, "An Introduction to 'The Flying Dutchman,'" in *The Flying Dutchman/Der fliegende Holländer*, ed. Nicholas John, ENO Opera Guide 12 (London and New York: John Calder and Riverrun Press, 1982), 13–26. The same issue and the same words, however, are placed in different contexts here not touched on in the earlier piece.

22. See John Deathridge, "The Invention of German Music c. 1800," in *Unity and Diversity in European Culture c. 1800*, ed. Tim Blanning and Hagen Schulze, Proceedings of the British Academy 134 (Oxford: Oxford University Press, 2006), 35–60.

23. "Über deutsches Musikwesen," SSD 1: 158; PW 7: 93 As already mentioned in chapter 1, all traces of tactical conciliatoriness toward the French in the article originally published in Paris in the *Revue et Gazette Musicale* on 12 and 26 July 1840 were later cut or ironically distanced by Wagner himself in this "official" German version. For structural and musical detail on how Wagner

used the strophic (or verse) song in the Dutchman, see Deathridge, "An Introduction," 14–24.

24. A dynamic made clear after the fact in writings such as *German Politics and German Art (Deutsche Politik und deutsche Kunst)*, written and first published in 1867 in anticipation of the Munich premiere of *Die Meistersinger von Nürmberg* in the following year. See SSD 10: 30–124; PW 4: 35–135.

3. WAGNER THE PROGRESSIVE

1. Claude Lévi-Strauss, *The Elementary Structures of Kinship*, rev. ed., trans. James Harle Bell, John Richard von Sturmer, and Rodney Needham (Boston: Beacon Press, 1969), 36.

2. Letter of 31 May 1851 in SB 4: 57–58 (original emphasis). For all documents and texts relating to the genesis and performance of *Lohengrin*, see SW 26, *Dokumente und Texte zu "Lohengrin,"* ed. John Deathridge and Klaus Döge (Mainz: Schott Musik International, 2003).

3. The citations are from the longer, book version of the essay, first published in a German translation by Ernst Weyden in 1852 and copiously edited with parallel French and German texts in Franz Liszt, *Sämtliche Schriften 4: Lohengrin et Tannhaüser [sic] de Richard Wagner/Lohengrin und Tannhäuser von Richard Wagner*, ed. Rainer Kleinertz, with commentary by Gerhard J. Winkler (Wiesbaden: Breitkopf & Härtel, 1989), 4–5, 32–33. The editors rightly point out (249) that the shorter version of the essay in a different German translation by Karl Ritter—a translation that was overseen by Hans von Bülow and Wagner himself and appeared in the *Illustrierte Zeitung* on 12 April 1851— was one of the most influential factors in establishing Wagner's reputation well beyond musical circles on account of the paper's wide readership.

4. SSD 4: 289–90; PW 1: 334–35.

5. SSD 4: 291; PW 1: 335–36.

6. Claude Lévi-Strauss, *The Raw and the Cooked*, trans. John Weightman and Doreen Weightman, Introduction to a Science of Mythology 1 (London: Jonathan Cape, 1970), 15 (original emphasis).

7. Otto Rank, *Die Lohengrinsage. Ein Beitrag zu ihrer Motivgestaltung und Deutung*, Schriften zur angewandten Seelenkunde 13 (Nendeln, Liechtenstein: Kraus Reprint, 1970), 19. [Schriften zur angewandten Seelenkunde, ed. Sigmund Freud, 13 (first published Leipzig and Vienna, 1911)].

8. Ibid., 97–99.

9. Ibid., 137–51. See Max Graf's interpretation of the same constellation in *Der fliegende Holländer* in the ninth volume of the same series: Max Graf, *Richard Wagner im "fliegenden Holländer." Ein Beitrag zur Psychologie künstlerischen Schaffens* (Nendeln, Liechtenstein: Kraus Reprint, 1970; first published Leipzig and Vienna, 1911). The essay by Freud on which Rank and Graf base this insight into Wagner was written in 1910 and can be found in "A Special Type of Choice of Object Made by Men," *The Standard Edition of the Complete Psychological Works of Sigmund Freud*, trans. James Strachey, with

Anna Freud, Alix Strachey, and Alan Tyson (London: Hogarth Press, 1953–74), 11: 163–75.

10. Charles Baudelaire, *Selected Writings on Art and Artists,* trans. Patrick Edward Charvet (Cambridge: Cambridge University Press, 1981), 331.

11. Peter Wapnewski, "The Operas as Literary Works," *Wagner Handbook,* ed. Ulrich Müller and Peter Wapnewski, trans. ed. John Deathridge (Cambridge, Mass., and London: Harvard University Press, 1992), 35.

12. Morse Peckham, *Beyond the Tragic Vision: The Quest for Identity in the Nineteenth Century* (Cambridge: Cambridge University Press, 1981), 250.

13. Cited in Geoffrey G. Field, *Evangelist of Race: The Germanic Vision of Houston Stewart Chamberlain* (New York: Columbia University Press, 1981), 144. Chamberlain's negative estimation of *Lohengrin* first appeared in the Paris publication *Revue Wagnérienne* in its January issue in 1886.

14. Cited in William Ashton Ellis, *Life of Richard Wagner* (London: Kegan Paul, Trench, Trübner & Co, 1906), 5: 208.

15. Strauss's preface to Hector Berlioz, *Treatise on Instrumentation,* enlarged and rev. by Richard Strauss, trans. Theodore Front (New York: Edwin F. Kalmus, 1948), ii.

16. For a transcription of the original version of Ortrud's narration, see John Deathridge, "Through the Looking Glass: Some Remarks on the First Complete Draft of *Lohengrin,*" in *Analyzing Opera: Verdi and Wagner,* ed. Carolyn Abbate and Roger Parker (Berkeley: University of California Press, 1989), 82–86. The (cut) second half of Lohengrin's narration is reprinted with critical apparatus in Appendix 1 to SW 7/III, *Lohengrin: Romantische Oper in drei Akten,* ed. John Deathridge and Klaus Döge (Mainz: Schott Musik International, 2000), 202–12.

17. Carl Dahlhaus, *Richard Wagner's Music Dramas,* trans. Mary Whittall (Cambridge: Cambridge University Press, 1979), 35.

18. SSD 10: 176–93; PW 6: 173–91.

19. SB 4: 241. Wagner is referring to measures 430–32 of the second act. All measure numbers after SW 7/I–III.

20. See Curt von Westernhagen, *The Forging of the "Ring,"* trans. Arnold and Mary Whittall (Cambridge: Cambridge University Press), 29. Westernhagen fails to note the interesting fact that Wagner's label "world inheritance" for the motif we know as the "ring" suggests a not insignificant disparity between his understanding of what the motif is supposed to stand for and that of Hans von Wolzogen, who was the first to give it the name it is usually given now, and indeed the first to undertake the task of systematically naming all the motifs in the *Ring.* Westernhagen also fails to note that the example does at least indicate that it was Wagner's idea, and not Wolzogen's, to label them in the first place.

21. Wagner's stage designs for *Lohengrin* and those into which he had substantial input are reproduced in SW 26: 43–47, 340–42.

22. SW 7/2: mm. 718–49.

23. SW7/2: mm. 1362 ff.

24. Further details in WWV 336–37.

25. Theodor Adorno, *In Search of Wagner*, trans. Rodney Livingstone (London: New Left Books, 1981), 73.

26. SW 26: 132.

27. See Deathridge, "Through the Looking Glass," 66–68.

28. Arrangements for military band became very popular during the 1890s, especially in Britain. See, for instance, Jacob Adam Kappey, *Grand Selection from Lohengrin arranged for military band* (London: Boosey & Co, 1893), and *Bridal March from Lohengrin*, arr. A. Morelli for Fife and Drum Band (London: J. R. Lafleur & Sons, 1898).

29. First published in 1854 as "Lyrical Pieces for Voice and Piano" *(Lyrische Stücke für eine Gesangstimme und Klavier)* and reprinted many times. For a critical edition of Wagner's arrangement, see SW 7/III: Appendix 3.

30. SW 23, *Dokumente und Texte zu "Rienzi 'der Letzte der Tribunen',"* ed. Reinhard Strohm (Mainz: B. Schott's Söhne, 1976), 111–34.

31. The relevant entries in CD are included together in SW 24, *Dokumente und Texte zu "Der fliegende Holländer,"* ed. Egon Voss (Mainz: Schott Musik International, 2004), 166–68.

32. CD, 23 January 1883.

33. SW 26: 24.

34. Letter of 2 July 1850 to Franz Liszt. SB 3: 343–47 and SW 26: 42–43.

35. SSD 9: 288; PW 5: 286.

4. FAIRY TALE, REVOLUTION, PROPHECY

1. Cited in Mark Berry, *Treacherous Bonds and Laughing Fire: Politics and Religion in Wagner's "Ring"* (Aldershot and Burlington, Vt: Ashgate, 2006), 145.

2. Cited in ibid., 90.

3. See particularly SSD 4: 314–15; PW 1: 360–61. Wagner's insistence here that "pure history," i.e., factual history, is unsuited to art because of its literalness has to be treated cautiously in the light of his tendentious presentation of his decision at the time to move decisively from history to myth. The adjective "pure" is at least of some interest (it is missing, by the way, in Ellis's translation) because it implies momentarily that Wagner was abandoning a certain kind of history, but not history per se. That is not the sense of the whole passage, however, which sets up "history" and "myth" as binary opposites that supposedly gave rise to the inevitable trajectory of the modern artist toward the latter. The momentary qualification "pure" suggests a less rigid opposition, which, had Wagner reflected further on it, would have led him toward a more differentiated explanation of how he mixed elements of myth with allusions to history and real life to create an allegory of the modern world in the *Ring*. The subject of allegory had low status for intellectuals of Wagner's generation because of its supposed crudeness, which is one reason why he tends to avoid the subject, preferring an idealistic and hence somewhat misleading version of

his enduring love affair with myth. See chapter 1 and most of chapter 8 in this volume.

4. *Entwurf zur Organisation eines deutschen National-Theaters für das Königreich Sachsen,* SSD 2: 233–73; PW 7: 319–60.

5. Morse Peckham, *Beyond the Tragic Vision: The Quest for Identity in the Nineteenth Century* (Cambridge: Cambridge University Press, 1981), 251.

6. The German word she sings in the original text, *dämmert,* can mean both "dawns" and "darkens."

7. Eero Tarasti, *Myth and Music: A Semiotic Approach to the Aesthetics of Myth in Music, Especially That of Wagner, Sibelius and Stravinsky,* Acta Musicologica Fennica 11 (Helsinki: Suomen Musiikkitieteellinen Seura, 1978), 178–79.

8. Heinrich Porges, *Wagner Rehearsing the "Ring": An Eye-Witness Account of the Stage Festivals of the First Bayreuth Festival,* trans. Robert L. Jacobs (Cambridge: Cambridge University Press, 1983), 39.

5. SYMPHONIC MASTERY OR MORAL ANARCHY?

1. Donald Francis Tovey, "Parsifal Act III," in *Essays in Musical Analysis,* vol. 4, Illustrative Music (London: Oxford University Press, 1939), 121, 119.

2. The critic of the Munich *Neueste Nachrichten,* a paper not normally favorably disposed toward Wagner, cited in Ernest Newman, *The Life of Richard Wagner* (Cambridge: Cambridge University Press, 1976), 4: 268.

3. "Notgedrungene Erklärung" (16 February 1874), SSD 12: 323–24.

4. Newman, *The Life of Richard Wagner,* 4: 268.

5. Charles Baudelaire, *Selected Writings on Art and Artists,* trans. Patrick Edward Charvet (Cambridge: Cambridge University Press, 1981), 344–45.

6. Cited in Erwin Doernberg, *The Life and Symphonies of Anton Bruckner,* with a foreword by Robert Simpson (London: Barrie and Rockliff, 1960), 21. Nicholas Attfield thinks that the anecdote has its source in a remark by Bruckner's notoriously legend-prone biographers August Göllerich and Max Auer, who claimed that during a performance of *Götterdämmerung* (they meant *Siegfried*) Bruckner nudged his neighbor Felix Mottl with his elbows during Siegfried's awakening of Brünnhilde (sung by Amalie Materna) and asked, *"Du, Felixl, was schreit denn die Materna a so!"* (Hey, Felix, what's Materna yelling about so much!). The point is the same, however, because Bruckner was obviously concentrating on the sweep of the music rather than on its motivation in the plot—or at least so the anecdote is suggesting—no matter where in the *Ring* it happened to be. See Nicholas Attfield, "Bruckner in the Theatre: On the Politics of 'Absolute' Music in Performance," in *Music, Theatre and Politics in Germany: 1848 to the Third Reich,* ed. Nikolaus Bacht (Aldershot and Burlington, Vt.: Ashgate, 2006), 162.

7. Susanna Großmann-Vendrey, *Bayreuth in der deutschen Presse. Dokumentenband 1: Die Grundsteinlegung und die ersten Festspiele (1872–1876)* (Regensburg: Gustav Bosse Verlag, 1977), 193.

8. Newman, *The Life of Richard Wagner,* 2: 526. For a full decoding of the messages to Mathilde Wesendonck, see Otto Strobel, "Wagners Leben im Lichte der Randbemerkungen seiner Originalhandschriften," *Allgemeine Musikzeitung* 59, nos. 12–13 (1932): 152, and Otto Strobel, "Die Kompositionsskizze zur 'Walküre'. Zu unserer Notenbeilage," *Zeitschrift für Musik* 100, no. 7 (1933): 710–11.

9. Thomas Mann, "Richard Wagner and *Der Ring des Nibelungen,*" in *Pro and Contra Wagner,* trans. Allan Blunden, intro. by Erich Heller (London and Boston: Faber and Faber, 1985), 178.

10. See the essay first published in 1933, Anatoly Lunarcharsky, "Richard Wagner (On the 50th Anniversary of His Death)," in *On Literature and Art* (Moscow: Progress Publishers, 1965), 346–47. Joseph Goebbels happened to be in a performance of *Die Walküre* with Hitler at the State Opera in Berlin as the election results leading to the overwhelming Nazi victory of 1933 were gradually emerging. Goebbels wrote in his diary for that day, 5 March 1933, "In Wagner's ravishingly beautiful music [for *Die Walküre*], there sounded from outside the march rhythms of columns of steel-helmeted troops marching by," and, a few sentences later, "Germany is awakened!" *(Deutschland ist erwacht!). Joseph Goebbels Tagebücher 1924–1945,* ed. Ralf Georg Reuth (Munich and Zurich: Piper, 2000), 2: 772–73.

11. Cited in a collection of responses to the question "Is the *Ring* a drama of today?" in the program of The Royal Opera, Covent Garden, London, *Der Ring des Nibelungen* (September and October 1991), 83.

12. Letter of 6 May 1857 to his friend and patron Julie Ritter, *Richard Wagner an Freunde und Zeitgenossen,* ed. Erich Kloss (Berlin and Leipzig: Schuster & Loeffler, 1909), 207; SB 8: 312.

13. Robert Raphael, *Richard Wagner* (New York: Twayne Publishers, 1969), 46.

14. He called it *Siegmund und Sieglind: der Walküre bestrafung* in a letter of 11 November 1851 to Theodor Uhlig. SB 4: 172.

6. SIEGFRIED HERO

1. Susanna Großmann-Vendrey, *Bayreuth in der deutschen Presse. Dokumentenband 1: Die Grundsteinlegung und die ersten Festspiele (1872–1876)* (Regensburg: Gustav Bosse Verlag, 1977), 70.

2. Ibid., 177.

3. Heinrich Porges, *Wagner Rehearsing the "Ring": An Eye-Witness Account of the Stage Festivals of the First Bayreuth Festival,* trans. Robert L. Jacobs (Cambridge: Cambridge University Press, 1983), 81.

4. Eric Bentley, *A Century of Hero-Worship* (Beacon Press: Boston, 1957), 177.

5. Letter of 5 May 1924 from Adolf Hitler to Siegfried Wagner in Michael Karbaum, *Studien zur Geschichte der Bayreuther Festspiele (1876–1976),* Teil II: Dokumente und Anmerkungen 66 (Regensburg: Gustav Bosse Verlag, 1976).

6. Thomas Mann, "The Sorrows and Grandeur of Richard Wagner," in *Pro and Contra Wagner*, trans. Allan Blunden, intro. by Erich Heller (London and Boston: Faber and Faber, 1985), 131.

7. Letter of 10 May 1851 to Theodor Uhlig. SB 4: 44.

8. Bernard Shaw, *The Perfect Wagnerite: A Commentary on the Nibelung's Ring*, in *Shaw's Music: The Complete Musical Criticism in Three Volumes*, ed. Dan H. Laurence (London, Sydney, and Toronto: The Bodley Head, 1981), 3: 457–58 (hereafter *Shaw's Music*).

9. Susan Sontag, "Wagner's Fluids," in *Where the Stress Falls* (London: Jonathan Cape, 2002), 208.

10. See the two essays *Art and Revolution* (1849) and *The Art-Work of the Future* (1850), SSD 3: 8–41, 42–177; PW 1: 21–65, 69–213 passim.

11. Bentley, *A Century of Hero-Worship*, 183.

12. Porges, *Wagner Rehearsing the "Ring,"* 103.

13. Letter of 25–26 January 1854 to August Röckel. SB 6: 69.

14. *Shaw's Music*, 3: 498.

15. Letter of 22 December 1856 to Otto Wesendonck. SB 8: 231.

7. FINISHING THE END

1. See Bernard Shaw, *The Perfect Wagnerite: A Commentary on the Nibelung's Ring*, in *Shaw's Music: The Complete Musical Criticism in Three Volumes*, ed. Dan H. Laurence (London, Sydney, and Toronto: The Bodley Head, 1981), 3: 408–545 (hereafter *Shaw's Music*), and Paul Claudel, *Richard Wagner: rêverie d'un poète français*, ed. with commentary by Michel Malicet (Paris: Belles Lettres, 1970), especially Malicet's introduction, 31 ff.

2. *Shaw's Music*, 3: 515.

3. Letter of 25–26 January 1854 to August Röckel. SB 6: 67

4. Letter of 23 August 1856 to August Röckel. SB 8: 153.

5. For a translation of the new ending, which Wagner in the end did not compose, see Ernest Newman, *The Life of Richard Wagner*, 4 vols. (Cambridge: Cambridge University Press, 1976), 2: 354–55.

6. *Shaw's Music*, 3: 494.

7. *Shaw's Music*, 3: 490.

8. Heinrich Porges, *Wagner Rehearsing the "Ring": An Eye-Witness Account of the Stage Festivals of the First Bayreuth Festival*, trans. Robert L. Jacobs (Cambridge: Cambridge University Press, 1983), 129.

9. *Shaw's Music*, 3: 497, 499.

10. *Shaw's Music*, 3: 500, 502.

11. *Shaw's Music*, 3: 496.

12. On the renaming of the work, see WWV 409. After toying with the idea of a new title for a number of years, Wagner did not decide finally on *Götterdämmerung* until 1862, while preparing the first publicly available libretto of the entire *Ring* (Leipzig: J. J. Weber, 1863).

13. See Gerhart von Graevenitz, *Mythos. Zur Geschichte einer Denkgewohnheit* (Stuttgart: J. B. Metzler, 1987), 262. I have been greatly stimulated by this wonderfully eccentric and fascinating book, which has been quite unnecessarily maligned by Dieter Borchmeyer in his mammoth, and otherwise by no means unjustified, philippic against German literature on Wagner. See Dieter Borchmeyer, "Wagner Literature: A German Embarrassment. New Light on the Case of Wagner," in *Wagner* (Journal of the London Wagner Society), n.s. 12, no. 2 (May 1991): 51–74 and 12, no. 3 (September 1991): 116–37, esp. 131–37.

14. *Shaw's Music*, 3: 420.

15. "... im Schoose der Kirche umsummt von Pfaffen und umnebelt von Weihrauch." Cited in Graevenitz, *Mythos*, 263.

16. *Shaw's Music*, 3: 507.

17. Cited in Friedrich Dieckmann, *Wagner, Verdi: Geschichte einer Unbeziehung* (Berlin: Siedler, 1989), 57.

8. *DON CARLOS* AND *GÖTTERDÄMMERUNG*

1. Walter Benjamin, *Gesammelte Schriften*, ed. Rolf Tiedemann and Hermann Schweppenhäuser, 4 vols. (Frankfurt am Main: Suhrkamp, 1980), I/3: 901.

2. On the early scholarly reception of the *Trauerspiel* book, see Herbert Jaumann, *Die deutsche Barockliteratur: Wertung, Umwertung. Eine wertungsgeschichtliche Studie in systematischer Absicht*, Abhandlungen zur Kunst-, Musik- und Literaturwissenschaft 181 (Bonn: Bouvier, 1975), 570–89.

3. Walter Benjamin, *The Origin of German Tragic Drama*, trans. John Osborne (London: New Left Books, 1977). The translation of *Trauerspiel* as "tragic drama" in the title of the book is unfortunate in view of the distinction Benjamin is at pains to make between tragedy and "mourning play," a more accurate translation of *Trauerspiel* that was probably prohibited from appearing in the title by the publishers on account of its esoteric nature. The translator has wisely used the German word *Trauerspiel* throughout the body of the translated text, although I prefer for the sake of variety to alternate it in this essay with "mourning play." I have occasionally modified Osborne's translation, and all references to it are preceded by the location of the German text in Benjamin, *Schriften*, I/1: 203–409.

4. Charles Rosen, "The Ruins of Walter Benjamin," in *On Walter Benjamin*, ed. Gary Smith, Studies in Contemporary German Social Thought (Cambridge, Mass., and London: MIT Press, 1988), 135. Rosen's review first appeared in 1977 in the *New York Review of Books* (27 October and 10 November).

5. "Just as every comparison with tragedy—not to mention musical tragedy—is of no value for the understanding of opera, so it is that from the point of view of literature, and especially the *Trauerspiel*, opera must seem unmistakably to be a product of decadence." Benjamin, *Schriften*, I/1: 386; *Origin*, 212.

6. Benjamin, *Schriften*, I/1: 242; *Origin*, 62.

7. Rosen, "The Ruins of Walter Benjamin," 142.

8. Benjamin, *Schriften*, I/1: 317; *Origin*, 138.

9. Rosen, "The Ruins of Walter Benjamin," 143.

10. Benjamin, *Schriften*, I/1: 250; *Origin*, 70–71.

11. Benjamin, *Schriften*, I/1: 252; *Origin*, 72.

12. Benjamin, *Schriften*, I/1, 271; *Origin*, 92.

13. Benjamin, *Schriften*, I/1: 232; *Origin*, 52.

14. For an overview of the discussion about the concept of allegory in stud-ies of German literature, see Burkhardt Linder, "Satire und Allegorie in Jean Pauls Werk: Zur Konstitution des Allegorischen," *Jahrbuch der Jean-Paul-Gesellschaft* 5 (1970): 7–61, esp. 15–40.

15. Benjamin, *Schriften*, I/1: 336; *Origin*, 160.

16. See Michael Rumpf, *Spekulative Literaturtheorie: Zu Walter Benjamins Trauerspielbuch*, Hochschulschriften: Literaturwissenschaft 49 (Königstein im Taunus: Forum Academicum, 1980), 106.

17. Benjamin, *Schriften*, I/1: 343; *Origin*, 166.

18. Friedrich Lippmann, "Ein neuentdecktes Autograph Richard Wagners: Rezension der Königsberger 'Norma'-Aufführung vom 1837," in *Musicae scientiae collectanea: Festschrift Karl Gustav Fellerer zum siebzigsten Geburtstag am 7. Juli 1972*, ed. Heinrich Hüschen (Cologne: Volk, 1973), 374. See also John Deathridge, "Reminiscences of Norma," in *Das musikalische Kunstwerk: Festschrift Carl Dahlhaus zum 60. Geburtstag*, ed. Hermann Danuser, Helga de la Motte-Haber, Silke Leopold, and Norbert Miller (Laaber: Laaber-Verlag, 1988), 226.

19. Benjamin, *Schriften*, I/1: 364; *Origin*, 188.

20. Cited in Benjamin, *Schriften*, I/1: 291; *Origin*, 112.

21. Benjamin, *Schriften*, I/1: 386; *Origin*, 212.

22. Benjamin, *Schriften*, I/1: 387; *Origin*, 213.

23. See, e.g., Georg Wilhelm Friedrich Hegel, *Aesthetics: Lectures on Fine Art*, trans. Thomas Malcolm Knox (Oxford: Clarendon Press, 1975), 940, 930.

24. Letter to Schiller, 30 December 1797. Among the many editions of the correspondence between Goethe and Schiller where the letter can be found by date are *Der Briefwechsel zwischen Schiller und Goethe*, ed. Siegfried Seidel (Munich: Beck, 1984), and *Correspondence between Goethe and Schiller, 1794–1805*, trans. Liselotte Dieckmann, Studies in Modern German Literature 60 (New York: P. Lang, 1994).

25. Letter to Goethe, 29 December 1797. See n. 24.

26. "A me piacerebbe, come in Schiller, una piccola scena tra Filippo e l'Inquisitore . . . Amerei inoltre un Duo tra Filippo e Posa." Verdi's letter to Emile Perrin, 21 July 1865, cited in Ursula Günther, "La Genèse de Don Carlos, Opéra en cinq actes de Giuseppe Verdi, représenté pour la première fois à Paris le 11 mars 1867," *Revue de Musicologie* 58 (1972): 30. See also Julian Budden, *The Operas of Verdi*, 3 vols. (London: Cassell, 1973–81), 3: 6–9.

27. Mark de Thémines, *La patrie*, 12 March 1867. Reprinted in *Giuseppe Verdi: Don Carlos. Dossier de presse parisienne (1867)*, ed. Hervé Gartioux, Critiques de l'opéra français du XIXème siècle 9 (Heilbronn: Musik-Edition L.

Galland, 1997), 87. Thanks to Roger Parker for drawing my attention to this source.

28. Giuseppe Verdi, *Don Carlos,* Edizione integrale [vocal score], ed. Ursula Günther (Milan: Ricordi, 1974), 1–10.

29. Many examples from Josquin to Britten are cited in Deryck Cooke, *The Language of Music* (London: Oxford University Press, 1959), 148–49.

30. "Carlo V appare vestito da Imperatore!! Non è verosimile. L'Imperatore era già morto da diversi anni. Ma in questo dramma, splendido per forma e per concetti generosi, tutto è falso." Verdi's letter to Giulio Ricordi, 19 February 1883, in *Der Briefwechsel Verdi-Nuitter-du Locle,* ed. Gabriella Carrara Verdi and Ursula Günther, Studien zur italienisch-deutschen Musikgeschichte 10 (1975): 340.

31. Mark de Thémines in *La patrie* and Charles Monselet in *L'Etendard.* Reprinted in *Giuseppe Verdi: Don Carlos,* 87, 118–19.

32. Budden, *The Operas of Verdi,* 3: 152.

33. Verdi, *Don Carlos,* Edizione integrale, 667–69.

34. The mise-en-scène for the 1867 production in Paris, published in Italian translation by Ricordi, describes the image as follows: "In questo momento ad un colpo di tam-tam s'aprono i cancelli della tomba, e Carlo V apparisce in abiti da frate, con manto e corona imperiale ricchissimi: la sua figura è illuminata da un raggio di luce elettrica." See *Disposizione scenica per l'opera Don Carlo di G. Verdi compilata e regolata secondo la mise en scène del Teatro Imperiale dell'Opéra di Parigi* (Milan: n.p., n.d.), 54. The same description in the third edition of the mise-en-scène, which corresponds to the 1884 and 1886 versions of the opera, simply reads, "Al colpo di tam-tam il cancello si apre ed appare Carlo V col manto e la corona reale." *Disposizione scenica per l'opera Don Carlo . . . terza editione* (Milan: n.p., n.d.), 42.

35. As noted in chapter 7, the original version was called *Siegfrieds Tod* (Siegfried's death). The various versions of the libretto and some musical sketches were drafted between October 1848 and November–December 1852. Most of the music, on the other hand, was composed some twenty years later, between October 1869 and November 1874, by which time Wagner had renamed the work *Götterdämmerung.* The description *"Eine tragödie"* is to be found in the first layer of the fourth draft of the libretto of *Siegfrieds Tod.* It was probably written down in May 1850, when Wagner was planning a publication of the libretto that did not materialize. See WWV 395.

36. In November 1848 Wagner decided to change his handwriting from German to Latin script, though he continued to write in German script to people he regarded as belonging to the "old" order (including his wife, Minna!). This means that a number of documents from this period can be dated differently from the way he himself dates them in his autobiographical writings. For example, contrary to what he stated publicly, he was making sketches for a project called *Friedrich I,* which, because of its disposition in five acts, was probably intended as a grand historical opera, long after he had completed the first draft of the libretto of the "mythical" drama *Siegfrieds Tod.* We know this not only

because there are later prose sketches in Latin script, but also because of remarks made by his contemporaries, including Eduard Devrient, his dramaturge colleague at the Dresden opera, who was witness to his continuing interest in the project in 1849. See WWV 329.

37. Between the completion of the first draft of the libretto of *Siegfrieds Tod* in 1848 and the decision in 1851 to provide it with three more dramas to form the cycle we now know as the *Ring*, Wagner worked often in great detail on the following dramatic projects, which he never completed: *Friedrich I, Jesus von Nazareth, Achilleus,* and *Wieland der Schmied.* See WWV 328–43. On the way he attempted to set *Siegrieds Tod* to music in 1850, but he soon gave up. The best transcription with facsimiles and commentary of what remains of this thwarted first attempt at the music is included in Jean-Jacques Nattiez, *Les esquisses de Richard Wagner pour* Siegfried's Tod (1850). *Essai de poïétique* (Paris: Société Française de Musicologie, 2004).

38. For a detailed description of the surviving sketches and drafts of *Götter-dämmerung,* see WWV 397–99.

39. Thomas Mann, "The Sorrows and Grandeur of Richard Wagner," in *Pro and Contra Wagner,* trans. Allan Blunden, intro. by Erich Heller (London and Boston: Faber and Faber, 1985), 74–76.

40. Letter from Cosima Wagner to the chemist Edmund von Lippmann: "Geehrter Herr, Außer Stande Ihnen persönlich zu antworten, trägt mir mein Mann auf, Ihnen zu sagen, daß das Motiv, welches Sieglinde der Brünnhilde zusingt, die Verherrlichung Brünnhilden's ist, welches am Schluß des Werkes gleichsam von der Gesammtheit aufgenommen wird. Den Empfehlungen meines Mannes füge ich den Ausdruck meiner Hochachtung bei. Frau Richard Wagner 6. September 1875." First published in John Deathridge, "Review of Books on Wagner," *19th Century Music* 5, no. 1 (Summer 1981): 84.

41. See SSD 6: 256.

42. SSD 9: 306; PW 5: 303. The short essay "Über die Benennung 'Musik-drama' " (On the term "music drama"), which contains these famous words— *ersichtlich gewordene Taten der Musik*—first appeared in the *Musikalisches Wochenblatt* on 8 November 1872.

43. Theodor W. Adorno, *In Search of Wagner,* trans. Rodney Livingstone (London: New Left Books, 1981), 46.

44. Theodor W. Adorno, *Alban Berg: Master of the Smallest Link* (Cambridge: Cambridge University Press, 1991), 25–26.

45. See, e.g., Theodor W. Adorno, "Was ist Musik?" *Gesammelte Schriften,* vol. 19, ed. Rolf Tiedemann and Klaus Schultz (Frankfurt am Main: Suhrkamp Verlag, 1984), 614–19.

9. WAGNER'S GREEKS, AND WIELAND'S TOO

1. Wolfgang Schadewaldt, "Richard Wagner und die Griechen: Drei Bayreuther Vorträge," in *Hellas und Hesperien,* 2 vols. (Zurich: Artemis Verlag, 1970), 2: 341–405. Only the first lecture, "Richard Wagner and the Greeks,"

has been translated into English (by David C. Durst). See *Dialogos: Hellenic Studies Review* 6 (1999): 108–33. The present chapter first appeared in slightly shorter form as a response to Schadewaldt in that context.

2. Wolfgang Golther, *Die sagengeschichtlichen Grundlagen der Ring-Dichtung Richard Wagners* (Charlottenburg-Berlin: Allgemeine Musik-Zeitung, 1902).

3. Robert Petsch, "Der Ring des Nibelungen in seinen Beziehungen zur griechischen Tragödie und zur zeitgenössischen Philosophie," in *Richard-Wagner-Jahrbuch,* ed. Ludwig Frankenstein (Berlin: Hausbücher Verlag, 1907), 2: 284–330.

4. ML 22, 38.

5. Letter of 12 June 1872 to Friedrich Nietzsche. SSD 9: 296; PW 5: 292–94.

6. H. Lloyd-Jones, *Blood for the Ghosts* (London: Duckworth, 1982), 142.

7. Schadewaldt, "Richard Wagner and the Greeks," 131.

8. Lloyd-Jones, *Blood for the Ghosts,* 141.

9. SSD 8: 64–65; PW 4: 74–75.

10. Schadewaldt, "Richard Wagner und die Griechen," 2: 386.

11. Ernest Newman, *The Life of Richard Wagner,* 4 vols. (Cambridge: Cambridge University Press, 1976), 4: 106–7.

12. Friedrich Spotts, *Bayreuth: A History of the Wagner Festival* (New Haven and London: Yale University Press, 1994), 239.

13. SSD 9: 338; PW 5: 335.

14. Schadewaldt, "Richard Wagner and the Greeks," 123.

15. Hugo Ott, *Martin Heidegger: A Political Life,* trans. A. Blunden (London: HarperCollins, 1993), 142–43.

16. Editor's foreword, in Helmut Berve, ed., *Das neue Bild der Antike,* 2 vols. (Leipzig: Köhler & Amelang, 1942), 1: 7. Schadewaldt's article, "Homer und sein Jahrhundert," 1: 51–90.

17. Spotts, *Bayreuth,* 193–98.

18. SSD 3: 30; PW 1: 54.

19. SSD 3: 35; PW 1: 58.

10. DANGEROUS FASCINATIONS

1. Bernard Shaw, *The Perfect Wagnerite: A Commentary on the Nibelung's Ring,* in *Shaw's Music: The Complete Musical Criticism in Three Volumes,* ed. Dan H. Laurence (London, Sydney, and Toronto: The Bodley Head, 1981), 3: 479–80.

2. Cited in Isolde Vetter, "Wagner in the History of Psychology," in *Wagner Handbook,* ed. Ulrich Müller and Peter Wapnewski; trans. ed. John Deathridge (Cambridge, Mass., and London: Harvard University Press, 1992), 153.

3. Strictly speaking, Liszt was the first to use it, in his song "Ich möchte hingehn," the first version of which dates from 1845. This has given rise to the legend that Liszt "invented" the Tristan chord a decade before Wagner "stole"

it. The song was not published until the early 1860s, however, and some careful detective work by Rena Charmin Mueller has shown beyond a doubt that Liszt inserted a modified version of the chord (heard later in the *Tristan* Prelude) together with the short musical progression that follows at some point in the latter half of the 1850s, after Liszt had become acquainted with Wagner's score. As the author of the poem of the song is none other than Georg Herwegh, who introduced Wagner to the works of the philosopher Arthur Schopenhauer and was also acquainted with Liszt, it is highly likely that the passage was intended as a straightforward and irony-free homage to *Tristan* and an emblem of earlier meetings of the three men in Zurich. For details and a fascinating interpretation of the whole affair, see Alex Rehding, "*TrisZtan:* Or, the Case of Liszt's 'Ich möchte hingehn'," in *Nineteenth-Century Music: Selected Proceedings of the Tenth International Conference*, ed. Jim Samson and Bennett Zon (Aldershot and Burlington, Vt.: Ashgate, 2002), 75–97.

4. See *Die Streichquartette der Wiener Schule: Eine Dokumentation*, ed. Ursula von Rauchhaupt (Munich: Heinrich Ellermann, 1972), 113.

5. See George Perle, *Style and Idea in the Lyric Suite of Alban Berg* (Stuyvesant, NY: Pendragon Press, 1995).

6. Friedrich Nietzsche, *Ecce Homo: How One Becomes What One Is*, trans. R. J. Hollingdale (Harmondsworth: Penguin Books, 1979), 61.

7. Michael Kennedy, *Richard Strauss: Man, Musician, Enigma* (Cambridge: Cambridge University Press, 1999), 393–94.

8. Ibid., 391.

9. Nietzsche, *Ecce Homo*, 61.

11. PUBLIC AND PRIVATE LIFE

1. SB 6: 299. The editors of the volume suggest 16 December 1854 as an exact date of the letter.

2. Letter of 23 August 1856 to August Röckel. SB 8: 156.

3. Egon Voss, "Die 'schwarze und die weiße Flagge.' Zur Entstehung von Wagners 'Tristan'," *Archiv für Musikwissenschaft* 54, no. 3 (1997): 218. Two of the most thorough and interesting accounts of the genesis of the opera can be found in Ernest Newman, *Wagner Nights* (London and New York: Putnam, 1949), published in the United States as *The Wagner Operas*, and Roger Scruton, *Death-Devoted Heart: Sex and the Sacred in Wagner's "Tristan and Isolde"* (Oxford and New York: Oxford University Press, 2003).

4. Letter of 16 December 1856 to Franz Liszt. SB 8: 228.

5. Letter of 30 September 1857 to the firm of Breitkopf & Härtel. SB 9: 46–47.

6. Letter of 15 March 1858 to Alexander Ritter, *Hans von Bülow, Briefe und Schriften*, ed. Marie von Bülow, 8 vols. (Leipzig: Breitkopf & Härtel, 1895–1908), 4: 162.

7. Letter of 4 January 1858 to Dr. Hermann Härtel. SB 9: 107.

8. See letters dated 17 March and 6 April 1859 to the firm of Breitkopf & Härtel. SB 10: 375 and SB 11: 23.

9. Full details in WWV 433–42.

10. Letter of 5 June 1859 to the firm of Breitkopf & Härtel. SB 11: 120.

11. This phrase is used by the Wagner scholar Otto Strobel to describe the earliest musical sketches of *Tristan*. See Otto Strobel, " 'Geschenke des Himmels.' Über die ältesten überlieferten 'Tristan'-Themen und eine andere—unbekannte—Melodie Wagners," in *Offizieller Bayreuther Festspielführer* (Bayreuth: n.p., 1938), 157–65.

12. To cite one instance, Breitkopf & Härtel acknowledged receipt of pages 255–74 of the manuscript score of the third act on 21 June 1859. See *Richard Wagners Briefwechsel mit Breitkopf & Härtel*, ed. Wilhelm Altmann (Leipzig: Breitkopf & Härtel, 1911; repr. Niederwalluf bei Wiesbaden: M. Sandig, 1971), 164. On the same day, Wagner wrote to Mathilde Wesendonck that "the day before yesterday I started the composition [of the third act] again with enthusiasm: yesterday it came to a halt, and today I can't even get going at all" (SB 11: 136). As he frequently did, Wagner blamed his difficulties on the weather, though the sketches themselves show that serious harmonic and especially structural difficulties with the music were the real cause. For a detailed account of Wagner's procedure in the first act, see Robert Bailey, *The Genesis of "Tristan and Isolde" and a Study of Wagner's Sketches and Drafts for the First Act* (Ann Arbor, Mich.: University Microfilms, 1970).

13. For opposed views on the issue of recapitulation, see William Kinderman, "Dramatic Recapitulation in Wagner's 'Götterdämmerung'," *19th-Century Music*, 4 (1980–81): 101–12, and chapter 12 of this book.

14. ML 588.

15. In a letter of 12 July 1862 to the publisher Franz Schott, Wagner wrote that he had overcome his "reluctance" to publish the songs, which he counted "among his best works" (SB 14: 207). The simple reason for this change of heart was that Schott had advanced him a great deal of money for *Die Meistersinger von Nürnberg*, which was proving more difficult, and therefore taking longer to compose, than Wagner had anticipated. The offer to publish the songs was one way of mollifying Schott and preventing him from asking for his money back. Accounts of the *Wesendonck Lieder* are few and far between. The only more-than-cursory one in English is Malcolm Miller, *Wagner's "Wesendonck Lieder": An Analytic Study, with Consideration of the Orchestral Arrangements of Felix Mottl and Hans Werner Henze*, Ph.D. dissertation, King's College London, 1990 (copy deposited in the Chancery Lane Maughan Library, King's College London). This and the following two sections of this chapter are an expanded version of a paper, "Public and Private Life: *Tristan und Isolde* and the Wesendonck Lieder," first read on 9 August 2002 at the conference "Wagner and Wagnerism: Contexts—Connections—Controversies, at the University of Limerick, Ireland. I am grateful to Gareth Cox and Christopher Morris for encouraging me to write it.

16. See SW 17, *Klavierlieder,* ed. Egon Voss (Mainz: B. Schott's Söhne, 1976), vii.

17. See Egon Voss, "Die Wesendoncks und Richard Wagner," *Minne, Muse und Mäzen: Otto und Mathilde Wesendonck und ihr Zürcher Künstlerzirkel,* ed. Axel Langer and Chris Walton (Zurich: Museum Rietberg, 2002), 119.

18. For detailed information on the genesis of the songs between November 1857 and October 1858, some of which exist in as many as three versions, see WWV 448–58.

19. Franz Liszt, "Robert Franz," *Neue Zeitschrift für Musik* 43, no. 22 (23 November 1855): 230.

20. Wagner himself sang some of Franz's lieder while Franz accompanied him on the piano. A conclusion difficult to resist from the mixture of faint praise and scorn lavished on Franz's visit in Wagner's autobiography is that although Wagner had been grateful to him in the early 1850s for helping to bring *Lohengrin* to public attention, he now (in summer 1857) clearly regarded Franz as a rival. See ML 552. For a more generous evaluation of Franz, see A. W. Ambros, "Robert Franz," in *Bunte Blätter. Skizzen und Studien für Freunde der Musik und der bildenden Kunst* (Leipzig: F. E. C. Leuckart [C. Sander], 1872), 295–325.

21. Liszt, "Robert Franz," 229–35 passim.

22. Liszt, "Robert Franz," 234.

23. See WWV 452. This was by no means Wagner's only public attempt to downplay the significance of Mathilde Wesendonck. The piano sonata he wrote for her in 1853—according to Wagner's own description at the time, it was his "first composition since the completion of *Lohengrin* six years ago"—is a far more ambitious composition than is suggested by the title Wagner gave to it when he agreed to let it appear in print in January 1878 in order to settle some of his debts with his publisher: *A Sonata for the Album of Frau M. W.* Not even with the greatest semantic license could anyone convincingly describe this lengthy one-movement sonata as an album piece. In private, Wagner tried to diminish its obvious ambition even more by calling it variously a "sketch," a "fantasy," and, most damningly of all, an "elegant triviality" *(elegante Nichtigkeit).* See WWV 348. Mathilde Wesendonck herself thought the discrepancy between the nature of the piece and its published title blatant enough to mention it in a short memoir, albeit without pointing to Wagner as the culprit. See Mathilde Wesendonck, "Erinnerungen," *Allgemeine Deutsche Musik-Zeitung* 23, no. 7 (14 February 1896): 92. Answering a letter of 21 November 1884 from the Wagner collector Mary Burrell, who was equally suspicious of the title, she had already stated that it was not a question of an "album sonata," adding that Wagner "profoundly detested this mania for albums." See Judith Cabaud, *Mathilde Wesendonck ou la rêve d'Isolde* (Arles: Actes Sud, 1990), 371–72.

24. CD, 15 January 1872.

25. Letter of 31 December 1858 to Franz Liszt. SB 10: 206–7.

26. Letter of 4 January 1859 from Liszt to Wagner. *Franz Liszt—Richard Wagner Briefwechsel,* ed. Hanjo Kesting (Frankfurt am Main: Insel Verlag,

1988), 599. Liszt's reply and Wagner's original letter were omitted from nineteenth-century editions of their correspondence.

27. *Franz Liszt — Richard Wagner Briefwechsel,* 589.

28. Beginning of the letter of 31 December 1858 to Liszt. SB 10: 206.

29. Undated letter, probably April 1859, to Mathilde Wesendonck. SB 11: 58

30. Slavoj Žižek, "Afterword," in *Revolution at the Gates: A Selection of Writings from February to October 1917 [by] V. I. Lenin* (London and New York: Verso, 2002), 207.

31. Mathilde Wesendonck, "Erinnerungen," 92.

32. Dena Goodman, "Enlightenment Salons: The Convergence of Female and Philosophic Ambitions," *Eighteenth-Century Studies* 22, no. 3 (Spring 1989): 332.

33. Philip Dutton Hurn and Waverley Lewis Root, *The Truth about Wagner* (London: Cassell, 1930), 164.

34. The portrait is usually reproduced without comment in the more lavishly presented Wagner biographies. See, e.g., Curt von Westernhagen, *Wagner: A Biography,* 2 vols. (Cambridge: Cambridge University Press, 1978), 1: 8–9, illustration 10b.

35. *Richard Wagner to Mathilde Wesendonck,* trans. William Ashton Ellis (London: H. Grevel, 1905), xl.

36. See Cosima Wagner's letter to Golther dated 5 January 1904, *Cosima Wagner: Das zweite Leben,* ed. Dietrich Mack (Munich and Zurich: R. Piper & Co., 1980), 650. See also Ellis's introduction to *Richard Wagner to Mathilde Wesendonck,* xxxix.

37. One event turned out to be politically extremely hazardous. The German victory celebration Mathilde organized with Otto Wesendonck's support in the Zurich Tonhalle in March 1871 at the end of the Franco-Prussian War resulted in a near-riot and an attempt to burn down their villa, after which they left Zurich for good. See Chris Walton, "Wagner, Otto and the Three Mathildes," *The Musical Times* 143 (Autumn 2002): 43.

38. CD, 9 February 1871.

39. Letter of 6 October 1903 from Cosima Wagner to Wolfgang Golther, cited in *Cosima Wagner: Das zweite Leben,* 859.

40. The letter was eventually sold to the collector Mary Burrell by Minna's daughter Nathalie and was first published in English translation in *Letters of Richard Wagner: The Burrell Collection,* ed. John N. Burk (London: Gollancz, 1951), 369–72. German text in SB 9: 228–31.

41. The fate of Mathilde Wesendonck's side of the correspondence is still a mystery. Copies of some decidedly uninteresting letters written relatively late in her relationship with Wagner, between 1861 and 1865, when the intensity of their exchange of views was in any case markedly diminishing, were discovered fortuitously by Cosima Wagner's daughter Eva and sent to Golther and the Wesendonck heirs to do with as they liked. In an unpublished communication to Mathilde's grandson Fritz von Bissing, Cosima assumed (perhaps correctly) that Mathilde herself destroyed all her letters to Wagner after he had returned

them—an act that has left posterity almost completely in the dark about the true extent of her contribution. "Die Briefe Ihrer theuren Grossmutter wurden ihr Alle zurückgestattet u[nd] sie hat sie zerstört" (Your dear grandmother's letters were all returned to her and she destroyed them), dictated letter of 28 December 1903 to Fritz von Bissing (not in Cosima's hand, but signed by her), sold as part of Lot 167, *Sotheby's,* London, 19 May 2006. An admittedly inscrutable entry in Wagner's so-called Venice Diary addressed to Mathilde suggests that her letters to him were expected to be many: "I've had a beautiful case made here, expressly to keep your keepsakes and letters safe and secure. It can hold a great deal, and whatever is put there will not be given to naughty children. Take good care what you send me in future. You won't get any of it back." Entry dated August 24 [1858], *Richard Wagner an Mathilde Wesendon[c]k. Tagebuchblätter und Briefe, 1853–1871,* ed. Wolfgang Golther (Berlin: Duncker, 1904), 36. Mathilde's letters are relegated to an appendix (341–62).

42. "[Ich] brachte das Opfer vor welchem Ihre Mutter sich scheute," dictated letter of 2 June 1904 to Karl von Wesendonck (not in Cosima's hand, but signed by her), sold as part of Lot 167, *Sotheby's,* London, 19 May 2006.

43. *The New Grove Dictionary of Opera,* ed. Stanley Sadie (London: Macmillan, 1992), 4: 819.

44. *A History of Private Life, IV: From the Fires of Revolution to the Great War,* ed. Michelle Perrot (Cambridge, Mass., and London: Harvard University Press, 1990), 2.

12. POSTMORTEM ON ISOLDE

1. Brigid Brophy, *Mozart the Dramatist: The Value of his Operas to Him, to His Age, and to Us* (London: Libris, 1988), 35.

2. Paul Robinson, "It's Not Over Till the Soprano Dies," *New York Times Book Review* (1 January 1989).

3. Robinson, "It's Not Over Till the Soprano Dies."

4. Catherine Clément, *Opera, or the Undoing of Women,* trans. Betsy Wing, foreword by Susan McClary (Minneapolis: University of Minnesota Press, 1988), 54. Originally published as *L'Opéra, ou la défaite des femmes* (Paris: B. Grasset, 1979).

5. Clément, *Opera, or the Undoing of Women,* 56.

6. Ibid., 59.

7. Ernest Newman, *The Life of Richard Wagner,* 4 vols. (Cambridge: Cambridge University Press, 1976), 4: 547.

8. Margaret Higonnet, "Suicide: Representations of the Feminine in the Nineteenth Century," *Poetics Today* 6, nos. 1–2 (1985): 103.

9. Carl Dahlhaus, "The Music," in *Wagner Handbook,* ed. Ulrich Müller and Peter Wapnewski, trans. ed. John Deathridge (Cambridge, Mass., and London: Harvard University Press, 1992), 298.

10. Jean-Jacques Nattiez, "The Concept of Plot and Seriation Process in Music Analysis," *Music Analysis* 4, nos. 1–2 (1985): 107–18. A useful anthology

of musical analyses can be found in Richard Wagner, *Prelude and Transfigura-tion from "Tristan and Isolde,"* ed. Robert Bailey, Norton Critical Score (New York and London: Norton, 1985), 149–303. See also the analysis included in Allen Forte, "New Approaches to the Linear Analysis of Music," *Journal of the American Musicological Society* 41, no. 2 (Summer 1988): 324–38, where, with justi-fication, the *Tristan* Prelude is described as "the primary musical experiment of the mid-nineteenth century."

11. Benjamin Boretz, "Meta-variations, Part IV: Analytic Fallout (I)," *Perspectives of New Music* 11, no. 1 (Fall/Winter 1972): 146–223, esp. 206–17.

12. CD, 11 December 1878.

13. Theodor W. Adorno, "Richard Strauss. Born June 11, 1864," trans. Samuel Weber and Shierry Weber, *Perspectives of New Music* 4, no. 1 (Fall/Winter 1965): 28. English translation modified. "Ästhetische Autonomie von Musik ist nicht deren Ursprüngliches, sondern ein spät, mühsam und widerruflich Erworbenes." Theodor W. Adorno, "Richard Strauss. Zum hun-dertsten Geburtstag: 11 Juni 1964," *Gesammelte Schriften*, vol. 16, ed. Rolf Tiedemann (Frankfurt am Main: Suhrkamp, 1978), 582.

14. See Carl Dahlhaus, *The Idea of Absolute Music*, trans. Roger Lustig (Chicago: University of Chicago Press, 1989); Lydia Goehr, "Writing Music His-tory," *History and Theory* 31 (1992): 182–99; and Andrew Bowie, *Aesthetics and Subjectivity: From Kant to Nietzsche* (New York: St. Martins, 1990), 176–264 passim.

15. Goehr, "Writing Music History," 192.

16. Friedrich Nietzsche, *The Birth of Tragedy and The Case of Wagner*, trans. Walter Kaufmann (New York: Vintage, 1967), 126–27.

17. SSD 9: 108–11; PW 5: 109–12. Wagner adapted his theory of the alle-gorical dream from the fifth part of Schopenhauer's *Parerga und Paralipomena*, a collection of essays on disparate philosophical subjects he first read at the time he was beginning to conceive *Tristan*. An interesting question, which I cannot pursue at length here, is the extent to which Wagner was familiar with the co-pious literature on dreams that already existed at the time. Schopenhauer drew on the writings of the second-century Greek interpreter of dreams Artemidorus (published in various German translations at regular intervals since 1597) and—with scathing criticism—G. H. von Schubert's *Die Symbolik des Traumes* (Bamberg: Kunz, 1814 [rev. ed. 1821 and 1840]), both well known to several prominent literary figures, including E. T. A. Hoffmann. It is not out of the question that Wagner knew these sources too, and many others besides. In 1844, for instance, he added this description of Senta's behavior during Erik's dream narration to the first vocal score of *Der fliegende Holländer:* "at the start of Erik's narration, it is as if she [Senta] sinks into a magnetic sleep, so that it seems as if she, too, is dreaming the dream he is telling her about." The stage direction is not in the autograph score of 1841, but similar descriptions are to be found in Joseph Ennemoser's book on sleepwalking, dreams, and miracles, *Der Magnet-ismus im Verhältnis zur Natur und Religion* (Magnetism and its relation to na-ture and religion), which first appeared a year later (Stuttgart and Tübingen:

J. G. Cotta, 1842). At one point Ennemoser describes a state of "magnetic sleep . . . in which consciousness, as in a mixed-up dream, returns more clearly at times, and thus, so to speak, awakens in sleep" (section 17). For the sleeping Senta, Erik's accurate prediction in his dream that she will eventually escape from the real world with the Dutchman is clearly a significant moment of "awakening." In a sense, Isolde's *Liebestod* is an elaboration of this key moment in one of Wagner's earliest works.

18. "Ersichtlich gewordene Taten der Musik." Wagner called it a "truly artistic-philosophical title" *(ein recht kunstphilosophischer Titel)*. See SSD 9: 306–7; PW 5: 303.

19. Albrecht Riethmüller, "Nikolaus Lenau's 'The Bust of Beethoven'," in *Music and German Literature: Their Relationship since the Middle Ages*, ed. J. M. McGlathery (Columbia, S.C.: Camden House, 1992), 192–93. To facilitate the comparison, Riethmüller halves the four stresses of Lenau's trochaic lines into two stresses. Wagner, incidentally, changed "waves" *(Wogen)* in the fifth line of the example to "clouds" *(Wolken)* in the final score, though he retained the first version in his collected writings (SSD 7: 80). I am grateful to Professor Riethmüller for drawing my attention to his article.

20. "Der rein musikalische Ausdruck [fesselt] den Zuhörer . . . in einer, keiner anderen Kunst erreichbaren Stärke . . . in seinem Wechsel ihm eine so freie und kühne Gesetzmäßigkeit offenbarend, daß sie uns mächtiger als alle Logik dünken muß." SSD 7: 110; PW 3: 318.

21. *E. T. A. Hoffmann's Musical Writings: Kreisleriana, the Poet and the Composer, Music Criticism*, ed. David Charlton, trans. Martyn Clarke (Cambridge: Cambridge University Press, 1989), 236. Translation slightly modified.

22. The elaborate stage direction at this point was contained in a full libretto in Hoffmann's hand, which has unfortunately been missing since 1945. The scenic image was realized reasonably faithfully in the design for the original production by Karl Friedrich Schinkel and survives in the form of a well-known gouache reproduced in *The New Grove Dictionary of Opera*, ed. Stanley Sadie, vol. 4 (London: Macmillan, 1992), 865. The full text of the stage direction can be found in E. T. A. Hoffmann, *Undine: Zauberoper in 3 Akten*, ed. Jürgen Kindermann, Ausgewählte musikalische Werke 3 (Mainz: B. Schott's Söhne, 1972), 513.

23. Bailey argues plausibly that Franz Liszt's influential 1867 piano transcription of Isolde's monologue, to which Liszt gave the title "Isolden's Liebes-Tod," was a factor in establishing *Liebestod* as the title of the opera's closing pages. See *Prelude and Transfiguration*, 42–43. An ultimately far more influential publication, however, is the first separate full score of the concert version of the Prelude and (so-called) *Liebestod*, which was issued without the voice part by Breitkopf & Härtel in 1882 (plate numbers 16052 and 10000) with the title "Isolden's *Liebestod*" at the head of the concluding section (14). In this chapter, I shall continue to refer to the scene as the *Liebestod*, by which it is best known.

24. Jean-Jacques Nattiez, *Wagner Androgyne: A Study in Interpretation,* trans. Stewart Spencer (Princeton: Princeton University Press, 1993), 154.

25. For details of the genesis of *Tristan und Isolde* and its documentation, see WWV 431–48.

26. Richard Wagner, Prose sketches, B II a 5, Nationalarchiv der Richard-Wagner-Stiftung, Bayreuth, 53. The writing in the notebook containing the sketches is no longer visible and was deciphered with the help of special cameras kindly lent by the Bavarian Criminal Investigation Department.

27. CD, 25 April 1882.

28. Richard Wagner, Prose sketches, B II a 5, Nationalarchiv der Richard-Wagner-Stiftung, Bayreuth, 76.

29. Julia Kristeva, "Stabat Mater," *Poetics Today* 6, nos. 1–2 (1985): 149.

30. See Leonard B. Meyer, *Emotion and Meaning in Music* (Chicago: University of Chicago Press, 1956), 99–101, 112–15. These passages are reprinted in *Prelude and Transfiguration,* 297–303.

31. Gottfried von Strassburg, *Tristan,* trans. Arthur Hatto (London and New York: Penguin, 1967), 148. Peter Ganz points out in his notes to Reinhold Bechstein's edition of the German text that Gottfried borrowed the image of the "windows of the eyes" from medieval religious literature, though he does not cite an instance of its use in relation to the Virgin Mary. See Gottfried von Strassburg, *Tristan,* ed. Reinhold Bechstein (Wiesbaden: Brockhaus, 1978), 352. I am grateful to Carolyn Abbate for drawing my attention to this moment in Strassburg's text.

32. Tovey, "Wagner in the Concert-Room," in *Prelude and Transfiguration,* 151.

33. Michel Poizat, *The Angel's Cry: Beyond the Pleasure Principle in Opera,* trans. Arthur Denner (Ithaca, N.Y., and London: Cornell University Press, 1992), 166.

34. Transcribed by Bailey, in *Prelude and Transfiguration,* 107–12. The rewritten vocal line is from mm. 1664–80.

35. Nationalarchiv der Richard-Wagner-Stiftung, Bayreuth, MS: A II a 5, 16–18. The musical illustrations, written on thin blue paper, were brutally scissored out of the original letters. To judge by the fine notation of these scraps of music and the beautiful handwriting still visible on the reverse sides of them, the calligraphy of the letters must have been especially exquisite.

36. Richard D. Chessick, "On Falling in Love: The Mystery of Tristan and Isolde," *Psychoanalytic Explorations in Music,* ed. Stuart Feder, Richard L. Karmel, and George H. Pollock (Madison, Conn.: International University Press, 1990), 468–69. The letter, dated 7 April 1858 and provocatively headed "Just out of bed. Morning confession," is included in *Selected Letters of Richard Wagner,* 381–83.

37. Denis de Rougement, *Love in the Western World,* trans. Montgomery Belgion (New York: Schocken, 1983), 18.

38. Ibid., 52 (original emphasis).

39. Ibid., 53.

40. John Updike, "More Love in the Western World," *The New Yorker*, 24 August 1963, 90. Given de Rougement's obvious lack of faith in the ability of the West to come to terms with its refusal, as he sees it, to let passion coexist with civilization, it is not surprising that Updike's argument that de Rougement is captivated by a somewhat Thomistic trust in, and almost religious insistence on, an uncompromising and total supremacy of mind over instinct should be greeted warmly by psychoanalysts interested in the positive and creative aspects of certain narcissistic modes of relating. See, e.g., Helen K. Gediman, "Reflections on Romanticism, Narcissism, and Creativity," *Journal of the American Psychoanalytical Association* 23 (1975): 407–23, esp. 408. Gediman continues the discussion in a further article in which, incidentally, she points out that "*Liebestod* fantasy" was coined by J. C. Flugel as early as 1953 as a psychoanalytical term used to refer to fantasies of love and fantasies of death that coalesce into fantasies of "dying together." See "On Love, Dying Together, and *Liebestod* Fantasies," *Journal of the American Psychoanalytical Association* 29 (1981): 607–30, esp. 621.

41. De Rougement, *Love in the Western World*, 284.

42. Lawrence Kramer, *Music as Cultural Practice, 1800–1900* (Berkeley: University of California Press, 1990), 148.

43. Bailey, in *Prelude and Transfiguration*, 118.

44. In contrast to the Prelude and Tristan's death, the pitches of the cadence—an E-major 7th chord with an added major ninth progressing to an F-major chord, this time in first inversion, focused around an A tonic—are distributed differently, though it is still in essence the same object seen, as it were, from a significantly altered perspective.

45. CD, 14 March 1879.

46. Tovey, "Wagner in the Concert-Room," 151.

47. Ibid., 150.

48. Boretz, "Meta-variations," 201, 206.

49. Ibid., 206 ff., and Kramer, *Music as Cultural Practice*, 160 ff.

50. CD, 14 July 1879.

51. Elisabeth Bronfen, *Over Her Dead Body: Death, Femininity and the Aesthetic* (New York: Routledge, 1992), 59.

52. Ibid., 218.

53. Tovey points out that "though the vocal writing of Isolde's *Liebestod* is perfect both in declamation and singability, it is so little essential to Wagner's invention that Isolde's *Liebestod* is a complete piece of music without Isolde at all." See Tovey, "Wagner in the Concert-Room," 151. Tovey also noted correctly that Liszt included just seven independent notes and a grace note from the vocal line near the start of his famous piano arrangement and ignored the rest. Wagner himself conducted the first concert performance of the *Liebestod* in St. Petersburg on 26 February 1863 (Russian calendar) without Isolde and instructed other conductors to do the same. Isolde is also nowhere to be found in the first published orchestral score of the concert version, issued in 1882 by Breitkopf & Härtel. See WWV 440, 445.

54. Poizat, *The Angel's Cry*, 177–78.

55. Walter Benjamin, *Ursprung des deutschen Trauerspiels, Gesammelte Schriften*, ed. Rolf Tiedemann and Hermann Schweppenhäuser, vol. 1 (Frankfurt am Main: Suhrkamp, 1980), 364.

56. Ibid., 317.

57. Adorno, *In Search of Wagner*, trans. Rodney Livingstone (London: New Left Books, 1981), 87.

58. Susan Sontag, "Fascinating Fascism," *New York Review of Books*, February 6, 1975.

59. Ernst ("Putzi") Hanfstaengl, *Hitler: The Missing Years* (London: Eyre & Spottiswoode, 1957), 119. The phrase "with Lisztian embellishments" indicates that the piano version of the *Liebestod* that Hanfstaengl played to Hitler was probably Liszt's.

60. "Wie stark die Kunst ihm inneres Bedürfnis ist, das hätte man schon wissen und ahnen müssen, wenn er vor der Machtübernahme manchmal, in schwersten politischen Verhandlungen oder aufreibensten taktischen Kämpfen stehend, abends allein oder mit ein paar wenigen Kampfgefährten irgendwo in der unbeachteten Loge eines Theaters saß und aus den heroisch gesteigerten Takten eines Wagnerschen Musikdramas den künstlerischen Gleichklang mit seinem politischen Wesen vernahm." Joseph Goebbels, "Der Führer und die Künste," in *Adolf Hitler. Bilder aus dem Leben des Führers* (Hamburg/Bahrenfeld: Cigaretten-Bilderdienst, 1936), 66–67.

61. For a discussion of the term and its relevance to Isolde's *Liebestod*, see Chessick, "On Falling in Love," 478–80.

62. Thomas Mann, "Richard Wagner and *Der Ring des Nibelungen*," in *Pro and Contra Wagner*, trans. Allan Blunden, intro. by Erich Heller (London and Boston: Faber and Faber, 1985), 201.

63. Hanfstaengl, *Hitler: The Missing Years*, 49, 50, 65.

64. " 'Meine Mutter starb als sie mich gebar / nun ich lebe, sterbe ich / daran, geboren worden zu sein: warum das?" / —Refrain Parzivals—vom Hirten wiederholt—/ 'Die ganze Welt nichts wie ungestilltes Sehnen! Wie soll es / denn je sich stillen?'—Parzivals Ref[rain]." Richard Wagner, Prose sketches, B II a 5, Nationalarchiv der Richard-Wagner-Stiftung, Bayreuth, 77.

65. Cited in Édouard Conte and Cornelia Essner, *La quête de la race* (Paris: Hachette, 1995), 16. For a detailed account of the 1935 ceremony and its ruthless appropriation of Catholic symbols and practices, see Klaus Vondung, *Magie und Manipulation. Ideologischer Kult und politische Religion des Nationalsozialismus* (Göttingen: Vandenhoeck and Ruprecht, 1971), 159–71.

66. Poizat, *The Angel's Cry*, 166.

67. Liszt conducted the second performance of the *Tristan* Prelude at the first *Tonkünstler-Versammlung* (meeting of musicians) held in Leipzig at the beginning of June 1859 to commemorate the twenty-fifth anniversary of the *Neue Zeitschrift für Musik*, an important periodical devoted to the promotion of progressive musical causes that was founded by Robert Schumann in

1834. Liszt clearly programmed the Prelude as an important landmark of "German music," a concept celebrated by the meeting as both a universal and a modernist category not limited by geographical boundaries. The meeting included a keynote speech by Franz Brendel in which he coined the term "New German School," claiming that its most important members were Berlioz, Liszt, and Wagner. For a report on the meeting, see Richard Pohl, "Die Leipziger Tonkünstler-Versammlung," *Neue Zeitschrift für Musik* 50 (1859): 290. The first performance of the *Tristan* Prelude, conducted by Hans von Bülow, had taken place in Prague only a few weeks before, on 12 March.

13. STRANGE LOVE, OR, HOW WE LEARNED TO STOP WORRYING AND LOVE *PARSIFAL*

1. Eduard Hanslick, "Briefe aus Bayreuth über Wagner's *Parsifal*," in Susanna Großmann-Vendrey, *Bayreuth in der deutschen Presse. Dokumentenband 1: Die Grundsteinlegung und die ersten Festspiele (1872–1876)* (Regensburg: Gustav Bosse Verlag, 1977), 97.
2. Peter Wapnewski, "The Operas as Literary Works," in *Wagner Handbook,* ed. Ulrich Müller and Peter Wapnewski, trans. ed. John Deathridge (Cambridge, Mass., and London: Harvard University Press, 1992), 91 (hereafter *Wagner Handbook*).
3. Lucy Beckett, *Richard Wagner: Parsifal,* Cambridge Opera Handbooks (Cambridge: Cambridge University Press, 1981), 126.
4. Hartmut Zelinsky, "Die 'feuerkur' des Richard Wagner oder die 'neue religion' der 'Erlösung' durch 'Vernichtung'," in *Richard Wagner: Wie antisemitisch darf ein Künstler sein?* ed. Heinz-Klaus Metzger and Rainer Riehn, Musik-Konzepte 5 (Munich: Text + Kritik, 1978), 99.
5. Tzvetan Todorov, *Literature and Its Theorists,* trans. Catherine Porter (London: Routledge, 1988), 187.
6. Letter of 17 January 1880 to Hans von Wolzogen, in *Richard Wagner, Ausgewählte Schriften und Briefe,* ed. Alfred Lorenz, 2 vols. (Berlin: B. Hahnefeld, 1938), 2: 376–77.
7. CD, 5 January 1882.
8. Roland Barthes, *Camera Lucida: Reflections on Photography,* trans. Richard Howard (London: Vintage, 1993), 36.
9. Slavoj Žižek and Mladen Dolar, *Opera's Second Death* (New York and London: Routledge, 2002), viii (original emphasis).
10. Carl Friedrich Glasenapp, *Das Leben Richard Wagners in sechs Büchern dargestellt,* 6 vols., 3rd–5th ed. (Leipzig: Breitkopf & Härtel, 1908–23), 6: 555.
11. "*drei* Hauptsituationen von drastischem Gehalt." Letter of 29–30 May 1859 to Mathilde Wesendonck, SB 11: 107, and SW 30, *Dokumente zur Entstehung und ersten Aufführung des Bühnenweihfestspiels "Parsifal,"* ed. Martin Geck and Egon Voss (Mainz: B. Schott's Söhne, 1970), 16 (original emphasis).
12. Großmann-Vendrey, *Bayreuth in der deutschen Presse,* 97.

13. Letter of 5 September 1865 to Wagner, *König Ludwig II. und Richard Wagner. Briefwechsel*, ed. Otto Strobel, 5 vols. (Karlsruhe: G. Braun, 1936–39), 1: 170 (hereafter *Ludwig-Wagner*).

14. Letter of 7 September 1865 to King Ludwig II, *Ludwig-Wagner*, 1: 174.

15. Entry 21 September 1865 in Diary to King Ludwig II, *Ludwig-Wagner*, 4: 19.

16. Letter of 19 September 1881 to King Ludwig II, *Ludwig-Wagner*, 3: 223.

17. Letter of 11 October 1881 to Wagner, *Ludwig-Wagner*, 3: 226.

18. Letter of 22 November 1881 to Ludwig II, *Ludwig-Wagner*, 3: 229–30.

19. "Heldentum und Christentum" (1881), SSD 10: 284; PW 6: 284.

20. See, e.g., Hartmut Zelinsky, "Die 'feuerkur' des Richard Wagner"; Dieter Borchmeyer, "The Question of Anti-Semitism," trans. Stewart Spencer, and John Deathridge, "Wagner, the Jews, and Jakob Katz," both in *Wagner Handbook*, 166–85, 220–23; Marc. A. Weiner, *Richard Wagner and the Anti-Semitic Imagination* (Lincoln and London: University of Nebraska Press, 1995); Jens Malte Fischer, *Richard Wagners "Das Judentum in der Musik,"* Insel Taschenbuch 2617 (Frankfurt am Main and Leipzig: Insel, 2000); and Udo Bermbach, *Der Wahn des Gesamtkunstwerks,* 2nd ed. (Stuttgart and Weimar: Metzler, 2004), 261–82.

21. See, e.g., Robert Gutman, *Richard Wagner: The Man, His Mind, and His Music* (New York and London: Secker and Warburg, 1968), 120–21, 421–22; Joachim Köhler, *Richard Wagner: The Last of the Titans*, trans. Stewart Spencer (New Haven and London: Yale University Press, 2004), 250–55. Köhler overstates the influence of Hegel on *Die Wibelungen*, however, and ignores its deliberate anti-Hegelian posture against history and philosophies of reason.

22. Ernest Newman, *The Life of Richard Wagner*, 4 vols. (Cambridge University Press, 1976), 2: 18.

23. SSD 2: 123; PW 7: 266.

24. SSD 2: 118; PW 7: 261.

25. SSD 2: 118; PW 7: 262.

26. Isolde Vetter, "Wagner in the History of Psychology," trans. Stewart Spencer, in *Wagner Handbook*, 119.

27. Tzvetan Todorov, *On Human Diversity: Nationalism, Racism, and Exoticism in French Thought*, trans. Catherine Porter (Cambridge, Mass., and London: Harvard University Press, 1993), 140.

28. Joseph Arthur de Gobineau, *Versuch über die Ungleichheit der Menschenracen*, trans. Ludwig Schemann, 5 vols. (Stuttgart: Fr. Frommanns [E. Hauff], 1898–1901).

29. Ludwig Schemann, *Gobineaus Rassenwerk* (Stuttgart: Fr. Frommanns [E. Hauff], 1910), 237.

30. CD, 28 March 1881.

31. M. A. [Joseph Arthur] de Gobineau, *Essai sur l'inégalité des races humaines*, 4 vols. (Paris: Librairie de Firmin Didot frères, 1853–55), 4: 357.

32. August Friedrich Pott, *Die Ungleichheit menschlicher Rassen hauptsächlich vom sprachwissenschaftlichen Standpunkte, unter besonderer*

Berücksichtigung von des Grafen von Gobineau gleichnamigem Werke (Lemgo and Detmold: Meyer, 1856), xxxii.

33. Glasenapp, *Das Leben Richard Wagners*, 6: 436.

34. Gobineau, *Essai*, 4: 34–45.

35. CD, 12 May 1881.

36. Schemann, *Gobineaus Rassenwerk*, 237. See also Eric Eugène, *Wagner et Gobineau: Existe-t-il un racisme wagnérien?* with a preface by Serge Klarsfeld (Paris: Le cherche midi éditeur, 1998). In contrast to the present chapter, Eugène recognizes the elective affinities between Gobineau and Wagner, but he insists on an "essential opposition" (177) between them that allows Wagner to escape into a seemingly humane world of racial unity without serious interrogation of his ideology of male heroic supremacy and essential racial difference.

37. SSD 10: 280–81; PW 6: 280.

38. SSD 2: 155; PW 7: 298. Also SSD 12: 229 (original ending).

39. SSD 2: 144; PW 7: 287.

40. SSD 2: 151; PW 7: 294.

41. Robert J. C. Young, *Colonial Desire: Hybridity in Theory, Culture and Race* (London and New York: Routledge), 103.

42. SW 30: 72. (Citations from the original text of the prose draft written for King Ludwig II of Bavaria at the end of August 1865.)

43. SW 30: 70.

44. SW 30: 118.

45. Young, *Colonial Desire*, 107–9.

46. SSD 10: 276–277; Ellis 6: 276–77.

47. Egon Voss, "Die Möglichkeit der Klage in der Wonne: Skizze zur Charakterisierung der *Parsifal*-Musik," in *Der Opernführer: Wagner "Parsifal,"* ed. Ulrich Drüner (Munich: PremOp, 1990), 187.

48. CD, 3 February 1879.

49. Bryan Magee, *Wagner and Philosophy* (London: Allen Lane, 2000), 366; Frederic Spotts, *Bayreuth: A History of the Wagner Festival* (New Haven and London: Yale University Press, 1994), 166, 192; see also Robert R. Gibson, "Problematic Propaganda: 'Parsifal' As Forbidden Opera," *Wagner* (Journal of the London Wagner Society) n.s. 20 (May 1999): 78–87.

50. Joachim C. Fest, *Hitler*, trans. Richard Winston and Clara Winston (New York and London: Penguin, 1974), 137.

51. Ian Kershaw, *Hitler 1889–1936: Hubris* (New York and London: Allen Lane, 1998), 225.

52. Magee, *Wagner and Philosophy*, 391.

53. Frederic Spotts, *Hitler and the Power of Aesthetics* (London: Hutchinson, 2002), 236.

54. *Die Tagebücher von Joseph Goebbels*, ed. Elke Fröhlich, II/2 (October–December 1941) (Munich: Saur, 1996), 344.

55. Alan Jefferson, *Elisabeth Schwarzkopf* (London: V. Gollanz, 1996), 230–36.

56. Drüner, *Der Opernführer: Wagner "Parsifal,"* 205.

57. See letter of April 1942 (draft) from Wieland to Wolfgang Wagner in Michael Karbaum, *Studien zur Geschichte der Bayreuther Festspiele (1876–1976)* (Regensburg: Bosse, 1976), 109.

58. Hartmut Zelinsky, "Rettung ins Ungenaue," in *Richard Wagner: Parsifal,* ed. Heinz-Klaus Metzger and Rainer Riehn, Musik-Konzepte 25 (Munich: Text + Kritik, 1982), 102.

59. SSD 10: 271–72; PW 6: 271–72.

60. Joachim Kaiser, "Hat Zelinsky recht gegen Wagners 'Parsifal'?" in *Richard Wagner: Parsifal,* ed. Attila Csampai and Dietmar Holland (Reineck bei Hamburg: Rowohlt, 1984), 257–58.

61. Carl Dahlhaus, "Erlösung dem Erlöser. Warum Richard Wagners *Parsifal* nicht Mittel zum Zweck der Ideologie ist," in *Richard Wagner: Parsifal,* 265–66.

62. SSD 10: 271; PW 6: 271.

63. SSD 10: 281; PW 6: 281.

64. Hannah Arendt, *The Origins of Totalitarianism* (New York and London: Harcourt, 1985), 158.

65. Ludwig Schemann, ed., *Correspondance entre Alexis de Tocqueville et Arthur de Gobineau 1843–1859* (Paris: Plon-Nourrit, 1908), 192.

66. Todorov, *On Human Diversity,* 140.

14. MENDELSSOHN AND THE STRANGE CASE OF THE (LOST) SYMPHONY IN C

1. Jiří Weil, *Mendelssohn Is on the Roof,* trans. Marie Winn, with a preface by Philip Roth (London: HarperCollins, 1992), 2–9. With humble apologies to Weil's admirers, I have had to coarsen this part of his narrative by compressing it into a smaller space.

2. "Nazi Dance Culture," Colloquium, King's College London, 15 October 1997.

3. "Meines Erachtens kommt das, was bislang an Ersatz geboten wurde, nicht an Mendelssohn heran. Halten Sie es für psychologisch falsch, das auch nach Außen hin einzugestehen? Ich finde, es ist viel propagandistischer, wenn man in solch' eklatantem Fall, wo man wirklich nicht von Zersetzung reden kann, erklärt, daß es bessere Beispiele als Mendelssohn gibt, um den zersetzenden jüdischen Einfluß in der deutschen Musik zu beweisen." Letter from "RU" (11 February 1937) to Dr. Rainer Schlösser, Bundesarchiv (Berlin) 50.01 Akte Nr. 618, S. 98. I am grateful to Marion Kant for drawing my attention to this document.

4. A vitriolic review of *My Recollections of Felix Mendelssohn-Bartholdy* by Eduard Devrient, who as a former *Dramaturg* at the Court Opera in Dresden had also been Wagner's erstwhile colleague, speaks of the "Hamlet-like tragedy in Mendelssohn's operatic destiny," pointing to Devrient as the arch-villain. Devrient clearly thinks of himself as having been Mendelssohn's "dramatic genius." As Mendelssohn's operatic ambitions never took flight, Devrient was clearly no

good at advising his friend in theatrical matters, the review states, strongly implying that a certain Richard Wagner could have done a much better job in the role. The review was first published as a brochure under a pseudonym. See Wilhelm Drach, *Herr Eduard Devrient und sein Styl. Eine Studie über dessen "Erinnerungen an Mendelssohn"* (Munich: Fritsch, 1869). It is reprinted in SSD 8: 226–38; PW 4: 275–88.

5. See WWV 98–101.

6. "Bericht über die Wiederaufführung eines Jugendwerkes," SSD 10: 310–11; PW 6: 314.

7. "Das Judentum in der Musik" (Judaism in Music) was first published on 3 and 6 September 1850 under the pseudonym K. Freigedank in the periodical *Neue Zeitschrift für Musik*. It was revised, expanded, and published as a brochure under Wagner's real name in January 1869. See SSD 5: 66–85; PW 3: 79–100 and SSD 8: 238–60; PW 3: 101–22. PW notes the differences between the original essay and its later revision. For Stewart Spencer's more up-to-date translation of the original version, see *Wagner* (Journal of the London Wagner Society) n.s. 9, no. 1 (January 1988): 20–33.

8. See the surviving fragments of Wagner's letter of 28 December 1868 to Oswald Marbach in the enlarged edition of *Family Letters of Richard Wagner*, trans. W. A. Ellis, ed. John Deathridge (London: Macmillan Press, 1991), 369.

9. SSD 8: 240; PW 3: 101–2.

10. SSD 10: 313; PW 6: 319.

11. See Marc A. Weiner, *Richard Wagner and the Anti-Semitic Imagination* (Lincoln and London: University of Nebraska Press, 1995), 88–89.

12. Letter of 26 June 1875 to Johannes Brahms, in *Richard Wagner an Freunde und Zeitgenossen*, ed. Erich Kloss (Berlin and Leipzig: Schuster & Loeffler, 1909), 570.

13. "Einzig—die Symphonie wieder kennen zu lernen hätte ich mich ungemein interessiert—vielleicht geschieht dieß auch mit Enttäuschung. Doch muß ich meine Schwäche eingestehen, daß ich mir hierbei etwas erwartete, und um so begieriger war, als ich neuerdings Brahms [erste] Symphonie durchsah und wirklich ganz einfach darüber erstaunte, wie sich ein gelernter Komponist helfen kann, ohne daß ihm irgend etwas einfällt. Das habe ich allerdings nie gekonnt, und vermutete mir an meiner eigenen Symphonie Studien hierüber machen zu können, ob ich das zu irgend iner Zeit auch vermocht hätte. . . . Nun muß [die Symphonie] mir Seidel in Partitur setzen. . . . Das dauert nun noch lange, bis ich dennoch zu der Selbsteinsicht gelange, die mich sehr wahrscheinlich dahin bringt, mich Brahms verwandter zu erfinden als ich dieß glaubte." Unpublished letter to Wilhelm Tappert, dated by Wagner: "Bayreuth den soundsovielten Febr[uar] [18]78" (Bayreuth, Febr[uary] the something-or-other [18]78). Copy in Richard-Wagner-Gesamtausgabe, Munich.

14. CD, 19 April 1879.

15. CD, 10 January 1875.

16. CD, 3 January 1879.

17. CD, 18 February 1881.

18. CD, 23 November 1882.

19. Wagner's letter of 11 April 1836 to Mendelssohn in SB 1: 259.

20. CD, 30 March 1878.

21. CD, 4 May 1874.

22. CD, 8 February 1876.

23. See, for instance, Friedrich Schlegel's reflections on the novel in his *Athenäums-Fragmente,* mentioned in Marc A. Weiner, "Reading the Ideal," *New German Critique* 69 (Autumn 1996): 60.

24. Wagner, "Das Judentum in der Musik," SSD 5: 79.

25. SSD 5: 84.

26. Weiner, "Reading the Ideal," 69–78.

27. In the first version of *Götterdämmerung,* written in 1848 (its title was then *Siegfrieds Tod*), Siegfried tells Hagen and the assembled company just before his death that "als Meister lehrte Mime mich schmieden" (Mime the Master taught me how to forge). See SSD 2: 218.

15. UNFINISHED SYMPHONIES

1. CD, 16 August 1879.

2. Ludwig Nohl, *Beethoven's Leben,* 3 vols. in 4 (Leipzig: E. J. Günther, 1867–77).

3. Hannah Arendt, *The Human Condition* (Chicago: University of Chicago Press, 1958), 51.

4. Friedrich Nietzsche, *The Birth of Tragedy and The Case of Wagner,* trans. with commentary by Walter Kaufmann (New York: Vintage Books, 1967), 176.

5. See Thomas Mann, *Pro and Contra Wagner,* trans. Allan Blunden, intro. by Erich Heller (London and Boston: Faber and Faber, 1985), 102–3; Theodor W. Adorno, *In Search of Wagner,* trans. Rodney Livingstone (London: New Left Books, 1981), 28–29; and Egon Voss, *Richard Wagner und die Instrumentalmusik: Wagners symphonischer Ehrgeiz* (Wilhelmshaven: Heinrichshofen, 1977).

6. Igor Stravinsky and Robert Craft, *Themes and Episodes* (New York: Alfred. A. Knopf, 1966), 139.

7. For details, see John Deathridge, *Wagner's "Rienzi": A Reappraisal Based on a Study of the Sketches and Drafts* (Oxford: Clarendon Press, 1977), 25–28.

8. Letter of 13 September 1834 to Theodor Apel. SB 162. The sketch of the symphony is lost, but Felix Mottl's orchestration of the torso resurfaced in the late 1980s, and Wolfgang Sawallisch recorded the first movement with the Philadelphia Orchestra for EMI in 1995.

9. SSD 10: 313; PW 6: 317.

10. For details see Egon Voss, *Richard Wagner: Eine Faust-Ouvertüre,* Meisterwerke der Musik 31 (Wilhem Fink: Munich 1982), 8–9.

11. See WWV 506–9.

12. SSD 3: 97; PW 1: 127.

13. The philological discussion in this and the following section is an adapted and expanded English translation of a text I wrote with Martin Geck

and Egon Voss in WWV 520–25, in which more details about the sources discussed can be found.

14. A II a 6, fol.

15. See, e.g., Ernest Newman, *The Life of Richard Wagner*, 4 vols. (Cambridge: Cambridge University Press, 1976), 4: 666–67.

16. For details, see WWV 460–61.

17. CD, 29 November 1882.

18. CD, 19 March 1878.

19. Nietzsche, *The Birth of Tragedy and The Case of Wagner*, 158–59.

20. Ibid., 172 (original emphasis, translation modified).

21. "*Zukunftsmusik,*" SSD 7: 129; PW 3: 337.

22. Ibid., SSD 7: 112; PW 3: 320: "[der Dichter], welcher die Tendenz der Musik und ihres unerschöpflichen Ausdrucksvermögens vollkommen inne hat und sein Gedicht daher so entwirft, daß es in die feinsten Fasern des musikalischen Gewebes eindringen . . . kann."

23. Alfred Lorenz, *Das Geheimnis der Form bei Richard Wagner: Der musikalische Aufbau von Richard Wagners "Tristan und Isolde"* (Berlin: M. Hesse, 1926), 181; Hans Grunsky, "*Tristan und Isolde:* Der symphonische Aufbau des dritten Aufzuges," *Zeitschrift für Musik* 113 (1952): 390–94. Both authors refer admiringly to an earlier article by an author close to the Bayreuth "inner" circle, Grunsky's father; see Karl Grunsky, "Wagner als Sinfoniker," in *Richard-Wagner-Jahrbuch*, vol. 1 (Leipzig: Hausbücher Verlag, 1906), 227–44.

24. CD, 28 September 1878 and 11 December 1878.

25. "Über die Anwendung der Musik auf das Drama," SSD 10: 176–93; PW 6: 173–91.

16. CONFIGURATIONS OF THE NEW

The epigraph to this chapter is from Carl Dahlhaus, "The Musical Influence," in *Wagner Handbook*, ed. Ulrich Müller and Peter Wapnewski, English trans. ed. John Deathridge (Cambridge, Mass., and London: Harvard University Press, 1992), 550. A shorter version of the chapter was read at a colloquium entitled "Die Oper nach Wagner," held in memory of Carl Dahlhaus (1928–89) at the Technische Universität Berlin in October 1989.

1. The advertisement subsequently appeared in a number of other "serious" daily national newspapers (e.g., *The Times*) and one or two "glossy" weeklies.

2. Gianni Vattimo, *The End of Modernity: Nihilism and Hermeneutics in Post-Modern Culture*, trans. Jon R. Snyder (Cambridge and Oxford: Polity Press, 1988), 10.

3. Friedrich Nietzsche, *The Birth of Tragedy and The Case of Wagner*, trans. Walter Kaufman (New York, 1967), 156.

4. Arnold Gehlen, "Die Säkularisierung des Fortschritts," in *Einblicke* (Frankfurt am Main: Klostermann, 1975), 56–68.

5. Franz Brendel, *Geschichte der Musik in Italien, Deutschland und Frankreich: 22 Vorlesungen gehalten zu Leipzig im Jahre 1850* (Leipzig: Hinze, 1852), 532. See also John Deathridge, "Germany: The 'Special Path,'" in *The Late Romantic Era*, ed. Jim Samson (Englewood Cliffs, N.J.: Prentice Hall, 1991), 61–62.

6. Adolf Bernhard Marx, *The Music of the Nineteenth Century and Its Culture*, trans. Augustus Wehrhan (London: R. Cocks & Co., 1855), 58.

7. Gehlen, *Einblicke*, 126. Gehlen says he found the term in a book published in 1951 by the Belgian politician and philosopher Hendrik de Man, who in turn took the idea from the French mathematician and economist Antoine Augustin Cournot (1801–77).

8. The adjectives "strong" and "weak" are not evaluations; nor is the difference between them synonymous with that between the "progress" and "reaction" that Adorno claimed to see entwined in Wagner. Rather they mark the gap between two philosophical positions—roughly speaking, the antithesis between metaphysics and nihilism. On the concept of "weak thought," see *Il pensiero debole*, ed. Gianni Vattimo and Pier Aldo Rovatti (Milan: Feltrinelli, 1983). Jürgen Habermas, a vibrant, polemically "strong" thinker, is discussed briefly below.

9. Readers interested in the debate about postmodernity could do worse than begin by consulting the bibliography in Matei Clinescu, *Modernism, Avant-Garde, Decadence, Kitsch, Postmodernism* (Durham, N.C.: Duke University Press, 1987), and the articles in *Postmoderne: Alltag, Allegorie und Avantgarde*, ed. Christa Bürger and Peter Bürger, Suhrkamp Taschenbuch Wissenschaft 648 (Frankfurt am Main: Suhrkamp, 1988). For the comparatively meager literature on music and so-called postmodernity up to the late 1980s, see Niksa Gligo, "Die musikalische Avantgarde als ahistorische Utopie," *Acta Musicologica* 61 (1989): 218. To this list should be added Helga de la Motte's refreshingly critical article "Die Gegenaufklärung der Postmoderne," in *Musik und Theorie*, ed. Rudolf Stephan, Veröffentlichungen des Instituts für Neue Musik und Musikerziehung 28 (Mainz: B. Schott's Söhne, 1987), 31–44, and Robin Holloway, "Modernism and After in Music," *The Cambridge Review* 110 (June 1989): 50–66. The literature has ballooned since. For the best overview, see Jann Pasler, "Postmodernism," in *The New Grove Dictionary of Music and Musicians*, 2nd ed., ed. Stanley Sadie and John Tyrrell (London: Macmillan, 2001), 20: 213–16.

10. Even Vattimo and Habermas, two philosophers diametrically opposed in their attitudes to the postmodern, are agreed on this point. See Vattimo, *The End of Modernity*, 164, and the fourth of Habermas's twelve lectures, "The Entry into Postmodernity: Nietzsche as a Turning Point," in *The Philosophical Discourse of Modernity*, trans. Frederick Lawrence (Cambridge: Polity, 1987), 83–105. For some dissenting voices, see *Nietzsche as Postmodernist, Essays Pro and Contra*, ed. and intro. by Clayton Koelb (Albany: State University of New York Press, 1990).

11. Friedrich Nietzsche, "On the Uses and Disadvantages of History for Life," *Untimely Meditations*, trans. Ralph John Hollingdale, intro. by Joseph Peter Stern (Cambridge: Cambridge University Press, 1983), 104–5.

12. Ibid., 120.

13. See, for instance, CD, 23 February 1874: "great courage, great fervor, very acute judgment. R's example has opened his [Nietzsche's] eyes to the triviality of the whole modern world."

14. CD, 9 April 1874.

15. Letter of 27 February 1874 from Wagner to Nietzsche, *Nietzsche Briefwechsel*, ed. Giorgio Colli and Mazzino Montinari, II/4 (Berlin and New York: Walter de Gruyter, 1978), 396.

16. Habermas, *The Philosophical Discourse of Modernity*, 7.

17. "Modern," SSD 10: 55.

18. SSD 10: 57.

19. Cited in Habermas, *The Philosophical Discourse of Modernity*, 387.

20. SSD 10: 56.

21. Charles Baudelaire, *Selected Writings on Art and Artists*, trans. Patrick Edward Charvet (Cambridge: Cambridge University Press, 1981), 333. The only English translation of *Opera and Drama* in existence in Baudelaire's day was anonymous and first published in serial form between 19 May 1855 and 26 April 1856 in *The Musical World*.

22. Richard Rorty, "Posties," *London Review of Books*, 3 September 1987, 11–12. Cf. Habermas, *The Philosophical Discourse of Modernity*, 51.

23. Habermas, *The Philosophical Discourse of Modernity*, 4–5.

24. ML 431.

25. See the third part of *Opera and Drama*, "Poetry and Music in the Drama of the Future" *(Dichtkunst und Tonkunst im Drama der Zukunft)*, SSD 4: 131–33; PW 2: 269–71.

26. SSD 3: 97; PW 1: 127.

27. SSD 3: 60–61; PW 1: 88–89.

28. SSD 3: 304; PW 2: 98.

29. SSD 3: 301; PW 2: 95.

30. SSD 3: 304; PW 2: 98–99.

31. SSD 3: 231; PW 2: 17.

32. For details, see WWV 380, 405–6.

33. Bürger and Bürger, *Postmoderne: Alltag, Allegorie und Avantgarde*, 10.

34. See Theodor W. Adorno, "Wagner's Relevance for Today," in *Essays on Music*, selected with intro., commentary, and notes by Richard Leppert, trans. Susan H. Gillespie (Berkeley: University of California Press, 2002), 594.

35. Nietzsche, "Richard Wagner in Bayreuth," in *Untimely Meditations*, 201 (translation modified).

36. Rainer Franke, *Richard Wagners Zürcher Kunstschriften* (Hamburg: Verlag der Musikalienhandlung K. D. Wagner, 1983), 167.

37. See, e.g., SSD 3: 98; PW 1: 128: "In dem großen allgemeinsamen Kunstwerke der Zukunft wird ewig neu zu erfinden sein" (the great, all-embracing artwork of the future will mark the creation of the endlessly new).

38. Letter of 2 May 1860 to Mathilde Wesendonck. SB 12: 137. Werner Breig calls these words "astonishing" (*Wagner Handbook*, ed. Ulrich Müller and

Peter Wapnewski, English trans. ed. John Deathridge [Cambridge, Mass., and London: Harvard University Press, 1992], 467); but they are quite logical in terms of Wagner's reaction against, and insight into, what Arnold Gehlen was to call, well over a hundred years later, the "secularization of progress." See Gehlen, "Die Säkularisierung des Fortschritts."

39. The oboe and English horn solos in Berlioz's *Symphonie fantastique* at the start of the third movement *(scène aux champs)* could have served as a model. They are also unaccompanied, obviously similar in tone color, and consciously structured to give the impression of natural, "naïve" musical expression that is freely improvised without rigid bar lines. The idea has a pedigree in early-nineteenth-century writing on music, in particular the theories of Gustav von Schlabrendorf and Ernst Wagner (no relation) about the origin of music as measureless, recitative-like song; see Hermann Danuser, *Musikalische Prosa* (Regensburg: G. Bosse, 1975), 51–54. Ernst Wagner is mentioned by Schumann in his well-known critique of the *Symphonie fantastique* in the *Neue Zeitschrift für Musik*, which Richard Wagner, himself a contributor to the periodical in the mid-1830s, had almost certainly read. (For the full version of the passage on Ernst Wagner, which Schumann later shortened, see *Neue Zeitschrift für Musik* 4 [August 1835].)

40. Joseph Kerman, *Opera as Drama*, rev. ed. (Berkeley: University of California Press, 1988), 165.

41. Nietzsche, "On the Uses," 76.

42. Kerman, *Opera as Drama*, 168.

43. Theodor W. Adorno, *In Search of Wagner*, trans. Rodney Livingstone (London: New Left Books, 1981), 156.

44. Paul de Man, *Blindness and Insight: Essays in the Rhetoric of Contemporary Criticism*, 2nd, rev. ed. (London: Methuen, 1983), 150.

45. Wagner himself emphasized that *Tristan*, in terms of its deeper mythic significance, was in effect another version of *Siegfried*, though he was more reticent about the precise affinities between the two works (SSD 6: 267–68). In a letter of 9 July 1859 to Mathilde Wesendonck, he remarked on the link between the Shepherd's "new" melody in C major in the third act of *Tristan* and the much bolder, jubilant C-major melody dominating the end of *Siegfried* (from the words *Sie ist mir ewig*), both of which seem to have occurred to him at the same time (SB 11: 157). Another idea common to both works relevant to the present context is the use of a quasi-improvisational melody with flexible meter to represent each hero's relationship to Nature. The difference in emphasis is significant: while the cheerful, metrically free song of the Woodbird in *Siegfried* reflects, in a bright E major, the hero's oneness with Nature and provides him with a clear pointer to the future, the melancholy, equally metrically free F-minor strains of *die alte Weise* in *Tristan* convey the sense that the hero's relation to his "natural" origins, and hence also his vision of the future, have been damaged almost beyond repair.

46. Vattimo, *The End of Modernity*, 39–41, 58–60. Vattimo uses Heidegger's term *Verwindung*, which can mean a variety of things, including

recovery from an illness, resignation to something, and acceptance of another's opinion.

47. Vattimo, *The End of Modernity*, 41.

48. In a letter of 29–30 May 1859 to Mathilde Wesendonck, Wagner was already predicting that Amfortas would be like Tristan in the third act of *Tristan*, but "with an unimaginable increase in intensity" (mit einer undenklichen Steigerung). SB 11: 104 and SW 30, *Dokumente zur Entstehung und ersten Aufführung des Bühnenweihfestspiels "Parsifal,"* ed. Martin Geck and Egon Voss (Mainz: B. Schott's Söhne, 1970), 14.

49. See, for instance, Robert Gooding-Williams, "Nietzsche's Pursuit of Modernism," *New German Critique* 41 (Spring/Summer 1987): 99.

50. Adorno, *In Search of Wagner*, 47.

51. Adorno, "Wagner's Relevance for Today," 598.

52. See Jean-Jacques Nattiez, *Wagner Androgyne: A Study in Interpretation*, trans. Stewart Spencer (Princeton: Princeton University Press, 1993), 64–68. Nattiez, who sees the *Ring* as a metaphorical reenactment of the history of music as it is presented in *Opera and Drama*, convincingly highlights allusions to the dramaturgical technique of *grand opéra* and the lilting gait of French *opéra comique* melodies in its opening scene. These, he says, are intended as an anti-Semitic allusion to Meyerbeer and a metaphor for the negative historical influence of French opera.

53. See Theodor W. Adorno, "Music and the New Music: In Memory of Peter Suhrkamp," *Telos* 43 (Spring 1980): 132, 143: "the new musical language . . . takes the form of a positive negation of traditional language"; "tradition is not imitation, a reaching into the past or a direct continuation of the past, but rather the ability to grow away from the demands in the past which this past did not fulfill and which left behind their mark in the form of mistakes. New Music assumes responsibility in the face of these demands." See also Karlheinz Stockhausen's preface to *Kontra-Punkte* (rev. ed. Vienna: Universal Edition, 1977): "No Neo . . . ! What, then? Counter-Points: a series of the most clandestine yet palpable transformations and renewals—no foreseeable end."

54. Arnold Schoenberg, "Criteria for the Evaluation of Music," in *Style and Idea*, ed. Leonard Stein (New York: St Martin's Press, 1975), 129.

55. Carl Dahlhaus, " 'New Music' as Historical Category," *Schoenberg and the New Music*, trans. Derrick Puffett and Alfred Clayton (Cambridge: Cambridge University Press, 1987), 13.

56. See Deryck Cooke, "Wagner's Musical Language," *The Wagner Companion*, ed. Peter Burbidge and Richard Sutton (London: Faber, 1979), 236–38.

57. Cited in *Kurt Weill: The Threepenny Opera*, ed. Stephen Hinton (Cambridge: Cambridge University Press, 1990), 27.

58. Cited in Ralph Scott Grover, *Ernest Chausson: The Man and His Music* (Lewisburg: Bucknell University Press, 1980), 171.

59. See Craig Ayrey, "Salome's Final Monologue," in *Richard Strauss: Salome*, ed. Derrick Puffett (Cambridge: Cambridge University Press, 1989), 130.

17. WAGNER AND BEYOND

1. See Michael Kennedy, *Richard Strauss* (London and Melbourne: Dent, 1988), 7.

2. Cited in Vera Stravinsky and Robert Craft, *Stravinsky in Pictures and Documents* (New York: Simon & Schuster, 1978), 400.

3. Igor Stravinsky, *Chronicle of My Life* (London: V. Gollancz, 1936), 67–68.

4. Igor Stravinsky and Robert Craft, *Themes and Episodes* (New York: Alfred A. Knopf, 1966), 189.

5. See Franz-Heinz Köhler, *Die Struktur der Spielpläne deutschsprachiger Opernbühnen von 1896 bis 1966* (Koblenz: Verband Dt. Städtestatistiker, 1968). Thanks to Aine Sheil for drawing my attention to this source.

6. See the instructive discussion in Katharine Ellis, "Wagnerism and Anti-Wagnerism in the Paris Periodical Press, 1852–1870," in *Von Wagner zum Wagnérisme: Musik, Literatur, Kunst, Politik*, ed. Annegret Fauser and Manuela Schwartz (Leipzig: Leipziger Universitätsverlag, 1999), 51–83.

7. See, e.g., the illuminating discussion of Massenet's *Esclarmonde* (1887–89) in Steven Huebner, "Massenet and Wagner: Bridling the Influence," *Cambridge Opera Journal* 5, no. 3 (1993): 223–38.

8. SSD 3: 96–97 and 5: 74; PW 1: 126–27 and 3: 88. For a different interpretation, which to a large extent reflects the standard view in Wagner scholarship, see Jean-Jacques Nattiez, *Wagner Androgyne: A Study in Interpretation*, trans. Stewart Spencer (Princeton: Princeton University Press, 1993), 128–38.

9. Theodor W. Adorno, *In Search of Wagner*, trans. Rodney Livingstone (London: New Left Books, 1981), 107.

10. Bryan Magee, *Wagner and Philosophy* (London: Allen Lane, 2000), 130.

11. Jack M. Stein, *Richard Wagner & the Synthesis of the Arts* (Detroit: Wayne State University Press, 1960), 85.

12. Carl Dahlhaus, "Wagner's Musical Influence," *Wagner Handbook*, ed. Ulrich Müller, Peter Wapnewski, trans. ed. John Deathridge (Cambridge, Mass., and London: Harvard University Press, 1992), 547.

13. Edward Lockspeiser, *Debussy: His Life and Mind*, 2 vols. (Cambridge: Cambridge University Press, 1978), 2: 215.

14. *Cosima Wagner: Das zweite Leben*, ed. Dietrich Mack (Munich and Zurich: R. Piper & Co., 1980), 204.

15. Richard Wagner, "Einleitung zu einer Vorlesung der 'Götterdämmerung' vor einem ausgewählten Zuhörerkreise in Berlin," SSD 9: 308–10; PW 5: 305–6.

16. See the editor's postscript to Richard Wagner, *Oper und Drama*, ed. Klaus Kropfinger, Reclam Universal-Bibliothek 8207 (Stuttgart: Reclam, 1984), 525, 531–32.

17. Theodor W. Adorno, "Wagner's Relevance for Today," in *Essays on Music*, selected with intro., commentary, and notes by Richard Leppert, trans. Susan H. Gillespie (Berkeley: University of California Press, 2002), 588–89.

18. Alfred Kühn, "Manon Lescaut von Puccini," *Neue Zeitschrift für Musik* 61 (1894): 62–64.

19. Reported in *Neue Zeitschrift für Musik* 79 (1912): 241.

20. Adolphe Appia, *Staging Wagnerian Drama*, trans. and intro. by Peter Leoffler (Basel, Boston, and Stuttgart: Birkhäuser, 1982), 41–42. The original French text of the essay is in Adolphe Appia, *Oeuvres complètes*, ed. Marie L. Bablet-Hahn, 4 vols. (Lausanne: L'Âge d'homme, 1983–92), 1: 261–83. Thanks to Patrick Carnegy and Eoin Coleman for persuading me to look at Appia's work more closely.

21. The lecture is published in full in English in H. F. Redlich, *Alban Berg: The Man and his Music* (London: John Calder, 1957), 261–85, esp. 267.

22. Joseph Goebbels, "Der Führer und die Künste," in *Adolf Hitler. Bilder aus dem Leben des Führers* (Hamburg/Bahrenfeld: Cigaretten-Bilderdienst, 1936), 67.

Acknowledgments

Most of the chapters in this book have been revised, abridged, or expanded since their first appearance. For permission to print some of the chapters, I am indebted to the following editors and publishers of journals and books, who printed them in their original form, or are scheduled to publish them:

Chapter 1: "Wagner Lives," in *The Cambridge Companion to Wagner,* ed. Thomas Grey (Cambridge: Cambridge University Press, forthcoming). © Cambridge University Press. Printed with the permission of Cambridge University Press.

Chapter 8: "Verdi, Wagner, and Walter Benjamin's concept of Trauerspiel," in *"Schlagen Sie die Kraft der Reflexion nicht zu gering an":* *Beiträge zu Richard Wagners Denken, Werk und Wirken,* ed. Klaus Döge, Christa Jost, and Peter Jost (Mainz: Schott Musik International, 2002). © 2002 Schott Musik International, Mainz. Reprinted with the permission of Schott Musik International.

Chapter 12: "Post-mortem on Isolde," *New German Critique* 69 (Fall 1996). Special issue devoted to Wagner, ed. David J. Levin.

Chapter 14: "Wagner and Mendelssohn," in *Nineteenth-Century Music: Selected Proceedings of the Tenth International Conference,* ed. Jim Samson and Bennett Zon (Aldershot and Burlington, Vt.: Ashgate, 2002).

Chapter 15: "Richard Wagner's Unfinished Symphonies." Permission to reproduce a revised and abridged version of this essay from *Late Thoughts: Reflections on Artists and Composers at Work,* ed. Karen Painter and Thomas Crow, has been granted by The Getty Research Institute, Los Angeles, CA. © 2006 by The J. Paul Getty Trust. All rights reserved.

Chapter 16: "Wagner and the Post-modern," *Cambridge Opera Journal* 4, no. 2 (July 1992). © Cambridge University Press 1992. Reprinted with the permission of Cambridge University Press.

Chapter 17: "Wagner and Beyond," in *The Cambridge Companion to Twentieth-Century Opera*, ed. Mervyn Cooke (Cambridge: Cambridge University Press, 2005). © Cambridge University Press 2005. Reprinted with the permission of the Cambridge University Press.

Other chapters appeared in previous incarnations in the following publications:

Chapter 2: "Wagner's 'Pale' Senta," *The Opera Quarterly* 21, no. 3 (Summer 2005), published by Oxford University Press.

Chapter 3: "Wagner's 'Alter Ego,' " *Lohengrin: Richard Wagner* (London and New York: John Calder and Riverrun Press, 1993), English National Opera Guide 47; "The Beginning of the Future," *Lohengrin*, Program of the Royal Opera House, London, February 1997.

Chapter 4: "Fairy-tale, Revolution, Prophecy," *The Rhinegold*, Program of the English National Opera, London, January 2001.

Chapter 5: "Symphonic Mastery of Moral Anarchy?" *The Valkyrie*, Program of the English National Opera, London, January 2002.

Chapter 6: "Siegfried Hero," *Siegfried*, Program of the English National Opera, London, December 2002.

Chapter 7: "*Götterdämmerung*: Finishing the End," Booklet accompanying CD recording of *Götterdämmerung*, conductor James Levine (Hamburg: Deutsche Grammophon, 1991).

Chapter 9: "Richard Wagner, the Greeks and Wolfgang Schadewaldt," *Dialogos: Hellenic Studies Review* 6 (1999).

Chapter 10: "Gevaarlijke Fascinaties," *Iconen van het Fin de Siècle*, Program of the 10th Gergiev Festival Rotterdam, 10–17 September 2005.

Chapter 13: "Strange Love, Or, How We Learned to Stop Worrying and Love Wagner's *Parsifal*," in *Western Music and Race*, ed. Julie Brown (Cambridge: Cambridge University Press, 2007).

Index

absolute music, 136–39; commodification of, 149–50; crisis of, 216–17; human affairs and, 142–43; *Liebestod* as allegory of, 148, 154–55

acciaccatura, 87–88

Achilleus (unfinished opera; Wagner), 258n37

Addresses to the German Nation (Fichte), 105

Adorno, Theodor, 152; on absolute music, 136, 149–50, 153; on Benjamin, 100–101; Benjamin's influence on, 79; on *Götterdämmerung*, 99, 222; on *Lohengrin*, 42; on New Music, 280n53; normative view of music, 101; on number convention revival, 233; *Parsifal* and, 170; on progress vs. reaction, 222–23, 226, 277n8; on *Tristan*, 220–21; on Wagner's "dilettante" traits, 191

adultery, 143

advertising: Wagner's music as, 150; Wagner in, 209–10

Aeschylus, 80, 102, 108, 235

aestheticism, 126, 132, 144

Aida (Verdi), 89–91

alienation, 214

allegory: dreams as, 137–39, 265–66n17; *Liebestod* as, 148–49,

154–55; motivic, 94–99; in *Parsifal*, 169; *Ring* as, 251–52n3; symbolism vs., 81–84; Wagnerian influence and, 236–37; Wagner's passion for, 83

androgyny, 25, 140

"Annals" (Wagner), 7, 13–14

Antigone (Sophocles), 103

anti-Semitism, 107, 166; fellow exiles alienated by, 107; Greek revival and, 103; Ludwig II's disapproval of, 107; Mendelssohnian influence and, 185–86; during nationalist phase, 106; in *Parsifal*, 160–61, 175–76; public shrugging off of, 49; in Wagner's works, 135, 280n52; in Wagner's writings, 164, 182, 213

Appia, Adolphe, 235–36

Arabella (Strauss and Hofmannsthal), 116

Arendt, Hannah, 176, 190

Aristophanes, 102

Armageddon, 159

Arme Heinrich, Der (Pfitzner), 231

Art and Revolution (Wagner), 106

Artemidorus, 265n17

Artwork of the Future, 106–7, 213, 219

"Artwork of the Future" (Wagner), 229–30

285

Aryan race: miscegenation and, 176;
purity of, 165, 166–67
Assumption of the Virgin Mary, 140
Assunta dei Frari (Titian), 140–41
"Asyl" (Wagner's Zurich residence),
117, 130
atonality, 114–15, 221, 236
Attfield, Nicholas, 252n6
Auber, Daniel François Esprit, 13,
73–74
Auden, W. H., 227
Auer, Max, 252n6
Aufstieg und Fall der Stadt Ma-
hagonny (Brecht and Weill), 237
"Autobiographical Sketch" (Wagner),
11–12, 29
autobiography: gender relations in, 6;
as process, 8; Wagner's understanding of, 4. *See also* Wagner,
Richard, autobiographical
writings

Bailey, Robert, 145, 266n23, 267n34
Bakunin, Michael, 48, 64, 66, 73
Ballo in maschera, Un (Verdi), 69
Barbarossa, Friedrich, 12
baroque mourning play: Benjamin's
research on, 79; Greek tragedy
vs., 80–81, 91; *Liebestod* and, 149;
opera vs., 84–85, 255n5; *Ring*
compared to, 94; romantic borrowings from, 82–83, 86
Barthes, Roland, 160
Baudelaire, Charles, 36, 56, 133,
214–15, 278n21
Bauer, Bruno, 48, 66
Bavarian Hoftheater (Munich), 153
Bayreuther Blätter, 213
Bayreuth Festival Theatre: amphitheater of, x; criticism of, 227; first
Ring performance at, 55–56, 62,
197; influence of, 231–32; *Lohen-*
grin production at, 37; *Parsifal*
performed at, 173–74, 190, 227;
post-WWII de-Germanification
at, 107–9; as reincarnation of
Greek rites, 107; Schadewaldt

lectures at, 102; Wagner (Cosima)
as guardian of, 7; Wagner invites
Gobineau to, 165; Wagner's disil-
lusionment with, 203
Bayreuth Nationalarchiv, 194, 197
Beethoven, Ludwig van: absolute
music and, 136, 139; Adorno as
music critic and, 101; French Revolution and, 65; influence on
Wagner, 148, 181, 191, 192; revisions made by, 122; Schröder-
Devrient sings, 8–9, 24; Wagner
moves away from, 122, 202; Wagner objects to biography of, 189
"Beethoven" (Wagner), 137–38
Beethoven, Ludwig van, Symphony
no. 9: as "last" symphony, x, 183,
205, 215, 216; Wagner's commitment to, 245n27; Wagner's obscene parody of, 193
"Beethovens Büste" (Lenau), 138–39,
142, 266n19
Bellini, Vincenzo, 24, 83
Benjamin, Walter, 75, 79; on baroque
mourning play vs. classical tragedy, 80–81; on baroque mourning
play vs. opera, 255n5; on confused "court," 83, 94; music and,
100–101; significance of, 101; on
symbol vs. allegory, 81–84, 149;
theory of melancholy, 83–84
Bentley, Eric, 63, 65
Berg, Alban, 42, 100–101, 114, 173,
237–38
Berlin State Opera, 253n10
Berlioz, Hector, 192, 270n67, 279n39
Berry, Mark, 48
Beyond the Tragic Vision (Peckham),
36
Biedermeier, 181, 185
binary opposites, 72
biography: antichronological, 10; gender relations in, 6; Victorian era,
4; Wagner's understanding of, 4
Birth of Tragedy, The (Nietzsche), 135,
137
Bismarck, Otto von, 73, 182

Text: 10/13 Aldus
Display: Aldus
Compositor: Binghamton Valley Composition, LLC
Music Engraver: Don Giller